Michelina's Letter

Michelina's Letter

Co-Authored and Edited by
Victor R. Pisano

Published by
NightOwl Productions, Inc.,
Martha's Vineyard and
Savannah, Georgia
nightowl@vineyard.net
www.EllisIslandÉmigré.com

ISBN: 13: 978-0-578-44933-3

CONTENTS

Helps her father and brother already here
Michelina is pursued by many suitors, both past and present
Self-discovery and challenges to a woman's identity
Courtship Italian style
Succumbs to custom but embraces self-evaluation
Michelina discovers writing
More troubles with church doctrines, romance and mariage

Act Three
(339)
Michelina creates a home in Lynn, Mass. with husband Louis Pisano
Conflicts with the "Temporary" Emergency Immigration Act of 1921
Michelina's mother and siblings stuck in Italy
Adjusting to a strict Italian marriage
Michelina reflects on World and American politics, post-WWI
Michelina's sons, Reno and Geno, are born - two cultures
Michelina recounts Women's Rights, the depression, pre-WWII
Acting career denied, writing career realized
More church and self-identity conflicts
Debates future archbishop and becomes a perennial philosopher
Michelina's mother and siblings come to America
Family branded "enemy aliens" by US government, WWII
Michelina's brothers and two sons go to war as US combat enlistees
Son, Geno, trains as a Navy combat pilot
Son, Reno's, 51st battalion receives the French Croix de Guerre in the
"Battle of the Bulge"
First house. Marital strife. Final identity determined
After years of polite but living separate lives, husband Louis passes

Denouement/Epilogues:
Twenty years of traveling, exploring, writing, and reminiscing.

BOOK SLEEVE

We've all seen them - in books, travelogues or even in person, those gloriously ancient hillside villages of Italy. They seem to be cut out of the face of the mountain itself - in color and in form. Most hang precariously on a precipice, proclaiming and protecting a view of the valley below that has gone unchanged for centuries. The narrow streets, passageways and cuts, each surround and connect upward to an ancient church and its bell tower. A bell tower that reminds everyone within earshot that there is a reason for its being perched at the highest point, of the highest structure, in the highest village.

The question begs - who lives up there? What was it like a century or more ago - before electricity - before the age of a different Cloud, when old was ancient, really ancient, even for then? What marvelous stories do these old communes hold - cloistered within their multi-stucco walls?

"Michelina's Letter" recounts one such individual story - of living, growing and ultimately leaving a mountain commune in Italy. My grand-mother, Michelina Pirone Pisano, "invaded" America rather than immi-grated and proceeded to put pieces of her village and her life in a jar like candied fruit of Christmas. She was born in the mountain village of Pratola Serra, Italy, in 1901.

As a teen, Michelina left a place of boundless beauty for a place of boundless promise. A young woman on her own who was of spiritual bent; a rebel - an historian - an essayist - a poet - an intellectual - and an Ellis Island emigre. Michelina Pirone Pisano - this is her story - in her own hand - bound with sewing needles and hemming pins and speaking to us directly from the near distant past.

FOREWORD

(Special thanks to: Matzo Mauriello, a little family gnome who again whispered in my ear, "It's time, Victor. Finish 'Michelina's Letter.'" And none too soon, for I have now been newly grandfathered as well.)

I'm not really sure as to the number of people who will actually read this account of Michelina's life as a young woman through the early part of the twentieth century - honestly, it really doesn't matter. For me, it was a simple request that I made of my dear "Nonnie" and that she, in turn, set out to accomplish.

Admittedly, it was I who wanted a private letter of Michelina's amazing life in coming to America - a letter from my grandmother - my inspiration. She and I were the firstborn, each to different eras eons apart - a tough responsibility, especially in her case having been born "where" she was and "when" she was. Upon both our arrivals, we each made brand new fathers, mothers, grandparents, aunts, and uncles - all at once. As Zorba recounted in a movie he named after himself, "the whole catastrophe." So, it would stand to reason that I would inherit through some archaic right of primogeniture any family heirloom of note - any family treasure. And this woman was indeed a treasure.

I confess, there was a part of me that wanted to keep the ancestors all to myself - to listen to their speech and to their calling out to me - me, a family member way off in some distant future and village the ancestors could only imagine. But that notion was not to be. My grandmother Michelina wrote for posterity as opposed to her offspring and their offspring. Michelina transcended convention. She considered herself bigger than life, and in the context of the life she led, she obviously was correct in believing so. Michelina wrote as if people one thousand years from now would be interested in what she had to say. And who is to argue that point effectively? Not I, so, I gave up my private audience with this remarkable woman and set out to accomplish what she herself already knew - that Michelina Pirone Pisano was a woman ahead of her time and, in many ways, still is.

The mere fact that my grandmother wrote down her life's story at all was reward enough. Not many people of her generation or circumstance did or were capable of it. Ultimately, in no way was I the expectant sole recipient of this material. In my back recesses, I was perfectly willing to share her Letter with at least other members of the immediate family. However, after laying out her material on the desks of some neutral observers, they indicated to me that keeping a penned letter such as this under wraps or to simply letting it fall solely in the hands of family members or some dusty shoebox hidden in an attic somewhere, would be a sacrilege.

So, let the games begin.

Way back in 1979, I was under a screenwriter's contract at 20th Century Fox. My grandmother Lena (anglicized for "Michelina") was bugging me about publishing some of her short stories and poems - as if somehow, I could. I told her at that time, that the best thing she could do and something that would make the most sense would be to write out her Memoir in the form of a "Letter" for the family and for posterity. The idea was that that chore would keep her busy for a while. She bought a bunch of yellow legal pads, commandeered her worn-out fountain pen from her stationary box and then began her letter to me in blue-black- uninterrupted.

A few months later, she sent me a six-hundred-page handwritten letter of her early life on yellow legal pads, in first draft form - an unbelievable open letter. "Ooofa!" I made a promise to her then and there that I would transpose her handwritten "Letter," edit it, and make it available to at least her heirs and the heirs of her heirs after she left us. A handful of Michelina's immediate family got unedited copies of the entire six-hundred-page Letter several years ago. Obviously, I kept the handwritten original for proof of origin and as background for the back cover of this book.

———— ·⊂⊃· ————

Thirty-nine years ago, Michelina set out on this task knowing that she would most likely never receive a response to her Letter, outside of me of course, but that didn't matter to her. What mattered was that her children, their children and their children's children (ad infinitum), would be left with a legacy and direct connection to their immediate and distant past.

They could visit their heritage - pure Italy - pure America - pure struggle by a woman - by simply turning a page. And now that I have grandchildren of my own, all girls of course, they can plug into their great-great grandmother's voice as soon as they are able to read.

It also ventured into my mind that this woman, my grandmother, was a truly gifted if not egocentric writer (is there any other kind when the term "gifted" and "writer" appear in the same sentence?). My grandmother wanted her personal work to be lifted up, held to the light of day and heralded by the masses. Who could blame her considering the place and time in history for her gender and of her circumstance? She was a paradox of defiant decorum - an interesting combination when one considers.

Against all odds and above all else, Michelina was a self-taught intellectual, wrapped in a hand-sewn bundle of silk of her own design, in the middle of thousands of other inspired Italian immigrants, who then set off to find salvation in the bowels of steerage-class.

Michelina was born in February of 1901. She was the Forrest Gump of our family in the sense that she seemed to touch every key historic nerve ending of the twentieth century. Her life started at the very beginning of the century and finished almost at the very end of it. And what a life. She was an immigrant girl of eighteen from a medieval mountain village in Italy - a feminist - an intellectual with virtually no formal education whatsoever - a pseudo-Catholic who was essentially kicked out of Italy for starting a book club for girl's contrary to the doctrines of the church - a born-again Buddhist - an Humanist - a Suffragette - a practitioner of perennial philosophy - a journalist - a poet - a wife - a mother of two and a "builder" - of women's apparel and original silk wedding gowns. She backs all of these roles up here in her own words.

I sometimes like to write in a style that my grandmother Michelina was fond of calling "familiar formality." Twain was the best at it. Thousands of "easy" thoughts, none of them repetitive. It was the way she approached life. She would say to me as a child that words themselves are wondrous things; "Just look at them. Look at the way they spread out in a contiguous chain, connecting individual meanings but ultimately sacrificing their own singular definitions for the overall good and integrity of the sentence to which they serve - a sentence which too is just a singular piece of a larger cause." Yes, my grandmother started off as a cottage collectivist. In her mind, the common sentence was made up of individual "workers." Not a bad way to look at language actually. My grandmother had a pragmatic working-class perspective of composition. As importantly, she taught me to be a storyteller - an honorable profession - mostly.

In editing "Michelina's Letter," I tried not to detract from her unique style of delivery. It was told to me that Michelina learned English by translating Dante's "Inferno" from Latin into Italian and then into English. For most of her life, she could speak all three fluently even though one of those languages is dead. Her writing was flowery, descriptive and insightful - truly a style that had its roots in 19th century Italian prose which poured itself out unabated into the velvet parlors of early twentieth century English. I never used more commas, nor had more fun doing so. Again, a writing style choreographed by my hero, Samuel Langhorne Clemens. Little pentameter rest stops in a sentence, waiting for the readers to catch up, to collect themselves, to consider, and then to amble on at their own leisure.

Michelina's manuscript-Letter is essentially a first draft. It was written in longhand, much of it in fountain pen and on yellow lined legal paper. Wonderfully, it was all fastened together in bunches of tens and twenty pages with the tools of her trade - common "hemming" pins and sewing needles. In essence, she forwarded a six-hundred-page "Letter" hemmed together in sections of cloth for anyone who wanted to read an account of her life or the rarified era in which she lived.

And, it all "fit" perfectly.

It is also important to remember that English was Michelina's "second" language. The additional papers she left us in cardboard boxes still contain reams and reams of handwritten short stories, poems, and personal observances - all in what is no doubt flawless Italian.

However, she came to the English language with a sense and application derived from the classic romanticism of 19th century Italian literature. It shows up everywhere in her Letter.

Parts read like the libretto of a Verdi opera. I did not dare alter her way of composing sentences, for they were very much the way of her thought processes and equally how I remember her forming sentences as she spoke. Nevertheless, her Letter to us remains virtually as written.

There were times in editing her Letter that I was uncertain if the word she used was actually a word - an "English" word that is. I would check the largest English dictionary that I could find by necessity, and invariably the word was not only found to be a meaningful word, but it was also the perfect meaning for what she had intended the word to contribute. However, there were times, where my grandmother's choices of words were archaic and, dare I say, old-fashioned. But, they are her words, and there they shall remain in context.

As for expurgating text. I trimmed out some, consolidated, mended some rough patches and then sewed her patches back together - a family genetic acumen. But I was always sensitive to my grandmother's vernacular, her writing style, her approach and always who she was talking to.

In many instances, Michelina would "invent" words that not only conformed to the sentence perfectly, but, should be inducted into any new modern English dictionary. For English, after all, is the most malleable of all modern languages. My grandmother would attest to this by suggesting that the British like to reminisce that the sun never set upon their empire. I remember as a child, my grandmother telling me that the English language is so flexible because of the sheer number of peoples who were subjugated by the English over the centuries. People manipulated that foreign, non-indigenous language into their own need - who, in turn, kept the English language upgradeable and alive by the necessity of having identifiable, culturally protected colloquialisms. And, Michelina would tell you this in flawless Italian - over a roasted capon laced in a sweet white wine reduction and pine nuts along with handmade gnocchi as a lead-in to a long Sunday afternoon feast - opera blaring away on the 33 1/3 record player. You get the scene.

Examples of her literary prowess and ingenuity, however, can be found when she described going to a village festival as a child where all the people there would "festivate" like the Romans did. Or how she describes candles in her village church as "wax luminosities" and the ring of mountains surrounding her village in central Italy as the "altitude circumstant." My spellcheck just keeps staring at me. I could not, nor would not, alter such marvelous invention. Her Letter is full of such wonderful contrivances.

Michelina was also blessed with a tremendous memory and a gift of visualization and storytelling. She would keep me, the firstborn grandchild, spellbound for hours with stories of the old country, of Greek mythology and stories manufactured of her own design. I could never bring myself to blink.

What I found to be amazing when I first went through her openended letter was that so many of the accounts were in "dialogue form." Think about it. Actual conversations that she remembered having taken place more than seventy-five years ago in her own past - that's about 525 in dog-years. As you read her Letter, remember that she is recounting conversations that took place over a century ago. Being a screenwriter, I knew first hand just how difficult this particular form of writing discipline can be. The idea, always, is to bring reality to your reader into the present tense - "their" tense. And nothing accomplishes this better than written conversation. Reality presents itself in a splash of cold water and in a few short words. "We need a bigger boat." No one taught Michelina how to do this. That ability still intrigues me. Who of her time, of her circumstance, would have put conversation to pen? She just simply remembered conversations verbatim and wrote them down. It adds insight and texture to her Letter. We get to know the people around her, not only by what they did or how they reacted to situations, but by what they actually said and how they actually said it - a hundred plus years ago.

My grandmother also had a tremendous sense of history and how people such as herself fit into it. And, by the way, she would have let you know about it, too. She championed the workers' movement of the early teens and twenties of this past century and helped to establish the first Woman's Seamstress's Union in Massachusetts. The cause of working people and the plight of the less fortunate were always at the forefront of my grandmother's actions and concerns.

Michelina would always surround herself with people who could help satiate her overpowering need to learn and to expound on the free exchange of ideas. She was the first-born child born to a dominant Italian family; but born female, not male. She was forced to take her place at the table with that caveat, at that time in world history - but not for long. I often think, "what if."

Her intellectual pursuits included lectures, poetry readings, museums and garden groups, symphonies, operas, and libraries - "sempre" the library. As you will read, books were her most singular passion and they sometimes got her into much trouble. She was essentially "kicked out" of her village in Italy for starting a book club for girls with titles that fluffed-up the sacrosanct vestments of her encrusted village priests. This strength came from a young woman who was offered no more training or education, other than that of a career in domesticity, from village nuns, many of whom were related to her, until well into her teens.

Signora Michelina Pirone Pisano passed away in 1995 at the seasoned and venerable age of 94, way before I could even start to work on this piece to its final conclusion. Her ashes, by request, were scattered over three different prayer sanctuaries of three different religions. But Michelina knew that I would ultimately complete my part of the bargain. Now, I have the advent of the Cloud and a MAC at my disposal in this final leg of this monumental task. It is time to keep the promise I made to her so many, many years ago and to forward Michelina's Letter to those she ultimately left it to - the "people" - the "paesani."

Newfound technologies have given me a way of getting her old-world cursive into the hands of her new-world "heirs" - for you see, Michelina's spiritual bent dictated that her "heirs" include anyone who knows how to read.

My promise to her then will be fulfilled with the printing of this Three Act Letter. Take each Act as you would your own.

INTRODUCTION

The original six hundred handwritten pages were faithfully transcribed from longhand ink and set to CD disc by Michelina's great-granddaughter, my firstborn and noted Martha's Vineyard painter, Jessica Pisano. (jessicapisano.com). That was the hard part.

Last. About *[Asides:]* These Asides are not of my own device. I confess. Because of the classic nature and application of this work, Shakespeare's Elizabethan insertions duly influenced me - me thinks. I somehow felt that asides were the best way to go about it. Notwithstanding, Asides should be considered immediate footnotes supportive to pertinent material. They are literally my personal aside to the reader as he or she goes through Michelina's Letter - her Letter. They may be insights into what is being said or simply a clarification drawn from conversations I had with my grandmother on the subject when she was alive. They are mine and mine alone, and therefore I tried carefully not to let the Asides become too frequent or too intrusive.

ACT ONE

"Italy - as a Child"

August 7, 1979

"I start my memoir today with acute awareness of my own limitations but possessed with a desire to write whatever I remember of my long life.

I may lack the skill to do justice to the demand I force on myself, but the consistency I feel, it will help me. I promised my gifted grandson, Victor, to do this task and I will go through with it.

I begin my Letter

I was born in Italy on the 17th of February 1901, in a little town nestled under the Apennine Mountains a two-day carriage ride from Naples in a green valley surrounded completely by hills and mountains. The village, still called Pratola Serra, was lived in by people of many superstitions - people of almost atavistic habits. Looking back just eighty years ago is like peering back through unchanging centuries. No electricity - no motorized travel

- no refrigeration - no mass communication. Still, the surroundings were an enchantment. Reflecting now, I revisit childhood images as easily and as clearly as if I were looking out of my own kitchen window. I remember the silent evenings, the glorious mornings full of sunshine – the quietness of it all nearly a century ago. Yes, the quietness. It was as if one were alone with oneself and yet still in a crowd. Up until that time, up until the time of my birth, it had been breathily quiet and candlelit for thousands of years.

In 1901, Italy was recovering from the strains of war and of new laws, new ideas, and a resurgence of knowledge. The Industrial Revolution was not yet helping Italy, especially in the mountain villages south of Rome. England had already used the steamboat and had many miles of railroads, etc. Italy had too, but only on a very limited basis.

When Italy was finally united in the mid-18th hundred as a monarchy, (1861), then and only then did the industrial age take hold. Austria, Spain, France, and the Papal State powers of influence were destroyed, and Italy became free. But was it freedom? Some other powers were still there - the feudalistic powers. At the turn of the new century, the 20th century, the internal conflict of Italy began. Cries of freedom were heard. A newly formed Italy needed money for these fierce changes. The people who had the money hesitated to invest in the unification. Was it secure? Would it be profitable for them? They had felt secure until then when the peninsula was an amalgam of separate fiefdoms. Now? The Feudalists were against these phenomenal and drastic changes.

The King and his administration did very little to promote or to inform the people about the many innovations. Mostly the little towns of the South, like my own village, were kept in the dark. But progress always wins in the end, eh? It has a way of penetrating, perhaps slowly, but surely it happens. News began to touch the ears of the paesani (the masses) who were tired of working for a pittance of what they produced. Angry voices of the rebellious were heard, demanding more and more of the share they were permitted to have by the feudalistic landowners. This was a worldwide struggle at the time, not just in Italy.

The small towns had a hard time grasping anything new because of the many customs and influences set upon them by other nations that had ruled Italy. The towns had suffered more greatly, mostly the southern villages. No communication existed between one town to the other. They all embraced different dialects and their schools were not yet properly organized or directed on a unified basis. The Catholic Church, with its Latin dogma, ruled. This was Italy just prior to my birth.

Chapter One

My Father's Side

The Pirone Family

My grandfather, "Don Carlos" Pirone, was a Master leather-worker and owned his own factory. He used to make fancy harnesses for monumental horse carriages. He had no time for carts or other types of common transportation. He was a "Master" in the classic European tradition. Don Carlos had five dutiful sons and an educated wife - a beautiful family.

My grandfather's three oldest sons were also leather-workers - my father, Giuseppe, and two of his brothers. My father, Giuseppe was the second born son (and the best worker of all the brothers). Don Carlos called him, "L'ago d'Oro" - "the Golden Needle," for his prowess with elaborate leatherwork and technique. The other two youngest Pirone sons were educated in the art of metalwork mechanics.

The Pirone family all lived together under several big roofs joined to the harness factory - a compound in the middle of the village. Don Carlos was, of course, the patriarch. The order he maintained was indeed admirable. The only problem was that my father, Giuseppe, was the secret envy of his four other brothers. But one would never have known this. It was not out in the open. The sons had to obey their father, the "Don," without questioning, even as young men. That was how family order was maintained.

All five brothers could sing and play cord instruments. My father had a wonderful tenor voice and never hesitated to show it off. My "Nonno," (grandfather), loved it when his sons sang. This handsome stern man loved music - mostly opera. He often suggested that his sons sing some operatic arias whenever work was finished in the harness shop.

Don Carlos used to travel by carriage to Naples on many weekends with his friends to the San Carlo Opera House. My grandfather loved the opera "Don Carlos" by Verdi so much that he imitated the protagonist of the opera, Don Carlos, by making his own beard grow just like that of Verdi's character. Now, everyone called him just by that name. He rejoiced in the habit of rubbing his chin.

My Nonno Pirone sang softly the arias to his children as they grew, until all of them were able to sing together - harmony in voice anyway. Even my ultra-religious Nonna Pirone sang with her sons on candlelit Sunday evenings when the family was all together. It was how people entertained themselves then - simply and with their own contrivance. All together. Nonna Pirone was always humming tunes of Palestrina, Scarlotti and other church annotations.

My village, Pratola Serra, was full of music. Music was everywhere. There was always a good organist in the village church and the Sunday masses were a treat not only for Nonna Pirone, but of course for the entire town as well. There was also a band of very good musicians in our village, with a very gifted bandleader as Maestro. When the men rehearsed, their music resounded all over the quiet town. The village was a performance stage during these times. The music would often echo off the hillside and return to us again for a second appraisal. Most of the time they played new songs. Then, everyone in the village tried to learn those songs, and soon people sang what they had just learned. And the echoes were of constant support. In addition to the organ and the bells of the church, there were mandolins and guitars played in the town by many individuals. Pratola Serra was very musical.

Times were beginning to change, however, perhaps in some small way because it was also about to turn into a new century. The monumental carriages of an earlier time of the 18-hundreds were becoming very scarce, and my grandfather's little harness factory had lost some of its seasoned trade. Don Carlos, his three sons, and his three apprentices, had to come up with a different kind of harness work in order to survive. Finally, this fussy man had to find the humility to accept common horse carts and large mule-drawn wagons of transportation for work. His old clients, the nobility, now traveled by a new innovation - the first-class passenger train. The demand to place harnesses on noble carriage horses went to lower beasts of burden.

Well, the drivers of the food carts, mule trains, etc., were so thankful that Don Carlos had finally accepted to dress up their mules and horses with his harnesses that they began to leave lots of food and other goods in Nonno's harness factory. So much food, that it was impossible for Nonno, his sons, and the three apprentices to consume it all. *[Aside: At the time, barter trading was a proven way of doing business and was usually the first and sometimes only means of paying off debts. It kept business relationships close and personal. Every transaction was a re-evaluation of each man's worth, unlike settling debts with cold hard "official" currency, which was still scarce and especially mistrusted in rural Italy at the turn of the last century.]*

The harness factory now needed more workers. Oh, how busy everyone was. New apprentices finally came in to help from the nearby mountain town of Ariano. More and more carts and cargo wagons came by the factory; more food and goods were left as payment. All these carts were transporting foodstuffs to Avellino and to Naples, and all of them carried the produce from other regions - from opulent Apulia Basilica, etc. All the abundance of these regions passed through our little village of Pratola Serra. And who serviced them? The skilled Pirone men, naturally. The Pirone clan was as busy as ever, but this time building harnesses of function rather than form.

Ah, but now my sagacious Nonna soon concocted an idea. She would open a store to get rid of all the food and produce left behind by the drivers as payment. Perfect! This store of hers was right next to the harness factory. Nonna also had help from her daughter-in-law, Uncle Antonio's wife, Bernadina. The Pironi (plural of "Pirone") were an enclave of commerce of our little village tucked away in the mountains of South-central Italy.

Nonna Pirone had two servants - a man named Feluccio and his wife. Feluccio used to take care of the two horses and carriages we had and he did all the outside work. He used to transport our family when they needed to go to Naples or to other towns nearby. His wife used to help Nonna with the housework. Well now, poor Nonna was so very busy with the new store, she asked the servant woman to help in the store and also to cook. She was a wonderful cook. Together with Nonna, they managed to feed the growing Pirone family compound, take care of the store and dispose of the forever-abundant produce that came in as trade.

Chapter Two

My Mother's Side

The Fabrizio Family

My mother's family was named, Fabrizio - also of the village, Pratola Serra. The Fabrizio were a very old family of the region, going back to medieval times with many attributing the Roman general Fabrizius as to the name's derivation. His heirs were my mother's ancestors - an old and tenacious seed. The town records in Pratola Serra listing the Fabrizio's goes back 700 years to the 13th century. They were mostly rich landowners, road builders, shoemakers, priests and nuns - many, many priests and nuns. The Fabrizio had a tradition of producing many nuns and priests so as not to dilute their inherited power. Land was handed down for generations, and land for them was a base of power. Priests and nuns did not share in their family's wealth of course. Their lives were vested in the Catholic Church. They could not inherit land directly, so it would be split fewer times but still remain within the Fabrizio family. It was a perfect approach to having many children without dividing the family inheritance too many ways. Having ascetic priests and nuns meant it was less likely to having additional children to vie for all the family's possessions as well.

My mother's immediate family consisted of her mother, my grandmother Giuseppella and of course my grandfather, Luigi Fabrizio - and also, my mother had two brothers. My mother's name was Angelina.

My mother's older brother, Antonio, had a best friend in the village of Pratola Serra - Giuseppe Pirone - my destined-to-be father. My mother's brother and my father were the same age and two of a kind, happy-go-lucky showoffs born a little selfish from privilege. As young men of the village, they were both incorrigible and inseparable.

Now, about my mother's father, my other Nonno - Nonno Luigi Fabrizio - what a story to be told as well! He was a stoic and proud man - another Italian-Roman classic.

When my mother's father was a young man, in the mid-1800's, he had been a soldier under the regime of the Bourbons - the Empire who kept Italy from unifying by fighting against the eventual emancipator of Italy, Giuseppe Garibaldi. My Nonno Fabrizio served a total of eight years - four years for his own call of duty and another four years for his brother. *[Aside: Bourbons ruled in Naples from 1734-1806 and in Sicily from 1734-1816, and in a unified Kingdom of the Two Sicilies from 1816-1860. Luigi Fabrizio served the Bourbons as a soldier around 1856. Soldiers in many countries during the 19th century could add the mandatory time required of other family members to their own term of military service.]*

At this time, my grandfather's brother Gabriele, two years his younger, was making lots of money building the much-needed paved roads in Italy. When Nonno Fabrizio was through with both tours of duty, eight years in total, he had only a "thank you" from his brother and no other remuneration.

During his military service, my grandfather Luigi was caught in the middle of the transition time between all of the wars that marked the unification period of Italy. Garibaldi won, and Italy was unified. Both the rich north and the poorer south came together as a tentative one in 1861. His side, the longstanding Bourbon regime, had ultimately lost. Land was consolidated, precious Fabrizio land as well. Most of it now was taxed into absorption.

After those eight years of serving the Bourbons, my grandfather Fabrizio became a rash fanatic for honesty - one could say to a fault. Yes, he signed on to be a soldier with the losing Bourbons, and by God, in his mind, he had to be a good one - a good soldier. At times these principles became detrimental to his peace of mind because he thought the stability of Italy and of his family's long legacy had succumbed. And so, this perceived weakening of the Fabrizio land holdings was to haunt my mother's father for most of the remainder of his life.

As a young war veteran, however, Luigi fought more with his tongue - in any coffeehouse, bar or in the street. After the unification of Italy, everywhere my grandfather went, he had constant political arguments with the Garibaldini, the winning Nationalists. He was fatefully branded as a soldier of the Bourbons, branded inside and out.

In one of these fights, in the nearby village of Mercogliano, my grandfather severely beat up a Garibaldino who called him "traitor." Imagine the fire that this honest man felt in his heart, tormented as he was by his confusion of duty versus honor and love of country. He fought as if he had to defend his own life! Other men went against him. He was beaten up plenty. Finally, inevitably, he was arrested.

While Italy was trying to build a new nation, there were not many jails, and the authorities didn't dare to use the old dilapidated castles for jailhouses as the Bourbon's had done unless they absolutely had to. So, in the small towns and villages, especially in the south of Italy, the delinquents were brought to the private houses of whoever was entrusted to maintain order. This was sufficient for small crimes, but big offenders like murderers or thieves were brought to whatever city jails were available - often to medieval castles. So, after my grandfather's arrest for beating up a follower of Giuseppe Garibaldi, my grandfather was brought to the local jail-keeper's house for detainment.

As it turned out, it was also the house of his future wife, my grandmother Giuseppella - the jail-keeper's daughter!

The jailer's house was a large stone manse with an adapted cellar for the purpose of keeping prisoners. The commune paid him a goodly rent for this service. The jailer's house had enough security in this beautiful town of Mercogliano positioned between Pratola Serra and Naples.

So, as was told to me, my grandfather, dirty and bloody, looked like a monster just at the moment he saw this beautiful, little, darling girl, Giuseppella. She was no more than sixteen and very fair. He was being forced past her by two bullish guards. When confronting him, she crossed herself, "Dear God, what a man!" His beard, his hair, his entire attitude was devilish. The two guards had to forcefully hold him down. Luigi was roaring like a wild animal in front of his future love. Imagine.

After two days of rest on a padded rope bed with lots of good food and a bath in a wooden tub, Luigi was like another man. He stood tall and erect. He carried the Roman head of his ancestors, a mass of curly hair, and a ready smile showing his white teeth - a very handsome fellow indeed. Understandably, Giuseppella made more and more trips down to the cellar of her own house - the jail.

And so, it came to be that my grandfather, Luigi Fabrizio, and my grandmother, Giuseppella, fell in love together right there, in my great-grandfather's jail. The year was about 1862 - the year of the great American Civil War.

Luigi remained in the town of Mercogliano, Italy until he was able to secure permission to marry Giuseppella, which must have been quite a feat of talkmanship given his first introduction to the family. It must have been a long and arduous stay. I think finally Luigi's honesty and goodness came through to his future father-in-law, his jail-keeper. What a courtship that must have been, eh?

Luigi then took his little darling back home to Pratola Serra where he settled in as yet another leather-worker of the village - this grandfather, however, became a Master Shoemaker.

Nonno Fabrizio was extremely devoted to my grandmother Giuseppella right up until her death. He treated her ever so gently, with such love and devotion. I saw this every time I visited with them as a child. Devotion to her in an almost unbelievable fashion - an endearing countenance for such a rough-mannered and unpolished man of contention. I must add again, that my grandfather, in all of his life, had to defend his honesty, mostly from the Garibaldini of our village, a continuous torment for him. Nonno Fabrizio would defend himself until his voice became confused, then he would leave in a garbled rage. Poor fellow, he meant well, he just took the wrong road to champion his honesty. Honesty must also deal with injustice, an obsession that comes with a long stick that hurts when it strikes.

Chapter Three

The Unification of Italy

The Unification of the Pirone and the Fabrizio Families.

My Uncle Antonio Fabrizio was the firstborn to Luigi and Giuseppella. As mentioned, Antonio and my father, Giuseppe, grew up together in the village and were the best of friends. Like many firstborn sons, Antonio took up the trade of his father. He, too, became a Master cobbler in the village. In time, Antonio married a girl of Pratola Serra. *[Aside: Most of the names Michelina mentions in the early part of her Letter repeat their appearance throughout the body of the work.]*

My Uncle Antonio's separatist beliefs were like that of his father (and many others I might add). They were discontented with the orders coming out of the unificated Italy, which demanded more and more taxes from the people. These taxes for a "central government," as opposed to smaller states, made it impossible for these newly unified Italians to make a decent living in isolated villages of the south.

When his chance came, my mother's brother, Antonio, was one of the first of the village to leave for the United States. He had no solid prospects as a shoemaker; he just took his wife, picked up and left, taking with him only the tools of his trade. A paesano [a friend], a shoemaker from another village, received Antonio and his wife in his house in Lynn, Massachusetts - America. Antonio remained in the USA all the rest of his life, in Lynn, where he first landed. Lynn was home of a whole community of skilled shoemakers. Here, he became a very successful citizen and very content. Lynn Massachusetts in the late 1800's was part of America's shoe capital - the best in the world at the time. However, before Antonio left for America, he did a fine deed for his sister, my mother, Angelina. He also played a good trick on his best friend, my father Giuseppe at the same time. His last act was to play cupid for his reluctant friend before leaving for America.

As young men, Uncle Antonio often brought his best friend, Giuseppe Pirone, around to the house. They both had a lot in common besides being skilled leatherworkers. During these visits, my mother, Angelina, developed a not-so-secret adoration for Giuseppe. It simmered in her for years. My father, of course, being so perfect in his own mind and manner, did not dissuade her interests at all. In fact, he encouraged the adulation, but when he was sure of Angelina's love and admiration, he gave his attention to other girls of the village. I can say however that not much has changed in this area of courtship in Italy - or America.

At this time, before leaving for America with a new wife, Uncle Antonio planned a surprise birthday party for his father, Luigi. He invited all of the Pirone to attend - a gathering of his best friend and his family - leatherworkers all of course. He especially invited Don Carlos Pirone to attend this sumptuous supper. The stage was set for Uncle Antonio's plan. Then, at the feast's toast for all to hear, Antonio cautiously, but intentionally, brought up the subject of Giuseppe's escapades with other girls in the village. My mother Angelina said nothing. It was not her place to. The room went silent.

Don Carlos Pirone, right there and then, sitting at the head of the table, very honorable and imposing, asked his son, "Is your long love for this beautiful girl wavering?! Seven long years she has thought of nobody else but you!" My mother blushed. My father hesitated to answer. Then Don Carlos stood up saying, "Giuseppe, answer me!" "No, Papa. I love Angelina and nobody else."

Don Carlos sat back down and looking toward my mother's father, Luigi, and said, "Well, Luigi, let's plan their marriage then!" My grandfather gave my mother's hand away with the lift of a wine glass and a smile. Next? My two Nonno's planned everything at the table. Yes, only them. The future bride and groom had nothing to say about it. Only Ferdinando, my mother's younger brother, whispered to her at the table, "This man, Giuseppe Pirone, will never make you happy! You deserve better!" He excused himself and left the house in a huff. Both Angelina and Giuseppe got up and embraced each other. What choice did they have? Sure, love had a hand in it - almost as much as my Uncle Antonio, who smiled to himself I'm sure. He tied up his best friend and his sister in a tight package and then left happily to go to America.

Three thousand lire, that was my mother's dowry, a small fortune in those days. The dowry also included a full trousseau of 20 Garments – 20 pieces of linen sheets - half that amount for spreads - 20 tablecloths - 10 dresses - 10 underwear, etc., etc. The money was handed over and entrusted to Don Carlos Pirone with a gentlemen's handshake agreement. The agreement would eventually cause dissension between my father and his brothers and also be a derisive contention in my parents' marriage as to ownership and usage.

That night, the two old Master leather-smiths came to an agreement. The money in my mother's substantial dowry would be held by my father's father, Don Carlos and Don Carlos alone. It would all go into the Pirone harness factory. The reasoning was that my father, Giuseppe, worked most closely with his father and lived in his father's house. The long-term plan was for my father to eventually inherit the factory outright, and the dowry was to be a seal for that purpose as a down payment. After Don Carlos' death, my father, Giuseppe, would then be the sole inheritor of the harness business even though he was not the oldest son. He was the heir harness-maker apparent, however - "L'ago d'Oro," - remember? The Golden Needle. These two old and venerable Dons of leather drank their wine in consummation of everyone else's future at the table.

So, it came to be. My parents, Giuseppe and Angelina were married in the month of February 1900.

Exactly one year later, I was born!

———————

Chapter Four

My Day of Birth – Rebellion

(As recounted to me in childhood by my Nonno Fabrizio – the Roman rebel). Sunday, February 17, 1901. Pratola Serra, Italy

The day of February 17th, 1901 was a typical winter day in the mountains of southern Italy. The sun at this time of the year has a calm luminosity - dry, cool weather - very salutary!

Pratola Serra was in turmoil, however, for there had been a little rebellion that very morning. About fifty armed farmers and peasants appeared in the town square - squadron-like. There they stood, carrying on their shoulder's muskets and aggressive-looking farm tools. They stood there in silence with an air of stern expectancy. People from every corner of the village came to the square with frightened curiosity. Everyone in town had gathered around these men. The mayor, other dignitaries, the two priests - all were present and appalled. They asked the armed men what they wanted. "Are you joking?" the mayor demanded. But there was no answer. The silence became very painful. Finally, the two priests approached the group, confident that the armed farmers would respect what they represented. One of the priests who arrived was a Fabrizio, my grandfather's cousin - Domenico. He confronted the men pleading, "Please, move away. You give us an apprehension of trouble." One of the men answered, "We are waiting for our lord, Il Signorino, to talk to him." The Signorino was the feudal lord, a land baron, the one most of them worked for. ("Signorino" is an endearing name for "lord.")

The priests sent for this man. Soon, Il Signorino showed up - a proud, arrogant man of about forty years of age. He barked at the armed farmers, "What in hell do you want standing there fierce and audacious?" The peasants lowered their farm tools and one of them spoke. "We will not work for you anymore, Il Signorino. We asked for a better share of the crops that we grow, and you refuse us. We will leave this town. We will go away from here! Perhaps to other parts of the world where people like you are not around! You and yours have kept us in misery long enough!" The armed men began to push forward.

Before the Signorino could say another word, Father Domenico spoke to the farmers. "You will cause disturbances, more misery, scarcity, and disorder!" A young man who was at the back of the group, pushed forward, straight and ready for any debate. He said to Father Domenico, "You, as a man of God, should perorate our cause and not encourage him," pointing to the Signorino, "to get richer and richer!" More shouts came forth. Then addressing the other priest, the young man said, "When you preach again your Sunday sermon, do not talk about obedience for our baron lord who gives us work. We work! He does nothing! Preach, yes, I love to listen when you make sense, and imitate Jesus. Jesus is the Lord, not this man." Then with more ardor, he said, "Tell me what Jesus would say now with all this misery that confronts us. I can't buy my mother a new dress! I can't afford the medicine for my old father! My brother works in Tufo, in the Signorino's mine of sulfur for 12 hours a day. Still, he can't make a decent living! All we work for is to make this man rich!!!" He went on and on. The mayor came forward and said to everyone in the square, "All right, enough! Go home - all of you! I will see that things will get better!" The peasants, military-like, held their muskets on their shoulders and left peacefully. Each and every farmer, however, left his farm tool right there, in the middle of the town square. Nobody dared to touch them. Later, in the dark of the night, the tools all disappeared.

There was a continued unrest after the square was emptied. People congregated in groups to discuss what had happened. They left stunned. Never had anything like that ever happened before in the village that anyone could remember. "Why would anybody dare to address a man of God that way?" one man said. Other comments followed. "All right, they left their jobs, but others will take over. There are so many people in need!"

Well, my two grandfathers, Pirone and Fabrizio, were there, too, of course. Luigi was having an argument with some women of the crowd about the rights of landowners - the Fabrizio family discourse. More joined in against him, as was his history. They accused him of being too strict with the peasants, etc. He defended himself, hotly, getting all nerved up. Nonno Pirone approached him and said, "Luigi, please, go home now." Mamma Mia, that made my Nonno Fabrizio still madder, and he shouted back, "You, Don Carlos, will not tell me what to do! I shall go home when I feel like it!" Although there was a longstanding working relationship between my two grandfathers, they were so different from one another. They were friendly but with a restraint.

My Nonno Fabrizio mostly resented my Nonno Don Carlos. Perhaps it was a jealousy, for Don Carlos Pirone had a sharp tongue. He could say things that would hurt Nonno Fabrizio with direct politeness - things that confused the rugged old soldier. Yes, Don Carlos was loquacious, sharp, and direct. He could convince even a devil with his imposing personality and mannerism. He was the Capo Di'Maestro of the village after all.

At this instant, my very pregnant mother ran up to Nonno Fabrizio and, together with the help of my father, brought him back to his home several streets away. My grandfather, Luigi, was spitting venom all the way there.

Once inside the house, my grandmother Giuseppella made some hot lunch and so tried to pacify her irate husband. They all sat at the table close to the stone fireplace. My mother, happy, beautiful, with olive skin as fine as silk, sat next to her father in a large chair. She straightened up her father's hair and embraced him dearly. She jokingly said to him, "Papa - the Fabrizio temper got to you again, eh? Now you look like Saint Anthony penitent." They all laughed. After composing herself, my mother suddenly felt a sharp pain. It was I who was knocking to be out. She stiffened. Everyone became alarmed.

Nonna Giuseppella, said, "Good! You shall have the baby here! In this house!" But my father suddenly jumped up, "No, no! Impossible! We must go home before the pain becomes more severe." His child, his firstborn, had to be delivered in the house of the Pironi - that was his thought.

So slowly, but surely, my father escorted my mother back over the many stone streets to his father's compound. It took them countless minutes to get there. They walked close together and nobody noticed my mother suffering - people were still in the square recounting the conflict and milling about.

My father had to bring his wife home because of his father's domination - he had to.

Soon, my father and mother reached the door to the Pironi main house and slowly went upstairs to their quarters, which were right over the harness factory. My grandmother Pirone saw them. The attitude of my mother and father told her just what was happening. She ran upstairs after them. She was sure that the time had arrived for her grandchild to be born.

Nonna Pirone advised my mother to get undressed and to go right into bed. The knocking of my arrival occurred every ten minutes. Nonna said, "There is still lots of time." Nonna then assured my mother, "Stay quiet, dear, and don't be afraid. You are becoming a mother. Bless you."

Nonna ran downstairs to look for Don Carlos and to find somebody who could run to fetch the village midwife. Don Carlos was still out in the square discussing the farmer's revolt of the morning with his friends. The harness factory was empty. It was the siesta hour. A little distance away, in the middle of the street, was one of my grandfather's apprentices with his fiancée. They were laughing and having a good time teasing each other with some flowers that the girl had in her hair. Nonna Pirone called to him, "Luciano! Please run to Signora Lida, the midwife, and don't come back until you bring her here!" The young man returned the flowers to his girl and ran.

From afar, Nonno Pirone saw the boy running. My grandfather left his companions and joined his wife. He then ordered her to close her store and to go upstairs again to my mother. Don Carlos then called to my father and ordered him to get the workers back from the street and to maintain order. Nonno Pirone then went upstairs himself, approached my laboring mother, and pleaded for her not to call out for her husband adding, "I will be here outside the door and will let no one in. Only my wife and the midwife will be with you, Angelina. No confusion, please!

20

Now try to be a good girl." He bent down and kissed her on the fore-head. Being kissed by this stern, prominent man was a thrill, and she felt honored. She answered, "Yes Papa, I will be good. I promise!" So, it was. Don Carlos shut the door and sat on the top of the stairs, in front of the door, as my mother vocally anguished in the room, alone - wait-ing in pain for the midwife - waiting for me to arrive.

My father appeared again at the large Roman type portal below the stairs of the apartment. Don Carlos raised his voice, "Giuseppe! I told you! Go back and finish what you started this morning! Take care of the workers! I will call you when the baby will come. Go, go!" Nonna from another balcony gave orders too. She told her other daughter-in-law, "Bernadina, keep the store closed! There is a baby coming!" Orders, orders, orders - what a time I chose to be born!

My grandfather's young apprentice, Luciano, felt honored to be com-manded to fetch the midwife. He ran like a Greek Olympian through the narrow ancient streets. In a few minutes, he came back with the old woman - Signora Lida, the village midwife. She was so full of impor-tance, dressed all in loose folds of immaculate brushed white wool, with a heavy shawl over her shoulders. She talked to no one, looking like an old priestess. The midwife flew up the stairs and past Don Carlos with-out even looking at him. There was no question as to who was the boss of this hour. In she went to her patient who was lamenting with unbear-able pains that were now only a few minutes apart. Nonna Pirone was getting hot water ready and the inevitable black coffee. All the town's attention was turned away from the rebellious square toward the Pironi compound. They watched from their own front doors as people went in and out of my grandfather's house - everyone expecting news. They knew what it was about.

Father Domenico Fabrizio saw the midwife run into the Pirone house and went straightaway into the church followed by a few paesani. He solemnly prayed, "Oh God, give us a healthy child, free from birth-marks and deformity! Please, God, please!" They always burdened their God with all their desires and problems.

In the meantime, my mother, at age 22, healthy and very proud, kept on being good, as she had promised. She suffocated the intense pain of birth with dignity. She knew that the old man on the top of the stairs outside her door would be proud of her. Was this man bad? Was he a dictator? A tyrant? No, it was only his deep sense of family duty and honor that made him appear so. Tradition. It was also his place in that world to do so. After all, Don Carlos Pirone was not just Master of his trade, he was the Master of his house. He was beautiful in appearance with a loquacious tongue, sometimes a little sharp, but always to the point and always convincing with his deep logic. Yes, he was lord of his household, and his household was now growing.

At this point, my sweet grandmother Fabrizio came running up the stairs to the apartment, but the old man advised her not to go in yet.

Gently he said to her, "Please, Giuseppella - here, sit down with me." Holding her hands, he continued, "It is better not to disturb your wonderful daughter, the joy of our lives." The loving little darling obeyed - and prayed silently next to Don Carlos.

After an hour of soft lamentations from my mother, a baby's cry was heard. My cry!

Nonna Fabrizio and Don Carlos embraced each other both saying, "God bless our new child." They got up.

After a short while, the door was opened. Nonna Pirone came out holding me in her arms bundled up in white flannel - part of the midwife's shawl. She said to them, "Michelinella (baby Michelina) is born! Here she is - healthy and beautiful." My mother, now free from heavy pain, smiled. Her own mother crying, embraced her, "This is my first granddaughter." My father came up, looked in and he said with disappointment, "A girl?" Don Carlos jumped back harshly, "Yes! A girl!" Nonna Pirone kept on repeating, "Yes, this child shall be called after me - Michelina."

And, so it was.

Nonna Fabrizio could only glow with pride. Poor dear, forced to listen from behind a door as her first grandchild was born and given the name of the other grandmother. And of course, a cry of joy was heard from the town, "the Pironi have another girl grandchild!" My equally poor grandfather, Luigi, must have heard the commotion behind his own closed door. When I was later told all of this by him, he also told me that both he and Nonna Fabrizio were overjoyed, for I was their own grandchild.

Not all were that joyous, however. My father's acknowledged disappointment of my birth was woven in the fabric of custom. Here was another firstborn who could not inherit, who could not vote or influence, who could not be trained in the family business or carry on some preconceived legacy - a legacy that had not even been fully realized yet. A girl. Not all of the prayers were answered that day - yes, another female Pirone born into the world. But no future doctor, no future dignitary or priest, no person of high station, no promise except to perpetuate the hope and the name of some other family. Plus, the burden of a dowry. My father knew he had to eventually provide my own dowry as well. A loss from what my mother's dowry provided? No, he could only hope for some other child, the next child to come to him in the future - to be a male Pirone. Looking back, I can almost understand my father's disappointment. Almost.

Right after my birth, it was Nonna Pirone who took charge of me. Naturally. She had in her store next to the harness shop a little cradle that had been used for her own children - her five sons. My mother was only called in to nurse me and to wash my clothes in the well by the garden. That was it. Those were my mother's duties in the house. Poor Momma. Only at night did she have me all to herself in the large but lonely apartment above the factory. My grandmother Pirone had her help for the store and to cook for her husband and sons when they finished work - my mother was just one of the two wives of the Pirone sons living at the compound.

So now there were two little girls in the Pirone compound. Me and little Fortunella, the infant daughter of Don Carlos' third born son, Antonio. Don Carlos was very attached to his first grandchild, little Fortunella, so much so, that it became a point of jealousy between my father and his younger brother. Which female grandchild - which Pirone girl would now

23

get the Don's complete attention? For after all, Don Carlos and Nonna Pirone only had five sons to raise all these years, and baby girls were not in his disfavor by any means.

But providence answered that question. My Uncle Antonio Pirone, being the third born son behind my father who undoubtedly knew the terms of my mother's dowry, made an independent decision. He saw his future at the factory as hopeless and with no future to expand his own self-perceived gifts. So, he declared one solemn day that he was leaving, for America - he would take his wife Bernadina (a poor farm girl with no dowry of her own who was pregnant before their marriage) from Don Carlos' house and leave.

Well, they did go. However, they decided to leave behind their only child, Fortunella for Don Carlos and Nonna Pirone to take care of. It was said that Nonno Pirone couldn't part with his firstborn grandchild and that my little cousin was forced to remain behind because of my grand-father's wishes. But I think it was not so hard for my father's brother to leave with just only his wife. Of course, Don Carlos might not have had to put up much of an argument from his son under the circumstances. Don Carlos wanted his firstborn grandchild to stay - even if a girl - and everyone knew that Don Carlos always had his way.

So, America now would have two Antonios from my families - my mother's older brother and my father's younger brother. Antonio Pirone would bring a wife and leave a child. He vowed he would make his way in America and would soon come back for the child. No one believed otherwise.

Thus, I was born in Italy that February in 1901 amongst village and family politics - neither of which was of my choosing or control.

Chapter Five

Family Dissention: Coming to terms with a large dowry

My brother Ralfo was born

My First Years

My father Giuseppe, like his father, Don Carlos, was a Master in the trade of harness making. As I mentioned, he was nicknamed the "Golden Needle." But he was still too obedient and subservient to his own father in the factory and in the household. Never could he relax. My father never dared to disobey Don Carlos or his mother either. After younger brother Antonio left for America, my father's older brother, Raffaele, the firstborn son, was the only son left competing with my father in the harness shop. It became too much for Uncle Raffaele to bear - the curse of my mother's dowry - of being the firstborn son of Don Carlos with no meaningful inheritance. How he must have felt. So, in 1901, he too left for New York, following and joining his brother Antonio there. My father was left alone with Don Carlos to work in the harness factory as the only son. My fathers' other two brothers were of a different trade. Metalsmiths. I will recount these other two uncles shortly. *[Aside: It is clear why both of Guiseppe's harness-making brothers, Antonio and Raffaele, left the village for America. They knew of the deal consummated between Don Carlos Pirone and Luigi Fabrizio where their brother Giuseppe would ultimately inherit the harness factory as part of the marriage arrangements which was sealed by the large Fabrizio dowry. Their fortune was elsewhere.]*

Soon, after arriving in America, Raffaele married a girl in New York who happened to be born and raised in the nearby town from us called Montefalcione. They were happy - for a while. It was no surprise then when Antonio and Raffaele opened a shop together in the Bronx, New York, as harness-makers. They did pretty well. At that time, in 1902, there still were horses for transportation, even in America - mostly milk or ice wagons and carriages for rich people's stables. Back in Italy, the old harness shop was left only to my father, my grandfather, and the apprentices. No wonder my father himself would sometimes enviously look off in the direction where his two brothers had fled. He was to find himself in an arranged marriage to a woman he professed to have loved and to her large dowry. Still, he should have been grateful for such a circumstance. But he wasn't.

⎯⎯⎯⎯◦⎯⎯⎯⎯

In the first eighteen months of my life, I developed acute colitis, a condition which I carried in various forms until this day. As an infant, I could not digest anything other than my mother's milk, only my mother's breast had become dry before long. So, Nonna Pirone got me a village wet nurse - the healthy, beautiful, Melella, (Little Apple). She was called this because of her abundant beauty. She also had plenty of milk to feed me with, and also her own child. Everything else in the household and the village stayed the same during this time - uneasy, expectant times.

Then, in 1904, when I became three years old, two major events happened in my young life. First, my dear baby brother and kindred spirit for life, Ralfo, (Raffaello) was born - a big, plump, healthy and happy newborn boy! I remember the joy that was abundant in the house. Don Carlos had now a firstborn grandson to carry on the family name, and of course to learn the trade of harness-making. (Ralfo, I'll mention later, for he obviously broke the perceived jinx of the Pironi having no legitimate heirs. I should mention here that it is custom for us to say "Pironi" for more than one "Pirone" and "paesani" for more than one "paesano." Also in this year, 1904, my Uncle Ferdinando's homecoming has an equally memorable recounting in my mind. It reflects for me a measure of another custom in Italy at that time.)

The second event of importance that year was that my mother's younger brother, Uncle Ferdinando Fabrizio, came back from America. He left soon after my mother's marriage, following his own brother Antonio to Lynn, Massachusetts, and then he came back three years later. He was the brother who advised my mother very strongly not to marry my father. However, all these brothers from both families leaving to seek a new life in America played into my father's unrest. One set of Pirone brothers and one set of Fabrizio brothers had left, including my father's best friend.

Uncle Ferdinando, too, had become a master cobbler like his brother, Antonio, and their father, my Nonno Luigi. However, Uncle Ferdinando was the first of my mother's two brothers to come back from America after leaving the village. Why? To bring a wife back to America of course. His success in America emboldened him to reach for the stars.

My mother's brother was not exactly a handsome man. He wasn't an unattractive man either. He did carry himself well, dressed well, and knew his own special abilities. Yes. He was another Master leatherworker from our village - a prodigal son. And he came home to "declare" a wife.

So, in the summer of 1904, my Uncle Ferdinando came back to Italy with the sole intention of being married to his beloved - and supposedly waiting - Margherita. It was like the true love he as an Italian man cherished - a love he placed upon his one and only, Margherita.

Well, the irony was that Margherita's affections were not as equally devoted to my poor Uncle Ferdinando. Still, after many unanswered letters, he came back with an unwavering purpose - to bring back a "highly cherished female" as a wife to America from his own village. The village, after all, was transplanting - westward. [Aside: My grandmother's overriding dictum of the period was that a man's self-worth was measured in social context by what he could eventually acquire as a female counterpart. To the Italian male of that era, this was obviously a requirement of life when custom dictated that it was time to declare a co-propagator. Again, there was also a dowry factor. The young girls and women of the time understood this, and it is little wonder then that their primary occupation was to become expert in the preparation of that selection. Granted, this ritual is cross-cultural and relentlessly timeless. However, Michelina, later in life as it turns out, was not so inclined to accommodate that expectation.]

This practice of coming back from America to take a wife was not uncommon. Most of the men who went away from Pratola Serra usually came back with the money they had earned elsewhere. They bettered their conditions. Some bought land, fabricated their own homes, and remained in the town, but only a few. My Uncle Ferdinando was not a farmer however; he was a shoemaker in Massachusetts - and he thought that making

27

shoes in the U.S.A. was more profitable. What better place to be than in America and in a spot, that championed the family enterprise? Ferdinando, the gifted leather craftsman, was in his element - except, of course, without his ultimate dream - the jewel of his distant eye - Margherita.

Once my Uncle Ferdinando had established himself amongst his envious peers in the new world, he felt the need to solidify that position with heirs - lots of heirs to his mind, I'm sure. Something he could never have done if he had stayed in our village, I would suspect. Thus, his thoughts returned to Pratola Serra and to the idealized completion of his ultimate dream. Ah, the beautiful Margherita. He must have felt himself invincible, "If only, if only" he could add the last brick to this vision of his. Margherita. So, Uncle Ferdinando, with conviction and confidence, came home to Pratola Serra to be married - with his hat in his hand.

On a late Saturday night, out of nowhere, Uncle Ferdinando secretly arrived in Pratola Serra. He told no one that he was coming - so dramatic - such assurance. He had boarded a train in Naples, which took him a long and winding six-hour trail to get to the local station. Then, from there, he had to lug his suitcases one more hour in the dark, to get home to his father's house in our village. What a welcome he had. "Surprise!"

But his mind was on only one thing - the lovely, cherished, Margherita. I'm sure he must have asked secretly upon his arrival. "Do you think she knows I might be coming? Have you heard? I sent letters to her. Is she preparing?" It was a small village after all, compared to Lynn, Massachusetts, U.S.A. - shoe capital of the entire world.

Well, one must assume the young woman had read the letters, as one must also assume that she knew of my uncle's intentions. It must have been a long, long first night for the poor fellow and his expectations. It was too late to go and see his beautiful, naïve, Margherita, whom he had not seen in almost three years. Three years of unanswered promise.

As it was told to me, at nine o'clock the next morning, a Sunday, Uncle Ferdinando Fabrizio, of prosperous Lynn, Massachusetts, waited in front of our village church in not so prosperous Pratola Serra, Italy, knowing that his love, Margherita, would have to arrive on foot with her two sisters to attend holy Sunday mass.

Uncle Ferdinando had only ragged photos of his intended to console him for all those years. Then, to the penetrating ringing of the church bells, Margherita and her blushed sisters all appeared, like Beatrice of Dante, three virgins gliding along together out from under the shadows of Roman tuffa - Margherita buttressed and brightly framed in the middle.

Well, the long expectation and fermented desire was all too much for my poor Uncle Ferdinando to bear. The poor man actually fainted when the three sisters were close enough for him to confront his intended. No words came out. He just dropped into a pile of himself. Margherita simply passed by and calmly looked down at him in the street where he lay - motionless. She then kept on going into the old village church with her sisters. Believe me, I've heard this story from more than one family source.

Across from the church was a café serving liquor and small biscuits. Some friends helped revive Uncle Ferdinando there. The many male friends consoled Uncle Ferdinando and plotted to pass the time, while waiting for the mass to end. My uncle could find no words. There was no color in his face. It must have been an eternity for the distraught fellow before the exit of the messa began.

Finally, Margherita appeared from inside the church and again proceeded to walk by my uncle as if he were a corner gas lamp. Propped up from behind, Uncle Ferdinando somehow found the strength to remove his hat, saluting her. Shaking, he touched her hands - she remained cold. "Margherita, it is I - Ferdinando. How are you?" "You are back?" she said indifferently. "Yes, yes. I am back." "Yes, I see that," she said and continued away with her siblings. And so she was all of her life, just a beautiful, indifferent, dull doll - but he loved her.

The courtship lasted for six months with my dear uncle bumbling about for words of devotion and promise. Six months of courtship would pass in Pratola Serra between the virginal Margherita and the equally neglected Ferdinando Fabrizio. Sometime during the procedure, she probably came to the realization that America might not be all so bad. As for Uncle Ferdinando, his time was spent in wooing and practicing being married and in getting a passport for his future bride who eventually accepted his offer. They were married in modest splendor with an equally modest dowry, but my Uncle Ferdinando was victorious all the same. He had his village trophy - small dowry or no dowry, it didn't matter.

During their long marriage and lifetime settlement in Lynn, Massachusetts, they would have five children together - and perhaps five other sweethearts between them.

During my uncle's long courtship, however, there was an inevitable confrontation that would act to pull my two families further apart.

My mother's brother didn't need to work for money while he waited for his lovely mannequin to be ready. Ferdinando set out to make shoes for all his family instead. Heavy shoes for his father - boots for the winter. Uncle Ferdinando also made fancy shoes and slippers for his little, darling mother, Guisepella and for his sister, my mother. For me, he too made many shoes, some for the foot of a three-year-old and some for later. And to be in good rapport with Don Carlos, the Maestro leather-smith, Uncle Ferdinando made a pair of beautiful soft leather shoes for him as well. Don Carlos was very thankful.

Everything was going very well - until - one Sunday morning.

Uncle Ferdinando came to the Pirone compound, then up to my mother's apartment above the harness shop. He asked my mother to let me, his little niece, spend the day with him. He was going to take his fiancée, Margherita, for a walk over the top of Pratola Serra to where there was a beautiful view of the neighboring mountain village, Prata, just across the valley. Uncle wanted to see all those roads over and under the hills that formed a beautiful design. This was the place that men of the village would take their "inamorata" (sweethearts) to walk. I think he also thought that having a little child along, me especially, might enlighten his future wife to the pleasures of little children - especially Fabrizio children, which of course he considered me to be. But uncle had to ask my mother permission first. Sure that he would not be denied the pleasure to take his little niece with him for a walk, my mother said, "Wait, let me ask Papa Pirone if this is okay." Uncle Ferdinando got concerned and said, "What has your husband's Papa got to do with me taking my niece for a walk?"

Mother began to worry. She knew her brother well. He was quick to temper like their father. "Now, now," she repeated, "Don't get upset." They walked down to the sidewalk, and my mother went into the harness shop. She soon returned with a disappointed look on her face. She shook her head, "no." Uncle Ferdinando needed no other words from his sister. His face quickly reddened.

The factory was empty on Sundays. Don Carlos was holding my cousin Fortunella and me on his lap telling us a story. Before my mother could say anything, my Uncle Ferdinando burst in and took me up away from Nonno Pirone's lap. Surprised, Don Carlos said, "What do you want, Ferdinando? What are you doing?" Uncle answered rather harshly, "I want to take my niece with me today. I seldom see her or even my little nephew Ralfo!" Nonno Pirone put little Fortunella down and abruptly pulled me away from Uncle Ferdinando. "No, she will not go with you! You will not take good care of her! She has been sick and just now she is better. I do not trust anybody with her!" My uncle then pushed Don Carlos - hard. "Oh!" My mother screamed, "Ferdinando! You should never have done this!" Don Carlos shot back in a rage of his own, "You! You can't help but to be rough like your father - you are born an animal and you want to take this child with you!? - Never, never!" the old man yelled. I started to cry, which of course didn't help matters any.

Confused and perhaps sorry, Ferdinando quieted down for a moment. But when Don Carlos said to him, "Get out of 'my' factory! Now! Quick!" Oh boy, Uncle Ferdinando lost his temper again - the Fabrizio pride against the Pironi. "Yes, I will get out, but give me back the shoes I made for you!" Don Carlos had the shoes on. He sat on the chair and one by one took the shoes off and threw them at Ferdinando - an insult of the highest order. My uncle picked them up, stopped for a second at the door, then dropped the shoes into a waste barrel of scrap leather and left. Mamma Mia!

My poor mother took the shoes and was going to help put them back on again, but Nonno said, "I shall never wear them again. Get me my slippers!" After a while, Don Carlos retired to his bedroom and laid down on that Sunday morning. He was offended deeply but would never mention the incident again.

My mother then took me up and brought me over to Nonna Fabrizio's house where Uncle Ferdinando stormed off. Soon, after all the fuss, Uncle Ferdinando finally took his romantic walk with his Margherita and his little niece, Michelinella. But the day was spoiled for him as well. Not even the beauty of his girl all dressed up could make him entirely happy. Ferdinando was thinking hard about the outburst.

That night, my mother took me home from her mother's house, and she washed me up, fed me my donkey's milk, and then brought me into the Nonni's big bedroom and placed me next to the old man to say good-night to him. Don Carlos had remained in bed the entire day. He had the beginnings of diabetes and sometimes bouts of high emotions would make him dizzy. He hugged me and told my mother to light a new candle on the bedroom altar, which was framed inside a bureau, adding, "let her sleep here tonight. I shall put her in the cradle myself. Good night, Angelina." My mother, of course, did what she was instructed. "Good night, Papa."

My father, Giuseppe, wasn't at home that evening. He missed the entire altercation. As was becoming common practice for him, my father had snuck out early and was passing time by playing cards in the café, mostly because Don Carlos was not around to check.

Also, that night, Uncle Ferdinando, came to my mother's apartment hoping to find her alone. He had ample time to talk sense into her for my father was still not home. "Why all this fuss about the old man? Why do you let him keep Michelinella? Who is he really? He bosses everybody around as if he were a God. Even your brother-in-law, Francesco, is not allowed to leave the compound and to move out on his own. And, he too, is married!" My mother did not answer at first. "And Angelina, why do you keep eating with them and working like a jackass in their store?" My mother then meekly responded, "Now that the old man is getting more sick, how can we separate?" Ferdinando continued, "Yes, you can! You have two children now. Your dowry has kept Don Carlos Pirone in money. Demand to your husband that you want to cook for him and the children yourself. Tell him to demand wages. And you learn to be a wife and mother on your own. If you continue to live this way, I never want to see you again!" He left in a huff, which came naturally to him - he really was a Fabrizio after all. *[Aside: Ferdinando, obviously ascending, had a habit of demanding then leaving, unlike Don Carlos who simply demanded and didn't have to leave. But member's leaving both families was becoming ingrained, and Ferdinando was successful in a place where world-class leatherworkers ruled. Two of Don Carlos' own leather working sons were now gone as well, one leaving a child behind. Ferdinando Fabrizio and Don Carlos Pirone - two master leatherworkers and family spokesmen going in two different directions. Don Carlos obviously sensed this drain on the life that he knew and was desperately trying to hold on. He had his harness factory and he had one leatherworking son left - the eventual heir to that factory - a talented and troubled young man imprisoned in the terms of a dowry and in the consummation of a fixed marriage.]*

When my father came back from playing cards, Mother was ready. She told him what had happened that day and she told him to ask for wages or he would end up leaving Pratola Serra like his other two brothers had done. My father saw my mother's determination. He also felt guilty, for he had just lost lots of money from their allowance in the card game. He commented, "Only when my father gets better. Right now, he is in strict need of me." As it turned out, soon after, my father did demand wages from Don Carlos and freedom for his wife to independently cook for him and for his two children. Permission was finally granted.

I guess after the scene with Ferdinando, Nonno Pirone expected something of the sort. Silently, the old man nodded, "Yes. Yes." It was done. My mother was a real wife now. She shopped for clothes and she got everything else free from Nonna Pirone's store. Everything went very well - for a while.

———————

Chapter Six

Transitions

One day, my grandmother, Nonna Pirone, during the siesta hours, came up to my mother's apartment above the harness factory with a pot of coffee and some sweets. Pleadingly, Nonna asked my mother to let me sleep in the big house with them, Don Carlos and Nonna - not all the time, but just sometimes. The new independence that my mother had acquired was slowly being chipped away. "After breakfast," Nonna said, "Michelinella will come back to you. Please. Angelina. You have a baby son who needs you, too, now." My mother reluctantly consented. I was sentenced to sleep at the big house with my grandparents - as it turned out, more and more, almost all the time. My mother had lost.

But in all verity, as a little girl, I loved the Nonni's bedroom in the big house. It was so rich and full of everything. Yes, I was only three, but I value my visual memory above all other blessings. There were seven bureaus, one with a large mirror sitting right in the middle of it. On each side of the door of the lodge, there were two beautifully carved, tall-back chairs. Next to one of the chairs was a cabinet and a large copper vat with hammered swirls on it full of water. All around the walls of the bedroom were elaborately framed pictures of various Saints. One bureau was made into an altar featuring a painting of a beautiful Madonna posed as if looking out into the room. There was always a candle burning in front of the Madonna and scented fresh flowers of the season arranged next to her. I remember the image of this room as if I were in it this morning.

The other bureaus were covered with heavy marble tops, and there were statuettes of the Madonna or other Saints in the style of the 18th century - all dressed up with beautiful silks and kept inside round-glass tubular cases. They were so richly adorned, standing on artificial flowers. My eyes could never get enough of them.

On one side of the room, next to the huge wooden bed, was a large china closet that reached almost to the ceiling. It was three yards wide with eight massive shelves going across. Four shelves on top were full of beautiful blue dishes - a set. Anytime Nonno Pirone went to Naples, he would bring back with him another addition to add to the collection - a pot or a sugar bowl, and many other curios - salt and pepper shakers, etc.

The other four shelves of the bureau were full of the books Don Carlos had in his collection. They were his treasure. He was a voracious reader. And books were not that easy to come by. Boccaccio, the poet, was always in the back of other more puristic storybooks. There were books of mythology, of Biblical stories and even scientific reference books. Also books about the Renaissance - about the French Revolution, etc. This master bedroom of the Nonni had a profound effect on me at a young age - and then further on in life. It was deeply spiritual, profoundly artistic and above all, full of answers to unanswerable questions. It embraced fresh cut flowers, the Virgin Mary, and the guillotine.

———————

One of my father's younger brothers who still lived in the Pirone main house was my Uncle Costantino - a master metalsmith. Uncle Costantino would become my favorite of all my uncles - even including my mother's two brothers. He would always smile and conspire plots of mischief with me, his little niece.

Uncle Costantino was Don Carlos' youngest son of his five. He slept in the room next this Nonni enclave I described. When I was a little older, I sometimes would try on Nonna Pirone's dresses from one of her large closets. Well, when Nonna was approaching, Uncle Costantino used to warn me in a loud whisper, "Take off the dress, Michelinella and close the closet! Your Nonna is coming!" I guess he enjoyed seeing me acting my age. I was so curious. I had to look into all the bureau drawers, full of silk spreads, embroidered towels, sheets with cutwork or Venetian lace and boxes filled with costume jewels. And the effusion was so rich. Oh, how I loved everything in that storied bedroom. I was like Alice in a Land of Wonder.

Yes, I wanted to sleep with my two Nonni, but I resented my older cousin, Fortuna, who was also in the main house. She was very spiteful when we sat in the large kitchen for breakfast each morning. *[Aside: Sometimes in the Letter, little Fortunella, is referred to simply as "Fortuna," meaning "luck." She was the first grandchild born to Don Carlos and the one waiting to join her parents in America. She would later play a major role in Michelina's indoctrination into the New World.]*

In those morning hours, I usually sat next to Uncle Costantino during breakfast. Such childish things happened which I now remember. My uncle often combed my hair before he sat me on the chair with a pillow to make me reach the table. Cousin Fortuna used to pull the pillow out from under me and made me spill my milk on my clean dress. Once, she pushed me and made me fall. Another time, Ralfo, my baby brother, then only two years old, threw a fork at her, hitting her right on her forehead. It left a scar for life. Don Carlos didn't even punish Ralfo. He said, "Listen here young man, go there (pointing to Fortuna) and kiss her." Ralfo ran away instead. Nonno loved Ralfo in the same way he loved Fortuna. Why such love for a rascal I thought?

Well, I always loved breakfast time because we were all together, except for my parents. I loved to be in that massive country kitchen with the long brick stove with the many burners and the little hollow oven on the side. In the middle, ran the long, hand carved, wooden table and the stucco walls were covered with bronze utensils and cookware. Sometimes the sun would shine on my Nonna's large bronze pots just right way and make them look like hanging armor - the armor of ancient Rome. It was all so wonderful.

As all this was going on, my Uncle Ferdinando finally married his beautiful and aloof Margherita after six months of stay in Pratola Serra. I do not remember his wedding so well. But I do remember when Uncle Ferdinando said goodbye to my mother and to me before going back to America with his village trophy - Margherita. I remember how he cried and how I cried because he did. He hugged his sister until they could hug no more. It would be many, many years before we saw Ferdinando Fabrizio again.

1905 – 1906

In December of 1905, my sister Allessandra was born. We were three now, me, Ralfo and Allessandra. One boy smudged between two sisters and a precocious older girl cousin. Ralfo, however, was obviously the idol of Don Carlos. My brother was seldom with us now. He was a constant little Pirone terror, lurking in the shadows of the harness factory. Allessandra was so small, so petite, we used to call her Fregolina - a "small crumb." She was a quiet child, a beautiful, quiet child. She still is.

Then, one day in 1906, Uncle Antonio Pirone, Don Carlos' third son, the first to leave, came back from the Bronx in New York to fetch his daughter, Fortuna. He had worked and saved enough money in his own harness shop to return as he had promised he would. He stayed only a few emotional days and then left with his daughter - now the first Pirone grandchild to leave.

Don Carlos was inconsolable. He cried openly as if in desperation. Only my little brother, Ralfo, could console the old man. Many times, Nonna had to remove Ralfo from the big bed where he would sleep alongside his Nonno. Nonna would pick my brother up and place him in the cradle beside their bed. It was hard for me, too, when I realized that my cousin Fortunella would no longer be with us. I did not think that I would miss her - but I did, as soon as she was gone.

Every morning of the year, cold or hot, Nonna Pirone would get up at six AM. She would wash, dress and then go to church for the first messa (mass) every day except on Sunday. She liked the last messa on Sunday because it was the only one sung.

Don Carlos got up after Nonna was out of the bedroom. The first thing he did was to cross himself while, with his bare feet, searched for his slippers. He wore a long flannel gown, long and spacious with a cap on his beautiful head. With hands in prayers, he made his rounds to all the paintings on the wall until he reached the altar in the bureau where he stopped. He knelt down with his head bowed, making his last prayer aloud, "Oh, Madonna, give me peace this day. Let my family flourish and behave as they should. Help me. Amen."

Once, I remember asking Uncle Costantino, "Why were the Nonni so religious and why does Nonno pray so much in the morning?" He answered, "They gather strength by their religion. They want to keep on being good." I asked him, "Do you pray?" "Yes of course," he said. Then I said, "I never see you pray like Nonno does." He thought for a moment then added, "I pray in my own way."

At seven AM, Nonna would come back from church, and we were ready for breakfast. After breakfast, as agreed, my brother and I would be returned to my mother's apartment over the harness shop.

The mornings in Pratola Serra smelled of strong coffee and hot bread - everywhere. Fresh. It was intoxicating. The air was so pure that any odor was experienced right away. Later, at dinnertime, we knew just by the odors in the air what our neighbors were having for dinner. We used to open the lodge doors wide. We felt the odors of the garden as if we were right there amongst all the vegetables and flowers.

A time came when it was my father's youngest brother, Costantino's, turn to get married. I was then about five years old. While my uncle was dressing up for the wedding, I distinctly recall that he couldn't tie his necktie right - his mother had to help him. I stayed with him until he finished his nervous primping. He looked so beautiful in his black suit and white shirt, his brown eyes shining, his chestnut wavy hair, well combed.

Uncle was rather short. When he was at the young age of six years old himself, he fell off a wall and broke his back right in the middle. That injury interfered with his growth. But he was handsome anyway. In the big house, all of Nonno's apprentices and workers were moving beds, tables, and chairs, making room for the bridal banquet, what we call now the wedding banquet. Don Carlos ordered a caterer from Avellino just for the occasion. It took weeks of preparation.

I remember the wedding well. The bride was named Peppina - a quiet but wise girl of twenty. She was healthy and beautiful and escorted in her pinkish bride's gown by her three future sisters-in-law, one being my mother. The wife of Uncle Francesco, Zia Filomena, was on the other side of the bride. She was dressed in a bluish gown. (At that time, brides did not dress all in white, not always. It was optional).

When I went to the church just across the square, I could hear the bells ringing, and everyone was singing a very happy tune. The organ was playing the favorite messa of my grandmother Pirone - it was "Palestrina." My brother Ralfo and I were led by the hand into the church by the Pirone manservant, Feluccio. He managed to keep Ralfo quiet even though Ralfo was a little devil, spoiled by Nonno Pirone.

I remember the sounds of the bells still calling everyone for the bridal messa. They started the ceremony. The Nonni looked so nice all dressed up. Nonna Pirone had on one of her silk gowns of a violet color. She looked so very young and refined. My other grandmother, Nonna Fabrizio, was there as well, and also looked adorable. She always had that angelic purity of soul look about her that one sees but never is able to explain because it is so hard to describe.

The cortio (procession) started with three young women entering the village church with the bride in the middle. It was not custom then to have the bride be escorted last by her father. The bride came first without her father. Next, my uncle the bridegroom, entered with my father, who was his best man. Then, Uncle Francesco Pirone along with the brother of the bride. My two Pironi grandparents followed, then mother and father of the bride, her family, then the dignitaries of the town. The Signorino (the lord) and his wife, the mayor, my mother's parents, etc., all paraded down in a line filling the front of the church first. The whole village of Pratola Serra seemed in attendance.

I cried for joy. It was so beautiful to be in such harmony. The people so well dressed - the church so illuminated with all kinds of candles - the many altars adorned with flowers - the pulpit dressed up with Persian carpets. Even the priests had beautiful vestments and gowns on, and the main altar had a long scarf embroidered by my mother with her name on it - "From Angelina Fabrizio Pirone." I cried when the messa was on, and Ralfo, at a bossy three, told me to shut up! I retorted, "You leave me alone, everything is so beautiful. I can't help it!"

The priest raised the challis, and the incense ambula was shaken. The odor of the incense mingled with the odor of melted wax and of abundant flowers. Echoes. I was into another world. I hugged our babysitter, Feluccio, and stayed close to him. He held me in his lap and said, "Yes dear, one could cry for joy." Was it Joy?

Yes, but it was also the awakening in me of many things - emotions that conquer or disperse fear. Never before had I seen the unity of all these beautiful dresses, church ornaments, and wax luminosities. I was new to the splendor of it all - the continuous chanting of the priests - the answers of the people - the organ - the silence in between - the altar all dressed up. Even the priests looked majestic in their arcane gestures. Mostly, it was the incense that made an impression of purification. I was asking, why? Only the echo of my young mind answered. Why?

I also was happy to be so well dressed up. I remember vividly my white shoes and stockings, my blue batiste dress with embroidered hem and collars, and a blue cap adorned with white roses. But this happiness had a tinge of fear with it. What was it? When the messa was at the end, everyone got up. I felt dizzy.

The bridal party passed by when I saw my Uncle Costantino looking at me, smiling. I then knew my fears. I am losing him now. I cried again, this time with tears all over my face. Feluccio cleaned me and made me blow my nose. He said, "Now, dear child, why cry so much? Do not spoil your toilette. Nonno will want to see you poised." At the thought of my grandfather Pirone, I went into another sphere of thoughts. I turned and saw him sitting, staring off into his own dream.

I asked Feluccio, "Tell me, will the bride stay at the big house at night with us?" "No," he answered, "they will leave. They have their own apartment, away from the compound." As we were going out of the church, he pointed across the square and said, "Right up there on the second floor of Marano's apartment."

I felt a void in my heart. I said, "Uncle, too, will live there?" "Oh!" he laughed, "but of course!" I didn't cry, but at that moment, I began to hate my new Zia (Aunt) Peppina, the bride.

I was scheming many ways of how to retain my uncle's affection. Will he love me just the same?

The bells began to ring again - a very happy tune. We walked across the square of the village. The bells rang until the cortio (procession) reached our home. The entire big house was full of people. Long tables ready with food - one table set. The bride and groom sat at the head of the table. My Uncle Costantino looked around until he spotted me, then he called to me saying, "Michelinella! Come! You will sit next to me Precious child." Well, that did it. I forgot all the hate I had borne for the bride. I even went to her and kissed her. I sat next to my uncle, the bride's maid, and my mother next to me. They all sat according to their status and rank.

I don't remember the wedding dinner at all. I was happy again, and, after a while, I fell asleep. It had been a very emotional day. They made room, opened my couch, and I slept in my blue dress, while mandolins, guitars, and organs were playing. I slept on and on. I woke up when my father was playing his mandolin and singing the beautiful Verdi's, "Va Pensiero Sulle Ali d'Orate." Oh, that magnificent voice of my father's, it haunted me for days afterwards. I thought it was perhaps that song.

This first family wedding experience was all so very new and different for me. I remember thinking, "I had to learn. I must learn." Soon after, I slept more and more in my own bed in my parents' apartment above the factory. Time to reflect.

My favorite uncle - Uncle Costantino Pirone (circa 1916)

Chapter Seven

1908 - 1909

Volcano's, Gnomes, Ghosts, and other

"Natural" Phenomena

Christmas had just passed by only a few days. My brother, Ralfo, and I had finished breakfast with my Nonna and Nonno Pirone in the big house. I remember then going back to my parents' apartment above the harness shop pulling my little brother's hand - he objecting of course. It was just another bright December morning. Then, at about 10 o'clock - everything went completely dark. The morning light went away, disappeared. There were no voices heard in the town, only some whispers. We opened the balcony doors to see and sheets of ashes blew into the apartment as black as coal. It was snowing ashes! The sun was gone. My father said nothing, but I could tell he was in some manner of concern. We closed everything tightly and stayed together quietly in the main room. Ralfo made the only noise of objection.

We heard the people of Pratola Serra who began to call each other from their houses - a few at first, then many voices joined in. Then Nonna Pirone called up from the big house to mother, "Angelina! Bring the children down! Hurry!!!" Father took the baby and covered her up. My mother took me and covered me with a blanket. When we came down and opened the large front portal to the apartment, my parents found themselves knee deep in two feet of volcanic ash.

Mount Vesuvio's volcano was angry again.

At the big house, we had some breakfast, and we all prayed together. Uncle Costantino came in with his new wife, Peppina. And then in came Uncle Francesco and Zia (Aunt) Filomena. Everyone was covered in choking soot. We were all together - huddled in Nonna's kitchen. Naturally, I liked it, not being completely conscious of the danger of the occasion. I liked it because it brought the whole family together, to pray and to console each other. No one was panicked even though Don Carlos was not there to direct us in how to behave.

About four in the afternoon, there appeared some hint of sunlight. We prayed again - this time thankful prayers. People began to clean up the streets, the roofs, etc. It took many, many days of clearing to see that along with the smothering ash, fell millions of stones, volcanic stones like sharp marbles that settled beneath the residue ash. Yes, small crushed stones all over the earth - some stones not yet melted and fused like the large lava slabs that had formed in Avellino and other important cities closer to the volcano. We had no way of knowing until much later that an earthquake nearly totally destroyed cities in the South of Italy. In Reggio di Calabria and Messina Sicily, it was determined that over 100,000 people lost their lives. Prayers and superstitions were especially abundant that Christmas week. As usual - they believed it went hand in hand. *[Aside: (A Victor Pisano side note): Semi-related to this incident, on my maternal side of the family, my mother's mother, Constantina Peccora, was living on her large family farm in Reggio di Calabria where the epicenter of the earthquake of 1908 hit. Her side of the family's stone farmhouse collapsed on the sleeping area of her and two of her sisters. My grandmother, Constantina, was fourteen years of age at the time - the second of four sisters. One of her sisters was crushed to death by the weight of the collapsing structure. Constantina herself survived only by the quick actions of her brother Muomo, then 20. He extricated her from the rubble, barely alive, and frantically squeezed lemons into her mouth to revive her. Later, Muomo Peccora would become a private chef of the last King of Italy, Vittorio Emanuel, and Constantina would become his young sous chef.]*

There were many superstitions all around my region. I often heard people repeating that they saw ghosts. Every crossroad in the village had a sacred cross to scare the evil spirits away. I often heard my mother say that in the big house, in the Nonni's bedroom between the two large chairs on the side balcony that opened on the lodge, often would appear a gentleman in the costume of the 17th century with a silver coat, short pants, light stockings, slippers and a silver-white wig. The ghost was about 5 feet 3 inches tall and was holding a tobacco box and sometimes an embroidered handkerchief. The family never knew who he could have been. I saw him once myself at this time. When I tried to talk with him - he disappeared. Truly, I was not afraid.

Every town in the region had a master thief as well - another medieval vestige. These clever men or women, not afraid of ghosts, would dress in fantastic habits and roam about the vegetable gardens or farms as apparitions, loading themselves with fruits and vegetables, chickens, even lambs or goats - anything available or portable.

During the year, whenever we killed pigs, we would kill only one or two, because there was no ice at that time or Frigidaires. We left the killed creatures out, cut in half and then they were put into the lodge cellars to cool them off. Even these sides of pig went sometimes missing if the people were not careful. With many people about, there was always something stolen. At times, the culprits were found out. But still, the thieves kept on blaming the ghosts. They would plead, "Spirits! It was the spirits, you know that." Or they would say, "We were taking these things to help the poor people in other parts - away from the town." At least that's what they would claim. Nobody, rich or poor, ever found anything of the sort to be true. But still, people believed that some ghosts or spirits were walking about, stealing things from the village to help the poor. And in some ways, they were.

The people of our village also truly believed in gnomes. There were two of these little men dressed in red in town. One was with a rich family in Pratola Serra, the Acone family. The Aconi were mostly professional people - professors, doctors, pharmacists, and wine merchants. Wine was one of the most profitable kind of business. Well, the Acone gnome was named "Midas." He was excreting gold for them, or so the villagers declared. The Acone used to feed him a lot. "Oh, yes," the butchers would say, "the Acone buy most of our meat. You know why? For their Midas! He demands our meat!" People believed. They would swear by it!

The other gnome in town was "Matzo Mauriello." We, the Pirone family, had him.

Matzo Mauriello didn't excrete gold like the Acone Midas; he was an artistic sort of little fellow - a whisperer. Everyone in town knew that Matzo Mauriello had a capacity to whisper into the ear of the Pirone family about how to make those beautiful harnesses, how and where to go to get that soft leather, etc. The little gnome was even thought to design mechanical items for my Uncle Francesco and Costantino at night. He went into their shops and made models of beaten iron - inventing machines to spray sulfur and elaborate gas lamps to illuminate the town. Matzo Mauriello would whisper to them instructions! The townspeople truly believed this. It was always on the wing of gossip. It gave everyone reason to believe they were just as good - if only they themselves had a family gnome. These two little creatures - these gnomes - were also known to be immortal and could be visible or invisible as they wished. And I must write they did actually exist, at least in peoples' minds.

I again confess that I saw our Matzo Mauriello, yes, twice in one day. A little bit of a man about two feet tall, rather fat, moving about our kitchen in Nonna's house, and later in my mother's kitchen, whispering how to cook a turkey. Turkeys, even today, are rare in Italy and no one knew the best way to cook it, especially then. My mother was going to boil it. But I heard Matzo Mauriello in my ear, "Bake it Angelina, bake and stuff it.'" I asked my mother, "Are you going to stuff and bake the turkey like Mauriello told you?" My mother, astonished said, "I didn't see him! What did he whisper?" Well, I was afraid to say more. My mother did bake the turkey and stuffed it. It was a new invention at that Christmas. No one ever heard of a baked stuffed turkey for Christmas before. Such a big bird! It hardly fit into our little oven in our kitchen heated with coals. It was all Matzo Mauriello's doing. He whispered it in my ear.

There were other spiritual incantations floating about Pratola Serra as well. There was an old lady who was well respected in our town, the wife of Don Giannini, the schoolteacher. Donna [Dame] Simonetta was her name. She used to come to Nonna's store most every night to buy cheese or whatever. Dame Simonetta Giannnini had a way of narrating a story with such conviction that it was impossible not to believe her. Her family, however, had no gnome of their own which may have attributed to her forceful convictions and exaggerations.

I remember one of her famous stories. She, with awe's attitude, said that every Monday night, every Monday, at twelve sharp, the souls' penitent would go to church. They came out from their cemetery graves not too far from town and walked in line all dressed in black with heads covered, murmuring a cantilena litany. At precisely one o'clock AM, they would go away in line and in prayer back into the cemetery. She swore by this story in her high-pitched voice. Well, of course, as an imaginative child, I really believed her. My Nonna, my mother, Aunt Raffaella, and the others all believed her too, or showed no signs of not believing her. Dame Simonetta was so convincing in her delivery and gestures that it was impossible not to believe her story of dead spirits strolling the streets of the village every Monday night at midnight. She was the wife of a schoolteacher after all.

I was then eight years old, and the front room of my mother's apartment above the harness factory was right directly across from the church. "Perfect," I thought. The very next Monday night, I was ready. I sneaked out of bed and crawled to the front room. I first heard the midnight bells of the village Prata across the mountains. The bells rang from afar, declaring the hour. I wrapped myself with a blanket and without awakening anyone, I sat like a bundle at one end of the balcony and waited. This was going to be an experience, and I promised myself that I would try not to be afraid by what I was about to see. The bells of my own town church then joined in with an echo harmony - one - two - three, until twelve. I felt as if I were waiting for a volcano to open wide and that I would be engulfed in fire. I hugged myself still closer. I must have looked like a round-bundle of shivering flesh. I waited. And then I waited some more. I did see ghosts before and even our family gnome, Matzo Mauriello. "What now?" I thought. The air and the fear shook me to my insides. Every little thing I focused on. No stars out and there was a soft wind blowing. Still, I waited.

The church doors were closed tight. I felt suffocated with fear and expectation. I opened the blanket a little more, wide away from my face. Nothing happened. There I was, the whole hour, all by myself until the clock sounded one o'clock. Not a soul - not even one ghost - nothing! Dame Simonetta's balcony was a little bit away from where I was. I saw no light there or anybody on her balcony looking for the penitent souls going back and forth from the cemetery to the church. I was stiff and very disappointed. Then I was angry. I had believed her. She lied to all of us - even Nonna. Why?

Slowly and quietly, I joined my little sister Allessandra in bed. I couldn't sleep. Many thoughts confused my mind. I repeated aloud - "Yes, Dame Simonetta lied. She lied to us!" This woman told a story so sure in a way that the others would believe her. She had nothing else to say, only that story. That lie gave her pleasure - to have the attention of my Nonna and the rest of us there in the store. Are all people like her? Were all the stories I heard about ghosts not true? But why then even tell these stories? Didn't even I see the silver dressed gentlemen in the big bedroom? And what about Matzo Mauriello in my mother's kitchen? Was I crazy? I couldn't sleep one minute that night. I didn't know what was real or not real.

For days, I tried to push Dame Simonetta's story away from my mind. But one evening, there she came to the store again, talking about the penitent souls of that past Monday night. I couldn't help but to answer her. I blurted out, "It is not true!" All heads turned in my direction. I continued almost angrily, "I stayed on the balcony the whole hour of twelve, until one o'clock. On the balcony of my parent's apartment. The balcony straight across from the church! No spirits came from the cemetery Monday night! No hoods. No lines. No people dressed in black. It's all a lie!"

Oh, boy. Dame Simonetta kept quiet for a while, then with lots of pity in her countenance, she said to me, "You, poor child. You did not see the souls because you are not pure of heart." I defended myself, "Not pure?! I am a good girl! I respect everybody, but sometimes people just invent stories to be important!" I was surprised that Nonna let me go so far. She looked at me and said, "That is enough, Michelina. Go into the house and pray for better thoughts and deeds. You expect too much from yourself and others." I stood my ground instead, just staring at Dame Simonetta, not blinking at all.

Dame Simonetta then stepped backward and left, just saying, "Good night." I looked at her walking away. Her steps were uncertain. Her long dress was interfering with her walk. Nonna was confused. My young Aunt Raffaella had a quiet smile on her face.

That night, I was told to stay in the big room of Nonna's house and pray as my punishment. I prayed and prayed, sure, but no answers came. Dame Simonetta lied, but I was the one to be punished - and why should prayer be my punishment? Was lying not a sin, even for an old woman? Am I to ask forgiveness for saying so? Still more questions.

Nonna came in later and lit another candle and gave me her own blessed rosary beads to pray with, then left. I was thinking hard. I went to bed in the big room. The holy beads fell from my hands – unnoticed.

Later, when Nonna came in, she thought I was asleep. She picked the beads up from the floor, covered me, then kissed me murmuring, "Oh God, guide this child in other fields. She is precocious. Help her not to waste time on pursuing the truth. People mean well. They are frustrated with nothing else to do or to think. They are lost in fantasy. God help this dear child, the joy of my days!" Left alone - I cried myself back to sleep.

Nonna was right about people. But why? Oh, dear God, why does she listen to all those false stories without a challenge? Was it hypocrisy or piety? I was more confused than ever.

For days after, I tried to keep quiet. Only to my Aunt Raffaella, I said, "I was awful, wasn't I?" "Oh, no," my aunt answered with a smile. "Just last night, Dame Simonetta came in and she had nothing to say - nothing at all to anyone. Your Nonna did all the talking this time." "What did they talk about?" I asked. "Nonna told her that no, you were not to be punished, but in fact, she was planning a trip with you to Pompeii on the Madonna's feast - on the 8th of May." "What?! Yes, oh yes!" I said excitedly. "Pompeii?" My aunt had second thoughts about telling me this. "Please do not mention it to anyone, promise?" she replied. "Yes, yes, I promise."

Promise I did. But I did tell Uncle Costantino the good news - how could I not tell my favorite uncle? I couldn't help it. I didn't tell him though how I found out about it. I had made a promise of that anyway.

I was so excited. My first big trip with Nonna!

The next day, Nonna found out that I had told Uncle Costantino that I was going with her on a surprise trip to Pompeii. Nonna thought that I had found out about the surprise by hiding and listening to Nonna while she was talking to her friends. "No," I said, "I wasn't hiding - I wasn't spying." "No?!" she said, "Then who told you? How do you know about this surprise? Did Matzo Mauriello whisper this trip to you in your ear!?" For a second, I refused to answer. I did not want to say that Aunt Raffaella told me. I had promised her. Again, I was so confused. Did Nonna really believe in Matzo Mauriello? My family, the Pironi, was nicknamed, "Mauriello." Even now, after so many years, we would be addressed, "You are of the family of the Mauriello's, no?" Nonna stood waiting for an answer. Should I lie and blame a family gnome that everyone believed in - even me?! To protect my promise to my aunt I said, "Yes, Nonna. It was Matzo Mauriello who told me." My Nonna just turned without a word and left. Yes - I lied to her. I lied like Dame Simonetta lied, no? But then I thought, "Perhaps the little gnome might have whispered it to me if my aunt didn't speak of it first."

Oh, what trouble it was to grow up. I believed no one, not even my own mind.

Chapter Eight

1909

Destiny - Books -

First Communion and the Passing of an Era

One afternoon, after my schooling, (which I shall describe soon), I again went and helped my Nonna Pirone in her store next to the harness shop. By this time, my grandfather Don Carlos and my father were working six days a week with many long hours to keep up with the demand put upon the harness shop. So many pieces they made. And still, mostly the payment came in a manner of goods for their harnesses. What cash money they did receive had to go mostly to materials and to pay the salaries of the apprentice workers - now four.

So many different goods and products now appeared on Nonna's shelves to offer both the village and to drivers of the wagons and carriages. Wine, bunting cloth, flour, dry goods - everyday necessities and even products for farmers and hunters.

On this one afternoon, little did I know that I would first meet the man I would eventually marry many years later in another country - how could I know? I was only eight years old.

I was in the front of Nonna's store when in came a monk and a handsome, very tall, young man in his twenties who had to duck to enter the door. They were from the neighboring mountain village called, Prata. Prata was the sister village to Pratola Serra - same in size and all manner of custom. It was another hilltop village in the ring of the mountain circumstant.

Both the young man and the monk had muskets on their shoulders. They came to buy bullets for their guns. This was the first time for me, I think, to have seen a priest carrying a gun. Nonna said to them, "How many, Luiginio?" The young man replied, "Two dozen, please, Signora."

"And you, Father?" "The same," replied the monk. Then, turning to me the monk smiled and added, "You are your Nonna's big helper, eh? Will you collect our money?" Instead, I ran up to the young man and went to touch the gun which he had placed against the counter. He and the monk noticed my interest. The young man playfully tugged me away by my braided hair saying, "No, no. Not to touch," and then lifted me high up to the ceiling saying, "Do you want to come with us hunting little one?" I said, "No, you brute! Why do you want to kill birds?" He let me down laughing. Even my Nonna was amused.

They both went out of Nonna's store full of humor and armament. *[Aside: This "brute," Luiginio, was the young Luigi Pisano, Michelina's eventual husband - my grandfather. He was sixteen years older than she.]*

It was June of 1909 when my second brother was born to us and he was named Costantino. My new brother was obviously named after my father's youngest brother. Uncle Costantino was very honored at the choice of names for his new nephew, even though it was a longstanding family name.

I had one year of schooling by this time, but I had already learned to read on my own and with a little help from my mother and my Nonna. I could read almost anything at a very early age. Reading books came easily to me. I was hungry for words. School felt like a detraction from this passion, as if I was going backward.

The books on Nonno's shelves in his room were always in my hands, even books of Latin. I could not get enough and I was reading far above my age level. I was like a sponge. I burnt many pages with candle wax, which stuck the pages together. When I didn't know the word, I would think of a possible meaning and see if it made sense. Then Nonna would arrive and correct it, and I would never forget the meaning after that.

The teacher at the school in the village was named Signora Piscopo - this was a common name in our village. Mostly, it was the name of the land barons. She was also a sour type of woman. She was sour to me because I was always ready to answer any question with my arm up before she even finished asking the question. And sometimes, I would help some of the girls - even older girls. I was continually punished for these behaviors, but I had to obey even when I felt like telling her that she was cruel. Signora Piscopo used to hit us with a wooden spatula - hard, on our hands if we stepped out of order. It hurt terribly, and likewise, we hated her. She was a nervous type and seldom smiled. Once she did smile, and she looked even worse.

We were a mixed group of many ages and therefore of many abilities. We were mostly separated by age, but also by gender. To make matters more difficult, there was only one main schoolhouse in Pratola Serra.

At this time, I also had Sunday school where the priest taught dogmas, which made me confused. Much of what he preached didn't make any sense, especially after having gone through most of the books on my grandfather's shelves. I could go on and on about this discrepancy but perhaps later in the story, it will be more propitious.

The memory of my first communion was nothing I ever want to wish on anyone. Not because of the communion itself, but because of the tragedy which happened around it. It brought our family to its knees - literally.

Well, I had everything ready for my first communion, except for my dress. Don Carlos himself went by carriage with his servant/driver, Feluccio, all the way to Naples and bought me a beautiful white dress and white undergarments, a veil, white silk stockings, white shoes, etc. Oh, everything was just wonderful. He was so proud. The communion was to be the last day of June 1909. Then disaster. My Nonno got desperately sick. He accidentally pierced his hand with a long needle while sewing a harness strap. This wound was disastrous because he was a suffering diabetic, and the penetrating needle turned out to be soiled. Don Carlos' hand became severely infected, and soon my grandfather had gangrene.

Doctors from Avellino were called. The doctors decided that they just couldn't amputate my poor Nonno's hand because he would be too weak to survive the operation. Such a simple accident now quickly diminished this self-assured and confident man. I am reminded by the works of Freud, who postulated that there was no such condition as an accident.

Oh, the turmoil in the house - the village even. My Nonna was forever preparing Nonno's hand bath with hot water and some disinfectant. But my grandfather was dying, and everyone knew it. My father would disappear for hours at a time, unable to bear the thought of losing his father - the leader.

One day, Don Carlos called me. He looked at me and said, "Please darling, Michelina, dress up as virginella (a little virgin) as you will for your communion. I want to see you all in white with the beautiful clothes I bought for you." I knew then that he was dying. I could see it in his eyes. I quietly cried, but he insisted. I went downstairs to my mother, and she dressed me up as the little virgin. I went back up into Nonno's great bedroom, walking all around slowly in front of him, and then, just turning in place. I prayed at the altar in the bureau and then went to him. I knelt down and poised my head on his good arm. He had tears in his eyes. Then he said to me, "When you walk into the church for your communion, walk just the way you did here, but do not cry, eh? Have your head high - always. You are a Pirone my child. You are just a wonderful girl. My little Michelinella."

Inside I kept on crying. It just came out. He put my head on his chest and he kissed my hair, which was covered with orange flowers and a veil. I kissed him again and again until Nonna came in to take me out.

Right then, the priest entered with an incense ampula and accompanied by three attendants. The priest was dressed as if he was going to say a messa under an embroidered umbrella - an umbrella brought to perform Nonno's own last communion. It was a scene that I will never ever forget. I stood sobbing at the doorway watching them - dressed for my first communion - while my Nonno received his last.

The day after, Don Carlos cried out, "God, come! Take me!" He went on in agony for three more hours murmuring, "What a long beautiful road!" Adding, "Wait, wait for me!" My beautiful Nonno, Don Carlos Pirone, died, and an era died with him.

Don Carlos' funeral was beautiful. His younger brother came from Ariano Irpino where Nonno was born. All the town of Pratola Serra was mourning for him, for this beautiful wonderful man of just 60. That day, Monday, June 14th, 1909 will be forever remembered.

Life after my grandfather, Don Carlos Pirone

Nonna did all the preparations for her husband's funeral arrangements. She told my father to go on with the factory as before. It was his harness factory now. He was the heir - the harness "Maestro" of Pratola Serra - the "Golden Needle." Yet, it was a simple needle that took his own father's life - the unassailable Don Carlos. My father's grief came in two forms, that for his father and that for himself. His resentment grew. He started thinking more and more of his own freedoms. *[Aside: Giuseppe Pirone now inherited and was the reluctant and sole purveyor of a harness factory which was predetermined by the marriage arrangements and terms of a dowry set up by Luigi Fabrizio and Don Carlos Pirone. This inheritance was more like a "fixed obligation" to Michelina's father in a fixed circumstance. He found himself inheriting a business he didn't want in a country he didn't want to continue to live in while his two leather-working brothers, and his wife's own two leather-working brothers, propagated and flourished as successful leatherworkers on their own in the new world. It's obvious he felt abandoned and overwhelmed with the responsibility at hand upon his father's death.]*

Nonna Pirone told the workers of the harness factory and the apprentices that her son, Peppino, had now inherited the harness factory. "Behave as you did with your Master, who was my husband." Nonna tried. She desperately tried and believed that it would all continue smoothly. But her voice did not have the same conviction or authority as that of Don Carlos.

She managed to keep her store going as before. Everything went on beautifully - but just for a while. The weight of my grandfather's passing pulled on his remaining family dramatically. The house and harness shop he left behind was built only of a tower of cards.

My father was used to playing cards - and mostly losing.

One day, out of nowhere, my father decided to go visit his two harness-making brothers in America, Antonio and Raffaele. Nonna, my mother, and his two remaining brothers all thought he was crazy. "Why are you going to America?!" everyone asked. Well, nobody really knew why. Perhaps it was because he could. So, my father left for the United States. The workers and apprentices soon left, and the old harness factory fell into silence - an empty space. It was a selfish and foolish plan on my father's part. He said he "needed a break" from the world, but the world only followed him. My father left his family, a productive shop and everything else behind to make a visit to America. He didn't come back to Pratola Serra for a year.

In the meantime, Nonna had kept all the tools and materials for my father's return - she sold nothing. She kept the horse, the carriage, and the servants - Feluccio and his wife. With no harness work being done, however, the cart and wagon drivers now left very little foodstuffs and items for Nonna's store. Income was barely a trickle now. My two remaining uncles looked after Nonna and my mother looked after her four children - as best she could.

When my father finally came back, he moved the harness factory and all of our belongings directly across the square from the old factory. We moved our apartment as well, above the new shop. It, too, fronted directly the village church, but only a bit further away. Plenty of room, yes, but it was not the same. It was a separation for my father mentally as well. He needed a different space. I think he tried to purge the thought of the old ways and his dependency on anything relating to the past - especially the aspect of the old factory being connected with my mother's dowry. My father soon got the apprentices and some of the old workers back. And, like a miracle, he got all of his trade back again as well. I don't think the "Golden Needle" ever understood just how talented he was in his father's chosen profession. Or maybe it was, he just didn't care.

My Nonna Pirone set up her new store where the old harness factory used to be and kept on being busy. My father and his two local brothers managed to build back up the inventory on Nonna's shelves. At this time, I was constantly at Nonna's side. My mother did not miss me much. She was feeling the effects of trying to maintain a complete family on her own. She was not good at it, but she made an attempt. She and my father were also not as comfortable in the presence of each other as they once were - or at least it seemed that way. The trip to America that my father had taken and the length of time he had stayed, weighed heavily on her, I believe. It was a slap to her face in many ways.

After my fathers returned from America, he never stopped talking about that country. He was really trying to convince himself (and others) that being free from any responsibility was what really mattered - or at least, what really mattered to him. I think he came back to Pratola Serra to prove to himself that it was his choice to come back freely - that he could again leave for America any time he wished and as easily return. He needed permission from no one. And who could stop him? No one. Not even the ghost of Don Carlos.

Chapter Nine

My father, Giuseppe "Peppino" Pirone

My mother, Angelina Fabrizio Pirone

My father. How can I describe him? Outwardly, Giuseppe "Peppino" Pirone was handsome, loquacious, and well-mannered, yes. He was not the tallest of the Pirone brothers, but I remember my father always standing tall - proud, even when working alone. He had a marvelous singing voice and used it with skill. He sang for the pleasure of his own company. He was a unity; of honesty, of selfishness, of an artist, of a lover of music and of anything that was beautiful and useful. But there was always something going on in my father's mind. He was always in a state of deep thinking when not speaking. About what? About everything. He was also short-tempered and abusive at times.

Passionately - and to a fault, my father played cards. One could have forgiven him, but intelligent as he was, he never realized how badly he played. In so many things, he was a master - a master at leatherworking, singing operatic arias, playing the mandolin, etc. But at cards, he was a buffoon. Why? I think he was too anxious, too avid, and too guilty from the love of it. So, he constantly lost. Once, he came back home on foot without our family horse and carriage. My father's passion for the cards was a ruination of our family. There was a deep discord in my mother's character and his because of it. He was religious, yes, but he never went to church. It wouldn't have helped anyway.

My mother, on the other hand, having so many Fabrizio priests in the family, was always in church for the morning messa and for the Sunday prayer. She would leave early with my Nonna Pirone and stay behind in the church after Nonna came back to her store. If anybody needed to dress the church altar, the holy Saints, or the Mother Madonna, my own mother was there in the company of the sacristan, helping, suggesting, and always forgetting home, her children and everything else. She was as married to the church as any nun would be and as dedicated. If anybody was sick in town and needed help, my mother was there. She was always there - for others.

Now, who managed the home? I say, nobody and everybody.

At eight years of age, and being the oldest of my mother's children, I was called from Nonna's store often to go home and to cook. I rushed with my duties at Nonna's house or in her store and ran to my mother's house, trying the best I could. When my mother came home from her mission, she was exhausted, and so was I.

One day when I realized that my household duties had forced me to miss school, I cried. And because I cried, my father slapped me and kicked me hard. (For me, something I would never forget). He said, "Women do not need too much schooling. Keep quiet!" Oh, the horror, the pain in my heart. I had to suffocate what I loved most - learning. But I understood one lesson - never, never to be either like my mother or like my father. I vowed to myself - I would be different than them.

It was at this time that I missed my Nonno, Don Carlos the most.

One day, Uncle Costantino sent for me from Nonna's shop. He knew what had happened about my discipline when I objected about missing school. I know it concerned him. I went to my favorite uncle's metal shop ready to hear him support my father - but to my surprise, he didn't. Instead, he hugged me, and then he gave me his daily newspaper to read. He promised to give me the paper every day after he got through with it. So, he did. Almost every day when there were no duties and while he was working on his bronze candelabras or iron balconies, etc., I would read to him. I preferred to be in his shop and not my father's. When I mispronounced a word to my uncle or hesitated on other words, he corrected me. I felt he loved me and knew the deep desire I had in my heart for knowledge. Many times, I wished he was my father. Sometimes we sang together the new songs. Banging on the anvil with a hammer was how we kept time for our songs.

On Sunday evenings and most holidays, Uncle Costantino and my father often played the mandolin and guitar and sang together. They both had wonderful voices. My other uncle, Francesco, was somehow kept away from these musical affairs by his wife, Filomena. There was a petty jealousy among the three sisters-in-law. But I loved my Aunt Filomena from working with her in Nonna's store. She always supported me. Always a wink from her. I also loved her because she wore beautiful clothes, and she never spoke one word in dialect - just pure Italian. I wanted to be just like her when I grew up.

As I mentioned, we always had music and song in my Pironi family. There were no radios or movies or any form of entertainment that we have today - no TV obviously. So, everyone sang. The town folks used to call us the Mauriello - the happy Pironi - the singing family of the town. Neighbors came in - it was the most joyful family when all together. Oh, sweet memories! I still feel and hear those memories with deep nostalgia.

Chapter Ten

1910

To Pompeii with my Nonna

Finally, the day came when Nonna Pirone took me to Pompeii - an old promise. I was nine years old and shaking with excitement. I had been waiting for many months on this promise, and I kept thinking that perhaps my Nonna had forgotten - but she didn't. She packed one suitcase for the both of us, and Uncle Costantino took us to the train, down the mountain and some distance away from the village. My first train ride. My heart could not be contained. Again, I remember the sound of it vividly. Loud, rough and uncomfortable to sit. I loved it!

We first went straight away to Pompeii, that ruined city of Roman times. I was now bewildered by the trip itself, overwhelmed really. I couldn't understand the tragedy of what happened in 69 AD. There was so much to see at one time. It went on and on as we walked. All ruins. Oh, why didn't I read more about the history of it? Even now in the distance, Mount Vesuvio, the old volcano quietly puffed back at us - quiet, yes, but still breathing. Old Pompeii, that wonderful ancient city, gave me a sense of the painful unknown - why all the ruins? I was trying to connect the distant volcano with the ruined walls I touched with my fingertips. It was all impossible for my young mind to fathom. I kept thinking of the rainstorm of ashes that nearly buried our village only two years earlier. Nothing was really destroyed under the blanket of that eruption, just a deep blanket of dust, but this - Pompeii - my God!

Through it all, my poor tired Nonna, all she did was pray amongst the antiquity. I wanted to know who built the beautiful golden church inside Pompeii? Who created the small painting of the Madonna studded with diamonds? The ancients did not know of the Madonna, or did they? I realized then just how much there was I still had to learn.

Nonna prayed and prayed in front of every picture there was of a Saint all around the Pompeian church. Poor Nonna, she had a good education, but she wasn't using it. She never had a chance to. She worked so hard all her life as the wife of a maestro. Me, I just had too many unanswerable questions.

Well, fortunately for me, we couldn't find lodging in Pompeii. So, we went to Naples and found a room near the section "Margellina." And there it was - endless and bright - an explosion of blue. I had never seen the ocean before!

When we got off the trolley from Pompeii, I was drawn to the sea with eyes wide open. I was out of my internal self. I felt as if I were flying across that beautiful blue blanket. Oh, how wonderful! Nonna understood my feeling and for a long time, she sat alone at a nearby coffee-house, drinking her special drink - strong black coffee and watching me. I was in a fantastic revelry and in my first ecstatic moment. After a long while, Nonna finally had to lead me away. We went silently to the hotel.

That night, I dreamt of the ocean. I was levitating - walking on it - feeling the soft cool wind on my face - saluting Mount Vesuvio and its puffing volcano. I dreamt of the sanctuary of Pompeii, screaming out in my sleep, "Tell me, oh, God, who created all this beauty!?" Then the Madonna with the diamonds answered me! "The people. The people!" Nonna shook me, "Quiet, Michelinella, sleep." She patted my shoulders and I became wide-awake all the rest of the night. I kept perfectly still so Nonna could sleep. I reviewed in my mind all I had seen that day. It was like two years had happened! Thomas Mann was right. When he analyzed time, he said, "Time is measured by what you put into it."

In the morning, nearby the railroad station, I bought a detailed text-book of Pompeii for me and another for Appia Motta, my next-door neighbor. I also bought a travel book about Naples for my mother and many other small souvenirs for my friends and family. For my dear Uncle Costantino, I bought a tobacco box.

I would not see that wonderful bay nor the ocean again for almost ten years when I myself left across that blanket of blue for America.

Chapter Eleven

The Adjustments of Life

Another male child was born to us - my brother Mikele, just nine months after my father returned from America. Now there was me, Ralfo, Allessandra, Costantino, and Mikele. Two girls, three boys. My mother could make babies, that she could do, but all the family knew she was disorganized and now with five children and a husband, she found herself overburdened by even simple tasks. I was the oldest and a female, so naturally, a lot of that mother's burden was passed on to me - a birthright so as to speak. Nonna thought it would be too much for me to handle. She knew that the job of caring for the new child would be on me mostly. I was still going back and forth from my Nonna's house to my parents' house, for as I said, they were just across the square from each other, and Nonna's house had more room in it. My duties, however, were in both households now, and both houses were changing fast.

Soon after Don Carlos' death, Nonna's longtime servant, Feluccio, and his wife left Nonna and became bakers, like his mother. So Nonna Pirone then hired a new couple as help - also man and wife. They were a couple from our village who desperately needed work, and they came just in time, too. We badly needed them as well because Nonna's own mother was now coming to live with her! My great-grandmother, Mamma Maria, was a lady 98 years old, who came from Montefalcione (another town, Falcon Mountain) to live out the rest of her life. She was now too old to take care of herself, so as was Italian custom, she came to live with her family in her final years. It is interesting to think that she did not consider herself old enough when she became 90 to make this move.

My great-grandmother, Mamma Maria, was born in 1810, just at the beginning of yet another century. She was close to being deaf and blind but very alert for her age. There were now four generations living under two separate roofs. *[Aside: Interestingly enough, all through Michelina's letter, she never once mentioned Nonna Pirone's maiden name which would have been Mamma Maria's married name. Pity. Still, to read in detail about her, someone in the family who was born over two hundred years ago, is a special gift.]*

The new servant couple was very efficient. The woman, Carmela, was also deaf, like Mamma Maria. She helped with the housework and took care of the old great-grandmother. Her husband, Pellerino, helped with Nonna's store, cleaning, delivering, getting the water, shopping, etc. What a relief! But Nonna also had her own sister, Great-Aunt Raffaella, staying at her house just to help with their mother. So Nonna had two new grateful servants to help with the rest of the work and her sister. In the end, Nonna had a hand in everything and with everyone. Don Carlos would have been very proud of her.

Finally, I was able to enjoy whatever schooling was available at that time for a country girl of nine. After three years of being in a rudimentary school, I was able to move to another level - of sorts.

A nearby Catholic convent for girls offered the teachings of domesticities and some basic literature, good manners, sewing, etc. I was sent there. But the continuous religious lectures were a little confusing for me. I trained myself, however, to accept silently what religious instruction I disagreed with and I managed to survive without too much trouble. But my favorite part of the day was not religion or domesticity training - it was the literature. But those lessons were so small compared to the constant repetition of church doctrines.

I once asked my father to send me to a better school in Avellino, a real school where I could at least be with real teachers, not Sisters of the cloth. He firmly refused. He even discouraged Nonna from helping me. It was at this early point that I realized that I might well be denied any real education outside of keeping a religious household like Nonna or my mother did, and that was not me. I loved them both, yes, but I didn't want to be like them. "I must do something about it," I thought. "But what?" I would have to wait many more months before the answer came.

Chapter Twelve

1912

Our Girls' Book Club

Salvation. In the spring of 1912, five other girls of the village and I organized a secret reading club. Why was it secret? Because we all thought we would be punished if the materials we read were not first approved. And we decided the things we would read we would choose ourselves. Of course, we never took into consideration how to acquire these reading materials, but we would figure that part out later. We did promise ourselves, however, that they would not be religious books.

The girls were all girls from Pratola Serra. Amalia, Appia, Adelina, Antonetta, Rosina, and me. Amalia Pisano, many years in the future, would become my sister-in-law. She was tall, beautiful and came from a proud family - the Pisano family, who were distributors of regional wines. Very successful. Anyway, we girls were almost all of the same age, eleven or twelve, and with the same aspiration toward self-betterment.

This group was a savior to me. We planned our daily activities around our reading club specifically. A first, we found books from our parents' shelves. Some were hidden and not meant for display. Romanticism yes, but none of those books were ever lurid or sordid. Those kinds of books would never be found anywhere at that time. But these first books of ours were still not approved reading for "girls." We were taking a risk, and somehow that made the readings of them aloud even more exciting.

The meetings were planned so that each girl would read aloud in rotation to the group; then we would discuss and explore the work together. In this way, we planned to learn from one another. We had a good program.

On the few occasions Nonna would allow our reading club to meet at her house, we all had to say the rosary at some part of the meeting. Most of the girls didn't mind so much - they were used to it and just did it. This would please Nonna. She thought she was giving us a little of her deep sense of religion while we explored the world of modern literature. There was no malice in her about it though, just old ways. Most of us young girls were different, however. We believed in God very much, yes, but we never openly showed it in front of Nonna unless she asked. Nevertheless, we felt it was our duty to keep her happy in her efforts to enlighten us - and, it was her house.

Our club prospered. All together, we had two dozen books to begin with. We were advanced readers for our age. We read Manzoni's, "The Betrothed," which was (and still is) a book that was studied in the university as literature of the last era of romanticism.

Amalia Pisano was the oldest and was the smartest of us all and used to read aloud so well and so efficiently. It was her detailed interpretation of the author's meaning that excited the curiosity in all of us. The obvious problem we didn't plan for, however, was that we soon ran out of books!

Well, off we all went to Avellino - a brigade of pre-pubescent girls, trudging on foot the entire twelve miles, both ways. We needed a chaperone of course, so I asked my Aunt Peppina, Uncle Costantino's wife, to accompany us. She was an educated woman who always spoke pure Italian, not dialect, and she supported our cause.

In Avellino, we each bought two books at once. That was an extravaganza indeed. Even still, Appia and Amalia had to contribute extra of their own money toward the purchases. They did it so graciously, so unobtrusively, that none of the other girls felt inferior in any way.

The two books we chose were written by Matilde Lerao and another of Gabriele D'Annuzio. Aunt Peppina treated us with some pastry and candy. Oh, how good it all tasted. We bought a bottle of mineral water and walked arm-in-arm all over the town of Avellino. We finished at the villa there and rested, seated under those beautiful opulent trees. Impatient, we read our new books - aloud and together.

Going back home, walking those twelve miles, we passed Lake Sabato and the aqueduct of Serino, which flowed water to Naples. Also, in the distance, there was the high and beautiful Mount Vergine, ("Mountain of the Virgin") - the holy sanctuary of miracles, right there looking down on us. We agreed that our next outing of our club would be to go up to Mount Vergine - afoot. "Oh," one of the girls exclaimed, "It is too far!"

But Aunt Peppina said, "It is far, yes, but I went there as a young girl myself with a group of people - and on foot! I will talk to my husband. Maybe he will make that trip with you." "Yes! Oh, yes!" we cried.

The Habit

Really, my father could have been one of the richest men in the village for when he came back the first time from America, his factory was busy and prosperous. But the poor devil played cards every day and every evening - always losing. During afternoon siesta, he never rested like we all did. Instead, my father ran next door to the coffeehouse and played cards endlessly. If Don Carlos were still alive, he would have tempered his son's habit. Because of this addiction, however, my father had no physical rest. Instead, he developed a feeling of failure and guilt. He became more and more nervous and irritable - ready to explode with anyone. He usually took his frustration out on me or out on my mother. The latter was a fighter however. My mother never spared his feelings, either. With propensity, she made my father feel what he was - an irresponsible man, who cared only about himself.

There were times, under pressure, that my father stopped playing cards, but the temptation was always too great. The coffeehouse was right next door and when his comrades called, he went back to the table.

During these days of heavy gambling, my mother's father, Nonno Fabrizio, made it a point to visit us every day. On occasion, when my grandfather came late from his retirement duties as overseer of the area farms, he would stop in at the coffeehouse himself and watch my father gamble. Nonno Fabrizio wouldn't say anything. He would just sit and watch as my father lost his money. My father soon stopped playing cards and went home. What other choice did he have?

About my one remaining and dear Nonno - Nonno Fabrizio. He retired from making shoes when his hands developed arthritis. So, he retired to what he knew second best, overseeing Fabrizio land holdings - those that were still left. He was an honest caretaker of shutdown family estates.

71

The old Roman always wore big caretaker jackets with pockets opened all around. Every day, he came by our house and left fruits of all kinds for us children that he would pull out of these bottomless pockets. He often sat in my father's factory with all of us children around him, begging him for stories. Nonno Fabrizio had read, "The Count of Montecristo" of Dumas and other books of adventure, but what we all wanted to hear was his own stories - his own adventures. And there were plenty. Everyone, especially Papa's leatherworkers, would listen to him as they worked. Of course, we never mentioned the name Garibaldi to him - never. We also wanted to keep him calm.

At this time, Nonna Fabrizio, "Mammapella" we called her, the sweetheart, would never come to our house except on holidays. She resented my father for his traveling and keeping us poor with his gambling. But we as children went to her house almost every day. She was so very generous with all of us.

Also, in 1912, another child was born to my parents - Josephine. Three boys - three girls now. Baby Josephine was a beautiful girl - she was like a daughter to me. But even at eleven years of age, I was wondering how my mother could stand so much burden. She looked rather frail - yet so beautiful. Still, having children for my mother was like having fun with nature. She always came out better. This was her "habit" perhaps. And Papa? Oh, he was just the commander - and not a good one at that.

My sister, Josephine, was born just after Italy invaded Tripoli and Cyrenaic, (later to be called Libya). Two of my father's apprentices were involved in this war. Letters came back from them, which made me think of how horrible it all was. Why kill to get what raw materials Italy needed? God created the world for all to enjoy - whatever was on earth. Who demarcated the land? Of course, man did. Yes, but in my young mind, I thought that it would be more effective and obedient to the laws of God to discuss difficulties with the other nations and to find a way how to distribute God's given materials that were needed. I discussed this concept with my Uncle Costantino while we read the newspapers. He laughed, "You forget, dear, that man is greedy. What you want is one world united." "Oh, yes," I added. "Not now - not yet," he said. "We still have to refine our human nature." "How?" I asked. He looked at me smiling and said, "Enough for today. Let's sing now, eh?"

Uncle Costantino Pirone was an artist and even a good businessman. Besides being a master metalsmith, he also sold Voga bicycles, which were a new invention at that time. He sold them and fixed them, as well. He also sold and repaired sewing machines with his brother-in-law as partner. They also owned a mine together to make soft coal which he used free in his metal shop. Uncle Costantino accumulated some money. He saved enough to educate all of his children, formally. He had five children - four girls and one boy. He lived very well, almost in luxury at that time.

The other Pirone brother who remained in Italy, my Uncle Francesco Pirone, he too continued to work his mastery on metal in his own shop in the village. He and Uncle Costantino had the monopoly on these works in the area. Uncle Francesco made beautiful balconies, gas lamps, utensils and knickknacks out of any metal available. His wife was an excellent dressmaker. They too planned to educate their children in Italy. Unlike my father, these brothers of his didn't feel there was a better life to be had in America. If so, why did so many Italians return with just money to invest? These youngest Pironi brothers already had what they wanted. Their skills would be recognized anywhere, so why move they thought? What could be better for them or their children? Besides, they had the family gnome, Matzo Mauriello, to assist them in their success.

Had my grandfather Don Carlos lived a little longer, his heart would have at least been partially pleased that three of his five sons were not lost to immigration. Perhaps my father would never even have gone to America either, had Don Carlos not died the way he did and when he did. And likewise, perhaps, I would never have followed after my father there myself.

———————

Chapter Thirteen

1913

Book Club Trip to Monte Vergine

(Mountain of the Virgin)

Our girl's book club finally planned our trip to Monte Vergine, the "Mountain of the Virgin." But again, we needed, of course, to find a chaperone and decided to take my Aunt Peppina's advice and ask my Uncle Costantino to be our chaperone and guide. There was a day or two of careful thinking before he agreed to this monumental task. He was busy as usual in his metal shop, but the gentle pleas of his wife and the determination on the faces of our group eventually persuaded my dear uncle. And oh, what a splendid journey it was!

This trip was big for us. Almost every young girl in our region, at one time or another, planned the same trip up to Monte Vergine. It was, in a way, our "rite of passage" and reaffirmation of our faith. And now here we were, six book-starved young girls of Pratola Serra, planning a pilgrimage to a mountain named after the patron Saint of all purity - the Virgin Mother of God. It was also deemed the holy place of miracles, and we had plenty to ask for.

The mountain was far off in the distance across rough country. The shortest way there had no roads at all and it would be at least a day's journey each way on foot. Girls who made this pilgrimage mostly walked in a procession there as part of the ritual.

Anyway, before we started on our trip, all of us girls made a basket full of food and strong coffee in bottles, enough for us and my uncle.

At nine o'clock, on a Wednesday evening in July 1913, we started. We got to the base of Monte Vergine at nine the next morning - twelve hours of steady walking and climbing through the middle of a midsummer's night dream. My uncle's trail map was proven, and he was a master guide - bless him.

We had a flame torch and a bright moonlight. Now, to think of it, we must have been quite a sight. In the middle of the night, here was a group of young virgins carrying baskets led by a short, stocky, troll-like man with a torch traversing dimly lit fields and valleys.

We went through farms and forests before we got under the mountain itself. Then, there was only one way to climb - straight up. We did a sacrament, singing religious songs as we climbed to our communion. All six of us girls were good singers. We sang together in the girls' church choir. Well, we sang with harmonious voices going higher and higher up our Mountain of the Virgin. At times, we pulled close together so we could stop to get the high notes just right and to catch the echoes as they returned. It was all so surreal for us. Monte Vergine was very green with many types of trees. In some places, a dense forest, at other places it opened up, and we could see the illuminated reflections of towns like Avellino just below the mountain.

At one special place on the climb, right about at sunrise, we saw the beautiful green canyon of Irpina just as the sun began to appear - first like a pinpoint, then growing into a little ball of fire. This ball burst on one side and a little lake of yellow and red appeared. Then other parts opened, until the sun became a big round ball of fire with rays all around, showing the blue sky. I had never seen the sun so big! It was twice as big as the full moon that still was somewhere in the vast sky above. We became washed in splendor until it blurred our senses. Uncle Costantino then barked an order to us in mock military manner, "Let's go. March!"

Nobody could eat or drink before the communion - it was not allowed. But I never was too religious, (I was sorry). I began to pick up the very tempting strawberries on the bushes showing their beauty between small leaves of green with a touch of yellow. All along the roadside, these strawberries kept on tantalizing me - until finally, I ate one. "Oh!" my friend Rosina exclaimed, "How in the world can you take the communion now?! Eating is forbidden before this communion!" Just as she says this, the other girls ate the wild strawberries as well - so did my sweet uncle with a smile. Uncle Costantino said, "Let's rest here for a while." He had spotted a place where we could view the distant lakes and the waterfalls running along the green hillside which fed them. From our virgin mountain, we saw little towns attached to these hillsides or in the valleys below. We spotted our own town of Pratola Serra and even the village of Prata where Amalia Pisano's family first came. Amalia hugged me and yelled pointing, "Oh, Michelina! Do you see?! How beautiful! My Pisano village! There! Prata!" It was wonderful for all of us. For me, this climb, the wild berries, these forests and the mountain itself was my holy sanctuary.

We got up to the sanctuary just as Uncle Costantino had predicted, at nine o'clock in the morning. We entered the big church - a small cathedral really. I remember the sudden change at leaving the outside warmth of a summer's morning and entering the dank stillness of this cavernous place of worship. Everyone was pulled by some mysterious hand to the back of the sanctuary wall. And there she was - the Vergine. The painting of the Madonna was in a rather large frame and she was painted with a dark brown face. They called her, "Mamma Scheavona" - "Mother of the Slaves." Why she was painted this way I never knew. It was a pre-Renaissance painting with a gold and yellow background - to me, a large and rather ugly painting, I thought, but I didn't dare say it to the others.

Everyone knelt down praying - including myself. There were lots of other people there too. Some of these people came with open carts and horse-pulled wagons carrying young girls (virgins) with rose garlands on their heads. The Madonna had fame. The painting was mysteriously found right on the spot where the church was built. Very miraculous. Or so they made us believe.

My Uncle Costantino and I got out of the church before the others. I think he felt uncomfortable in there, as well. Outside I asked him, "Do you believe that prayer in front of this painting brings special miracles?" He replied, "Oh, maybe." Then I said, "If you lost a finger in your shop and you prayed to the Madonna and asked her to grow it back, would it?" He looked at me, saying, "You are a little too smart, you know that? A thing like that never happens. People ask only for what is possible. Subconsciously, they know the limits of miracles."

"So, miracles have limits then?" I asked. "Then why are they miracles?" He did not answer. The others finally came out.

At that time, no one was allowed to eat meat while on Monte Vergine. It did not matter what day of the week it was. On the side of the church, however, there was a coffeehouse with pastries, bread, and fish sold in cans. There was also a monastery. The monks of this monastery were all from rich families who retired there, away from the sinful world. The monks had an underground passageway that led them from the monastery down to the foot of the mountain. They all went there after the messa for their meals and then came back up for their Ave Maria hour. Many people believed that none of these monks ever ate meat. But this I didn't believe.

After a little rest and restoring our stomachs with some of the delicious coffee, we went up on the very top of the mountain where Naples could now be seen way off. On the summit of Monte Vergine was an enormous cross that beckoned the pilgrims. We could also see another road far below with some carts coming up, carrying even more virgins with garlands of flowers in their hair. A few of these girls were gliding along on the backs of donkeys or horses. But most of the young girls that we saw were like us, climbing on foot.

Coming back to Pratola Serra, we all felt tired but happy. We reached home about ten o'clock that night. I was so exhausted. We all hugged my uncle goodbye and thanked him for being such a good chaperone. When I got home, I don't even remember if I took my clothes off. I just crawled into bed with my sister Allessandra and her cat. I didn't dare to go to Nonna's house that night. I knew that as tired as I was, she would still make me recite the rosary with her before going to sleep. I had had enough penance for one day.

The morning after the trip to Monte Vergine, I went to my other Nonna's house, Nonna Fabrizio. I brought her a souvenir from the mountain - a medal medallion with the dark-faced Madonna on it. She kissed the medallion and asked me how it had been. I kept on talking about everything I had seen on the mountain and the march to and from until I was hoarse. All Nonna said was, "Boy, Michelina! Can you talk!" Oh, how I loved her so.

Chapter Fourteen

A Life's Career Fabricated

At almost 13 years of age, I became more conscious of my personal needs - my body was leaving the awkwardness of childhood and taking on a new form. I was beginning to bloom, and I wanted different clothes. I thought the clothes that I had looked shabby and I took to wearing one dress continuously. There was never enough money to go around with Papa's gambling and our growing family. And, the style that Nonna Pirone would find for me was dated and plain, I thought.

More and more, I wanted beautiful things to wear, but I could never get them. I then remembered Nonna Pirone's closet was full of magnificent gowns of silk, of velvet and of wool. She never could use them anymore - they were too dressy, too formal. Old women at that time wore simple long skirts and jackets. These fancy dresses that were kept dormant in her closet were there just to remind Nonna of when she was once young and traveling with her husband, Don Carlos and she were a stunning pair in their early marriage. Then I thought, "I could remake some dresses for myself with them. Oh, yes, they were so full and long! They could be cut down and re-stitched to fit my smaller body. No?" Modern styles didn't require as much material as in the past. What an idea!

I got enough courage to one day ask Nonna Pirone if she would give to me one of her old dresses. I told her what I had in mind. She refused, of course. She dismissed it out of hand as a "girl's fantasy." Well, then I told her I would prove to her that I could make my own dress and not ruin anything, except of course one of her old dresses. I had studied with these nuns who trained me, trained me in something at least. "And I am the best in my sewing class the nuns say." This last part stopped her objection. She didn't answer. I didn't know just how

I would succeed, but I knew I would. "Okay. Show me something, but do not use any of the dresses." A challenge!

The very next day, I brought to her an old doll that I had. I had copied the dress of the doll perfectly and made another just exactly like the first. "Look, Nonna. If I made the doll's dress, I can make mine own, too." Nonna smiled and said, "Okay, child, listen. I have an idea. In my room, I have an old bed sheet. Try to make your model dress with that. If you can succeed with that, then I will accommodate your wish."

"Oh, oh," I thought, "I need a template just exactly my size for this challenge to work. Where would I get one?" I thought and thought - then I asked Rosina, one of the girls in my reading club, to assist in my dilemma. Rosina was just exactly my size, so I begged her to give me one of her old dresses that I liked the style of. "I will return it unharmed!" I begged her. She reluctantly did. What a good friend she was to trust me like that.

I carefully cut the stitches of Rosina's dress and pulled it apart into sections - then I carefully ironed the sections out. I added style fixtures of the day and pinned the sections onto Nonna's old bed sheet and ironed everything once again. I cut the template as measured. Well, I made a good dress out of Nonna's old bed sheet - only, it was still a dress made from a bed sheet. I even re-hand stitched Rosina's dress and returned it to her - practically unscathed. What a job - but I did it. I had learned everything that I needed to know at the convent school and some of my own invention. The dramatist, George Farquhar, once said, "necessity is the mother of invention," so, I invented new clothes. I showed the trial dress made from the old bed sheet to my Nonna, and she was truly surprised and impressed. "Okay. Yes," she said, "take two dresses from my closet - the blue silk one and the red velvet one." "Two?! Oh, joy!"

That evening, I stayed with Nonna, and I was so happy. I even recited the interminable rosary prayer with her - without boredom. Before I went to bed, I kissed her thankfully. She hugged me tight. Seldom did she, almost never. But this was a big moment for both of us. True to form, Rosina came by and was so patient. She helped me greatly with her constant assurances that I could make a beautiful dress out of old gowns and that I would do it. After all, the new dresses that I was about to build would fit her as well. She made a smart investment of sorts.

One of the two dresses Nonna gave me was of heavy and lustrous blue silk. Nowhere today, anywhere, can such quality of silk be found. The dress was substantial, long and lined with a fine white linen. The other dress she instructed me to take was of velvet material of reddish color - a deep, dark red. The fullness of this dress was because it was lined with a fine cotton material of the same color. I mastered the handling of both materials.

When the big moment finally came, I held my breath and put my scissors through the exquisite silk dress first, almost as if in slow motion. It was the sensation of prayer, of fear, and of a certainty that I was a grown-up person - all at once. "I can do this," I heard myself say. Of course, I was thinking maybe that the little fellow, our family gnome, Matzo Mauriello, was also in my ear.

To shorten this episode, I will only say that I made a beautiful and stylish new silk dress to perfectly fit myself. And with the lining of this same dress, I made another dress and still had material left over. Later, I made two more dresses from Nonna's dress made of velvet - two warm velvet dresses for the winter. I had made four new beautiful dresses for myself out of two of Nonna's heirlooms. Yes, I did share them also, on occasion with Rosina until her own body changed differently than mine.

Well, Nonna was very happy with my results, so happy, that she bought me many pieces of beautiful underwear and six pairs of stockings to compliment my success. She also bought me a new dress for everyday use and even gave me some pocket money for needles, thread, and other necessary things to repair what I had just constructed. I guess, in her mind, I was heading in the right direction, especially in domesticity and in prayer. She was partially right.

Soon after that, my other Nonna, (Fabrizio), bought for me two pairs of shoes, one for everyday use and another for Sunday best. When the Occurrent Feast occurred, I was now the best-dressed girl in Pratola Serra.

Later, Rosina said to me, without provocation, "I bet Matzo Mauriello helped you with all of this! Didn't he? You are such a lucky girl to have him, Michelina!" I was left speechless. How did she come to think this without my saying anything? I had to think about it. Sure, the Pirone gnome was still well known in the village. But did Matzo Mauriello really help me do this thing? Did he instruct me as he did with the stuffed turkey on Christmas? Did he instruct me on how to build wonderful dresses for myself? Did he whisper instructions in my ear without me knowing, like he did others in my family? Well, perhaps he did. Perhaps the little fellow suggested something in my dreams. Who is to say otherwise?

Chapter Fifteen

Nursing Nonna Fabrizio

All this serenity didn't last long. My grandmother, Giuseppella Fabrizio, the little jail-keepers daughter, began to suffer with her eyes. As I have mentioned, she didn't care much for my father. But all the same, she respected his intelligence and the ability he had in solving problems.

One summer afternoon, Nonna Fabrizio unexpectedly came to our house and asked my father to take her to Avellino to see an eye doctor. My father carefully looked at her. Both eyes were badly infected. He said to her, "Why did you wait so long? They are very inflamed," then declared, "We will go tomorrow." My Nonna Fabrizio added quickly, "I want Michelina to come, too." "All right, all right," he said, but he didn't seem too pleased about it. But there was no school, and Nonna Fabrizio was insistent.

The doctor in Avellino said, "You need an operation on this, today. I can do this here in our hospital. This is glaucoma." Well, we didn't know what glaucoma was. We had never heard of it. Papa asked the doctor, "Will she go blind?" "Not if she will have the operation right away."

Everyday people were mostly ignorant of things of this sort, so doctors often told their patients whatever it pleased them to say with impunity. The people would always believe without question or another opinion. They would never question, no matter how serious their plight might be.

The doctor in Avellino operated on my grandmother Fabrizio's eyes that very same day. After, we called a carriage to go to a local hotel. Nonna had her head completely wrapped in bandages and had to be led by me and Papa by her arms. She had to go to the doctor's clinic every morning for a week. Papa let me stay with her for that week to care for her needs.

The operations of that time were so different from what they are now. Nonna was forced to wear two pieces of flat, round silver discs, two inches in diameter, to cover each of her eyes. I think the doctor made a small hole in the middle of the pieces, but perhaps I am wrong.

When Papa came to get us after a week, Nonna Fabrizio's eyesight was pretty good - for a short while. She continued a normal life again and went out alone. But every morning before she went out, my little Nonna had to remove those two silver discs from her eyes and clean them with boric acid.

The operation was successful the doctors said. But Nonna was very weak when she came back home. Hugging me one morning she told me, "Oh, how I suffered. It was awful! Thank God, I saw you again, Michelina. To see your face." I kissed her.

Then, one day, two months later, she had a fever, got pneumonia, and then she died. The little darling was no more. She was born sometime near 1830, but still to this day, I don't know her exact age.

I felt a void in my heart for a long, long time. My grandfather Fabrizio cried like a child when his little Giuseppella died. What love they had together, right until the end - the jail-keeper's daughter who loved her old warrior soldier so much. My Nonno never would recover. And for me, it was the same, an immense loss - a love that will be with me, forever.

Chapter Sixteen

1913 - 1914

Village Antidotes Remembered

I was quickly into my teenage years, full of promise and self-confidence. I now wore fine dresses of my own design and hand. I especially remember the Christmases at this time of my life. The feast of the birth of Christ was highly celebrated in our home.

My family always had an open house at Nonna Pirone's house where many of our friends and relatives came. In the Christmas of 1913, for instance, we had Amalia Pisano and her family, Rosina's family, all the neighbors, uncles, aunts, cousins and both Nonna Pirone and Nonno Fabrizio. The house was full of festive music, singing, and dancing. I made all the traditional cookies and pies - all by myself. My two remaining Nonni were so proud of me. That Christmas, each of them got up to the crowd and made a toast in my honor. Nonna Pirone said, "To Michelenella and her delicious specialties!" I was surprised. Everybody clapped their hands, even my father.

As with other Christmases, for two weeks before, the musicians, four of them, would go to every house in our village to play Christmas music and cantatas. When they reached the shop of my Uncle Costantino, they kept playing for half an hour straight. Yes, they played and watched while my uncle put together the figurine crèche that he had built himself. Each year, my dear uncle would add more figures or pieces of scenery to his Christmas masterpiece. Crowds would gather to watch this ritual. Across the way, in celebration of the season, the gaslights of the church would be put on for one hour in the morning and one hour in the evening. What a beautiful thing Christmas was in Pratola Serra. We would festivate just as our Roman ancestors did. Later, much later, my Uncle Costantino gave all the figures of his nativity crèche to the church. I would imagine that they are there still.

About this time, I remember a few small but interesting family episodes. These are so vivid in my memory as if they had just occurred. I must put them to paper here.

As I said, in front of my house and my father's shop, across the square, was the Catholic Church. Once, because of the summer heat, my father and a few of his workers brought all their workbenches outside on our sidewalk. There, my father prepared the work - cutting or adjusting the leather harness ornaments, etc, while the others worked on their small benches.

Well, the Ave Marias at the church were administered exactly at six o'clock every evening. On one of these evenings, the church was full of the faithful who were chanting the rosary, "Ave Maria," "Pater nostri ...," etc., etc. My father and his assistants were still working across from the front of the church and paid no attention to any of the droning prayers coming from inside. Now, when my father sang, he was at his best, and he could really project that beautiful tenor voice of his. As a habit, while working, he often sang without thinking, to the delight of his workers. Imagine this beautiful voice booming out from across the church, "O Sole Mio!" Well, all the Ave Marias inside the church were drowned out - the poor worshipers were lost in place. People inside the church suddenly stopped reciting the rosary and turned their heads toward the lyrical voice coming from outside. My siblings and I were there that day and giggling to ourselves. We all knew this voice. My mother was also inside the church - mortified - she knew that voice, as well.

The priest, alarmed and very indignant, immediately summoned the church custodian, the sacristan. Under strict orders, this poor fellow was told to run out from the church to my father and to shut him up. The sacristan meekly crossed the square, tiptoed up to my father and humbly requested, "Maestro, Peppino! Please! Do not sing now. In a half hour, we will get through with the Ave Marias. Then you can sing all you want." My father glared silently at this poor fellow. Without waiting for a response, the little man then quickly ran back to the priest as if he were preparing to be nailed onto the cross himself. My father was caught completely off guard.

After the messa, my mother, the children and I came out from the church. She went right up to my father with a fire in her eye. He, very embarrassed, said to all of us, "Why didn't you tell me that the Ave Maria was in session?! I did not hear anything!" My mother bristled.

Only she answered him. "Ooffa! Peppino! Didn't you hear our voices praying? The church door is wide open! Sometimes I think you are the anti-Christo!" "What!? Angelina - what did I do wrong?! Explain to me!" On and on they went - more loudly than his singing.

As Mother angrily took us inside the house, I saw the priest come out from the church and walk over to my father. He stopped right in front of him and just stood there. He did not say a word. Mutely, the priest must have been telling him, "Shut up you, big show off." My father, looking back at him without answering, must have been thinking, "Go to hell where you belong." Neither man actually spoke.

Another time, the church sacristan was forced to sweep up a mess in front of the church doors that was made by my brother Ralfo and his obedient follower, our brother, Mikele. The two of them had thrown stones at the nesting pigeons high up on the cornice of the church and had made a resulting mess of the place. My brothers continually ignored the sacristan and his warnings of not to throw stones at these birds. Finally, the priest himself came out from inside of his sanctuary with a stick, sending my brothers home with a series of well-placed swings on their backsides.

Each afternoon, after the siesta, mostly in summer, there was a rather old couple, a man and his wife, who went all over the village pushing a huge wooden barrel of lemonade on two large cartwheels. We children were always ready for them.

The man and wife sang at every stop. It was how they proclaimed their presence. First, the man would sing out, "When you are near death, oh, how you will wish I was there with my delicious lemonade!" The wife would then answer in song, "If he is not there, I will be! A woman is always more faithful!" We too answered in song, "Yes, Yes. This is all true!"

Another remembrance. Sometimes a bunch of traveling Gypsies came to Pratola Serra - beautiful, dirty, artistic and persistent people. The men used to position themselves on the square or near the village church and fix or shine bronze utensils - or to sharpen knives, while the women went to every household, reading fortunes with cards or interpreting the palms of people's hands. At night, they all slept in their covered wagons outside of town - happy Gypsies.

There were chickens all around town. It was permissible to have domestic animals inside the house at that time - (not anymore). Well, most of the chickens and many other things disappeared when the Gypsies left town. They were so very bold, audacious, and defiant of any law. Mostly, they were from Albania and Romania - only a few Gypsies were from Italy. Still, there were many things about them with which I could identify.

Also, there were mendicants who came to our village - derelict old men asking for alms. They were always in rags, crippled or half blind. Almost everybody just gave them loaves of bread. They usually carried a sack on their shoulders full of this bread. No common sense. How could one person ever eat so much bread?! Sometimes, however, Nonna Pirone or Nonno Fabrizio would give them a hot dish or a little money instead. Even my mother made underwear for them and gave out stockings. Still, the old men would sleep on our stairways and then leave in the morning. Many times, they would leave loaves of bread on the steps.

On very rare occasions, a little Chinese girl and her father used to come to Pratola Serra just to sell their paper flowers. The girl was so dainty and delicate - very exotic for us to see. She had very small feet and she walked so carefully - so gently. So was her father - gentle, courteous, honest. We never knew from where they came or where they went back to. It was a mystery. Whenever they came to town, however, we always bought some of their handmade flowers.

The meat butchers of Pratola Serra used to kill their animals right in the front room of their own houses or in their basement cellars. These front rooms would also be where they would sell the meat. As I wrote before, there was no refrigeration or ice. They would mostly preserve with smoke or with salt, or they would sell quickly. (Of course, now they have modern ways.)

There was only one family, two brothers, who sold meat in our village - no competition at all. So, they always agreed on the price and helped one another. All members of this family had one insufferable smell about them. Children of this group in school were seated far from everybody else. The grownup members, oh, one could smell them coming from twenty feet away for sure. There was yet no understanding of personal hygiene. Now, not even an unkempt chicken is tolerated, not even in the vegetable gardens. Before Louis Pasteur, hygiene was nil. It is a wonder how we survived.

Chapter Seventeen

1914

Our Girls' Book Club

vs

The Church and its Priest

Now, more about our girls' book club.

As nature would dictate, all of the girls in our group began to discuss more and more the boys of our town rather than books. We were doing less reading and more orchestrating. The boys were not helping either, because they would follow our group everywhere and disrupt the readings with shouts of amorous declarations from the street. At one of these meetings, we copied right out of a book of Greek mythology and decided to make the boys of our village our slaves - we would command, and they would obey. And it worked just like that. The boys were sent off to buy books for us in Avellino, sometimes even with their own money. Anything we needed, they would provide. The problem with this plan was that as a book club, all of us girls were equals, yes. But as objects of amorous attention? It was not always so.

Soon, jealousy began to enter our group. Some were resentful that Amalia Pisano and I were getting more attention from the boys who sought our company even if it was not encouraged. Many of our meetings now were in Amalia's house. The boys knew where to wait for us. When we came down, they told us what they themselves were reading that day in school. Some of the older boys used to tell us how wonderful our anatomy was working and how they dissected small animals just to study their internal reproductive structures. They smiled - we listened. And so, it went, for months. Then, something happened to bring our club back together as a cohesive group - at least temporarily. It became us versus the church and one priest in particular. And, of course, I started it.

93

As I have mentioned, the girls of our book club also were a large part of the all-girl church choir. Many times, we would take our club meetings right after choir practice. We would rehearse, then run off to read and discuss. But our latest book of choice got us into a lot of hot water. I shall never forget.

On one cold day in January 1914, all the girls of the choir were waiting for the head village priest, Father Viviani, for the rehearsing of the evening Novena. We girls jokingly called him, "Archiprete" ("the Bishop"). While we waited for him, we grouped together in one of the cloistered side chapels and seated ourselves on the steps. I told the girls who were not in our reading group of a new book we had just acquired for our book club. There was genuine excitement to hear about it. It was called, "The Physiology of Love," by Paolo Montegazza. It was about the purity and the physical structure of love. Each of these girls who were not in our club looked at me half in fear as if struck by lightning.

Well, I went on with a few details of the book, when the girls suddenly looked up behind me with fear. Standing there was the priest - Archiprete. He had heard me describing the mechanics in the book. This man was very petty and so very scrupulous. He never smiled and always carried with him a look of a martyred Saint. Imagine how he felt when he heard the words of reproductive anatomy between a man and a woman and why we make love - a serious discussion by me with other girls in the choir. Well, the priest screamed as if he had seen me with the devil. "You! Signorina, Michelina! Come to the main altar and kneel down with me! Pray, pray so the devil inside of you will come out!" Not one of the other girls moved.

The priest pulled me hard from the girls and at the main altar, we stopped. There, he pushed me down to my knees. He then knelt on the other side of the altar and prayed aloud and alone! His voice echoed everywhere inside the church. "Oh God," he boomed, "help this girl who tries to corrupt my choir. She is not a good influence on this church. Guide her better to serve, etc., etc." I was a little shaken until Amalia Pisano came and knelt right at my side - very close. Her touch silently was assuring me that I was not alone. The Priest did not ask her to come up, but when he saw that she too was praying, he probably thought his words were inspiring the others. Amalia and I knew otherwise. She came for solidarity.

After much outrage and prayer and after all that commotion, the priest stood and left us on our knees. He angrily went into the vestry to compose himself. He was shaking red as he left. Amalia and I looked at each other - just kneeling there at the main altar. What could we do? We waited and waited at the main altar, our hands clasped together in prayer. We shrugged and looked at each other. "Should we just stay in this position?" we thought, "How long?" The other girls also stood silent and motionless in the side altar, probably fearing for their own fates.

Then the door to the vestry flew open, and the church sacristan quickly ran out right past us to across the street to get some strong coffee for his boss. We all remained stunned. "What next?" I thought. Then, like a flash of light in my head, I knew. I crossed myself, jumped up from my knees, and pulled Amalia back to the still frozen choir. I said to the girls, "I did nothing wrong, and I am not going to rehearse. Enough of this! Are all of you with me!?" No answer. Then, one by one, all the girls of the book club said, "Yes," starting with Amalia. I continued with the others of the choir, "Did you not like what I was saying about the purity of love?" All said, "Yes." I spoke again, "Will you go out now with me - all of you? We can give the Archiprete a lesson! We can make him feel sorry. He is too much to bear. Everywhere this book is read. It is scientific literature. Ask the best scholars of Pratola Serra! They will tell you that it is a book of scholarship, and we don't want to be ignorant, do we!?" "No, no," came the reply. I added quickly, "Let's go together then! Avanti! The priest needs us to sing the Novena tonight. We don't need him!" "Yes! Yes!" We stormed toward the church doors all in a file. We were unified!

At this point, the priest came out of his retreat in the sacristy to go to the organ to start the rehearsal, when he saw us all about to march out as a group. He came after us shouting in an acrimonious manner, "Come back here, you devils!!!" Everyone froze in her tracks but me. I kept going out the door.

This was a bad move by me.

I ran to Nonna's store. I didn't dare to go to my mother's house; it would be the first place the priest would look for me. When I told Nonna what had happened, even she was indignant with me. "Yes, you can read books, Michelina, but why read about love of that kind!? - especially, to mention them in a holy place." She got me thinking. But in the store happened to come Don Andrea Lieto - a graduating student of medicine. "Dottore Lieto" was about twenty then and very progressive in his thinking. This helped me out immeasurably. He often stopped at Nonna's for some special things he wanted. Don Lieto was a good family friend who would soon become our family "Dottore" (doctor). He was also a compare and godfather to one of Nonna's sons. Well, Nonna was still fuming. Don Lieto asked, "What is all the fuss about?" He listened attentively, then explained to Nonna just who the author, Paolo Montegazza, was. He added, "Signora, how can you, an educated woman, condemn this girl who tries to learn. The book is a masterpiece. Montegazza explains simply what is love. I even had to study this author myself in medical school. The priest is ignorant and dominating. He doesn't know anything else but how to complain. He should be more interested in what is happening in the outside world." Don Lieto picked up a newspaper and showed it to Nonna, "Look, all the world around us is in dissension. War is coming. This priest should worry about these affairs and not about a simple book of human mechanics and emotion. Maybe I should go and have a talk with the priest myself."

Now I felt better - vindicated. It was exactly what I was saying, but I didn't think that even a student dottore could influence this village priest. Still, he nodded a confident smile at me.

Somebody else came in and joined the conversation. Giovanni Mancini, an old, venerable and respected man who had some land way up on the hillside - a Garden of Eden. He knew a lot about botany; we often visited his garden. Well, he agreed on the subject at hand, that I had the right and the privilege to read new authors and to learn. I loved this man. Everything about him showed wisdom and benevolence. I liked the Dottore, too, for he was very kind. Anyway, these two men spared me lots of trouble with Nonna.

Nonna was soon convinced that the Archiprete was wrong. He didn't even read anything of Montegazza! How in the world could he judge and why such a fuss? But this conflict wasn't over.

When my father, mother, and the parents of all the other girls heard about what had happened, we were in trouble - especially me, the leader of the uprising. There was even talk that some of us girls might be kicked out of the church - a modern inquisition. People obeyed the priest blindly. Thank God that there were some who didn't. I can tell you, however, that I was still scared for confronting the head priest of the village.

I went to Uncle Costantino's shop and stayed there the rest of the afternoon. I told him what had happened, in every detail. He said nothing, just shook his head, smiling. We read the newspapers together. As Don Lieto described, the news was very alarming. Germany and France were exchanging insults about the market, Germany asserting that France could never meet the perfection of their products, etc. My uncle commented on it, but I couldn't concentrate. My mind was on other things.

When the bells for the Ave Maria rang, my uncle put his tools down and said, "Come, Michelina, let's go to church." I was amazed. I said, "You seldom go to church!" He repeated, "Let's go! Let's see what this 'Archiprete' dares to do, eh? Don't worry," he said with a smile, "I will protect you." And so, we went.

My uncle's shop was a little far from the church, but the bells were still calling when we got there. All the girls belonging to the choir were there - standing in front with their parents - including all of my book club girls. They greeted my uncle and me, and we all went inside. My mother and father arrived later and saw me just inside the church with Uncle Costantino. I was afraid my parents would come over to scold me as usual - they never took my side. But I was glad that they remained outside the front door, away from us. My uncle and I stood quietly in the back of the church along with the entire girls' choir. I still felt that they were with me. But no one said anything which had me worried.

At this point, I had my answer. None of the girls in the choir moved forward to the side altar to sing as a choir. We all stood in quiet solitude away from our accustomed places - united.

The priest saw us all stationed in back and slowly moved to the main altar. He seemed like a person who had reconciled his anger. I could only think that Don Lieto had possibly his talk with him, but I wasn't sure. But there was no singing that evening at the Novena. The absence of the girls' choir was very evident. The priest simply played the organ on the side of the main altar - alone. That was all. Victory. We had won - but what? Was it over? No. The church in my village was never over anything. Eventually, the Archiprete would advance my leaving Pratola Serra altogether. To this day, I believe it all began for him with this episode.

The day after, the priest and the sacristan came to each of our houses, requesting that all the girls come back to rehearsal with a promise that there would be no more lectures by him but also there would be no discussion of any other books or teachings other than that of the church. We girls agreed. We really had no choice. We went back, and we all felt that we had won a big battle. But we never did discuss any of Paolo Montegazza's books after that, not in church anyway. So, in some way, it was a victory for the Archiprete as well. I'm sure he had convinced himself that his faithful prayers were answered.

After a while, our mothers and fathers stopped questioning the books we read and had chosen for our club. Quietly, but persistently, we defied both the church and our parents. As I think back about the priests of the church, all of them, they were the dictators of the town. They were so archaic, blaming all the trouble of the world on the sins and on the disobedience of the people. But also, I think this episode with the Archiprete took its toll on our club. It was losing its tight interest. Some girls dropped out, perhaps from family pressure, perhaps just from a growing disinterest. Anyway, girls were leaving. Only Amalia Pisano and I kept on analyzing books together. We talked about how we saw human nature to be. We began to understand how it worked in different people, even how it manifested itself in our club - and why we were dissolving. Sadly, we realized that we could not force everybody to study or at least to try as we did to know a little more than the ordinary. No, no. There was something in Amalia and me that urged us to ask and ask again. We often were stopped along the way of our questioning and had to do as we were told. We were walloped with a mass of ignorance all around us and were nearly drowned in the flood of it, but we never lost our love for perfection, for beauty, or for each other. Amalia and I used to repeat often that we knew our own mental limitations, but that we would use the little knowledge we had and try to do more for ourselves as young women and for others. As for the church? It had no interest in these matters.

Chapter Eighteen

Great-Aunt Raffaella Dies

Great-Grandmother Maria, Doesn't

Brother Francesco is Born

Francesco, (Frank) my new brother, was born July 29, 1914. I was the first one to see him arrive, besides the midwife of course - only then did my father come in. "Another boy!" he said, "Oh, how wonderful!" But not wonderful for me, I thought. Now we were seven children; me, Ralfo, Allessandra, Costantino, Mikele, Josephine and also, Francesco. I would have more responsibility especially with my mother bedridden. Well, what could I do, get mad with my mother who loved to have children?

More issues. Great-Aunt Raffaella, Nonna's old maid sister who came to live with her to help take care of their aged mother, Mamma Maria, too became sick and bedridden. I helped my poor aunt as best I could. I was constantly going back and forth from Nonna's house to our house. I think I must have worn a new path in those ancient cobblestones in the square. With the new baby, Mother recovering, a dying great-aunt at Nonna's house and young children everywhere, I had my hands full. And, my father expected his dinner.

I was only thirteen the day my Great-Aunt Raffaella died. She died practically in my arms just one month after Francesco was born. She died smiling saying, "Michelina. You are a brave girl. I thank you." In those days, everybody died at home in the company of loved ones, if they had loved ones. Almost always, the wake was at home as well, with family positioned around the body according to their rank. Death was more personal than now.

My great-grandmother had just turned one hundred years old when Aunt Raffaella, her daughter, died. Mamma Maria was outliving her own children who were dying of old age!

So, I had lots of responsibilities on my shoulders - cooking, making clothes for my brothers and sisters - watching after mother, etc. Fortunately, Nonna's new servants, Carmela and her husband, Pellerino, helped, even sometimes in my parent's house. It was a fulltime job for me. My little bedroom at Nonna's house was my private sanctuary, when I could get there.

But even at Nonna's there was still plenty to do. I had to bathe my great-grandmother - the old dear. This was no chore for me, really. She became as small as a child herself. Every night I gave her a bath. Sometimes in the tub, other times, just with a sponge. Somehow, I thought she felt better - her skin was so very dry.

Nonna bought some body oil, and when I rubbed the oil on my great-grandmother, she smiled. Sometimes she said, "I wish I could see you." Over her many years, she had become more and more blind - cataracts. One time, I took her hand and put it on my face. She touched my face, hair and got hold of one of my hands and kissed it. "Bless you. You are a wonderful girl," she said. It was a wonderful experience for me to have this contact with my Mamma Maria. I needed it at that time.

When Nonna's servant, Carmela, who was nearly deaf herself, dressed my great-grandmother up in the morning, they sometimes started a conversation. It was comical to listen to them. Mamma Maria would say how nice she had slept, and Carmela would answer, "Yes, the weather is good today," etc. They never heard one another. It was truly funny to listen to them. I couldn't help but laugh. My grandmother Pirone scolded me on this, but many times she couldn't help but to laugh herself. It wasn't ridicule. No, just a part of human behavior - a part of our lives. Nonna at this happening would look at me and smile. "Well, we will get old too, Michelina. Perhaps we will be just like my mother, eh?"

Two years later, in 1916, during the First World War, Mamma Maria, my old great-grandmother, passed away. Yes, passed, at the age of one hundred and two years of no real sickness. Actually, she didn't really "die" - she just stopped! She had had enough of this mortal world, I think, and was every bit comforted that she would be going "up the stairs now" to heaven. And so, she did. Blind, deaf, happy, intelligent, and so beautiful - only Rembrandt could have done justice to her.

Chapter Nineteen

1914 - 1915

The Great War Hits Home

I relate now this war because I was there when it happened - World War I and how it had its manifest in our little village of Pratola Serra. I studied hard to answer "why" and to read as much as I could.

Early 1914, as we know, the rapid growth of Germany in industrial and commercial areas caused a jealousy with other dominant nations, such as England and France, both of which had prestige and power of their own all over the world. This forced Germany, Austria, Hungary, and Italy to form an alliance called, the "Triple Alliance." The Alliance's charter was just defensive in purpose, mostly on the part of Italy. *[Aside: We had to cross-reference Michelina here who seemingly assigns four countries to the "Triple" Alliance - sure enough, it turns out she was correct.]*

There was another Triple Alliance. England, France and Russia - also for protection and to keep the balance of power. But France had an obstinate grudge toward Germany, because of Germany's victorious war of 1910 that took from France the Provinces of Alsace/Lorrainer. Austria had always looked toward the States of the Peninsula Balkan, not only to influence them but also to protect herself from Russia who always protected these Slavic regions. *[Aside: Balkan Wars.]* All these nations, and others around them, were getting ready with armaments and preparation - including Italy. They only wanted an occasion, an incident, to light up the flame of envy. It all came soon enough with the assassination of Austrian Prince Archduke Ferdinando and his wife, Sophia, in Sarajevo by a Serbian student on June 28th, 1914. These deaths gave vent to all these hostilities.

So, on the 28th of July 1914, the day before my brother Francesco was born, Austria-Hungary declared war on Serbia. Italy at this time prepared to join the war to protect and complete her internal struggle for national unity, an ever, ongoing process. War, war, war.

There were two political currents in the country - one for neutrality, directed by the old statesman, Giovani Giolitti. He believed that Italy could obtain plenty, even without involvement. The other current, more hostile and dominant, moved to agitate the people toward war. They wanted territory.

Also, there were shouts in the streets of, "Everybody to the front!" "Save the refugees of the Trentino!" (Italians in the Dolomite Alps), "War to Austria!" Etc. The village newspaper offered: *"Il popolo d'Italia,"* ["The people of Italy"], by Benito Mussolini, he proclaiming, "War to the enemy - now!" Gabrielle d'Annunzio, poet, and playwright, was forever writing long editorials as well - "War! War!"

In Pratola Serra, people were standing on balconies repeating what d'Annunzio, Mussolini, and others were writing. *[Aside: Michelina's personal memory of these events is remarkable. On April 26th, 1915, Italy was induced to sign the secret "Treaty of London" pact, bringing her into a "new" alliance, this time with Great Britain, France, and Russia, thereby surrounding the Austria-Hungary/ Germany Alliance. Italy had flipped sides.]*

I remember the mayor of Pratola Serra on his balcony proclaiming, "Let us not be cowards!" And the paesani (the people) answered him, "No! We won't be!"

Gabrielle d'Annunzio repeated that war is the only way we can liberate Trento and Trieste, (Italian territories lost to Austria). He inflamed the minds of the people. The agitation became uncontrollable until, with high scruples, Italy openly denounced the treaty of the Triple Alliance with Germany and Austria-Hungary that it had once belonged to.

The Italian government on the 24th of May 1915, declared war on Austria. In the same day, King Victor Emanuel III assumed command supreme, giving power to direct the Italian military to general Luigi Cadorna. Then began, even for Italy, that bloody and miserable war of the trenches as it was in France. It was here that we lost our dear Salvatore, one of my father's young apprentices. By the winter of 1915, Italy lost all that she had gained. Tormentous was the war on the Alpino front. Not any less arduous was the fighting on the Isonzo and the Carso - desolated battle areas with stones, caverns, etc. - really bad territory. Here, the Italian

Third Army produced an enormous offensive against Austria, which led to the liberation of Gorizia in this battle, north of Trieste.

At this time, our little town of Pratola Serra was becoming more depleted. The older men and young men were leaving by the dozens. My father and his apprentices had plenty of work now because of the big demand for making harnesses for war horses. He could not keep up because some of his own help now went to serve this war as soldiers. This is when my brother, Ralfo, at age eleven, began his apprenticeship with Papa in the harness shop.

All the women in Pratola Serra at this time were busy making wool stockings, gloves, and caps for the soldiers - free of course. Our town became desolate. Only women, old men and children remained in the village - and the priest, too, of course.

My father's youngest brother, Uncle Francesco, went, too, as a mechanical specialist. He served in the artillery, adjusting machines of war and anything mechanical. Thankfully, my uncle came back to us in one piece.

But by this time, the farms began to feel the absence of men - little was produced. Soon, we had to ration our needs accordingly. During these months, every morning, we would wait in line with our books of rationing. We would also forage. We got bread, some cereal, and seldom meat but never sugar, eggs or many other needs. Everything went to the front, to the military.

1916

There was at this time in Pratola Serra a sort of invasion as well. In the south of Italy and even to our village, there was an influx of refugees, northern Italians from Gorisia and from the Alps. They came by the hundreds into each town - we received them in the church. Old people or very young children dressed badly, hungry, sick. To Pratola Serra came a few young refugee men who were unable to fight because of wounds they received as civilians. Every family adopted a few of the refugees until the commune provided homes for all of them. We even took a few of them home with us - an old-women, two young girls, and a baby of one-year-old. We used Nonno Fabrizio's home to temporarily house them. Well, the refugees soon found an abode of their own, and they eventually became part of the paesani and fabric of the town. But we all believed that our little mountain village, our commune, would no longer be as little or as isolated in the world.

"Limit to strength?
There is no limit to strength.
Limit to courage?
There is no limit to courage.
Limit to suffering?"

Gabrielle d'Annunzio

Chapter Twenty

Papa Leaves for America – Again

Perhaps the World War, the strain of unending demand for harnesses for war, the lack of qualified help, the fear that it would all end badly, the desire to follow his leatherworking brothers to America and having been there himself - all played a role in the already troubled mind of my father. Papa didn't believe in personal sacrifice, so he ran away before he would be trapped further by the demands of war or by more family responsibility. Yet, he was the sole artist to all he designed and created.

One day, Papa abruptly closed his harness shop and told Mother he wanted her to move into her father's house until he could afford to send for her and all the children - he was taking Ralfo and was leaving for America. My mother was pregnant again, so she had little choice. She could not travel. Of course, Papa blamed everything on the Great War. His two brothers wrote from New York saying things were better there, not like Italy. My father needed little outside convincing, however - he had already been to America - he had already convinced himself to return. He had sacrificed enough.

On November 16th, 1916, my father and my brother Ralfo, now thirteen, left for America.

Papa took with him a good deal of money but also thought it would probably be worthless in America. No one knew anymore. He gave Nonno Fabrizio the rest to keep safe and hidden for his family. He also asked my Nonno Fabrizio to take his daughter back into his house with all the children. Another Pirone - Fabrizio deal made by the men.

My mother took the children and went to live with Nonno Fabrizio as she was instructed to do. I left Nonna Pirone's house and joined them there. My grandfather Fabrizio had a small but nice house. Of course, he was glad we all came, although I think he felt my father was making a big mistake to leave Italy when he did and how he did. I was with my grandfather's opinion on this matter.

In my Nonno Fabrizio's house, a classic stone farmhouse, he had two good bedrooms on the upstairs floor. One of them was where Nonno and my brother Costantino slept. Costantino was the oldest boy now that Ralfo left with Papa. The other good bedroom upstairs was where Allessandra and I slept. Mamma and the small children (Mikele, Josephine, and Francesco) slept in one large room downstairs in the back. I remember that room was damp. There was also a large outer-lodge or outbuilding that we used as a kitchen. The house also had a main front room with a fireplace. I didn't like that room at all. It always seemed dark to me and foreboding, uninviting. So, this was now our home - a grandfather, his pregnant daughter and a large concentration of grandchildren. Truthfully? I know he loved it.

I quickly missed Nonna's house though, but it was just too far from Nonno's - across the village. It was not practical any longer for me to go back and forth to be with Mother or to help her with everything. I resented my father for leaving, more and more by each day.

Still, I worried about Papa and Ralfo in the middle of the sea surrounded by the perils of war. Sure, Italy and England were now allies, and England ruled the seas, but there were others on that dangerous sea as well.

News came later of dangerous incidents they experienced on the sea. German submarine came within view of their passenger ship, and all were told to stay below in the bottom of the boat and not to move. We knew just how frightened they both must have been. It must have been especially awful for young Ralfo. Oh, how I cried when Ralfo left. He left me a bird to take care of, and I gave him a golden ring and a silk scarf. I would have given him all that I had if it would have been of use to him. I prayed and I cried until we got a telegram of their safe arrival in New York.

Glory be to heaven!

Later, in April 1917, the United States declared war against Germany because the latter used submarines and had sunk even American boats. This was why my father's trip with Ralfo in November of 1916, on the Atlantic, was so fearful for us.

The entry of America weakened the resistance of the German-Austrian alliance. Soon l'armista (the armistice) took place. Exhausted, the Germanic allies asked for the armistice. Three years of war. In her alliance victory with America, England, France, and Russia, Italy herself lost 650,000 combatants and a total casualty to her people of over two million. *[Aside: Michelina is correct here. In addition, Italy's adversaries suffered even heavier losses. Austria-Hungary lost 1.2 million men with 7 million total civilian casualties. Civilian deaths attributed to the War in Europe outnumbered all combatant deaths. Civilian losses were about 13 million.]*

Chapter Twenty-One

1917

Sweet Sixteen

As I said, at this time, Mother was pregnant with her eighth child, and she was expecting the new baby soon. But the baby came early. One damp day, a Wednesday morning in March of 1917, we were alone, my Nonno was not home when my mother began to have sharp pains. "Oh my God! Michelina!" she cried out. "Go quick - get the midwife! Get Lida!"

It wasn't too far to midwife Lida's house. I ran hard - nobody was home. I looked everywhere and asked everyone in the village. Someone said the midwife was away delivering a baby. What now? I was panicked. Nonna's house was too far away as was our new family doctor, Dottore Lieto. So, I ran back home emptyhanded. What else could I do?

Oh! When I came back into the house, I found my mother cutting something from the baby boy that had just been born in the thirty minutes that I was away. "My God! Poor Mother." I was sure that she was ashamed of me for failing to get help, but her mind was more occupied to separate the baby from the bloody mass it was struggling in. I was half in shock - frozen at the spectacle, while my mother continued to cut and pull my new brother away from his entanglement.

To me, it (the placenta) looked like a little monster! I said, "Oh my God, Mother! You had two babies! One is awful!" She didn't answer at first; instead, she covered the baby, then calmly told me to put the other part in a basin that she had ready in the closet. I hesitated in my ignorance. I had been present at two other of my mother's births, yes, but Lida the midwife had managed to shield me away from this part. "It is not a birth, Michelina, it is the baby's casing, please, listen." Then Mother told me to get the string in the bureau draw - the top one. I did. She tied the baby's umbilicus and covered him up again, then fell back on her pillow. "Oh, God, help me and this poor girl with this beautiful guy." The baby was

113

crying. Mother ordered me to wash him with body oil and to dress him up. This I knew how to do.

I cleaned mother's bed, changed her soiled gown, and helped her wash her body. Mother supervised everything, standing weakly at times, slowly moving about, until everything was perfect. Finally, though, she lay back down and slept. In her mind, she must have thought, "Now there are eight."

I wrapped up my new baby brother, put him in the cradle and I went out into the kitchen outbuilding. I was still shaking. What Mother had done all by herself was unbelievable. I felt so ashamed that I had failed her. The roles were changed. My shame turned to anger toward my father for not being there with us - but he never really was anyway. I made some coffee, and I cried alone for hours. Later, when Mikele came home, I sent him to bring Nonna, another thing I had failed to do in my panic.

When Mikele finally found Nonna, she came running right away. Nonna went straight into my mother's room and quietly assisted with what was left to do, which was very little. My mother actually told Nonna that I had given her strength. I was surprised to hear this when Nonna came out. She hugged me and then said, "Michelina, you did a good job in helping your mother. You are just like me. You can do anything you put your mind to!" "Except find Lida, the midwife," I thought.

My mother named this last child of hers - Luigi, after her father. This she did alone and without permission from anyone.

1917 was a good and bad year. I was sixteen - a very precocious time. Now that the Great War was essentially over and Italy had won its position, the people got back to regular habits. Unencumbered, the girls and boys of Pratola Serra were back again concentrating on the ritual of courtship. How quickly balance regains itself. Many of my old book club friends now were always in and out of love. But for me, I never fell in love. The passion inside of me to learn more was so much stronger than any other emotion. Sometimes, I hurt the boys who would make the effort. It is true; I first accepted their attention, and then I left them flat.

It was not completely planned that way. I knew early that I was not physically objectionable, and I did enjoy this part of life, especially in my early years. The attention of it. Yes, I was grateful for how I physically turned out, but could not, nor dared not, totally commit to what was expected of that arbitrary condition. In my heart, I also knew that there were other gifts that sometimes were given out, the special gift of the ability to know. This was less visible, except in the heart. What was expected of a man and what was expected of a woman are dictated by culture. To me, however, the mind had no gender.

I do not deny in this letter that I encouraged the attention of boys, and even played my part with it. What girl would not? But this problem of the mind vurses the heart would follow me for all my life. How can we separate love of self from love of life or from love of another individual? Why must we choose at all? I did not have these answers at sixteen years of age - or for many, many years after. But people all around me acted as if they themselves understood the difference - that somehow, they knew. I knew only that I wanted to explore mentally first as far as it would take me, wherever it would take me - while I had the chance. I understood what was expected of a girl and what was expected of a grown woman. I learned that part from the nuns. I saw it in my Nonna and also in my mother. But to advance the mind must be first for a girl. I committed myself to this concept. Being courted by boys back then? Okay, but only on my say so - while I was still free. This paradox would govern me for the next several years of my life. In some ways, in 1917, the clock for me started ticking.

My First "Job"

Letters came regularly from Papa and Ralfo in America. They were living in New York City with his younger brother, Uncle Antonio and his wife, Aunt Bernadina. My uncle and aunt had five children now, including my older cousin, Fortuna. Ralfo wrote me that he loved everybody there. He was going to school to learn English and thought that I would be proud of his progress. He was also still apprenticing in leatherwork, and things looked pretty good for him and Papa. Every month, Papa sent 200 lire - worth about $250 in 1917 - enough for the family for a month. Now it is worth about a package of cigarettes. This, along with the money that my father left in the care of my Nonno, was meant for the family, and not much was left over for me. I needed things. So, I decided to find a job. What were my talents? Building clothes, cooking, caretaking children - all the teachings of nuns. I had to think harder. Books! I knew and loved books. I was a lover of the printed page. "But how do I turn that knowledge into money?" I thought.

The idea came to me, and it was a good one. I shall find a job as a writer. I thought hard on how to offer this service when one of Ralfo's letters came to me in rough sentences of Italian and English. It was crude in form and I thought of what he really was trying to say. "Ah, ha!" I would be a reader and letter writer for the village! And yes, it worked! I promoted myself and took jobs writing letters for farm people and others who had family and relatives already in America. Our part of Italy was still about 70% illiterate at that time. These people would pay me for this reading and letter writing service. Letters back and forth to America were numerous and always in Italian. It was a good fit for me. I also started to branch out into basic English when those letters themselves became important. I learned some English when reading the English translation of Dante's Inferno. I had that book in Latin and in Italian as well, so I could compare all three languages together.

It was perfect - an independent writer with income. I was happy and sixteen years of age.

Pratola Serra, Italy - 1917 - Michelina at sweet sixteen
in a nit of her own design and making.

Chapter Twenty-Two

The Plague of 1918

As I mentioned, after the Great War ended, food was scarce in our region. The farmers had little left over, even for themselves. They had to sell most of their crops to cover their debt. And they somehow were not producing as much as before the war - not yet anyway. There were no battles fought in our part of Italy, no, but we still felt the results of battles elsewhere. The Americans helped us for a while with those juicy American baked canned hams and processed cheese. The cheese was different from anything we had ever had before. At first, the paesani didn't know how to cook with it or even how to use it. Hunger, however, is a good innovator. But we were forced to wait for even these few commodities. Of course, wild greens and mushrooms were readily available during some of the year, but not a constant food supply. Besides, everyone would be gathering them as soon as they appeared. Unbalanced diets and scarcity of meat, fish, and poultry, left the people vulnerable to sickness.

Then came word, in the spring of 1918, almost as a whisper, that an epidemic was going on all over Europe. The papers began to warn us not to be exposed to dampness and to take every precaution. They also gave a reason of how this pestilence occurred. In Spain, they said, they found a well full of human cadavers covered with some soil. All over Europe, this kind of putrefaction, along with malnutrition, had created a lack of resistance to sickness in the people who had survived the Great War. Dead bodies were found in bushes and in cellars - rats were escaping from war boats, etc. Just lots of talk we thought, rumors, but it was all true enough. *[Aside: Influenza was sometimes called "Spanish" Influenza as Michelina noted. There were more lives lost during the great influenza epidemic of 1918, (20,000,000 people), than the total combatants killed in every war ever fought. Even away from the theaters of conflict, there was no escape. In the United States alone, almost 600,000 deaths were recorded. Millions more died in Europe.]*

One day, in my Uncle Costantino's shop, he said to me that in Avellino, it was rumored that twenty people had died in one day with the same sickness. I thought he was joking. He had promised to take me there when next he needed to re-supply materials and to shop, so he brought up the subject. I noticed a note of worry and of pessimism in his voice - his attitude was different. I remember that he was hitting the anvil so that sparks came up. Then he said, "Michelina, I have to go to Avellino tomorrow. Do you still want to come with me? I will understand if you don't." "Of course," I said, managing to push this rumor out of my mind. We both agreed, "We will go anyway, eh?" Avellino was a big town, and the rumors were that, just rumors. Besides, how could I pass up a long-promised trip with my favorite uncle?

The day after, we went to Avellino in Uncle Costantino's small carriage. We did our shopping and then went for some refreshments afterward at a sidewalk café. Avellino showed no signs of any pestilence - the café tables were full. People walked on every street and passageway. My uncle looked so young - black wavy hair, trimmed moustache, and bright hazel eyes. I looked across the table, and I never loved him more than at that moment. I was thanking the fates that made him my uncle - my protector, the man who helped teach me to read from the newspaper.

The waiter came up and asked with a smile, "Signore - is the Signorina your fiancée?" Uncle Costantino looked so pleased at the question. "How did you guess?" he said with a twinkle. The waiter said, "Well, the way you talk to each other. Mostly the way she looks at you. We Italians are very romantic. We sense these things!" Uncle with his eyes shining and playing the game continued, "But she is so very young! Too young for someone of my age." The waiter responded, "Oh, Signore, but love is blind!" My uncle laughed and said, "She would have to be blind!" Then, we all laughed. Uncle was so pleased to make the waiter really believe that I was his inamorata, when he helped me to get up, he kissed me loudly on the cheek. The waiter beamed, "Ah, ha. I told you so! Buona fortuna - e grazie!" We left arm-in-arm in laughter - happy all day.

On the way back to Pratola Serra, we sang arias from all our favorite operas in uncle's open carriage. Our voices echoed off the hills. We sounded good. It was the last happiness for the two us. It was the last happiness for the family.

Two days later, Uncle Costantino got sick. He came down with a heavy fever and delirium. Aunt Peppina sent for me and also called for Doctor Lieto. She had just given birth to another baby two weeks before and was still weak herself.

When I got to my aunt and uncle's house before the doctor, I found Uncle Costantino hallucinating with fever - almost mad. My poor aunt was crying, trying to keep him in his bed, but he wouldn't stay there. He kept getting up - ignoring her pleas. When I came into the room, I don't think he even recognized me. He was walking in circles saying, "My razor. Give me my razor - I must shave." I didn't want to give him the razor. He was wobbling all around the room. "Please, uncle, go to bed. Rest. We can't find the razor!" Aunt Peppina and I still could not get him back into bed.

When Dr. Lieto finally came in, right away he knew what it was. The doctor gravely announced to us that there was an epidemic spreading across the land called, "Spanish influenza," and that these were the symptoms. "Just now, there are at least ten cases in Pratola Serra," he said. "My God," I thought. "Those rumors of Avellino were not rumors at all."

Dr. Lieto was able to make Uncle Costantino lie down and gave him some medicine. He continued solemnly to my aunt and me, "First, a headache with a murmur in the ear - then a fever - a very high fever. If you can abate the fever, then you can spare yourself. It won't come back." I said, "Please doctor, do not let him hear you." Then Dr. Lieto said, "He doesn't hear me - he is with fever. All he is thinking of right now is to walk out or to do something. They all act this way. You must keep compresses on his head to reduce the fever." Before leaving he said, "Go home, Michelina - you look pale yourself." "I want to stay with Uncle - I must," I said. He stared at me to make me go. I went to Uncle Costantino's bed and kissed his hand, "I will be here tomorrow to see you. Please listen to what the doctor says." Then he said, (I will never forget this), "Where is Michelina!? I haven't seen her today!" "I am here, dear Uncle, here!" I cried out. At this instant, I got a terrible headache and the room started to move. I don't remember much after that moment. I collapsed - I think. I was gone.

The next reality that I remember was not being in Uncle Costantino's house at all, but in my own bed with my mother and my sister Allisandra looking over me. I, too, was burning up, but I remember their faces. I remember their voices.

I was lying semi-conscious in bed when Doctor Lieto came in and was not surprised to see the state I was in. I don't remember anything of his visit, not even the instructions he gave to Mother. He came late because of all the cases that were now just appearing everywhere in our village. Dr. Lieto was busy going almost from door to door to tend the sick. Mother told me later that she had never seen this confident man of medicine so visibly shaken. That very same night, both village doctors, Dr. Lieto and Dr. Acone, also became sick with fever - as well as most members of their families. No one could believe how fast the disease was spreading. One strange condition of the Spanish influenza was that it would some-how completely pass by some people without effect while others it would debilitate - or worse. There was nothing in between.

Throughout that night, I was in and out of consciousness. My fever pounded in my head, and I felt like I had to run, but I could not move. It totally occupied my dreams. For the whole night, I felt as if I were in a close room - a tight chamber with kitchen utensils and dishes all about me on the floor. These objects began to multiplicate until I was covered, suffocated by them. I tried to get up, screaming. I found out later that I somehow managed to get out of the bed. I was kicking until I fell. My poor mother couldn't lift me up. Either Allessandra or somebody else helped get me back to bed. They put a cold cloth on my forehead, soaked with some vinegar. A compare of my mothers, an old woman in black, came to our house in the morning, and she injected some medicine into me with a needle. Now this woman was not a doctor and not a midwife, but practiced a sort of spiritualistic medicine, just the sort of mystical medicine Doctor Lieto was trying to eradicate. But old traditions die hard. When this woman injected me, it was so painful. It left a noceform on my right buttock, a hard, little ball like protrusion, innocuous, but even to this day, it is still there.

The day after, I was a little better. Was it the needle? I will never know. But I still was very weak and still had a mild fever. Then, in the background, I heard people inside my house crying, almost in a dream. "Oh, why is everyone crying?" Mother and Allessandra came bursting into the room in tears and cupping their hands over their mouths. They brought word. Uncle Costantino had died in the night with fever. I cried out, "No, this could not be! This is still a dream! Take it away from me!"

Mother sat on the edge of my bed where we cried alone for a long time. I cried until I could cry no more. At the same time, my fever came back then broke again. It was another day later - or it might not have been. I was left unable to move, with an inconsolable numbing pain, thinking of my dear, dear Uncle Costantino - my best friend. I couldn't even cry. I was so sad that tears just would not come. "Why - why?" More hours went by - days - I did not care. What is the meaning of it?

Near the end of my battle, I was perspiring so much, my mother had to change my clothes twice in a row - I was completely soaked through. I also temporarily lost the hearing in both ears, having just a dull ringing in my head. When I finally lifted my head to sit up, Mother looked at me with distress. Because of the high fever, all of my long tight curls were left behind on the pillow. Soon, all of my hair would fall out. I had gone entirely bald, but I didn't care.

For a long time, I was unable to get my strength back because all my family was now sick with influenza - Mother, my grandfather and all the children. Catastrophic. I was weak, but because I was the first to get sick, my fever was the first to lower. I survived! I remembered what Dr. Lieto said, "If you can abate the fever, then you can spare yourself. It won't come back." Yes, but why was I spared and not my poor uncle? Again, always, why?

I was the only one able to get up. "I must - I must get up." When I went to the kitchen to find something to cook for my family there was nothing there - no food - nothing. I had to go out. Somehow, I managed to get myself to Nonna's store. Nonna had no fever - she was spared, of the influenza anyway. But she was not spared of inconsolable grief. When Nonna saw me, she jumped up and embraced me hard crying, "Costantino - Oh, Costantino!" We cried together in each other's arms. She felt my head with the back of her hand and then sat down as in a dream. "Your hair, Michelina. Your beautiful curls?" She took the scarf from around her neck and gave it to me to wrap my baldness. I told her everyone in Nonno Fabrizio's house also had the fever, but all were slowly recovering. They escaped - everyone. Then neither of us spoke for the longest time - just tears came to both me and my Nonna.

I got up, and I took some of what little was left of the beans in Nonna's barrels which were now nearly empty. I promised my Nonna that I would help her to restock her store someday. She did not respond. The poor dear just sat there; she had let everything be taken away by those who were in need - the store was now nearly completely empty. It wasn't looting in the true sense, but it was close. Nonna Pirone was in a different world - mourning for her son, her youngest and closest son. She didn't care what was happening around her. She would just watch as people took from the shelves with promises - always promises, to make good. The people became irresponsible - they needed food - she had some - they took the food. I was no different.

I did not think that things could get worse in our village, but they did. All of Pratola Serra was sick. There were homes in the town where everyone inside was found dead - everyone. The mountain isolation that once protected us was now our most terrible enemy. Officials had no time to make or to buy funeral boxes. They were forced to carry the dead out on an open cart - body upon body, one cart after another. They placed the corpses into one big open grave away from the commune. All the men of Pratola Serra were forced to pick up the dead - they had to do it in rotation. No one questioned it. They had to register their names, and then they were called by the guards to bury the bodies when it came their turn.

Neighbors went into homes of neighbors searching for dead bodies - mothers, fathers, old people, and children, lots of children. They piled them up together. I saw one of these carts - the driver was swaying with illness as if drunk and so it seemed were his two horses. One never forgets such a horrifying sight. To compound this grief, one of the two village doctors, Dottore Acone, died from the contagion himself. But, in all of these deaths, our own beloved family doctor, Dottore Andrea Lieto, survived the influenza pestilence somehow and continued to care for all of Pratola Serra for the rest of his natural life. A true Dottore of the paesani. For some reason, he and I both escaped. Fortuitously or not, we also shared the same date of birth - February 17th.

Dott. ANDREA LIETO

médico condotto

· Pratola Serra

* 17-2-1894   † 1-5-1963

As I slowly walked around Pratola Serra at that time, I couldn't believe it. My little village was as good as destroyed. Half the people of the commune had died. Three men from the Red Cross came into town and whitewashed the fronts of the houses and the sidewalks; and they gave the paesani some disinfectant to wash the floors inside. I could see and smell these changes immediately. The odor of bleach and lime filled the air. *[Aside: There were no phones or easy means of village communications at this time. People were still afraid of leaving their houses because of the lingering possibility of infection. There was also no way of telling just who survived. The whitewash process Michelina describes must have given the townspeople some modicum of assurance that it was safe to venture out as she obviously did.]*

I looked inside the coffeehouse owned by the family of one of my book club girls, Appia Motta. But there was only darkness inside. I decided to enter into the coffeehouse anyway. No one. I began to worry, for it should have been open for business. Then, Appia appeared from the back. She ran to me with a hug and tears. I learned then that both her father and mother had died at the beginning of the pestilence. Also, Rosina, our little book club friend who could never remember things, my duplicate dress model comare, the girl we both loved so dearly, also had died. Appia and I cried in each other's arms. It was all too much to bear. For a long time, we just sat in silence together in her little café. Then I asked her, "What will you do now?" She said, "My brother is in America. He wants me to go there to be with him, but I told him no. He won't come back either, so I will carry on father's business, alone; that is all I can do?"

I began to fear for all my cousins in different parts of the commune and for my Uncle Francesco and his family. I later found out that even though they all had the influenza, they all too broke the fever and were spared. The same for Amalia's family - the Pisano - they, too, all had influenza - all spared! Thank God!

For weeks after, I was so grateful to meet familiar people in the village and was glad that they were alive. Another book club friend, Adelina, ran to me from across the square, yelling at the top of her lungs, "Michelina! You are alive! My God your hair?!" More hugs - more tears. "Yes, I passed the horrible influenza!" I told her how afraid I was to ask about people and their families - afraid that they were no more. Then I asked her. Adelina and her family were spared. These first chance meetings were always a relief. Then, you would go to a place where you expected someone to be and he or she was not there, nor would ever be again. This phenomenon happened a lot.

When the scourge was completely over, the paesani all gathered in the church, thanking God directly for having spared them personally. I too went - reluctantly. I sat there listening, numbed by the droning priest and the also droning voices of those in syncopated prayer. I thought instead, "Why did I survive? Why did these people survive and not the others? Was God having fun? Was he a cruel God? Why take little Rosina? Why Appia's parents and why my dear Uncle Costantino? Why - why?" I had to get out from the church. I felt like a hypocrite. I was suffocating in the echo of these prayers. To what was I praying - for what? I got up and ran out.

From across the church, Appia saw me run out during the middle of the prayer. She chased after me yelling, "Michelina! Michelina!!!" I stopped in the middle of the square. She caught up. We hugged.

One would never have believed what she said to me then. Crying she said, "You are right, Michelina. Why - why?"

Chapter Twenty-Three

Summer, 1918

Rebirth, Renewal, and Romance

Confessions of a Rebel

Even after the war, in 1918, there was no contentment. Italy felt left out from many things. The writer, Gabriele D'Annuzio, continued to preach about further rebellion. Small skirmishes still appeared on the old Northern front. Nobody was satisfied. Soldiers came back with a rancor about the state of the world in general. Farmers didn't want to dig or plant; many of them ran to the cities in the North. Only a few soldiers from the South returned to their old occupations. Yes, nobody was satisfied - including me.

I had a terrible period in 1918 of spiritual guilt and a deep questioning that tormented me - especially then with death touching my family, my friends and almost me. I told nobody of my doubts of formal religion except Amalia Pisano, for I already had a reputation of being a rebel - a bad influence towards people of regimented religious activities. But they were wrong about what I really believed. I was religious in the sense that I felt God in me. I had a feeling of belonging to a divinity, yes, but then I asked myself, why couldn't I simply pray as the others did and be satisfied? I found the repetition of the prayers of the messa inadequate - why repeat them over and over? No matter how I tried, it all made no sense to me. Was this questioning of blind faith a sin? Some would say so. Some did. I kept this in me for a long time, but oh how I needed answers. More of a problem, I had no access in that part of Europe and at that time to find those answers. I read everything now that I could possibly get my hands on.

Through it all, I decided to keep these thoughts and questions all to myself - to obey the system - to try to believe in something, even if it was the dogma of the church. I would at least try to make it work.

To better my situation a little, I dutifully and finally went to confession. I confessed without scruple - I had to do it. I finally confessed my sins to the priest who was hidden away in a cabinet confessional. "Have you sinned?" he asked. "Yes," I told him, "I have been bad."

He asked me, "What are your sins?" I almost choked out my response, "I don't know. I obey. I hate no one. I don't lie or steal. The only sin I am conscious of is that I did not go to confession." "For how long?" asked the priest. "For two years." I said. "What!" he exclaimed, "Two years!?" "Yes, two years." After a long pause, the priest said through the little window of the confessional, "This is bad. You must promise to amend this sin by confessing every month?" "Yes, I will." He gave his benediction. I could tell now by his voice that it was Archiprete who was listening to my confession. He gave me communion. Still, I felt neither blessed nor guilty of anything.

But for a long time after that, Archiprete looked at me without hatred. I kept my promise. Every month, I confessed, and every month I made sure that Archiprete was my confessor. I wanted no reprimands. I wanted peace, just finally peace. I wanted to please everybody. I learned lots of songs for the choir and sang all the time. I was a faithful mezzo-soprano. I took my spiritual refuge in music - my corner of my mind. I even became a godmother to a few children in the town. Yes, I was a good girl - but happy with myself? No!

Romance "Springs" Eternal

By this time, my hair had nearly grown back. It was like a miracle - all those curls reattached to my head, like small springs - one upon the other. When I took my scarf off one Sunday morning in church, everyone congratulated me. Such a beautiful crop of chestnut curls all over my head and across my forehead. Shorter, yes, but healthy.

I will say that the young men of my village considered me beautiful, in form, appearance, and deportment. I was quietly happy again in that respect. However, the death of my Uncle Costantino had made me very apathetic about everything, including boys. But time is a healer and the best teacher. Soon, my troubled mind was unavoidably turned in the direction of the opposite sex.

At seventeen, I had many suitors - all nice boys to think now about them. One was a distant cousin of my mother named, "Peppino" Fabrizio, the village bandleader of twenty-two. Peppino was also my father's nick-name, so I started with this as a negative thought. Mother encouraged him however, for obvious reasons. So, this distant cousin of mine got the notion that he wanted to be married right away and that I was the one that he picked out himself to spend the rest of his life with - a common theme. He knew my love of music, so to move the courtship quickly along, he proposed to teach me the mandolin, but only if I would accept his romantic intentions. When he arrived at my door with the instrument in hand, my response was simply to hand him a note. It read:

"Dear Peppino,

I am sorry I have to sacrifice the love I have to learn how to play the mandolin, but I do not love you. I love to hear you playing the organ and other instruments - you are an artist. The world is full of nice girls. You are a wonderful man. You will find a better girl who will love you as you deserve. But please, let us be friends in music and in good conversation.

Michelina"

After reading my note, Peppino Fabrizio never returned to my door. Mother was not happy.

The one suitor I liked most out of all of them was named Giacomino Fabbo. He had a friend who played the flute. Well, every night, in the small hours, he and his friend would come all the way from Prata, Amalia Pisano's old village, just to serenade me. They played and sang under my window - really!

Giacomino had a beautiful baritone voice, and he sang so well. His friend played that magic flute like a virtuoso and woke up the entire town. The paesani enjoyed the serenading a few times - then they rebelled! They needed sleep, so to stop him, I said, "Okay. We will try to be good friends, eh?" "No," he said shouting up to me, "not good friends! I love you and you will love me – otherwise, I give you no rest!" I suspect he really did love me, and I was touched by his resolve. The neighbors, however, were less receptive.

I remembered the first time we met. He was with some of his friends in the front of Appia's coffeehouse. I was with Amalia Pisano. Giacomino approached us, for he knew Amalia very well when the Pisano lived in Prata. He saluted Amalia, then he told her, "Amalia, please introduce me to your beautiful friend - please." He looked so eager. "Certainly," Amalia said. "Michelina Pirone, my best friend, this is Giacomino Fabbo." He was so romantic. With a voice soft and caressing, he kissed my hands and said, "May I call you Michelina?" "Yes, of course." It was all out of Shakespeare this meeting - ancient traditions with new characters in the parts.

Spring in Italy has a festive atmosphere. Just breathing in that fragrant dry air is enough to awaken all of the human emotions. You sing, and your heart expands, awakening the mind to the reality of being very much alive. Of course, being just seventeen had some influence on this emotion as well.

Was I in love? I thought so for a while. This was my first real infatuation with someone of the opposite sex. What was it that I liked in this brash and extroverted fellow? He was handsome, yes, with a full crop of dark, curly hair. Curiously, Giacomino was lame in one foot. He had fought in the Alps during the Great War and lost the toes of his right foot because of frostbite. Strangely, this lameness he had was attractive to me, however, for he was tall, and it forced him to have controlled movements. But what made me accept his attention? I was so careful not to waste my time with love. Was it his company? Too many questions, perhaps, but that one was still on my mind.

After asking myself over and over again, I realized, yes, it was his company I enjoyed. I liked his joyful, quick ways. He sang a lot, and talked and talked. Mamma Mia, could he talk. For once, I found an equal. Giacomino's boldness was also very endearing. If I was in church kneeling down during the Ave Maria, he would come and kneel down next to me. He was impulsive and a rebel. Once, he was expelled from the university for throwing a milk bottle at his professor's feet. The professor was an opinionated dictator. Giacomino left the university with only half-way to graduation because of his rebelliousness.

As I said, Giacomino was from Prata, the nearest town to ours. Every evening, he would come to see me. In addition, he had a cousin in Prata who came almost every morning with a love letter. My brothers, Costantino and Mikele, were always ready to bring my answer back to him. Too much attention, I thought, but it had an unusual sentiment. I stayed awake at night asking myself if this was truly love. No, no, I just liked to be with him. I liked him, yes, but love? Would he be my future? Knowing I could choose my future, my destiny, scared me. What possibilities would I be giving up if I did choose Giacomino? Doesn't that question alone mean that I wasn't in love? I was doing myself no good by worrying about it. So, not choosing was my choice. Too many times girls found that husbands were chosen for them. Again, I promised myself that I would never submit to such an arrangement. Still, I didn't mind being courted. It was flattering and reassuring in its own way, especially having lived through the recent past.

Well, Giacomino and I were together every evening, usually seated on the cold stone slabs of my grandfather's steps under Mother's supervision or walking and promenading through town with some of my friends. But never were we allowed to be alone, except in a crowd who knew me. I did not object to being protected by these customs and conventions, for the protection afforded me both control and time to think. These were also the steps - the dance - dictated to all the young men as rituals of courtship prior to marriage. Commitment was the scary part. To dance was fun. To commit to a life-long dance partner was not.

If it was raining, Giacomino boldly came into my house, which was not customarily permitted at that time. A fellow was not allowed just to walk into a girl's house. At first, I didn't say anything to him, but it definitely stirred up some consternation from Mother. So, I had to go and ask permission from my Uncle Francesco, the only adult male on my father's side of the family who was still left in Pratola Serra. My mother's father, Nonno Fabrizio, did not count! Nonno could not give permission even though I was living in his house - the house Giacomino was trying to visit me in.

After obtaining the necessary permission from my Uncle Francesco, everything seemed quiet for a while. In groups of girls and boys, on Sunday afternoons especially, Giacomino and I went for long walks. Still, the more he pushed to be closer, the more I resisted. It was not a game for me, however, although I think he might have thought so. And, the relationship stayed like this for weeks.

Also, during this summer, my mother was still having trouble with the size of my father's monthly allowance. It remained at 200 lire. She wrote letters to him constantly, demanding more money. The children were growing rapidly - especially my brothers. They were voracious eaters. We needed money for more clothing and for food now that it was more easily obtainable - the farmers were producing almost normally. The Sunday open market was back to functioning as it had before the Great War. Papa's harness factory, too, could have been rejuvenated had he chosen to remain in Italy. But of course, he didn't. Instead, we got letters from him saying that he and my brother, Ralfo, were having a difficult time trying to make a success of it in New York with Papa's two harness-making brothers. In 1918, there was less demand for horse harnesses, even in America. To make matters worse, my father now was having minor feuds with his two brothers. One, Uncle Antonio, even quit making horse harnesses and opened up his own general store like Nonna had. This ongoing Pirone brother feud was partly because of the old issue of Don Carlos' leaving the family business to Papa. The perception was that Papa turned his back on the family factory and to my mother's dowry that came with it. This was a sore issue all around, even with Mother, and they all gave my father no rest with it. Nonno Fabrizio never said much about the matter, but we all knew how he felt.

At this period, Father decided that he and Ralfo would leave New York and move up to Boston, Massachusetts to join my mother's leather-working brothers there. As I mentioned, my mother's brother, Antonio, was my father's best friend in Italy - so Boston it was. Also, Nonna Pirone's younger sister, Aunt Alfonsina, lived in Boston and offered to take Papa and Ralfo in. In all of this turmoil, my father was still our main provider.

Father sent some food from America, but it was sporadic. The 200 lire a month he was sending us was still not enough to provide for the necessities of a family of nine people left behind, even with the money he left with Nonno Fabrizio for insurance.

Adding to this insult, my father was sending the allowance directly to his brother, Francesco so my uncle could keep a check on my mother's expenditures. I personally felt so indignant about this practice. "How dare you, father!" I wrote him. "How dare you treat my mother this way!" After that, he stopped sending the money to his brother. It came again directly to my mother, still, only 200 lire though. I wrote again to him with admonishment.

Papa didn't answer my letters after that. He ignored me as if I were still a little child. Mother was continually crying. Finally, I got Nonna Pirone, his own mother, to write Papa. Then, and only then, did we get a little more allowance. At this point, I told Mother that I would somehow try to find more money for the family myself. How? I didn't know, but it was constantly on my mind after that.

I can say that I did resent the restrictions and different expectations put on me as a "girl" by my own family - by them and also by custom. I did not share this growing resentment. I kept to myself. To openly express my anger would have been a sin worthy of confession to them and to Archiprete. Keeping it to myself was also a sin perhaps - but a sin just between me and God. Only, as I know now, it was not a transgression. Still, in my heart, I thought there had to be better choices.

Marrying out of my family was not one of them.

Chapter Twenty-Four

The Seed to Immigrate Planted

All that spring and summer of 1919, I had a good time with the company of Giacomino. We seldom were alone. I must confess, I liked those long discussions we had about human behavior - of what we liked about each other's company and how lucky we were that we could really talk interminably together on any subject. Everything he knew, he discussed. But towards the end of the summer, as Giacomino rambled on, I remember thinking, "Too bad that he is in love with me. I am not in love back with him. Why could we not just be friends? And why is it that only women think this way?" Of course, I avoided sharing these thoughts with this determined suitor. But, given time, truth always reveals itself without prodding, eh?

In one of our long discussions, I decided to ask a risky question - I asked what was his idea of love and marriage? Giacomino answered without hesitation, "I believe that man is capable of great love and I shall love you forever! Marriage is sacred for a man - therefore, his wife must be as pure as snow - always." There was a pause and then he asked me, "And what is your idea of love and marriage?" I didn't answer about love specifically, but I had definite ideas about marriage. I said that in marriage I expected fidelity from my husband, as he should of me. I never would forgive the man I married if he ever betrayed this union. All the love would eventually end up as hatred for both. Giacomino was appalled at this notion. I added, "Do you think that it is too much to demand from a man? Fidelity? You are saying that fidelity would be expected of a wife. But faithfulness would be the only way that I could live with my husband." He then said, almost like a joke, "I don't think I know of one man who has never cheated on his marriage. Wait, wait - no, that's right." "Stop," I interrupted. "You have said all that is necessary to hear. Good night, Giacomino. It is time for me to go. Please don't ever come back to my house." I walked up the stairs, looked down on his puzzled face, and slammed the door behind me.

The next morning, I told Mother of my disagreement I had with Giacomino on the steps. "I know, I heard. Who could not?" she said. "Michelina, this is an old argument of what is a husband and what is a wife." It was obvious that Mother was troubled about other things. The tone of my father's letters came up again. "Your Papa is so mean - he never writes kind or endearing letters. Only letters of bookkeeping." She looked at me with a heavy heart and continued, "Listen to me, Michelina - I think you should go to America. There is nothing here for you." For a moment, I was shocked. What was Mother saying? Leave? "When I heard your argument with the Pratese ("one from Prata"), then it became so clear to me. Your future is not here in Pratola Serra. I said to myself, Michelina should go to America." "Mother," I said, "you need me here - the children need me here, Nonno too. I will find more work. I promise!" "No, no," she said. "I have been thinking about this for a long time - you should go to America."

I looked at Mother's determined expression and knew right away that she was very serious. Still, I was shocked. Perhaps it was the best for me, yes, but I could not help but to think that it would also be the best for her. She would send a powerful emissary - a determined representative to press Papa. Was he also still gambling lire away at cards? But, I also think she was thinking for my own well-being. "Go, Michelina. This is how you can best serve the family. Not here."

I studied my mother's soulful face for a long time and then said, "Okay. Perhaps I should go to America. But if I want, I can come back - no?" "Yes," she said without hesitation. "We will start by getting you a pass-port. Your Nonno has some money set aside for you to do this and for the trip. And - thank you." I loved my mother so much at that very moment. She was pure to us and to herself - also pure to her marriage in a way that I could not convey to Giacomino. She was faithful to my father and to their marriage in all manner. But was that enough? No. She wanted more. She needed more. She needed to dance closely again with the man only she loved. I carried this observation with me for a long time.

That very afternoon, Mother and I took a carriage to Avellino and applied with an agency of passage. I got my passport picture, the second picture I ever had taken. That little picture somehow confirmed my existence to the entire world. Today, we take pictures for granted - almost an afterthought. In those days, pictures were so much more important - so permanent and rare. Everyone planned for weeks, sometimes months, just to pose once for posterity. A photographic picture was to be "forever" after all.

All the way to Avellino and back, I silently watched the driver handle his expectant horses through the tips of his fingers down through the soft leather harnesses that guided them. They were the very harnesses that my own father made for this man many, many years ago. They were perfection. I wanted to go to America, yes, but I also did not want to go at the same time. Perhaps I should have been more excited, but I wasn't. My mother said almost nothing for the dozen miles back and forth to Avellino. She was almost in a dream of thought herself.

The agency gave us everything we needed for my leaving to America. It was almost too easy - like they had done this thing over and over without thinking. I briefly thought that perhaps Mother was so anxious to send me to America because of Giacomino's intentions. She did not think favorably of him. Was she protecting me? Was she worried about my being swept away at seventeen? No. Mother knew my mind better than that. I could see that she really wanted to send me to my father as an ambassador for our cause back home. She wanted a spokesman. She knew I was headstrong and would do this mission with resolve. And, of course, the cause was not just about money - it was about the salvation of her own marriage.

[Aside: The average cost of a one-way ticket to America on a steamship from Naples, Italy in 1919 was about 400 Lire ($30.00) for third-class steerage. That would exchange out to $440.00 in today's real dollar value.]

"Michelina Pirone" (18 yrs. old) - Passport picture: 1919

Another Arranged Marriage

Giacomino was still coming as usual from Prata, every evening. I could not be rid of him. He was so apologetic, but I had a resolve to focus on my agreement to go alone to America. I was hoping it would be soon. I didn't even go to church so he wouldn't have the opportunity to come in and kneel down next to me as usual. I sent words to Archiprete that I was sick and could not practice or sing in the choir. I was so afraid the priest would start again with our little holy war. I shut myself in Nonna Pirone's house, in Don Carlos' big bedroom. I stayed in - reading, sewing - hiding. Amalia, Adelina, and Appia, the last of our book club, came often to visit me there. We discussed my situation with Giacomino and secretly my pending trip. Each was supportive of my leaving for America. Each wanted to join me if only she could.

Giacomino continued to send letters every day. I sent them back unopened. He probably thought the dispute was because of our last conversation, but it was greater than that for me. My world was about to expand beyond all borders for me, and I could not nor would not give that idea up. Never did I tell him of my and my mother's plan to go to America. It stayed this way for many weeks. I thought for sure that my trip was imminent - that I only needed word from the agency as to which boat I was to travel on. It was not so quick in coming.

Then, Amaila Pisano came to my house one evening to find me. She was crying uncontrollably. She told me that her father had brought home a young man named Mario Marano, that he had just come back from military service and that he was the son of one of Mr. Pisano's associates in wine distribution. "Well," I said, "why are you crying?" "He wants me to marry this man." "What?!" "My father thinks that he is good for me. He tells me that Mario loves me and wants my hand in marriage, but I only met him once before the war." "Do you have a choice in this matter?" I asked. Her look told me, "No." "Oh, my God," I thought. "Another arranged marriage." Then Amalia said, "I am afraid that Mario Marano will be interfering with our own friendship too - with all of my friends. I'm too young. I don't want to be a wife yet, Michelina. Yes, he has my father convinced that he is the right husband for me."

This revelation made me feel angry again. Here was the most beautiful and intelligent girl of our book club being offered in a marriage to a man, not of her choosing. Even Nonna Pirone's old friend, Mr. Pisano, was guilty of keeping alive bad customs. "And your father goes along with this man's idea for your future?" "Yes, he says it would be a good decision for me. He has property, and he distributes wine like my father. But I don't know if I ever could fall in love with him, Michelina." "But how is it your decision?" I asked.

At this moment, I thought again of how I was about to leave my family, Giacomino, Amalia, the commune and everything I had ever known to go to America. Was I spared because of my own rebelliousness or just because of my mother's issues within her own marriage? The question had me thinking.

One afternoon soon after, I went down to Amalia's house. When I got there, she was alone except for her younger brother, Rezziero, and her mother, Caterina, who quietly sat in her usual corner. Amalia was still agonizing, so I stayed consoling my friend until that evening.

Amalia and I were still upstairs when Mr. Pisano called from the bottom of the stairway. He didn't know that I was there. "Hey, you - my girl!" He shouted. "Come down here! Your fiancé is with me!" Amalia looked at me so scared. She hugged me tightly and looked at me so painfully. I felt so sorry for her. I said, "Come, let's go down." We did.

Mr. Pisano, after saluting me, scolded Amalia. Mr. Pisano said, "What are you doing upstairs? Didn't you expect your fiancé tonight?" Amalia didn't answer. Mario Marano just stood there smiling sheepishly. He was a decent-looking man of twenty-four. He always wore a large hat - larger than needed. Facially, it was a fair enough match. But the man was about my height and Amalia was a head taller than me. Also, I still didn't like the way Mr. Pisano pushed his daughter at this fellow, she then only eighteen years old. She was tall, more than six feet, extremely beautiful and intelligent. And, like me, she could have had any man she herself chose.

Amalia's younger brother, Rezziero, was then asked to escort me home. All the way back, I kept thinking of how my Nonno Don Carlos Pirone and Nonno Fabrizio had planned my own parent's marriage with them present. Would Amalia suffer the same fate as my mother because of her own father's wishes? Would she eventually find love for this man before they married? At least my own mother was madly in love with my father - still, look at how she is. I was left with an ache in my heart for my poor, dear friend - Amalia.

"In Italy, 1920. Mr. Domenico Pisano, his wife, Caterina (seated), daughter Amalia, son Rezziero "Richie," and Mario Marano (Amalia's husband, seated with hat.)

Chapter Twenty-Five

The Last Feast

It was late August 1918. I had to get out of the house. The big feast was as good a time as any. Amalia and I made plans to go, but, as she feared, our time together now would have to be shared. During this feast, Amalia walked with her fiancé Mario and her younger brother Rezziero who was their constant chaperone now. I walked separately with my friends, Adelina, Appia and my older cousin, Angelina, daughter of my dear Uncle Costantino.

We girls were all dressed up in our best dresses while the procession was in session and we were enjoying ourselves. It was a magical summer night for a feast. *[Aside: "Feasts" are mentioned throughout Michelina's Letter. They are sometimes commonly called a "fiesta." They are a non-secular celebration of one or more designated Saints during a day and night of holy observance, usually in late summer. The largest feast, traditionally in August, is set aside for the patron Saint of special requests - the Feast of Saint Anthony, which, we presume, Michelina is describing here.]*

To be expected, Giacomino came to the feast - and Rezziero Pisano, smiling as if a dutiful matchmaker, brought him over to me. Boldly as usual, Giacomino approached me. Amalia came over too and just looked at me and said nothing. I knew anyway what she was thinking. Now, we all walked together as a group, Rezziero assuming a dual role chaperoning us older girls. He was very pleased with himself. Giacomino was keeping his promise - he would never give me rest. He praised my appearance and kept stride directly beside me. I tried to ignore him, but it was difficult.

I focused instead on the splendor of the decorations of the street and the illuminations - they were never better. The merchants proudly stood behind their pushcarts with all their bountiful goodies of the feast - candies, chocolates, nuts, trinkets, and specialty foods - everything boisterous and beautiful. How quickly forgotten was the great war and the influenza that nearly destroyed us all. The entire village of Pratola Serra had turned out, as well as hundreds of other people from other nearby towns. There was a crush of paesani. We had a new mayor at this time, and the sheriff and his guardian sons followed the official orders almost to a science. But for me, believe it or not, it was the church procession that was the thing to be remembered that crisp, clear night. The approaching drums and music signaled that the statue of the Madonna was going back into the church. The band, which came first, marched in random disorder but had a splendid program. I saw my mother's choice of suitors, Peppino Fabrizio, leading that band. I nodded at him, and he actually smiled back, still waving his baton. Everyone pulled to the side of the square like the parting of the Red Sea. Up the hill came the procession with glorious pomp and display, their shadows casting rolling images on the stone and stucco buildings that framed our square. Actual gasps of delight were heard.

Leading the entire procession were a dozen village boys of twelve years or so, dressed up like little priests - their hands clasped in a prayer vigil. All the priests of the commune followed the young boys. There was distant cousin, Father Don Domenico Fabrizio, proud to be so well dressed up in his white lace tunic made by my mother. Archiprete, himself, stiff and solemn as ever, so very dignified and aloof, was among the priests. He too dressed up with all the decorations a priest of his standing would be permitted, layers of red ribbons and a gold stole around his neck.

Behind Archiprete, keeping time with the slow rhythm of the drums, paraded the Loyalist Society of the Priori. My grandfather, Nonno Fabrizio, led this group of men all dressed up in a presidential white and red loose suit, beaming as he walked. "Nonno, Ciao!" I called out. "Michelina! Bella!!!" he boomed back to the vocal delight of his comrades. How I loved that old soldier - my Nonno.

Behind Nonno's group, leading the statue of the Madonna came an artistic and enormous ornamental candelabra carried by two tall young men. The men were dressed up all in white - they looked like angels approaching from afar. The magnificent sculpture of light they carried that night was about two yards long, one yard wide and three levels in height with each level made of different size gas lamps. The top level had the largest lamps, the second level, smaller. The bottom and front lamps were the smallest and glistened almost like gems. The entire piece was interwoven with ironwork of leaves, roses, and strips of beaten iron made to look like delicate ribbon. The weight was why it took two men to carry it. This beautiful, artistic work brought tears to my eyes, for it was the last piece ever completed by my Uncle Costantino. He was in those lights that stretched out like rays of heaven in lines through my tears. Cousin Angelina and I hugged with tears as her father's masterpiece continued on by. The music thundered in our ears.

Now came the statue of the Madonna, carried on a platform of flowers by several men. The booming of the band's music made the men and the heavy statue seem to sway rhythmically to an inner, hypnotic tempo. This statue was life-size, delicately gilded. The Madonna glided by above the heads of the paesani, as if gently stepping across water.

Finally, at the very back of the procession, behind the priests, the men of the Society of the Priori, the band and the statue of the Madonna, came the women of the village. This was a long interminable line of women walking in pairs on both sides of the street. Each woman carried a large, long, burning candle. Endless women - no men. Mother was among them.

After the procession, I said my goodbye to the group and started my walk to go back home across the square. However, Giacomino followed me for some distance in the crowd. He reached me and held my arm to stop me from walking further saying, "Finally! I can talk with you alone and explain to you." I said to him, "Please, I want to go home. Do not spoil this beautiful night for me." He continued as if he hadn't heard me, "I didn't mean what you so hastily understood about fidelity in a marriage." I tried to turn but he insisted. "All I wanted to say was that seldom are men faithful all their lives to their wives." I interrupted, "There you start again with the same cantilina. You will not make me accept that." He was still holding my arm. He went on again with more emphasis. "No, I wanted then, as I want now, to assure you that I would never do that to you - never. I swear to that! I explained it so in all my letters that you sent back." I didn't answer, but he kept me thinking. He continued. "I want to make myself clear. Please, Michelina! You must let me apologize and make peace."

The moment was full of sentimentality. If he was anything, Giacomino was indeed persuasive and convincing in person. Besides, at that moment, I didn't want any further discord. I quietly answered him. "I guess I am sorry, too. Perhaps I was too hasty." Then I said what I had to say, "I do not think I love you enough, Giacomino, to marry you. I didn't see you for two weeks and never once did I miss your presence. I missed the singing and our long discussions together, yes, but not the rest." A surprise to me, he was not offended - in fact, he was glad that I was in such a conciliatory mood. He almost shouted, "Brava! Let's be friends again then - okay?" With hesitation, I said, "Yes. I hope to be just friends with you." "That is enough for now," he said. But half joking he said, "Ah, but you shall love me forever."

As we walked back through the square, Giacomino kept up his persistent dialogue, which was obviously reinforced by my saying nothing in return. "We have what eternal love requires - friendship, rapport, and attractions to each other, attractions of all kinds, etc., etc." I didn't want to walk with Giacomino alone. Luckily, I found my cousin, Angelina, still where I had left her and asked her to join us. Giacomino did not object - he dared not to object. Again, customs saved me.

The three of us promenaded up and down the town in all its festivity with my cousin and I arm-in-arm listening to Giacomino's continual observances and opinions. At one o'clock in the morning, the feast was finally over. Little by little, everybody departed - even Giacomino, with just a kiss of the hand outside my door. Gone into the night.

I got word the very next day from the booking agency in Avellino. It was both good and bad news. I, and a number of other people from my village, including girls that I knew in my choir, were all finally booked on a ship called the "*SS America*." The bad news was that the date of departure had been moved up to November 20th. I would have to live with these thoughts for almost three more months.

Chapter Twenty-Six

November - 1919

My Destiny

My Time to Leave

I kept as busy as I could to take my mind off of the long wait for my departure. I went about the village contracting my services out as a letter writer for the paesani as I had done before. I sewed new clothes and even sold one or two dresses to my cousins who wanted so much to help. I even tried to look up some of the girls from my village who I would be traveling with to America. I did anything to pass the three months - anything also to avoid Giacomino. But, faithful to his word, Giacomino gave me no rest. He came night after night on his matrimonial mission from Prata, as happy and determined as ever, ready to take a walk. I gave up. What the hell? So, we walked, just me, Giacomino and Appia. God bless her. The three of us walked and walked. We talked about everything - everything except immigration of course. Then one night, with only about a month to go before my trip - a slip.

Appia casually said, "It must have been painful for you, Michelina, since perhaps this past feast was the last one for you." Giacomino answered, "Why the last one?" Appia, perplexed, in a hurry, said, "Oh, my! I better run home. I said too much. Good night." She ran off - leaving us alone! I had to face the situation completely - to resolve the matter one way or another.

Giacomino and I were just outside my house. We sat on the steps of the doorway for the longest time. Finally, I took his hand in mine and told him what my mother's financial dilemma was - sparing words and avoiding details. I told him of her and my decision to go to America - soon.

At first, Giacomino got sad, then true to his character, he said, "Do not worry - I shall follow you to America!" adding, "You know, my father is hard to be with. He doesn't want to hear about me marrying you now. He says that you are too delicate for our needs. We have a big business. He wants me to marry a paesana who can work, like my sisters do and not a proper Signorina like you." He stopped abruptly, perhaps sorry he had said too much. "Go on," I said, tempering my anger. He continued with a big smile, "But you know me, I will insist! I always win." I said nothing.

Giacomino's confidence in winning his father's permission to marry me was pathetic. I realized his father was right. I never could work like his daughters - lifting big sacks of grain - loading carts, doing a man's work. Then Giacomino said, "Michelina, I will make you a good husband - a faithful husband. We have so much in common to share - art, music, literature. To hell with my father's wishes. I am not angry that you will go to America. Only let me prove to you of my love. Who knows what will happen there? We could build a good life together anywhere we choose." I said, "Enough now, let's leave things as they are - no more tonight."

The next day, I sent my brother Costantino with a letter to Prata. In my letter, I requested, "Giacomino, please, do leave me alone for a while. I need to think." I really did need to think. Could I marry this man after all? I was not planning to move permanently to America. Just to serve my mother and to get away from all that I knew. Was my high expectation of love just that - high expectation? I thought a lot about what Giacomino said for several days. The more I thought, the more I was fearful of leaving and fearful of the uncertainty of my own future. There was no doubt, however, that Giacomino did love me and would sacrifice greatly to fulfill his matrimonial intentions. I came to the belief that he would, in fact, create a new life away from his father. That if my world came crashing down around me, he would be there to put it all back together. Dare I? I did.

A few days later, back on the steps of my mother's house, we formally decided. Giacomino would come to America, we would marry in America, and then we would come back together. We would open some kind of store in Avellino together - a bookstore with knickknacks, cards, stationery, more books, embroidery, etc. It was also agreed that there would be peace between us, no pressure on this subject of marriage.

Before I went away, Giacomino left me with a cherished gift that he had only one of - a picture of himself. It was a picture taken just before his battles in the Italian Alps against the Austrians where he lost the toes to his right foot from frostbite. There were no duplicates - of the photo either.

Giacomino Fabbo. 1915. Italian Army. World War I.

Farewells

One afternoon of peace away from Giacomino, we, the last girls of our book club, had a final farewell meeting. We decided to meet, read poetry aloud, and also say goodbye to each other. There were only Amalia, Adelina, Appia and me left. It was the saddest and happiest last meeting for our club. Sad because our friend, Rosina, had passed away from the influenza and also sad because it would be saying goodbye to our dearest friend Amalia Pisano. I would be leaving her to a marriage not of her choosing - a marriage I would not be able to attend. Amalia and I promised to write each other every week and to be diligent spies - me on my father - she on Giacomino.

The very good news, though, was that Adelina confirmed that she, too, was one of the village girls who would be going on the same passage to be with family in New York. This news brought happy tears to the room. It was even more joyous when Appia made an abrupt announcement. She could not contain herself. "Me too! My surprise! I will be going on that ship!" she said. "What!" I cried. Appia told us that her heart was not in keeping the family café by herself - it was too much now that her parents had died of the influenza. She would turn it over to cousins who would either rent it or buy it. She told us that she would answer her brother's pleadings to go to America and to live with him and his family. He insisted and sent the extra money for passage.

In all this good news, we almost forgot about our club leader, Amalia. Saying goodbye to her was the hardest part, she was our leader. Amalia was so gracious and kind, and we understood she wanted to come with us in the worst possible way. But then she said, with humor, "Ok. I shall continue with the battles of our book club with the Archiprete. He was about to kick us all out of the church anyway. I will keep the cause to make his life miserable."

We laughed, we hugged and we cried tears of joy for our forever comradery.

I left Italy for America on November 20th, 1919.

The day was just before my nineteenth birthday. I barely remember kissing my Grandmother Pirone and Grandfather Fabrizio goodbye at their houses before leaving. They wanted to say goodbye alone to me in their houses - both houses where I grew up with them. I don't remember much of those goodbyes, nor much that involved my sisters, brothers and many cousins. There was the grey veil of numbness about it. I do remember saying goodbye to my last remaining uncle, Uncle Francesco. He mockingly said to me, "Why do you have to go to America? What is wrong with this place, eh? Don't we feed you enough?" I hugged him dearly. The rest? I blocked the pain of it, I am sure. It was all a blur - all of it.

I took salvation in the thought that I would be going on this boat - the *SS America* - with three of the four survivors of our rebel book club. As I mentioned, there were other girls of Pratola Serra preparing to leave on that day as well - and of other villages. We knew these girls by acquaintance, but not as part of our club - they were friends all the same, all steerage class paesani.

Large horse carriages were to bring us on our first step to America from the village - down the mountainside to the train and then to the sea. Mother would accompany me all the way to my boat. What a painful day. What a vibrant day. At the carriage, I remember Amalia Pisano crying, two hands on her mouth. To leave her behind was one on my greatest pains. I do remember thinking, "Goodbye, Pratola Serra - remember my promise to you - remember. I will come back someday."

It was a short ride for us, the twelve miles to Avellino where Mother and I were to get the train for Naples. And of course, Giacomino was waiting there, coming in from the village of Prata. He was waiting for us at the station when Mother and I arrived.

Mother did not say anything to him. Instead, she simply got on the train ahead of me to find our seats. There was not much time to say goodbye to Giacomino. The moment was a very awkward moment. As I was about to board the train, he gently kissed me on the forehead, like he was kissing a delicate flower - our first kiss. I remember him very clearly as I was saying goodbye from the train's open window. He was waving his hand vigorously chasing after, "Goodbye! Goodbye, Michelina! Goodbye, my love! I will come to America for you! Remember our love together!" I waved and smiled back. No words. He looked smaller and smaller as the train and I ran further and further away.

Mother and I reached Naples at our scheduled time to sail, but we were forced to stay an extra day. There was another workers' strike, this time it was the dock workers. Finally, the day after, the three of us in our book club, the other girls and the other paesani from Pratola Serra, were ready to embark on *America* to America. I hugged and kissed Mother beyond tears - only our resolve was left. "Goodbye, Mother. I will do my best in America. I promise!" Mama held my face, "I love you. You are, Michelina - my firstborn. Write! Write to me!!!"

All the mothers and fathers of the other girls were saying their good-byes as well. All the way up the ship's stairway we shouted back and forth. Appia stayed quietly close to me at this moment - leaning her head onto my shoulder - remembering her lost parents. The rest of the people were moving forward, slowly, up higher and higher - half on and half off in their hearts. They were proud, handsome, clean and all of them poor. We all moved as one mass - one paesani. Tears. My God the tears. They could have floated that ship with them. This scene, I shall never forget.

As the *SS America* slowly moving away, we girls of Pratola Serra, shoulder to shoulder, stood at the rail and waved, "Goodbye, Mother! Goodbye, all." We said goodbye to Naples, goodbye to Italy and goodbye to everything we knew and held close to our hearts.

ACT TWO

Chapter One

Portage: On *"SS America"* to America.

———

The ship "SS America." Built in 1908 by Cantieri Navale Riuniti for Generale Italiana Line. She was scrapped in 1928. She carried 2,650 passengers (30 first class, 220 second class and 2,400 third class steerage.)

———

Naples that evening was beautiful. We girls of Pratola Serra stayed together on the stern of the massive ship until we couldn't see our people anymore. It was like a dream - my head was swimming - they all dissolved in a heavy ocean mist. My past was dissolving, as well, in front of my eyes. It was all so very dreamlike and also so very real.

Everyone looked tearfully back at Naples. Mount Vesuvio, smoldering, could be seen glowing above, and brighter than all the city lights. It came to our eyes as a Verdi opera. The inner fire of my countrymen - their passion - their volatility, was sailing away. San Marino, the city, up, up on the hill was illuminated, a beautiful sparkling jewel. We huddled there until everything slowly disappeared. Only the waves broke the gray expanse of the sea. Nighttime. Then, and only then, did I hear the noise, the murmur of the ship - people chatting - some crying. Was I crying, too? Yes, perhaps I was. On the deck, we three girls of the book club stayed close together, taking comfort in each other's silence. The other passengers soon identified and called us, "the three paesane," like the Musketeers.

Appia quietly pulled me from the railing and took me downstairs. I was numb with many confusing thoughts. She held my hand and led me down, down many narrow metal stairs, down into the bowels of the ship until we reached the open woman's dormitory way below. Appia's cot was in the same area as mine, near a porthole. There were upper and lower cots. That night, we slept on the top cot together like little children - side by side, to comfort each other. I was locked inside a huge metal coffin that pressed against me as an endless ocean murmured on the other side of a cold metal wall. The only other thing I remember of that first night was how quickly it all disappeared in a heavy sleep. I was exhausted.

The ship, *"America"* as it was called, was made in Italy and had been an Italian battleship during the First Great War. It was old, dirty, noisy and unhealthy. We were one large dank dormitory - over a thousand women and children - all crammed together on the lowest floor. The men had their own crowded dormitory area in another low section away from us. Families, if traveling together, were split up. Most of us, the paesani, moved about quietly, what movement we could make. It was a crowed silence most of the time - one island on top of another.

Appia and I got up early the next morning and waited in a long line to wash in a miserable cold shower. We did not have to be reminded that it was the end of November. It wasn't until about ten o'clock that same morning that we got through washing and dressing. We both were so hungry! We again went up all those cold metal stairs. Higher and higher, passing others squeezing us to go downward. Near the top, the smell of coffee hit us - it was so intoxicating. I never felt hunger the way I did that morning. I was famished!

We got up to the top deck, an open deck, and there again was a long, long line of paesani waiting for food. The wind swept across us from the open expanse of ocean. Fortunately for us, this first morning had cold but calm seas. We were served only coffee and stale buns. Appia and I took our breakfast to a side room where many people were standing - only the children were seated. We all ate standing up. For me, that coffee and bun became a world of flavor and awareness of what is acutely brought to us by our senses. I would have cried if it all hadn't tasted so good. Somewhere else, at some other time, perhaps I would have pushed it all away. But now it was time to focus on the smallest of positives, even if those positives consisted only of reminiscences and representations of what I valued as dear.

After a while, we found Adelina and we took a walk, exploring every corner of the pondering ship, or at least the areas that were allowed to us. It was wonderful to see the sea as calm as a lake back home. Blue - nothing but blue - with the sky reflecting on the water of the same color. I stopped by myself at the railing and remembered the last two days of my journey. I don't know how long I was standing alone there; it could have been hours.

Adelina and Appia joined me again. We three paesane were together all day. We made many quick friends along the way. Naturally, we even acquired the servitude of a few young men. Dutiful men, with purpose, of course. It is important to point out that even though most of us did not know each other, we all shared an attitude and a common foundation of language as well. We had a comfort place as paesani that was easy and familiar to see in everyone's eyes. Sure, there were a few detractors, but we were mostly all in this voyage together - all of us. No one really complained openly. Complaining wouldn't have made any difference anyway.

So, we had many eager fellows fetching our meals, our utensils - anything we wanted. We had plenty of experience in this skill in the earlier days of our book club. We all sat on the floor of the open deck together with the rest of the people. There was no other place for us to sit - just on the open deck. We sat with our backs against the ship's wall or against each other. We made due. We were all leaving Italy for one reason or another and we were all in the same boat, in the true sense. It is amazing to me still how quickly people, especially we Italians, adapt to adversity and seek communal harmony to comfort our collective souls. There is one other thing that I observed and will mention here in my letter. Most of the paesani wore layers of clothing - stacked up one upon the other, like walking suitcases. Perhaps that was the purpose, to do this. But everyone was so clean, especially the children who could find a place to play anywhere they found accomplices.

———

It was here, the very first day of the voyage, that we, the three paesane girls of Pratola Serra, met a beautiful woman of thirty-four. Her name was Margherita Moro. She had two little girls with her. Their names were Stefania, who was ten, and her little sister, Pina, who was eight. Beautiful, beautiful little girls with wonderful names that matched their faces. These two little girls called this handsome woman, "Mamma" Margherita, even though they were not her children. We soon found out they were the daughters of the woman's fiancé who now lived in New York.

Margherita was a real dye-in-the-wool "Neapolitan," one from Naples. She had beautiful black eyes, full black hair, supple form, and angular features. She could sing with a depth of feeling that brought back all the nostalgic folk songs of Naples with all their enchantment. She was a very striking woman - a handsome human being. She wore her long hair up and around and pinned in the back. Margherita also wore several beautiful and voluminous woolen scarves that circled her shoulders and neck like a gypsy, the layers of which the girls would hang on and play with incessantly.

Margherita was going to America, to New York, to marry her fiancé and to bring the girls to their father. Margherita had us captivated with her story, as much as any of the romance books we had read in our club. Her story was intriguing and poignant. It was also true, which captivated us even more. I will relate it now, for it played an important part for us paesane girls and deeply affected our voyage to America.

Margherita told us that once, many years earlier in Naples, she was engaged to be married to a man named Giovanni Salti - her inamorata. They had fallen in love as children themselves. But somehow or other, while he was in the military service, he was forced to marry another woman because she became pregnant and insisted the child was his. No one was really sure, but he married this other woman regardless, and they had two daughters together. Margherita then told us, "I resigned myself to be an old maid - never to marry. I swore I would never marry any other but Giovanni."

Right after gaining his freedom from the army, Giovanni went to America. She told us, "He was to call for his wife and these two girls once he was able, but his wife died during the influenza pestilence. I took care of her at the end of her life. She said to me, 'Margherita, please take care of Giovanni and my little ones - please - promise me to do this.' So, I did." adding, "That was more than a year ago. These two beautiful little girls became mine automatically. For over a year now, I've raised them and have loved them as I have always loved their father. I am taking them to America to start again - all of us, together, in a new place - a nice place. Giovanni is waiting for us. We are to be married." Stefania was listening to this story while her sister, Pina, was playing a little further away in a corner. When Margherita stopped talking, Stefania hugged her tightly. Margherita bent to kiss her. It was so touching to see the love they had for each other. We three paesane were moved deeply by her story.

Well, the three of us girls did very well. We were constantly together, singing, talking, etc. We always attracted other girls, and, of course, boys or young men.

Little Stefania, Pina and I also had many hours together. I told them stories of Greek mythology and sang to them songs of our region. The two darlings wanted to be alone with me. We sat in front on the deck, the bow, always looking forward because I often got dizzy if I turned my back to the oncoming sea. Our stories were of why people had to go to foreign lands. I composed so many stories for them of other people. I told the little girls of other children like themselves, in olden times, and how just going from one region to another was like us now going all the way to America. "They had no boats, no trains back then, not even carriages or horses; they were nomads, going from place to place - finding new things - meeting strange and wonderful people." I stopped, for the girls in their exuberance were asking too many questions. "We shall save some questions for another time, eh?"

After Margherita, I suspect that the two little sisters loved me. As soon as the two of them saw me in the morning, they brought me hand in hand to where Margherita was. I often think now of how children can take the most deplorable of conditions and yet still find some gaiety in the moment if two things are present - a loving adult whom they trust and a little food in their bellies. That's it - that is all they need. That's all anyone needs, really.

There was a place on this old ship, *The America*, like a long archway. It was large and tubular shaped, cut deep into a section on the side of the ship with an elevated floor where twenty people could sit comfortably. We were there most of the time. This was where we brought our food, water to drink, etc. They called this section the "Neapolitan Grotto."

Yes, there were no tables, no chairs, no napkins, no dishes, only paper plates and basic utensils. This was third class. Steerage. Whatever was in second class or first class we could not tell. In that section, they had closed doors and, nobody of the third class was allowed to trespass in that area.

The people of these two higher classes, however, were permitted to come down to us for their amusement. If we were singing and we saw them approaching, then we stopped. We called a sailor guard to remove them away. I saw enough class distinction in my hometown, but it was nothing in comparison of these upstarts so well dressed. Insipid, silly people who came down to listen to us sing. Margherita, as soon as she

160

saw them coming, made us stop. We dispersed all over the boat, finding a better place to be alone.

Our third class was packed like sardines. We, the three paesane girls, realized this situation and agreed to stay closely to Margherita and her two little girls for many reasons. First, nobody dared to occupy that small grotto-like place if we were all together. Second, Margherita had a sailor wash the floor every night, as soon as we left. It was the cleanest place in third class - and it was covered. Also, nobody dared, nobody, to take that designated space away from Margherita once she had rightfully claimed it. The paesani knew this. Once Margherita was late. We girls found the place already occupied by other people. Then Margherita came. Oh, boy! I wish I could paint that scene. She just stood there, irate - this tall, statue of a Neapolitan woman with fire in her eyes. Stefania and Pina knew well to stay behind their protector's dress. What passion! What presence! A few words uttered with a firm obstinate command and the other people moved away - quickly. They meekly acknowledged their mistake and never dared to return again.

This boat, *The America*, should never have been used for passengers. It was old and had been abused by the troops that Italy sent by sea during the Great War. I often wondered, even now, if it was ever destroyed or if it was reconditioned. *[Aside: See the above picture for the answer.]*

One terrible day, we heard that there was maybe a smallpox pestilence on the boat. It was hushed about. We thought perhaps people just exaggerated. "What was small pox?" we asked. "It is the plague," someone said, and these words made the entire steerage class shudder and withdraw - even though it was only rumored. Yet, crewmembers gave us some disinfectant soap and some pills for everyone to take. We thought perhaps the pills were to prevent seasickness. Not true. The pills were for something else because they made me seasick instead. This made the paesani even more suspicious. I was so nauseated by the pills, that I couldn't eat. I yearned for a piece of dry bread, but all we got was some American food that made me worse. I lost weight from being sick to my stomach. Appia took care of me like an older sister. When I became weak, I had the same feelings as I had during the influenza. Yes, I became scared.

Adelina told the boys who helped us to find something dry for me. We could have boiled beef steak every day and one of the boys of our crowd sometimes forced me to eat it. He used to cut it one piece at a time and made me chew it. His name was Gaetano. I always remember how kind he was. I recovered in time.

It was now already one week into our crossing - we began to feel time. The boat was very rough. Margherita demanded blankets for us and for her girls. We got them of course.

As we neared North America, we began to feel very cold. The dormitory was dank with an endless chill. We got the blankets, and we all huddled together - Appia and I on the same cot. We stayed close together every night, talking, remembering Pratola Serra, our dear, little silent town. We heard constantly the pounding of the ocean knocking on the walls of the ship. There was never rest from the damp or the nausea I felt.

Then, one morning, Margherita didn't show up on our spot on the top deck area. Her two little girls came running to us, crying. "They took Mamma Margherita away while we were asleep!" they cried, "We do not know where she is!" Appia, Adelina and I looked at each other in desperation; we all guessed what it was. We held the girls close to us. They were shaking hard.

I said, "Let's sit down and wait, after all, she might be somewhere to get something she wants." After a while, Appia told Adelina to sit there in our place. "Take care of the children while Michelina and I go to find out what this is about. Feed yourself and the children and be calm." Appia and I then left to make our way to the third-class office of the ship.

They didn't know, or so they said. Then, we went to the hospital for third class of the ship - another dormitory area. As we approached it, a heavily armed guard blocked us. He commanded us to stay where we were. "Do not go any further!" he ordered. "Okay," we said. We asked him if Margherita Moro was in the hospital. The guard went in. Soon he came out with the information, - "Yes, she is sick," he said. "She will be fine soon. Now move away."

Appia and I hugged each other and went back to our place on deck. They all were eating their breakfast - the boys had gotten ours, too. Appia and I both drank some coffee and ignored, for as long as we could, all the questions. Finally, grieved and sorry for all concerned, Appia said softly, "Mamma Margherita is sick." The children cried.

I will only say that the week that followed on the boat was like an eternity. It was a routine. Every morning, the first thing we did was to go to the hospital dormitory and inquire about Margherita. We always got the same answer, "She is better." I answered only once to them sarcastically, "Oh, really?!" The guard retorted rudely, "Move away, I said!" "Please tell Signora Moro that the children are fine. Please!" I said, calling back. There was no answer.

Appia and I took care of Stefania and Pina now ourselves. We comforted them, fed them and saw that they were clean and warm. They slept with us in our cots, one with Appia, one with me - we would alternate. Appia and I took good care of these beautiful little girls. We had to. We did not know how long their Mamma Margherita would be in the hospital ward, but we knew we would take care of what was needed to be done.

Then, one morning, land appeared in the distance - "America!" Again, Appia and I ran to the hospital ward in third class and asked the guard for our friend, Margherita. "We are about to land! We need to talk with her!" I said in my purest Italian. We were told, "Margherita Moro died four days ago with a fever."

We were approaching the statue of Liberty in New York. It was December 1st, 1919.

What is the use to cry anymore - why? I have spent all my tears. There was an evil in this world, and it followed me everywhere.

*(Main processing center, Ellis Island immigration station,
Jersey City, New Jersey.)*

Chapter Two

Ellis Island, November, 1919

We were brought to Ellis Island and its hospital for quarantine. Our ship was sick. We all had to strip off our clothes and be bathed by some obstinate nuns who looked like nurses or they were obstinate nurses who looked like nuns - it was hard to tell. They admired our young bodies. The children were brought to a different area. Appia, Adelina and I were told to go naked into a large bath stall, all tiles, even on the ceiling. There, they used a hose on us. They splashed forceful water on us everywhere. I felt so indignant, but we had to submit to them in order to get away from hell.

After this, we were instructed to wash and to scrub ourselves still again. Then, they sprayed some odorous liquid on us with hand pumps like I used to see done on farm animals back in Pratola Serra. The nurses then examined our skin and our body parts carefully. Again, they sprayed everywhere. Never did I think to experience such barbarity. "We may die of pneumonia before anything else," I said to Appia. "And I paid money for this?" She replied. Later, they gave us white cotton pullover gowns and some slippers to wear. We were all freezing! It was December, and we were on an island of rocks, off the northeast coast of North America, directly from steerage class of a quarantined ship.

The nurses brought us back to the clinic to take some tests. They looked into our eyes and checked our mouths, teeth and gums. They checked our hair for lice and even the coloration of our nails. We passed fine, but we had to remain there yet. We were, after all, quarantined. We were served our first meal in the clinic that night on our very clean cots, with sheets and clean blankets - and, they had heat for us. Finally, it felt good. I slept well for the first time in a long, long time. Appia and Adelina were near me. The day after, all of our clothes were returned to us. They smelled funny.

After that, we ate in a beautiful dining room - long tables with all kinds of American food. It is funny sometimes, what one remembers. I loved the boiled ham and mashed potatoes they served us. I hated that white stuff called gravy they put on the chicken. But I did love the cream they put in their coffee - so did all the others. We three paesane girls still remained together. The two little sisters, Stefania and Pina, finally joined us at our long table. All of us were somehow still alive and in America.

Quarantine Ends

We were allowed to go out into the fresh air and into a major courtyard bordered by fences, gates and large buildings. The shape of these processing buildings impressed me not only in their size, but also in a design that was foreign to me, but pleasing. I had seen them before in books of course, but confronting them in person was better.

As on the ship, we three paesane girls and the two little sisters always stayed closely together. We girls kept the spirit of the children up as best we could. Often, they would cry thinking of their Mamma Margherita - and what of their father? When would they see him? We promised them that they would be reunited soon with their father - that he was coming for them. We told them this story over and over so many times that we believed it ourselves.

Two days later, my own father came to Ellis Island, bringing with him my older cousin Fortuna who lived in New York City. They came to the outer gate together. I ran up to them and touched them both with outstretched hands through the gates. We all shouted, "Papa!" "Michelina! Here!" "Fortuna!" My cousin looked radiant and happy, but Papa much less so. We were barely able to touch each other and to kiss past the massive gates. But because the processing of the people was still going on, I couldn't come out just yet. There was more paperwork to do. I had to stay in my place with the others.

I could tell that my father was pleased to see me, yes, but he was very awkward in manner. He had come all the way from Boston, Massachusetts, and I had come all the way from Italy. Still, he didn't say much. He sort of shuffled and looked down at his feet. Fortuna, on the other hand, was exuberant and looked wonderful. I had forgotten how much I missed her. She had a real business mind and was studying to be a businesswoman, of course. She did so much to get me out and to help the family and friends who had come for my other two paesane girls, Appia and Adelina.

Finally, Appia and Adelina were free to go first. Appia's brother had come all the way from Syracuse, New York, and Adelina's two sisters were there to bring her to her new home in New York City. We three paesane all promised somehow to find each other in America and to stay in touch, but we never did. We hugged, we kissed, and we said our good-byes - always these goodbyes. But there were two lives still unaccounted for. Everyone was spoken for - except for little Stefania and Pina - the two beautiful children. Their father had not come for them - no one had even a word that anyone was there to get them. I had this very sick feeling inside of me about it.

Yes, I, too, could have left Ellis Island right then, but I asked my father permission to stay until Stefania and Pina's father came for them. I didn't know how long that would be, but I could not leave them. I did not want to leave Margherita's two little girls alone. I was convinced that the delay in reuniting the children with their father was due only to Margherita's absence. My father said, "Of course. Yes, yes, you can stay. I will come back for you tomorrow." He was so business-like. No sympathy - no other word of consolation. I turned and walked back into the clinic building to find the little sisters.

That night, at the long table, the camerieri, the waiters and waitresses at Ellis Island, were just the same as my father - no smiles for the children. Only one young waiter came by and pulled at my curls. He was very American-looking. I pushed his hand off. "Move away!" I demanded. He, with a silly smile, said something in English which I didn't understand and then in a very bad Italian accent he added, "Io piace a te." ("I like you"). I retorted in perfect Italian, "You have the face of a frog!"

The night passed. Back in the clinic, the girls wanted to sleep with me like they had done on the boat. I was certain their fear was that no one would be there for them when they woke up in the morning. "No," I said, "they won't allow us to do that here. I will stay with you for a while, but then we all have to sleep in our own beds. I will be close by - this I promise. Okay? Hush now."

While we were talking, another ignorant nurse saw us and came over and made some fuss about clinic rules. I would have to leave. I winked at her and made a "shhhh," sound. She stopped her admonishments which were all in English. Pina was already asleep. The nurse stayed there without expression, gesturing for me to leave. I thought to myself, "Was this woman truly devoted to healing?"

Stefania was slumping her head against me sorrowfully. The poor child was exhausted. I took her up in my arms and placed her into her bed next to her sister. The nurse stayed there, waiting to see what I was going to do next. Then I said, again, in perfect Italian, "I am waiting until the other girl will fall asleep." This nurse didn't understand Italian - or perhaps she did. Then I knelt down, taking Stefania's hand in mine. I told her a little story in a Neapolitan dialect. The nurse finally smiled a bit and left. She probably thought that I was praying with the child in Italian, but in truth, I told Stefania a story of a little princess who ran away from home and started her own kingdom - all by herself.

Stefania finally fell asleep. I went to my own bed. I was tired and a little afraid - my mind was busy with questions. I kept thinking and thinking, "Would I like America? Would I ever see my two paesane again - or my town - or my friends? Would this man, Giovanni Salti, come for his two little girls? What if he doesn't? How will you keep your promise never to leave them? No! I will not leave them. This I am sure. This I swore to God - my own God. Oh, why did Margherita die? Why does anyone have to die?" Then I heard again in my ear the voice of my Uncle Costantino when he was teaching me to read when I was Pina's age, "Be patient and consider all possible meanings, Michelina. Go slowly - slowly." "Yes. Slow. Oh, God, lead me right for once, will you? Will you?!" I slept hard.

The next afternoon, Papa, Fortuna and I found each other again at our accustomed spot at the gate. I could only stay a moment - the children were waiting for me. After a kiss of welcome through the fence, I told my father that no one yet had come to claim the two little girls. I told him that there must be some mix-up. My father fumed at me, "What?! We have to come again here tomorrow? Leave with us now, Michelina! You see how much trouble you caused in coming to America?" "What trouble, Father? Would you have me leave two little girls here alone with no one to look after them?!" He didn't answer. Then I reflected. "My own father is not happy to have me here. I must accept this from him - just do my job for Mother and ignore the opposition." I half heard him speak. I was thinking, "Oh, Mother, Mother, what made you so good - and yet so weak in front of this man?"

I went back to Stefania and Pina. The girls were patiently seated together in the parlor - waiting for me. To know they were waiting for me and that I had returned to them scared me greatly. How trusting and fragile is the faith of children? My God - my God. What if I had followed my father's wishes and did not come back to them? The thought sickened me to my heart.

The parlor was a beautiful room, like the hotel lobby in Naples where once I stayed with my Nonna Pirone. Deep carpets, large windows, beautiful paintings on the walls of sailing ships, and of sailors, etc. The two little darlings looked lost in sitting so close together in this huge room. Their dresses were clean and neat. I remember funny things. I remember how their feet couldn't touch the floor and the expressions on their faces when I finally entered the room. When the children saw me, they jumped up and hugged my waist. "Oh, Michelina - we love you!" I was very careful not to cry or to show my concern of their possible fate. I knew then and there, I would adopt them if I had to, like their own Mamma Margherita did. I would. I swore myself to God I would do this.

I took each by the hand and showed them the pictures on the walls. I said, "Here, look at the ship with the grand sails - not like the one we traveled on, eh? And look - the waves - see how they rebel at the intrusion on them from the ship." Pina, the little one said, "I hate ships. It made Mamma Margherita die." I swallowed back my tears. We went for dinner - just us three.

After dinner, I went to the processing office at Ellis Island and again took a seat and waited - and then waited some more. In respectful broken English, I asked if anyone had come to find the whereabouts of the two girls? No one listened to me. Then, I just spoke up with conviction, like "Mamma" Margherita would have done only in perfect Italian. "Was there someone asking for two little girls?!" I demanded loudly. "Any news? Anyone?" "No. No one," they said in broken Italian. I told the officials that I was absolutely sure their father had come for them. Absolutely certain. "He must have. I was told he would be waiting - even as we arrived here in America." I was insistent on this, that someone was here waiting for them. "There has to be a mistake somewhere, and I want to know where that mistake is." I said this in my most perfect and ardent Italian. Now the responses mostly came back in English, and, of course, I was at a disadvantage.

Frustrated, as I was leaving, there was a little man in a corner - a simple clerk, thumbing his pages in a journal. My brand of Italian must have caught his ear. He said in a quiet, perfect Italian, "Yes, yes, Signorina. There was some confusion - names and quarantines. It is all arranged now for tomorrow morning at ten o'clock. Their father will take them out." "Oh, my God! Really?! He's here?!" I was beyond joy! Then, the clerk told me with a smile, "You, of course, can arrive in America anytime you like." "And leave those two girls alone? No." I said, "They only know me. And, I would never miss this reunion." I ran back to the children with the good news. We cried - and we hugged. This time, we did say a little prayer of thanks before sleeping. No nurses or nuns were around to tell us otherwise.

That night, I dreamt I was fighting with both my mother and my father who were struggling to hold me with them down inside the hull of that damp ship. I yelled myself awake. I stayed awake all of the rest of the night, staring up, waiting for that fateful sunrise to arrive. I wanted desperately to break free from this purgatorial space they called Ellis Island.

The appointed morning finally came. The children and I dressed in a hurry. We primed the final touches. They were so excited. I fussed with them, just like my own Nonno Don Carlos had instructed me, "Come now. Make sure you are neat. Remember to stand tall. Be proud of who you are. You are about to meet your father."

Nine o'clock - there was still another hour to kill. Did I say kill? One should never kill time, ever. Nonna Pirone always said this. You commit suicide when you kill time! "Yes, yes, Nonna. I will fill this hour too. I will tell the girls how to meet their father after so long - how not to miss Margherita so much. She is in heaven, looking down on them. They will find her and their own mother again, someday. Yes - someday. I will tell them this." And so, in that last hour, I did.

My God, when will ten o'clock come? That was the best ten o'clock in the morning that I had ever experienced. They opened the gate. There came running in, ahead of everyone else, this handsome Neapolitan man with chestnut hair - Giovanni. He ran in searching - searching - eyes wide open, looking for his children. He was lean, tall and exactly how Margherita had described her Giovanni. He was about forty, but he looked so boyish. He looked just like his oldest girl, Stefania. They all found each other. This man hugged both of his little girls at the same time, lifting them up high, high to his breast - together - and so they remained for minutes, crying with happiness. I found that my own hands were covering my mouth in tearful joy. Thank you, God. Oh, thank you for this simple embrace. Thank you.

Giovanni tried his best to compose himself as he turned toward me. His eyes were full of tears. Stefania jumped down and ran up to me and cried, "Bobbo, this is Michelina! She took good care of us!" "Signorina," he said kissing my hand, "How can I ever repay you? You are an angel of mercy to have stayed with my children - God bless you. God bless everything for you." I said to him, "I love your girls." Then he sorrowfully asked how it all happened about Margherita? I told him as concisely as I could. The poor man looked so sad, adding, "You know, Signorina, Margherita was my first love. We grew up together in Naples. She was my beloved!" "It is okay," I said, "Take care of your little girls now. God, help you with your sorrow - goodbye." "Goodbye," he said. I kissed my darling little friends, straightened out their hats one last time and watched them disappear with their father into other departing paesani. Alone now, I turned and went back in to gather my things knowing that I would never see these two little sisters again, but also that they would be fine. They would be fine.

I heard myself give an open prayer, "Thank you, God - for this simple goodness. I know in my heart that you offer no other kind."

Just before I left the processing building of Ellis Island, I could think of only one question - where will Margherita Moro to be buried? To this day, I don't know the answer. But my faith tells me that Giovanni Salti and his two beautiful daughters do know.

———

| | RECORD OF DETAINED ALIENS | | | | | 53 |

S.S. America (Italia America Line) 12-3-19 arrived _____, 191 _____ M., _____, from _____

[Aside: *Quarantine List. "S.S. America (Italia American Line) 12-3-19, #5, "Pirone, Michelina, Group 31, Disposition (released), To cousin, Fortuna P, 1361 Jerome Ave, Bronx, NYC." Because sickness and death broke out on board the S.S. America on this passage, the entire ship was quarantined for three days on Ellis Island or one of its other two hospitals. The female passengers were processed separately by nurses and most likely assisted by nuns under the aegis of the United States Government. That would include "all" of the 2,650 passengers onboard and even the crew.*]

———

Chapter Three

Manhattan Island

Late Fall, 1919

[Aside: Personally, I vividly remember all the stories and related details of my grandmother's life as she told them to me over the years from this point forward - her coming to America. Hours and hours of wonderful accounting of this period in her life until the year I was born. Her Letter now continues in America, in her own words which still echo in my ear.]

After waiting alone at the gate, I saw cousin Fortuna, Papa and my Uncle Antonio coming up the entrance way to get me. My uncle was as jubilant as I had remembered him to be - a little puffed up now perhaps in his middle age, but this weight only made him look happier somehow. It had been thirteen years since his return to Pratola Serra to fetch little Fortuna and to leave shortly thereafter. Now it was my family in America who had come to fetch me.

Emotionally, I was ready to leave Ellis Island way behind. I had spent a lifetime it seemed crossing the Atlantic, being examined by suspicious nurses and nuns and waiting for their final approval as someone being fit enough to venture onto American soil. I brought with me no more than who I was. I was Michelina Fabrizio Pirone, eighteen, from Pratola Serra, Italy - and I was exhausted.

A small boat brought my family and me to the shores of New York. I did not have many belongings to transport. The short trip rejuvenated me and gave me strength again. The day was cold and grayish. A small observance here - the light around us was very different, more gray-silver, unlike the gray-brown November days I experienced back home in Italy. This light, however, seemed bigger and colder. Space was expanded - details more distant to the eye. Everything appeared to me as if in cold pastels. This wash of light was everywhere.

Uncle Antonio's automobile was parked near a restaurant house. "Your automobile, Uncle?!" My, how proud he was of this modern advance of his. We went past his car, entered the restaurant and had lunch there.

Most everybody inside the restaurant spoke different forms of Italian. It was like any restaurant in Naples. That was the problem for me. At first, it was hard to keep track of where I was. I was almost dizzy with the experience; familiar yet aged faces in a surrounding of familiar aromas with a strangely lit unfamiliar landscape outside. Dusty images came in and out of my head.

I had a simple woolen dress on and a light overcoat. This clothing was not sufficient enough for November in New York, America. I was very cold and I think it was obvious. As we sat to eat, I kept my coat on. Fortuna, now a real lady of twenty-two, quietly observed me from across the small table. She was so smart and so elegant looking. She watched me eat for several minutes without offering a word, then suddenly jumped up and suggested to uncle and Papa, "You two wait here in the restaurant for a while, okay? I have something to do with Michelina." They were stunned at the request but obeyed and kept eating and talking. Then Fortuna quickly took me up by the arm, and we left out the door of the restaurant, leaving my father and uncle behind. "Come with me and don't ask any questions," she said in perfect Italian. Fortuna confidently led me out the door in a whirl, into America.

I expected everything and yet nothing at what I saw. We boarded a trolley car not one block from the restaurant. We passed many amazing streets, mile after mile we went with high buildings guiding our way. The size and scope of everything - the energy! It all took my breath away - literally, making me dizzy. I was young and in America!

The marvel of it all, the people, the automobiles, even the old horse carts - all familiar, yet all uniquely different. I thought instantly of my Nonno Don Carlos, the master harness-maker and what he would have thought. So many horses - so many harnesses! I asked my cousin, "Fortuna, these buildings, are these the skyscrapers?!" "Oh, no," she laughed, "the towers are much, much higher -wait, you will see." She spoke Italian so well - without any hint of a dialect. It was a welcome to my ear. I congratulated her on this accomplishment, "Brava!" I said without thinking.

She answered me abruptly and with ardor, "Never mind bravoing me on my diction. You don't speak like a Pratola Serran yourself," she laughed. "Where did you learn Italian so well? It's perfect. Did your father send you to Avellino for your education?" "Oh, please," I said, "let's change the subject."

Finally, we got off the trolley at another very long and narrow street. Fortuna said, "Ah, here we go." We went into a small store - small, yes, but it had quality and taste, even the sales ladies were well-dressed. They all had perfect poise and manners. Fortuna spoke with them at length in English - how well I don't know, only they all beamed at her with complete understanding. "This is a language I will master," I thought right then and there. "I will."

Fortuna, to my surprise, bought me a winter coat. It was deep blue, my favorite color. The coat was well-made of beautiful material with large collars and it fit me to perfection. "I thank you, dear cousin. Thank you!" "The climate here in America is not like Italy," she replied. "In November, one needs heavier clothes." The spring coat which I had brought from Italy was beautiful, but not heavy enough. Now I felt so very comfortable. I was ready for anything - even my father. We returned back to the men who were still at the table having a good time chatting away as if we had never left.

———————

I was wonderfully amazed and pleased that it was Fortuna who got into the car and drove us. She took us for a long ride all over New York City. We passed the Italian section, the Jewish section, the Negro section, the Chinese section, etc., etc. Naively, I thought, "My God, New York is so complex, they even separate the people!" I also thought that only the Chinese section was a town unto itself because all I saw there were Chinese. The other sections had a mixture of every other race. Only once before, in Naples, had I ever seen a Negro person. He was so black, his teeth so white, so beautiful. I liked him. He was a gallery guard in one of Pompeii's museums.

I knew little of the reasons why the races were so conglomerated together. Did they separate people here because of prejudice - or what was it? Was it a government policy, or was it by choice? Perhaps language was a factor, too? Well, on this subject, I had lots to learn yet. I knew little then about all the hostilities that existed among different races here in this great melting pot.

Fortuna was the perfect guide. She and I instantly became the best of friends and we still are, even now, as I write this. She is so smart and so lovable. Later, she would become a successful businesswoman buying and selling wine grapes from California. We continued.

Then the "towers" appeared, as Fortuna called them. The skyscrapers were amazingly high - I could not believe them! "Why so tall?" "New York is a small island - so they build up," she said. We took a ride up one of the towers in a monster elevator. Up and up we went until we stopped at the very top of the building where we saw all of New York City in panorama. "Oh, my," I shouted, "what an immense mass of humanity all huddled together! And the architecture!" I didn't fully understand. It all felt unnatural to me. My only thought was that New York was too close - too far - too high - too exaggerated - too everything. I was always taught that too little and too much were two evils. I believed the teachings of the old Greeks - "moderation in everything."

I came to the eventual conclusion that New York was simply too big. Too big for me anyway. This impression was my first, of course, because I only knew a few cities in Italy; Naples, Avellino, and Benevento. But even there, there was space - no exaggerations - easy to remember - lovely to look at. New York was full of people! Here, they were all rushed, bumping into each other - even in those big stores - the minds of the salespeople were always elsewhere. In the restaurants, there was little courtesy; people just ran and ran. Why? Why all the madness? What purpose did it serve? Where was everyone rushing to? I felt confused. I couldn't be myself, just me, while walking on those streets or into those rich stores - rich everything. I always walk slowly and sing to myself. That habit seemed out of place here. I already missed the familiar antique ruins of Italy that reminded me of the glory of Rome and the splendor of the Renaissance. I was in America for less than a day, and I was ready to leave. Was all of

America like this boisterous and demanding city?! I would not survive here if such were the case.

We reached the Bronx where Uncle Antonio and his family lived, on the same street up from where Yankee Stadium is now. I joyfully met again my Aunt Bernadina and, for the first time, their children - all my little cousins - six more of them besides Fortuna. There was Flora, Maria, Tammi, Francesco, Mikele and Venera - clean and beautiful Pirone children with magnificent manners - all.

My father and I stayed a week in New York in the Bronx. My American cousin Fortuna and I were inseparable. She told me of her own experiences of growing up as a child in New York which she insisted was much different than growing up in America. She talked rapidly, with assurance and understanding, "Most of our people settled here, Michelina - in New York. Here, and in other older cities where they need hard laborers, skilled workers and tradesmen. There is even a new industry forming - supplying old world items to old world people so they can survive. What is America's strength? Her markets. She must grow. She must renew herself. Endlessly grow. Easy demand - easy supply - easy access - things lacking in Italy. Most who come from the old country, work hard, yes, they save everything, and then they go back. If Italy would be more politically stable like America, then most of these paesani would not have to come to America in the first place. I am sure of this. This place, America, is not really Italy for them." "What about for you?" I asked. "Me? I grew up here. I live in this wonderful place. It will not change for me. I don't really remember Italy that much. I take the best of the memories as I can - and only keep what is good about them." Fortuna had thought a lot about this choice and was sure of her own observations. She had a strong intellect. I had the feeling that I was the only one she ever confided in about this. I listened hard to her argument. Honored. Fortuna's convictions resonated for me - they still do.

Over the years, I have thought about this time and have written about it many times, in journals and in newspapers. I also know from my long studies on this subject, that even as our boat, the *SS America*, arrived on Ellis Island, we were near the end of the great Italian migration which started in the mid-1800's. Thousands and thousands of the paesani already had come here before, mostly from Sicily and also from the South of Italy. They came to the cities of the industrial east in America. A group also went to San Francisco and to California to fish. But half of all these paesani went back to Italy. Half of them. The other half stayed to make America their own - but on their terms. They integrated and melded without notice. I think American culture was only as good for immigrant Italians as to how much it kept them working and also connected to the old world - connected to the Italy they once knew but were forced to leave. Two thousand years of art, music and heritage were temporarily obfuscated in order to persevere in its purity - but never, never to be forgotten or abandoned. The modern nation of Italy had failed them, failed itself and failed its best hope to advance - failed its free-spirited artisans and seasoned workers, some of the best the world has ever witnessed. Giving themselves up and disappearing into the American culture would have been a downgrade for many of these paesani. What for? Why should they settle into less? So, they used America to support what should have been supplied but was denied them in their homeland. They were "Italians." And so, in lies the unique difference of their migration. They did not get here too late. They got here when they most needed to incontrovertibly connect and preserve their own heritage.

Many Italians in Italy to this day feel that the reason Italy never progressed as a super-nation since the times of massive immigration was because her life's blood and soul - "la forsa" - the spirit and the best of Italy, all left for the new world like legions of Roman centurions. The Italians came to pillage uncharted territory solely to proclaim and reclaim themselves. The best and most aggressive spirit of Italy, left Italy. In a way, they used America's resources to rejuvenate Italy and to keep her alive. Half of them left a dysfunctional country behind and then returned to it with enough resources of their own to make their irrelevancy relevant. The other half of the paesani who eventually stayed? Most intermingled their blood with the continent itself, and the only vestige they kept of the old world was the vowel at the end of their surname. And, over my many years, this paradox was expressed to me in many different forms often. This dilemma is what I write about and still believe to be true. My gifted family was proof of this manifestation.

My Uncle Antonio had made a successful change in his own occupation from being a harness-maker to a distributor of Italian food products for Americans of all cultures. He took advantage of the supply and demand concept that he had also witnessed in Nonna's store back in Pratola Serra, but he was more successful with it in America. We ate well in his house.

We also visited my Uncle Raffaele, the oldest Pirone son, who had settled into the Italian section of New York City itself. He also had a large, beautiful family. As for my Uncle Raffaele, however, well, he hadn't changed very much. He was still sour, with an irritating disposition. He remained a harness-maker like his father and also Papa. Perhaps he was still bitter at being Don Carlos' oldest son and not inheriting his father's harness business - a business that my father ultimately inherited - and abandoned for America. This contention between these two brothers eventually forced my father out of New York and up to Boston. Nevertheless, I enjoyed being all together with my two uncles and their big families. My father and his brothers had a peaceful enough reunion. I think my arrival had something to do with this, for I loved them all. I was reminded of the old times when my Nonno, Don Carlos, was alive.

Back in the Bronx, I noted that it was nice, with large streets, busy with the many Italian and Jewish stores - many of them side-by-side. There were all kinds of people, and the city was alive with many activities. This was just after the First Great War and hundreds of thousands of European immigrants had already arrived and settled in. Mediterranean people, the Jews and the Italians - they got along just fine. I asked cousin Fortuna, "Is Boston, the city I am going to - is it like this?" "Yes," she answered, "Almost. Where you are going is all Italians and Jews. It is called the North End. I visited it once. It's much like here." "Good," I thought.

I was beginning to understand why races settled into sections of New York as they had - culture, food, language, all had something to do with it, yes, but it was something more than familiarity. The English word "validation" is one of my favorite words in English to explain this phenomenon. It is a perfect word. Each area was like a safety net, protecting each group while still connecting them to their ancestral past in the new world. They validated themselves by their own presence and cultural reaffirmations. Will this safety net still exist a hundred years from now? Will it be needed? Who is to say?

I remember well the last night we had in New York. We ate supper at Uncle Antonio's. Everyone was there. Aunt Bernadina had order and respect in her house. She sat at the head of the table, tall and erect, looking so much like my friend, Margherita, lost at sea. My aunt had the same direction - the same strength of character. I loved her so much, and I loved the order she created in that large family. It was a peaceful, enjoyable time. But a part of me was anxious and excited to leave New York. I was in a new and wonderful country - America. I was so eager to go to this new American city called Boston - even if I had to go there alone - with my father.

"Michelina Pirone. First Picture Taken in America. January 1920."

Chapter Four

Boston or Bust

My father and I left for Boston by train, carrying all I had brought from Italy and some new packages - gifts from the New York Pironi clan.

It was a ten-hour train ride from New York to Boston in 1919. The train was larger and more comfortable than the train from Praola Serra to Naples - the windows wide and clear. Naturally, my Aunt Bernadina packed enough food for us to last ten days, not ten hours.

Papa and I rode in quiet reflection for a long time. But after a while, I had a good opportunity to tell him what was in my heart and why I had come to America. I told him that I not only came on behalf of my mother's sorrowful heart but also for my brothers and sisters who were still left behind. They all needed more support. "Papa, I must tell you now. I came to America to represent my brothers and sisters, to assure their interest - and Mother's." This I told him without fear. My father looked at me funny and laughed, saying, "That is a silly reason. You could have written to me instead." "But I did write you many times, and you never answered my letters. You did wrong, Papa." Because we were on the train with people around us, he restrained himself a lot - he didn't answer me.

I took advantage of his silence and continued. I told him calmly and softly what I thought he was. I was determined to do justice for my reason of coming to America, for my mother and my siblings. I told him, "You must send Mother more money. There is a growing family back in Italy that didn't ask to be born. You have been spoiled, Papa, by my mother's weakness to make good with what she has, and that weakness has made you very selfish and disillusioned. Too bad, you could have been anything in Italy, anything, because you had a good upbringing, an inheritance, and my mother's dowry. And you have intelligence besides! But now, what do you or our family have to show for it?" I stopped there; my father was red in the face. I could feel his indignation.

For a long time, I kept quiet, but on my face, was a look of expectation, of waiting - waiting for an answer. He looked at me and asked,
"What? What do you want from me, Michelina?" "What do I want?! I
want you to tell me what you are going to do!" He sensed my obstination
and quietly said, "Okay, yes. Perhaps you are right. I shall send 300 Lire a
month, not 200. Will that be enough? Will that suit you?" "Yes - for now."
We both maintained a long silence. Then I added - "And I want you to
form for me a plan as to when we will bring everyone here to America -
or..." "Or what?" he challenged. "Or, we go back to Pratola Serra with
Ralfo and make a new life with my mother - nothing otherwise for this
family." My father was now shocked at how I addressed him. I was not the
child he had left behind three years ago. I was demanding like a firstborn
son would - only I was not his son.

He stayed silent, then said, "We will talk of this further, but not now."
I just stared in his direction, determined not to let him get away with
another procrastinated promise to keep. "Okay," he said. "One way or
the other, we will reunite the family. It can't continue like this. I agree."
"The whole family," I said. "Yes. Everyone. Either here or back in Pratola
Serra. But you must give me time on this. I must have some peace first,
my God!" It was my turn stay silent.

Divorce was never an option for people of my mother and father's
age, coming from where they did. Once committed to a marriage - that
was it. It really wasn't an option later on in my life either. We Italians put
such demands on ourselves to be right the first time. I was living through
this question myself. It explains why so much passion is generated on the
courtships. The results are dear and permanent. What made the matter
so egregious was that women mostly were not permitted to choose what
would dictate the rest of their lives. Mother loved this man - she did. And
I suspect my father loved her, as well, in his own way, even though he was
a man who ran from everything, perhaps because both of their fathers
had arranged the conditions of their marriage. In those times, disputing
husbands and wives would simply drift apart, not necessarily physically,
but spiritually, under the careful gaze of their religion and the oath of
the Catholic Church which forbade them alternatives or freedom. They
would bury themselves first in their babies and the church - then in their
growing families - and finally in themselves alone - unless they died in

their children's houses, which most of them did. Rarely would a husband or wife just leave - but never would they be able to marry again.

That was the Italian custom, and it was unbreakable. So, my father had few choices, really. I just did not want him to shoot the messenger.

I was looking out the window of the train at all the places we passed. The rhythm of the scene soon overtook my mind. How beautiful now - the countryside, farmland and shoreline - so different from Italy, yet so simpatico. Connecticut. Rhode Island. And the trees! Never had I seen so many trees full of the promise of bloom even in the sleep of winter. I saw many roads which were interwoven. "Where do they go? When I learn English, I will go up there - and there too," I thought. They looked beautifully soft and inviting. We crossed shoreline and bridges which brought thoughts of the steamship *America*. And the many cities we stopped at in those States - all different from New York. There was hope for me in this vast country after all, perhaps. I drifted in and out of conscious thought as this amazing country passed in front of me. Before I knew it, we reached Boston, Massachusetts; it had the unmistakable lines of the old world. It welcomed.

Papa and I gathered our belongings on the train and exited in a gush of steam around our ankles. The station was loud and invigorating. More invigorating was when we found my brother, Ralfo, nervously searching for us in the crowd of the massive train station - South Station.

As soon as Ralfo saw us, he ran to me, and we embraced for many minutes. Oh, the tears of joy! He was now sixteen years old and such a fine young man. Big wavy hair piled on top of his head. I was so proud just to look at him - my brother! "After three years! Look at you! What a change!" I yelled out. "My God, you are so grown up - so handsome!" His smile was from ear-to-ear.

As we walked together, Ralfo held my waist for a long time - he was so happy for our reunion. We jumped along together. Father followed, walking in the back a few steps. I turned just then and saw him with a proud and soft expression.

Later that day, Father wrote a letter to Mother - maybe the first love letter in a long time. He left it on the desk, opened. My curiosity was stronger than my good manners, so naturally, I read the letter. Yes, he wrote about the money he was planning to increase, but mostly he wrote Mother about the reunion of Ralfo and me. He also expressed that he very much missed Mother's company. I remember smiling and replacing the letter in the exact position that I had found it.

In Boston, we stayed in the section called the North End, as it is still called today. We stayed in the large apartment house of my Great Aunt Alfonsina, my Nonna Pirone's younger sister. Great Aunt Alfonsina was a very intelligent lady, like Nonna herself. She was a force - the original Statue of Liberty! She was a natural born leader in the neighborhood too.

The North End of Boston was exactly as my cousin Fortuna had described - "little Italy," mixed with Jewish families and businesses. Even in the winter, there were produce carts on almost every corner, and each storefront window seemed to be full of hanging offerings for the table. The scale of it was very Mediterranean, very Italian - so full of the old world! Still, there was no mistaking it - I was in bustling America.

My Great Aunt Alfonsina welcomed us proudly into her expansive apartment house on Salem Street. I think the whole neighborhood heard her welcome. Her house was spacious with five bedrooms, two parlors, a dining room, and of course, a sit-down, large kitchen. The two-level apartment house was over a bakery. Today, another bakery called Bova Bakery occupies the spot on the street level.

Familiar fragrances and sounds kept me sleeping comfortably, uninterrupted, in my own room for two days. "Perfetto."

During my first week, my brother, Ralfo, and I explored all of Boston. I loved this city. Beacon Hill, the Boston Commons, the Public Gardens, etc. Not so big - not so exaggerated as New York. Boylston Street looked just like a street called Retofilo Strada of Naples. Even though Boston was old for America, still, I missed the antiquity of Benevento and of Naples. There were no ruins here to remind me of the grandeur of Roman times. However, most of the buildings were copies of the Renaissance period, Greek revival facades, and also Roman columns supporting Palladian cornices. For this reason, I fell in love with Boston - a love that is with me still to this day.

Ralfo and I walked and walked as if it were May and not December. The Boston Library - The Charles River - Beacon Hill, and the famed POSH Newbury Street with its displays of fine restaurants, boutiques and expensive galleries of art. Only on some streets, toward the waterfront, did we find those awful black elevated train platforms like in New York with ugly trams, running just above the streets, obscuring everything else.

The Italian section of Boston.

"Little Italy"

The "North End"

But, as I said, in 1919-1920, the North End was like old Naples in manner, except that it was a conglomeration of Jews and Italians. It was interesting. In all the businesses owned by Jews, they could speak not only in proper Italian, but in all kinds of Italian dialects - Sicilian - Abruzzese - Neapolitan - Calabrese, etc. Marvelous for them, such wonderful people. *[Aside: Before the North End of Boston became an Italian immigrant stronghold, the North End was settled by Jewish immigrants from Eastern Europe and Russia. Reading Michelina's account, the transition seems to have been a smooth one.]*

I soon became friends with everybody on Salem Street, the heart of the North End. Oh, my, the wonderful smells that I went to sleep with and woke up to. Even sometimes today, especially in the warmer months, that odor sometimes is mixed with the underlying smell of sweet molasses left over from a tidal wave of molasses that killed several people the winter before my arrival. *[Aside: In researching this curious notation, strange as it seems, Michelina's account evidently was correct. On January 15th, 1919, a sixty-foot railroad holding tank containing 2.5 million gallons of hot molasses exploded above the streets of the North End during a sudden warm spell. A series of ten-foot tidal waves of black ooze gushed out at an estimated 35 mph with a force of two tons per square foot. The tsunamis of molasses carried several freight cars with it and destroyed automobiles, buildings, and trestles. After it was over, newspaper accounts of the day described it as a scene from Pompeii. People stuck and smothered as they fell or were trapped. Twenty-one people were killed by burns and asphyxiation, and 150 people were severely injured by runaway molasses.]*

On that street, Salem Street, the neighborhood people all soon called me "Magi," - one of the Biblical wise men. I suppose that was because I didn't have a regional dialect or accent when I spoke Italian, and I spoke confidently when asked questions on any subject. Yet, I didn't like this nickname, so I shortened my real name and said to them, "Please. Call me 'Lena.' It is short for Michelina, Okay?" In America, they have called me by this name since.

On one of my first evenings, all the sons and daughters of Aunt Alfonsina came to meet me. My cousins were a fine bunch. They brought soft drinks, cakes and best of all, the most delicious food I found in Boston - what was it? - Ice cream! American ice cream was so different than our Italian gelati and cassata. Oh, how I loved it! We had a wonderful time! There were so many of these cousins and their spouses. Instantly, they all became my family.

Aunt Alfonsina was about sixty at this time. She was alert, robust, yet graceful, with white hair and a venerable carriage. She had a husband, yes, a little piece of humanity - a frustrated carpenter who never smiled. My aunt was so much more superior than he. There was no question that she ruled her house. I wondered why she had ever married this man. Perhaps it was arranged. I never asked.

Aunt Alfonsina and I went shopping a lot together. I felt I was with my Nonna Pirone again. My great aunt had the same tinge in her voice as her sister - the same inflections. This similarity was comforting to me in no small way.

The stores of the Italian North End of Boston were full of everything one could imagine. Nothing was like this back home. Not only were there plenty of products from Italy, but many different American varieties of things to choose from, as well, mixed in. It wasn't opulent, no - but there was one of everything, and everything was abundant. Fortuna's convictions echoed in my head.

I would need money for sure. I started thinking about how I would become independent enough to buy things that I wanted, and, oh, how I wanted what I saw. I said to my aunt, "I will need a job, Zia (Aunt). I am a good worker. I can sew, and I have also worked as a writer." "Sewing might be an easier profession to start with," she said smiling.

While walking through Prince Street, Aunt Alfonsina came upon this compare (friend) of hers who had his own tailor factory. She called out to him and then introduced us. "Don Pietro, this is my beautiful and talented niece, Michelina, who just arrived from my sister's village in Pratola Serra. She says she can sew - and - I believe her." He asked me if I felt like working for him! "Oh, yes, of course!" I answered confidently, "I am a good dressmaker." He chuckled, "Well, that might be a problem though, young lady, we make only men's clothes." "Okay. Women, men, no problem! I will come tomorrow if you like." "Fine," he said. He respectfully shook my aunt's hand, tipped his hat, and left still chuckling to himself. "My, how easy and quickly things are done in America," I thought. That night, I told Papa and Ralfo of the job offered by Don Pietro. They accepted and approved the job.

I had truly arrived in America. I was employed after my first brief interview and after only my first week in Boston. Yes, the Italians took care of themselves and of other Italians if it was beneficial to both in this close community. This was how it was done and was how people survived in America. Yes, I had arrived, but I was not even close to being an American.

Chapter Five

"Net" Working

Winter, 1920

That first day of work, Aunt Alfonsina came with me to Don Pietro's garment factory on Bedford Street. It was just off Washington Street in the heart of the clothes-making section of Boston. It was quite far from the North End - an intricate walk of almost an hour. There were street trolleys everywhere, but we walked. It was good for me to get my bearings this way.

We entered the building where Don Pietro had his factory. I was impressed, for it had an elevator. We got off at the sixth floor and entered an immense bustling workshop. Don Pietro greeted us and showed us around. I mistakenly called him, "Don" Pietro and he corrected me smiling, "'Mr.' is fine, Michelina - Mr. Pietro, please." He introduced me to his partner, a Jew, but I learned this fact only much later because, all day long, this man spoke nothing but Italian.

I kissed my aunt goodbye, and I started in right away.

Here I was, among all these mixed people from various places in Italy. First, Mr. Pietro gave me some finishing handwork to do on a man's jacket. Easy. Then, a Sicilian woman, who was the floor lady at this station, spoke abruptly to me in Sicilian. I was mindful not to disrespect either her or her regional form of Italian. She showed me the way to do it. Simple. *[Aside: It is interesting to read through Michelina's inferential tone, that Sicilians were thought of as simply part of the make-up of "mixed people." Many of those who immigrated from Italy, even the South of Italy, did not consider Sicilians true Italians at that time. Yet, a majority of those who immigrated to America were from the Island of Sicily, and most of the Italian immigrants who stayed in America were Sicilian. Also, Michelina labels Jewish people simply as "Jews." This I know is not disparaging, but how she and people referenced each other as friends and acquaintances back then. I chose not to modify this inflection.]*

191

With this first jacket, the floor lady affixed a tag, something of correction on my work, and it moved on. No words. I observed the correction and handled the second jacket just fine. And on that went. I did fine for the first day - no problems.

At noon, this first day, I opened my sack lunch and sat with another girl of my age - her name was Antonia. (Another Italian compare girl with a name that starts with "A" in my life?) I was actually thinking about this coincidence when Antonia sat next to me. Antonia was a pure-blooded Italian girl, yes, but she couldn't speak a word of Italian - only English. Antonia was a second-generation Italian-American with no understanding of the language of her parents. Curious - a pure Italian face but no Italian, working in a shop half-owned by a Jew who only spoke Italian. Ah, America - so many paradoxes in this wonderful country. I wasn't sure how well Antonia spoke English either because I was not yet bi-lingual. Nevertheless, Antonia and I instantly liked each other very much - a friendship all done with hand gestures.

<hr />

In the course of my working for Mr. Pietro, Antonia looked out for me and taught me lots of ways. For instance, she showed me how to get the elevator to operate by myself and how all the other workers did their different jobs. Some would cut, others would put cut pieces together; some were sleeve makers, collar makers, pocket makers, etc. Finally, the finished suit jackets were pressed and then hung. It was all very simple and organized - easy. It was amazing how even though neither Antonia nor I could communicate through speech, we understood everything that either of us was saying. Sometimes it's just that way between certain people.

During one lunch break, Antonia introduced me to a young Italian man of twenty-five. He was very clean-looking, tall and very kind. His name was Gianni Letto. Gianni lived in the North End also, not too far from Aunt Alfonsia's - of course, no one in the North End lived too far from my aunt's house. To my surprise and delight, Gianni was from the village of Prata, home of my dear friend Amalia Pisano and all the Pisano family. Also, of Giacomino Fabbo.

Gianni offered, in a most proper fashion, to accompany me back home to the North End after work. I thanked him, "Yes, I would like that." We became friends right away. During that lunch, we talked of nothing except the region of our birth. Prata, Pratola Serra, Montefacione, etc. Yes, this workplace was full of a mixture of people from all over Southern Italy, but they all found comfort and support from people of their own dialect patterns and even regional habits and superstitions. This identified and separated the Calabrese from the Napolitano, from the Abruzzese and the Sicilians, etc. Old way customs held a favoritism first - nationalism came only second. There was much infighting because of this - even hair pulling between the women. It reminded me completely of the madness and discord in Bizet's opera, "Carmen."

In my conversation with Gianni, a very strange coincidence happened. (I must also write now that I no longer believe in coincidences, as later I will relate.) Anyway, just before we were to leave and walk back to the North End, Gianni introduced me to yet another worker in the factory - a friend of his, also from our region - his compare. "Michelina, I want to introduce you my good friend from our area, Vincenzo Motta." "What?! What is your name?!" I exclaimed! He repeated it, shrugging his shoulders, almost apologizing, "Vincenzo Motta, Signorina." I jumped a mile in the air. He must have thought I was crazy. "Oh, my God! What an incredible coincidence! You must be related to a compare of mine - one of my best friends, Appia Motta! Is this possible?!" "Oh, my, Yes, yes! Appia - you know my sister, Appia?!" "I came with her on the boat from Naples! She was in my book club in Pratola Serra! She is my dear friend!" I yelled out. "No. You are joking! Oh, my God, it is not possible?! Is it true?!" "But she went to Syracuse, New York. She said her brother was there." "That is our oldest brother, Marco. But seriously. This is true?" He was so very happy about this revelation that I was afraid he thought I was making all of it up. The rest of the time was spent talking of nothing else but Pratola Serra - dear Pratola Serra. How sorry I was for him to have lost both parents to the influenza - how the family café was gone as well. And also, I described how his sister and I helped two little girls to find their lost father at Ellis Island. All of it.

How life works, eh? How wonderful and mysterious.

An Incident with Papa – Again

During the second week of my arrival, Papa brought some of his pae-sani friends up to the apartment house - nice people, young men from our village of Pratola Serra - farmers mostly. They all spoke the dialect of our region, a dialect which I liked to hear very much. But, as was my habit, I purposely spoke Italian back to them - pure Italian - and why not? It was the language from my books and of my ear, and books are not written in dialect. Besides, they seemed to enjoy hearing proper Italian as much as I was enjoying their old dialect.

Well, after these young men left, my father grabbed me by the arm and scolded me in a belligerent way. He was so angry at me; I thought he was about to hit me! Ralfo positioned himself between us, ready to stop his swing. Papa yelled to me, "What makes you so insulting?! Why did you make my friends feel so inferior to you? Why did you speak in Italian to them?!" I answered firmly, "I did nothing of the kind. Sometimes I forget the dialect. Why must I speak in a tongue that is not myself?" Then he said, "Well, from now on - respect those who come here before you - remember! You are not special, Michelina! You are just a girl in this family!"

Well, I stood firm - not to back down an inch. Then my Aunt Alfonsina stepped in and spoke up for me with fire in her eyes. Oh, boy! She got nose to nose to with my father. "Keep quiet, Peppino! You fell in the mud. The only reason you like those young men is because you feel big with them. They are your slaves. You will not involve this girl with anybody you play cards with. Remember, I told you this!"

At that moment, I felt instantly sorry for my father - he looked terribly humiliated. I also found out then, as well, that he still embraced his habit of playing and losing at cards - a habit that kept him poor but admired by the many souls he lost to. Papa, this sad man, left the room and went right to bed. I felt confused and hurt by it all. My brother, Ralfo, took my hand with a smile and quickly took me out of the apartment. "Where are we going?" "Don't ask any questions," he said. "Just come with me. It's my treat."

I followed Ralfo down the street, and he bought two tickets to my first ever movie theatre. I forgot the argumentative scene at home as soon as the piano player started his arpeggio. I forgot Papa, I forgot anger and I forgot every other ache I might have had. Movies had entered my life. I was lost in this lyrical dance of light. Ralfo just beamed at me all the way through. It all was totally new to me. Never before had I been to a movie. I was in ecstasy!

That moving picture, the first movie I ever saw was called, *Way Down East*. It was made in 1920 with Lillian Gish and directed by D. W. Griffith. I loved every second of it! The movie had projected English title cards which I couldn't read, but the piano kept the mood of each scene and along with the expressions of the actors - I didn't need the words. I actually understood everything that appeared right up there in front of me. The movie was so tragically like a Verdi opera in its story of a desperate unwed girl with child and a poor past struggling to exist. It was a living dream.

After that night, I became a movie fan - a fanatic. Every weekend, my brother and I went, no matter what was playing - everything and anything, we saw. I loved especially the cowboy westerns. Sometimes, we even invited Aunt Alfonsina, too. Tickets were ten-cents - sometimes a quarter. The theatre was always filled with a swirling cloud of cigarette and cigar smoke which made the illumination from the projector like a searchlight beacon to the screen. This atmosphere just added to the mysterious feeling of it all - the telling of the tale - the story. I wanted to be up there with the actors. "I could do this," I thought. "I could act - I could write these stories." But then all the lights came on.

I loved to be with my brother, Ralfo. He was so intelligent and understanding - a wonderful, wonderful human being, always quick with a flashing smile and softly uttered reassurances.

Well, in those first months, I was doing very well in Mr. Pietro's clothing factory. I was nineteen. The hour walk from the North End to Mr. Pietro's clothing factory got shorter and shorter. I made many quick friends, and my English was steadily improving, although I was reluctant to speak a lot of it until I was sure it was properly pronounced and my grammar was correct. "It must be perfect, like my Italian can be," I demanded of myself. I did not give up speaking Italian either - pure Italian I mean. Not because of any pretense as my father claimed, but from pride of myself - just as my Nonno Don Carlos would have wished me to do. His son could go to hell.

I came to discover that my newfound working compare, Vincenzo Motta, was married to an American girl, and it was a very unhappy marriage from the start. Poor fellow, he was so sad that it was affecting his health. Vincenzo was full of nostalgia for Italy, as well - our home village of Pratola Serra. He was constantly homesick. I think in part his sorrow stemmed from the loss of his parents during the course of the great pestilence. Still, he had the best-paying finishing job in the place, a pocket maker on men's jackets, and he pinned, tailored and balanced each and every suit jacket on a form before it went out of the factory. Perfect. He even had another man helping him.

Vincenzo asked Mr. Pietro permission for me to be his second assistant. Mr. Pietro said, "Yes, of course. I am sure that she will learn quickly, of course." Vincenzo taught me well with the patience of a father (a good one). I made pockets on jackets as he did, also the rudiments of design and nuance. This I liked best, even for men's jackets which had little nuance at all. Vincenzo was so proud of me and was pleased with my progress. Every day, at noontime, Vincenzo went out and brought me back a pint of ice cream with different flavors. My co-workers, Antonia and Gianni, would share it with me.

Then one day, Vincenzo's wife ran away. When he came home from work, she was not there - no note - nothing. He got even more sick and didn't bother taking care of himself after that. At work, he coughed continuously. The winter inside and out of the sixth-floor factory didn't help. Still, he worked hard and was the highest paid man in the shop - a good,

good man. He called me, "Commarella" (little comrade). What a gentle-man he was.

A month or so later, Vincenzo died due to tuberculosis - alone and very unhappy - away from our Pratola Serra. Again, to lose a dear friend so quickly to disease. Still, this demon follows me. Will this heavy shadow give me no rest?

I wrote his sister Appia a letter. I tore up many first attempts at it.

"My Dearest, devoted, Appia,

How can I start this letter? How can I end it and have it show the true depth and sorrow in my heart? How can I comfort you my dear friend, where there is no comfort. I can't even comfort myself. I loved

Vincenzo like my own brother - a big brother. Tell me that you will take this terrible blow quietly resigned and with resolve and know that he loved you so very, very much. Please. He told me this many, many times, how much he loved you - his little sister. And in your resignation and strength, please, Appia, will you share a little, just a little bit of that strength with me?

Your sacred heart,

Michelina."

Now the matter of Giacomino Fabbo - my estranged suitor who con-sidered us to be engaged. Yes, Giacomino wrote me many letters, love let-ters full of promise and passion, of undying love. He reminded me of our farewell kiss - the one he placed carefully on my forehead at the train station. None of it moved me. He was so far away, both in distance and in my memory. I answered his letters, a few times, then our correspondence became further and further apart. When his letters slowed to a trickle, I didn't answer. So now I felt completely free. It was good for me not to be losing my precious time. People were dying, and life was moving in all directions and all around me. Time was constantly in my mind - the freedom of it, yet the pressure of it. What little freedom and time I had left. I was not even twenty years of age and still I had so much to catch up to as to what was expected of a girl of my available age, my visage and my circumstance.

So, with the sudden death of Appia's brother, Vincenzo, I felt that I had to leave Mr. Pietro's clothing factory. Why? I needed to breathe. It was too much to follow my compare's job patterns. This, and after four months of factory work, I was tired of it - tired of just assembling men's suit jackets on a production line. Perhaps I should have been more appreciative, but it had all become mindless. Separately, I also was continuing to build my own dresses of my own design and style. I dressed myself well. This didn't help matters any.

Gianni was good company, yes, and a good work partner. We did exactly the same tasks at different stations on the line with sewing and final fittings, and we were both good at it. But Gianni was paid a man's wage of more than fifty dollars a week, while I got only twenty-five dollars a week. I didn't at all think that was fair. I was doing just what he was doing and just as much. I moved quickly up the line because of my ability and my being second assistant with Vincenzo. It didn't matter. I was paid half for the same results. I took my complaint to the two bosses and also with the agent of the union, but my words meant nothing to them. "It is what it is, Michelina," I was told.

Gianni felt for my cause but said nothing for fear they would think him a troublemaker. In every other way, he made my many hours there seem almost tolerable. But, I wanted to do more than to deliver men's suit jackets as a living. I also felt unworthy in some ways because my friend, Vincenzo, had spent so much of his lost life embracing that pursuit. Still, I needed something more my style and I hungered for independence in the place that was America. I could build any clothing I wished to build, I knew this thing, so why not build in a style and elegance of my choosing? A style of an independent woman? I put my mind into the obsession of this thought for nearly four months as I helped to deliver men's suit jackets into the world.

And so, in the spring of 1920, America did something to join and support my headstrong ideas. There was a revolution on the wing, not just of the organization of workers, but also for women. I was not an American citizen yet, no, but I was inspired by what was being talked about and in the air - even in the North End of Boston. The 19th Amendment would be ratified on August 18, 1920, in the U.S. Constitution. It granted American women the right to vote - a right known as "woman suffrage." As an immigrant, naturally I could not vote, but it inspired my resolve, both to someday become an American citizen and to join this revolution of women.

This all happened concisely at the same time of my own true independence. And what better place for me to accomplish this? America!

To the surprise of everyone, and disapproval of some, I resigned my job at Mr. Pietro's men's clothing factory. Gianni begged me not to go when he found out about it. "Oh, no, Lena! You cannot! This will go against me. Who will help me do fitting now? You should give notice - at least one week before you leave!" "I am sorry," I said. "I am not a Carmen!" "What?! I don't understand." I just hugged him and said goodbye. For me, I made my case. No response? No equal pay? Then, no notice. Still, Mr. Pietro, the dear man, was supportive and understanding.

It was on this final walk home from Mr. Pietro's clothing factory, the first day of summer, on a Monday, June 21st, 1920, my first summer in America, that I thought to make a decision. Did I want to stay, or did I want to go back to my village in Italy like Vincenzo yearned to do? Yes. I would stay, not only to stay, but I would somehow bring my siblings and my mother to America as well. It wasn't going to be just up to Papa and Ralfo to decide anymore. I would decide. I would make this decision for my family - and I did. That was the fastest and shortest walk back from the factory that I ever made. My only hindrance was the language of course. "I will ally myself with English - true, meaningful English, good diction; then I will thrive here," I thought, walking hard. This was my first really major decision about me. I would make this choice in my head first and then let my heart direct how I would do it, instead of the other way around. My heart would seal my determination. I would make a plan.

Of course, looking back, I was only nineteen, I had no job, I spoke no English and was not even close to becoming an American citizen yet. But, like stitching pockets in a man's jacket, it didn't matter. I could do this thing.

Forces and events were happening all around that would carry me along like a storm, and I was determined to be part of it. I could feel it in the air.

That day, I finally arrived in America. I declared myself a true suffragette - if only by proxy.

Michelina Pirone, Boston, MA, circa, 1920

Chapter Six

Resettling In

At this date, my father was making horse harnesses for a milk company, Ralfo assisted him as a journeyman. In Boston, Papa had regained his nickname and reputation as "The Golden Needle" of leatherwork. He had a large following, even outside of the North End. But also, Papa was still gambling as I mentioned. At these card sessions, he met and became acquainted with an influential and dynamic persona of the North End named, Franco Chambelli.

Mr. Chambelli was a very prominent man - prominent and one might say a little shady. He even had a reputation for keeping an illegal gambling place in the back of his long narrow tobacco store where, naturally, Papa spent many hours. Mr. Chambelli was both feared and respected. "Chambelli" (as everyone simply called him), cultivated and associated himself with powerful bankers, politicians, and other businessmen, even non-Italians. He had a way about him like my grandfather, Don Carlos Pirone, had, a leader of men, the "Don," the "Padrone." Chambelli was robust, handsome and about 50 years of age - an elegant man of style with his well-trimmed moustache and beard. He was so proud to be a successful Italian in America.

In his short time in Boston, Papa had made many powerful connections in our part of the North End, the Neapolitan section, and Chambelli was his finest catch. Or, maybe because of my father's lack of talent with the cards, it was the other way around. Both were certainly indebted to the other, but for some reason, Chambelli took a special liking to Papa. I think Papa's wide reputation as a gifted Italian artisan influenced him greatly.

Not long after their introduction, Chambelli talked with one of his friends and was able to provide my father with a better job, a job making harnesses for the Coleman Truck and Carriage Company - many more horses - much more lucrative work. Of course, Ralfo was invited to go along with Papa as well. Now Papa's debt to Chambelli tipped the scale toward Chambelli. But there was more still to come.

It was also time to move out of Aunt Alfonzina's large apartment house. Well, among many other of his enterprises, Chambelli owned a four-story apartment house on Prince Street with eight apartments. He made room for us. So, we moved from my aunt's house into one of Chambelli's apartments, four rooms and a bath on the fourth floor.

On the first floor of the building was a doctor's office and Alviti's Photography Studio - they, too, were friends and connections of Chambelli. Automatically, they became our friends as well, especially Mr. Alviti, the photographer. Oh, how proud he was to be a Roman from the Trastevere. Mr. Alviti and his wife had two young nephews living with them who were orphaned, two orphan-victims of the influenza plague in Italy. My brother, my father and I loved these people who lived below us. They would invariably photo-record our family as well.

We had a large kitchen, with two stoves, one coal stove to cook on and one gas stove, which also provided the only heat in the place, but that was enough. A bathroom opened into the kitchen, a large bedroom with two beds for the two men, a separate, smaller bedroom for me - and a living room with a couch that opened out into another bed. It was plenty of room for us Pironi. All thanks to Mr. Chambelli. *[Aside: The networking and early associations formed by Michelina at this time were incredibly important to her. She often described them to me as a reaffirmation of identity not only for herself, but of her newly found friends. In her case, she believed it took a village to raise a village.]*

No sooner than we settled into our new apartment when we received very bad news. Imagine, my dear Aunt Bernadina had died suddenly in her home in the Bronx. "Poor Fortuna," I thought, "Poor Uncle Antonio and the children! What will they do?" My father had to go immediately to New York for the funeral. When he came back, I could see in his face that he was completely drained. There was no reason for it - she was not old or sick. Then, more tragedy occurred. Not less than one month later, Aunt Bernadina's young son, Mikele, died of an aching heart, he just stopped eating without his mother there. The poor boy couldn't function anymore. Nothing they did could help. He just wilted like a flower. So, my father went again to New York for the second funeral. What sorrow for our family. Fortuna was not the type to mother those children nor was her sister, Flora. So, I offered to go there to take care of them all. I was not working. My father said, "What makes you so sure that you could do anything more for them? No, here you stay."

My mother wrote often from Pratola Serra. She was finally happy even though her husband and two oldest children were thousands of miles away. When she wrote, she thanked me again and again. She wrote that she felt guilty for pushing me to America to confront my father. I wondered if the occasion demanded, would she suggest it again? For as good as she was, when it came to preserving the love she had for my father, she would have done anything within her reasoning. I promised her in my return letters that I would secure a plan to bring them all to America - and soon. I know Mother believed me, but I'm also sure she had some doubts.

As for her writing about my ex-suitor and pseudo-fiancé, Giacomino, she said very little. I knew however that her concerns were growing about my marrying. I let these trepidations pass. I knew Giacomino Fabbo was not the one. I felt something was wrong about him. I didn't care. It was never meant to be. But what was meant to be? My belief (and hope) was moving more toward the Greek mythological style where the gods controlled day-to-day events and played with our situations rather than toward the idea of a predestined destiny. Did I believe in God? Yes. Was I destined to be a formally uneducated woman? Just a simple wife and mother? No. A thousand times - No! That is not my destiny. I was repeating myself. I was trying to postpone what I feared was the inevitable. Marriage. But I knew one thing, my chances for success would be better here in America. I knew also that because of our new living situation, my duties now were to include taking care of the needs of my working father and younger brother. Yes, it was custom, but I was reconciled with that. It was a good excuse for me, a diversion and also a static extension of time.

I had been out of work at this point for almost two months - what little money I had disappeared on buying cloth. I spent many hours building a fine wardrobe though. This I could do. Even so, my dear brother

Ralfo supplemented my purse many times. Father provided money for our household living and I took care of everything else during that summer period. All through this time, I kept planning and planning my next move and what it would take to reunite my entire family in America. I had plenty of time to think about it, too, as I stitched. I needed to work again though - but what to do? How to do it?

On the back, written in cursive: "Boston, Sept. 1920. Ralfo, Papa and me."

Instant Compare Cohorts

Another of life's mystery connections happened that answered this question. One spring morning, Mr. Chambelli came over to pay his respects to everyone in his apartment building. It was a Saturday, as I remember, and everyone was home relaxing, except Papa. We were standing about on the front stoop when Chambelli came strolling up Prince Street with this beautiful young girl on his arm. Everyone smiled as they approached. Chambelli was showing off and parading his oldest daughter, Annie, around the neighborhood. He was beaming, and so was she.

Well, Annie and I became instant friends as soon as we greeted. Her Italian was pure and flawless. What could I do other than to reply the same? I'm sure Chambelli enjoyed our puristic exchange of Italian, as well. "Amici!" From then on, Annie Chambelli and I became inseparable compare. She was my age, my style, fair in complexion and of my independent deportment. Had I found another of my rebel paesane girls here in America? Yes, of course I did. Chambelli himself formally introduced us, and that was it. We spent many days after that strolling arm-in-arm in the North End, talking of life, of men as suitors, and, how we were both determined to stay free of fatherly dictates. "Splendid!"

Annie Chambelli had to get ready for a gala dance at the Sons of Italy organization which her father was the President - naturally. Annie was very excited about the ball and invited me to go along with her to her dressmaker's shop on Boston's fashionable Newbury Street. This was the POSH avenue that I first visited with my brother. It was so fine, so cosmopolitan in its flavor.

We walked up and crossed over historic Beacon Hill and down past Boston Commons and through the familiar Public Gardens. It was a lucid July morning. A freshness in the air caused us to rest a spell in the opulent Garden before we advanced toward Newbury Street. It was another good opportunity for us to talk.

Annie had many problems on her mind - like a child, she confided in me fully. Annie was in love. She was in love with the local pharmacist, Frank Battone. She once introduced me to him in his pharmacy store. Well, Battone's doctor father and his snotty mother did not approve of either Annie or the Chambelli family. These people were well-established with prestigious airs. My suspicion was that they didn't approve of Chambelli specifically or his notorious dealings in the North End. Regardless, Annie bore the brunt of this bias. There was so much class prejudice in America, much more I thought than in Italy.

I listened and added my opinion. "If Frank Battone really loves you, he wouldn't listen to his family, Annie. It may just be an excuse to break up with you. Does he see you often?" I asked. "No, no. He avoids me." "I thought so." "Why, Lena?" "Well, when you introduced me to him, I could tell he had his own questions about you," adding, "you are too good, Annie. You never suspect anything. If you love someone, just because you do, right away you think he loves you as well." I went on. "Please dear, do not let your deep emotions spoil your kind, generous heart - love, yes, but not so intensely. Love yourself a little better first." "How?" she asked. "I wouldn't show him so much attention. I would dress every day not just adequate - dress with beautiful things. You have so many beautiful dresses, but they get old in the closet. That is a waste! You know and I know that clothes only get old in the closet - more so than if they were used." "Very well, Lena, I promise that I will put in line nice things of what to wear every day." "Good," I said.

We got up and started walking again toward Newbury Street when Annie stopped me by the arm with a smile and said to me, "Oh, my God, Lena, look what I have on! My housedress and my oldest shoes - and here I am going to a dressmaker who will charge me two hundred dollars for my evening gown!" At first, she laughed, then looking at me, she noticed my own dress of fine cotton and silk pattern. "What you wear now is so beautiful. It fits so well," she said. "I made this myself," I told her. "It cost me about ten dollars for the material." She embraced me saying, "I thank God that he sent you to me. I shall love you forever!" And she did. We kept on walking and laughing, passing displays of flowered offerings at our feet.

Two more blocks from the Public Garden, Annie and I came onto Newbury Street in Boston. With happy conversation, we ambled by fine boutiques, art galleries and stylish hotels. I treated her to some Italian coffee and French croissants at the famed Florian Café with its very elegant and cultured atmosphere. They played soft classical music there on the phonograph and the place always had many young students and artists sitting around tables conversing. It was an easy place for me to be - like a soothing bath.

While we sat there enjoying our cappuccino, I quietly asked Annie, "With Frank Battone, what are you going to do with your heart? Will you continue to listen to it or listen to your mind?" "Oh, him? Don't worry, Lena, I will forget him. I think I will have to. You convinced me that he really doesn't care enough about me. But I don't want to lose my friendship with him - he is so nice." I felt deep sympathy and love for her.

Finally, we arrived at Annie's dressmaker shop aptly called, "The Parisian Dress Shoppe." It was on the second floor of one of the most beautiful buildings on that phenomenal street. We entered through a large, long room past a few sewing machines. When we got to the end, we came to a long table that had a pressing machine on it. Next to this press was a long line of several body forms - so many of them, that each form had a name tag draping the neck. There we came to five girls who were sitting around tables in front of two large windows. They were in the activity of finishing fine gowns - even wedding gowns. Two of them were beading, and the others were doing hand embroidery on silk material - roses around skirts of all kinds. I loved that room - the light - the color - the creative feeling of it.

Annie found the two sisters who owned the shop - their names were Rosa and Agnes. Both were not much older than Annie or me, late-twenties I would guess. They both looked very professional. Later, I learned that they both had advanced schooling of design in Paris. They wasted no time in getting Annie's gown out to be fitted. At that moment, I got the feeling that I'd better step away. I thought Annie might ask me about her gown right then, and I didn't want to interfere. Naturally, I gravitated toward the girls who were the sewing magicians. I quietly watched them and their techniques. Classic. Simple.

A little later, one of the sisters, Agnes, approached me while as I was watching the working girls embroider. She came up and spoke to me in perfect Italian, "Signorina, you are very much attracted to this type of work, am I not right?" I nodded, "Yes." "Signorina Chambelli tells me that you can do these things, too, and that you made what you are wearing - is this true?" "Yes." Then she asked me, "The design as well?" I nodded a "yes" with a polite smile. Annie just then called to me. I went over to her, and Agnes followed, quietly studying my clothes as we went.

Annie formally introduced me to the two sisters, and then she asked me how I liked her new gown. "It is very beautiful!" I responded. "This is how you should look all the time." We all laughed. "This shade of blue goes so well with your blond hair and your skin." Annie beamed as I continued, "And the fitting! Oh, the fitting is so perfect." I turned to Rosa and said, "Madame, you must be a genius." Rosa smiled, thanked me then asked, "Do you speak English?" I answered her in the best, yet broken English that I knew, "Yes, but only a very little bit." "Who is teaching you?" "I am teaching myself English. But, I have only been in America eight months, and I have many expressions to learn yet. And diction of course." This last part I almost choked out. "It is hard for me still, but I will do better later. Now, I am busy doing nothing except straightening out my desires of what I really intend to do here. Decisions are the hardest work for our minds." Rosa and her sister smiled sympathetically at my crude but honest attempt to use what little I knew of the English language. I excused myself to rejoin the seamstresses under the light of the front windows.

When I got there, I was again fascinated by all the colors and quality of the gowns they were making. I started a conversation with the girls - in Italian of course. I was more comfortable with pure Italian in this formal setting, comfortable in that it was really who I was. They all understood my Italian, but when they answered me, they each answered in an amalgamation of half English, half Italian. One of them told me, "We are all born here in America. Our parents speak Italian, but they do not talk like you do. They have different dialects." I answered, "But I love Italian dialects. People who speak them can express themselves better as to what they really feel. It is what they are most comfortable with." I gave them an example of how a Sicilian dialect sounds when a Sicilian says, "I love you." Then how differently a Neapolitan dialect sounds when a Neapolitan says, "I love you." Just then, a young man's voice came booming from behind us in yet another Italian dialect, "I love you too!" Everyone turned and laughed with admiration. His name was Eugenio Mettola.

[Aside: On the back of this painting-styled photo-graph of Michelina, it says only, "1920."]

Chapter Seven

Finally, A Smile from Above

Eugenio Mettola was about twenty-five. He was a slim 5'-8" with dark olive complexion and free movements - almost elastic. He had dark hair, black, black eyes and bright teeth. He was very handsome. I introduced myself to him in Italian of course. "Hello, I am Michelina Pirone." He took my hand and bent down and ceremoniously kissed it saying, "And, I am Eugenio Mettola, at your command." He then dashed off after flashing yet another smile. I watched him as he approached Agnes and gave her a paper bundle that was tied in twine. Then he took his jacket off and sat at one of the pressing machines and began working on a formal coat. "Oh," I thought to myself, "he works here."

Rosa, Agnes, and Annie were still conferring about Annie's gown when I re-approached them. Annie Chambelli ran over to me and had a funny yet happy expression on her face. "Lena," she blurted out almost too loudly, "Agnes and Rosa like you! They are going to ask you if you want to work here!" "What?" "Remember what you told me yesterday? You needed a job, right?" "Oh, yes but Annie, you didn't impose on these two ladies in my favor, did you?" I nervously looked over to where Mettola was working. He had suddenly stopped to listen to what was going on. Rosa came over to us with a smile and said, "No, she didn't impose on us at all. We know by instinct who could work here. This dress that you made and are wearing is very impressive." "Thank you," I said softly in English. "Firstly, our seamstresses must love the work, for it can be complicated, and secondly, they must dress well and must know Italian. You are both, my dear. If you would like to work here, we would love to have you."

I was so glad and yet truly shocked - afraid to show too much emotion. I surely must have been blushing though, judging by the gleeful expression Annie was wearing on her face. I repeated in pure Italian, "Thank you, Madame, for the confidence that I inspired in you. I love this place and if you really want me to work here, then I will, of course, accept your offer with great pleasure." "Yes," "Yes," both sisters answered happily together in English.

So, it came to be. The very next day, I gratefully went to work again. This time for two talented designer-sisters in their elegant little "Parisian Dress Shoppe" in that elegant building on that most elegant of streets in Boston - Newbury Street. God was now smiling on me, yes. I knew this, and I was appreciative.

From the onset, I worked at the dress shop with both a certainty and quiet resolve of my own skills. In my young heart, I knew that I could build anything with scissors, a needle, some cloth and some thread. I could work cotton and silk the way my father and his father could work leather. I was a version of my father's own "Golden Needle" nickname. What applications I was not familiar with, the sisters taught me. I readily learned so much, so eagerly, so soon.

I loved everyone at the Parisian Dress Shoppe. It was no time at all that I was also fitting and making small design suggestions to some of the work that came to us - especially for the elaborate wedding gowns, which I loved to build. Those gowns could have such variety and style. I was so pleased that both of these learned sisters, only a bit older than myself, accepted many of my suggestions and encouraged me to go still further. I thought often as I sewed of how Matzo Mauriello, the Pirone gnome, guided my needle.

As I stitched, Eugenio Mettola kept his ever-vigilant smile in front of me. What a difference from Mr. Pietro's clothing factory for men's suit jackets. I had found my nest! As a consequence, my father and my brother were glad as well. Oh yes, they were glad. But now my thoughts came back to them - my father and my brother. Who were these formidable men in my life? Really. Who were they? I was still very much troubled. How much of me was my father, "Peppino" Pirone, and how much of me was Newbury Street?

I realized then if I was to survive as an indivisible woman in America, I would need collective support. Still, I had not seen my twentieth birthday, but I was ready to succeed.

I never had any doubts about my status or position at the Parisian Dress Shoppe. The assurances of Agnes and Rosa, these two wonderful sisters, were enough for me. They liked me, I loved them, and they liked my work. Unlike the factory, I never had a disturbance either with the girls, my co-workers, with whom I happily stitched away. I made pretty good money too for a young woman. $10.00 per day, $50.00 per week - almost the equal pay amount I had asked for at the factory before quitting when they refused to pay. All that was in the short past now. *[Aside: $50.00 in 1919 had the same buying power as $735.00 in 2018]*.

I spent my money freely on hats, shoes - lots of shoes - and more material for making my own coats and dresses. I bought only the finest of wool, silk and weave. I constructed my own image - my own wardrobe - on my own time. I even had the luxury of sending some good money home to Pratola Serra to my mother and to my brothers and sisters. I was proud. Yes. I did this. Michelina Pirone. I could breathe, freely - for a while.

Chapter Eight

The Courtship "Dance"

Okay, I must reflect and interject something here before I write further about this section. In this time, young women, especially if they were not unattractive, had little chance of doing anything "alone." Nothing at all. It was not a choice for us. Always, I was greeted or approached by men of different ages and from different backgrounds - less so, American men. I think they felt awkward with the language, although some tried their hand at dialectal slang in crude attempts and vague offerings. But Italian men constantly positioned themselves with me to the point of vexation. The part that was unacceptable was that it was acceptable. These annoying fellows were like pigeons, spinning about in circles and cooing as I walked. They came out of nowhere.

I suppose that is why we as girls and young women walked in groups for protection or why, as is custom in Italy, chaperones marched along behind us as part of the procession. One could argue that not much has changed since then, but it has. Sure, young men today still dance about and make funny sounds as they do, but for more primeval reasons. What I reference here is a time when there was only one true objective for swooning men - matrimony. Women knew this and were careful only to respond submissively if they felt likewise. Marriage carried a life sentence with it. There was no other objective for the behaviors of Italian men of that era. How did we think as young girls? Flattered? Yes. Annoyed? Just as much - at least some of us. For me? I was not in the possession of a submissive personality. This phenomenon made all parts of my life - even walking - troublesome. I had no desire to do this dance - this ode to matrimony. None at all. Or so I felt at the time.

So now I had a good job, a decent apartment with my father and brother, and I had many friends, among them a few well-intentioned suitors who were quickly rebuked. All this and I hadn't even been in America for a year! What could possibly disrupt all of this now? Mettola. Eugenio Mettola, the Neapolitan.

As I wrote before, Mettola worked with me at the Parisian Dress Shoppe. He was so very handsome. His manners were of great refinement. He was doing all the tailor pressing and the buying of materials for the shop. On the side, he could paint landscapes beautifully. We had some of his artwork hanging in the shop. Mettola also had a beautiful baritone voice which he often showed off as he worked. He even sang in clubs and sometimes in local concert halls. He had everything a young woman could want in a suitor, especially an Italian woman, for Mettola was the personification of Naples itself. Flamboyant, sensitive and handsome. I liked him very much. In the beginning, I was afraid to admit it perhaps - to myself - that I liked him a great deal. Love? Perhaps a slight infatuation was building over many weeks. And, of course, I think he knew it.

One morning, as we sat embroidering, one of the girls said to me in English, "Lena, last night, I dreamt of you and Mettola walking in Boston Garden together. You both looked so very happy." Some of the other girls chuckled without looking up. "Oh, really?" I said unimpressed. "What kind of flowers were there in the Garden?" That worked. I was afraid the world read my mind. I changed the subject as quickly as I could.

The very next day, I walked to work my usual way - through the Public Garden. Mettola knew the way I took over Beacon Hill and through the Garden. I saw him from afar seated at one of the garden benches with two cups of coffee in his hand - two steaming paper covered cups. I tried to go around that section of the Garden, stopping to admire the beautiful fall flowers. "Lena!" I saw him waving his hands in my direction. I had to go over.

I reached him. Mettola stood erect, smiled and in his distinctive baritone voice formally said, "Buon giorno, Signorina." I answered, "Buon giorno." "Please sit down." He offered me one of the steaming cups saying, "I hope it is still hot." Even through my gloves, I remember nearly burning my fingers. "Yes," I said, "it is hot. Thank you. What a nice thought."

We drank the coffee, quietly admiring what was in front of us. The morning was cool - the air radiant. I told him, "I am very happy to be living in Boston and not in New York. Don't you agree, I mean about Boston?" "Oh, yes, Lena. Boston is a little like Naples." "Yes, how true. I feel the same way," I said. We were talking as if we had all the time in the world - proper and courteous exchanges. I told him that the North End was like the old city of Naples to me. Mettola smiled that smile of his and said, "I think you like Naples." "Yes, I do," I responded. He paused then said, "I hope you like the Neapolitan as well." "Of course," I said quietly, then, "Oh, my! It is getting late!" We left. The shop was only a few blocks away, but we were a little late anyway. Nobody noticed, except maybe my co-workers smiling away as we entered.

So, it began my friendship with this ideal Italian man living in Boston. This Neapolitan with the operatic baritone voice.

Not long after, Gianni Letto, my old co-worker friend at Mr. Pietro's clothing factory, happened to be out one day. He dropped by the shop on Newbury just to see me at lunchtime. Gianni often visited me at my apartment on Prince Street after I left the factory. We were still friends and he knew where I was now working. He was happy for me to be sure.

It was a beautiful day when he dropped by, so Gianni suggested we take our lunch by walking in Boston Garden. From out of nowhere, or so it seemed, Mettola appeared. He asked in an awkward and suspicious way, "Hello there! Is this your brother, Ralfo, Lena?" Chuckling I said, "Oh, no. This is my friend, Gianni Lotto. He is from my village, Pratola Serra. Gianni and I worked together at the men's coat factory. My first friend there." A less threatened expression then washed over Mettola's face - almost apologetic. He half bowed to the man. I formally introduced them. When Gianni went on and on about Pratola Serra, he and Mettola became instant friends. And why not I thought. I was fond of them both.

On my behalf, and without direction, Gianni brought Mettola to his house on Salem Street in the North End where he lived with an older sister. This, of course, was only a few buildings down from my Aunt Alfonsina's house. And, to exchange the brotherly favor, Mettola brought

Gianni to his mother's house in Cambridge outside of Boston. And, after a while, on a cold November Saturday afternoon, they both made a plan to arrive at my house on Prince Street in the North End - anxious to see me. As was habit, however, every late Saturday, my father had a habit of lounging about in nothing but his long-johns. Knowing this, Gianni and Mettola came anyway.

They stopped first at the ground floor of my Aunt Alfonsina's house where there was a bakery of fine pastries and breads. The two men thought to bring me some pastry. When I answered the door, I saw the both of them standing together, sheepishly holding a white bag. I welcomed both Gianni and Mettola that day. It was a surprise visit both to me and to my half-naked father. The pastry was presented, and formalities and introductions were exchanged.

One or two Saturdays soon after, Mettola suddenly appeared again at my house with his mother, a very distinguished looking lady of about fifty-five. I was taken more by surprise on this occasion. I recognized clearly that Mettola was doing the ceremonial courtship dance in front of me and he brought validation with him. There comes that word "validation" again.

I had no choice but to be courteous, but I still guarded myself. Had I encouraged this action from this man, Eugenio Mettola? Well, I certainly did not discourage him either. So, I allowed this dance to continue.

From then on, Mrs. Mettola came practically every Saturday. There was a time that I think I saw her more than she saw her own son. Anyway, Mrs. Mettola and I shopped together for the men in my household. She would tell me, "If I am not at your house by two o'clock, then it means that I cannot come." This proved to be a bit of a problem because Annie Chambelli and I used to shop together on Saturdays too. Saturday was a crucial day for us, if for nothing else but to catch up on each other's lives. I didn't know whom to please. So, Annie and I agreed that we would instead now take walks together after supper on weekdays. We both hurried supper in mid-week just to accommodate Mrs. Mettola's Saturday visits to my house.

Early into our Saturday shopping excursions, I got the whole story. While squeezing melons for freshness, Mrs. Mettola told me of the conditions of her family. She told me that she was a widow and had three sons. Her first-born son was a troublemaker. He ran away with a married woman from the North End. No one knew where they were, perhaps New York or even Italy. "I suppose," she said, "that they are afraid of her husband, that he might kill them. Perhaps my son better not come back so soon, eh?" "Yes," I said, "I could understand that." Mrs. Mettola continued squeezing melons, "Eugenio is the sole supporter of our family now. My other son, the youngest boy, he is twenty but never grew up mentally. He is retarded - simple in the head." "I see," I said, filling a bag with the melons she handed me. "My poor Eugenio has a big burden. I cannot help him very much. Even now, while I am here with you, Eugenio takes his brother for a walk. We never leave him alone. A neighbor takes care of him when I need help. Eugenio is such a good, good boy." "Yes." Mamma Mia, what have I gotten myself into? Are my Saturdays to be forever occupied choosing melons?

Mrs. Mettola could not speak much English, but still, her Neapolitan accent was adorable. She reminded me a little of my grandmother, Giuseppella Fabrizio, the jail keeper's daughter. Mrs. Mettola continued by informing me that she helped her son, Eugenio, by making hats for a hat shop in Boston, "But I work at home," she said. She even boasted about putting a little aside for making her own clothes. Holding her arms up, she demonstrated her basic dress, "Do you like?" "Yes, very nice," I said. "It's a hard life," she lamented. Her husband was an outstanding lawyer in Naples. "He died of consumption. He was sick for a long time and not able to work. All of our money and property vanished. Eugenio was studying singing when his father died. Oh, that beautiful voice of his! He had to stop but couldn't find much to do in Naples. So, he found work helping a tailor. My first son was already in America - here in Boston," she said, "He seldom wrote - never helped us. But when his father died, he sent for us - the three of us. We came here to America only three years ago." On and on, this woman would go. I listened with polite interest but still could not comprehend why she was telling me all of her sad life's story.

She carried on in her Neapolitan dialect as we toted home the groceries to my apartment on Prince Street. "My Eugenio insisted on living in Cambridge. But easily, I could live here in the North End in order to save fare and also for the money we pay in Cambridge for three rooms. We could have four rooms here instead. But Eugenio says it is better to have less room but a better address. Perhaps he is right. But I wish he was a little more democratic, as I am." She rested for a while - obviously to catch her breath.

I suggested that we stop for tea, at which time she started back up again. "My heart aches to see my son so dedicated to his family - to care for his brother who is simple and also for me. He never kept company with any girl. He has to study for his voice, and he also does many other things you know besides working at the Dress Shoppe." I had to interrupt. "You are lucky Mrs. Mettola to have a son like him." "Oh, yes, yes. Thank you. I thank God for that." But I could not help myself from thinking why was this woman going on and on about all of this? I did not have the courage to ask her directly. In retrospect, I probably was afraid to.

Yet another Saturday arrived. It was raining hard, but Mrs. Mettola came just the same. This time, we had tea at my house. My father and brother discretely and eagerly left the house.

Oh, how I remember that day so well, for it strengthened my feeling for Mettola. She told me very directly. "Lena, my son loves you and, believe me, he never was so serious in his life. He loves everything about you. I do, too. I think he is planning to ask your father about marrying you," she said. She felt my shocked emotion and stopped there. I looked at her; then impulsively, she kissed me saying, "My dear, dear child."

Somehow, I felt an anxious note in her voice with that "dear, dear child" part. I patiently waited. I didn't commit myself. I said quietly that I was glad that such a man was in love with me, etc., but left it at that. She continued again, "But you cannot accept his proposal now - you must wait." "What?" I exclaimed incongruently. "Eugenio thinks, before anything, he must first become an American citizen so he could take care of himself better. My other son, Rudolfo, who disappeared, never became a citizen. His mind was forever on this married woman - causing trouble always. It takes time to become a citizen of this country. My son applied, but we are poor. He can't commit himself or sacrifice to anybody in marriage until he becomes a citizen and makes better money and until his brothers are no longer a burden. You should not accept this proposal, Lena. We want you to wait before you become his wife."

"My God," I thought, "this was it!" I could not believe my ears. Mettola's mother wanted me to postpone her son's intentions of marriage but she was the one actually proposing? A comical reversal. That is why he never mentioned marriage to me himself. He was afraid to - afraid of his commitment to his mother. He brought his mother to my house the first time to set up the talk of marriage, but she now works against such a notion. This is a twist that I was not thinking about. There was a big part of me that was stupefied but yet otherwise relieved.

I said very firmly, "I don't blame him at all." "Perhaps I said too much," she said. "Oh, no, Signora Mettola. I love your truth and directness. I understand perfectly and please do not worry, I shall never interfere or encourage your son into any disturbance in your plans for him."

It was still raining very badly. We had more tea and biscuits. I was thinking of so many ways of how to avoid seeing Mettola now. I would not be dutifully waiting to enter the holy kingdom of matrimony. If anything, I was dutifully waiting for something else. Signora Mettola noticed my seriousness and continued, "But Lena, I want you to keep company with my son, please. Do not deprive him of this felicitous feeling. Let him be your friend. Wait, and stay steady with him until you become his wife - until the time is right for everyone before you marry. Marriage would be one more burden for us right now." I said truthfully, "Yes. Of course. I plan to wait, Signora." My mistake was that I did not specify that I would not be waiting for her son to propose marriage. She had just completed that obligation for him herself.

Mettola was very quiet, almost cowardly when I saw him next at the dress shop. I realized only then, that, I being skilled, was making more money than he was. The poor fellow was poor. He gave no outward indication of any problem. But I should have known this. Another reversal. I was earning more than a would-be suitor. Only undying love could survive that kind of dilemma. But love of that magnitude was not yet in my grasp.

Only days later, I was not surprised when Mettola gave notice to Rosa that he was leaving. Our mutual friend, Gianni, had placed him in a better paying job at Mr. Pietro's men's clothing factory - a union job. Perhaps he was embarrassed with his mother's cry of poverty and the dutiful dictates she had set for both our futures. When Mettola left, I was glad for him. I cared for him a lot and knowing his struggling financial conditions, I had great empathy. Was I blind? I only confided with Annie on this question. I again was confused. Why didn't Mettola tell me about his conditions at home? Pride? Why did he start this courtship dance of his in the first place? Why send his mother to ask about marriage? Did he send her?

The shop did not suffer too much in Mettola's absence. Together, Rosa and I worked on pressing dress coats and wedding gowns - another girl pressed everything else. The other things that Mettola did, Agnes took over. She went out, bought the material and cleaned the office, etc. Sometimes she took me with her to shop for material, just for the company.

After Mettola left, I took long thoughtful walks all over Newbury Street until Christmas season came about again. I knew all the galleries of art, and they knew me. I was still only nineteen, but an old woman according to my father. He thought that I would never marry and made it a point often to say so. "Yes, father, someday you will be surprised. I promise you."

Christmastime in Boston always has a way to warm your heart - whether you want it warmed or not.

Then one day, out of the blue sky, came a letter from Giacomino Fabbo - my old suitor from the next-door village of Prata. In it, he wrote of his still undying love for me and of his plans to come in America, to marry me and to return to Italy, together. "Oh, my God," I thought, "again?" More trouble from this man. Will he not ever cease? Giacomino also wrote that his plans included staying and working in New York with his mother's cousin. Oh, boy, that is not good news. I was hoping that something would go wrong with this plan of his - praying that it would. I disposed of the letter.

Just before Christmas, 1920, gifts started to come to me and more cards and letters from Giacomino Fabbo. He boldly announced that he was coming to Boston as soon as he could and take me back to Italy with him. "Dear God, what am I going to do now?" I didn't answer his letters. I became worried. Giacominio even wrote to my father, formally asking for my hand in marriage. My father answered him back saying in his letter, "After so much time of silence between you and my daughter, do not expect any preference. She is promised to somebody else. Accept with dignity the fact that she doesn't love you anymore." Of course, I was not promised to anyone else, but this was a good conspiracy for my father to take. Instinctively, and with some correspondence with Mother, neither of them liked or approved of Giacomino. Maybe Papa's letter of support for me was enough just then. Maybe.

Meanwhile, Back in Pratola Serra.

Nonna got sick in the fall of 1920 - too sick to be alone anymore. Nonna Pirone was forced to sell the Pirone big house and compound along with her attached store. The store that provided so much for the commune was now finally closed for good - the shelves finally bare. Everything, gone. Uncle Francesco was the only son left in Pratola Serra to take care of matters. And he did, as it should have been.

Nonna was brought to Uncle Francesco's house where she had many months of terrible suffering with cancer. They made her as comfortable as they possibly could. She had visitations from all of her family and friends who were in the area. Nonna Pirone had outlived most of them, except for my Nonno Fabrizio. They came from nearby villages to visit with her in her sickbed, and to "pray" their respects. The munificent shopkeeper. Nonna had supplied many of them with their daily lives - things that they had needed for so many years. My worldly Nonna had never ventured anywhere in her long life further than the ruins of Pompeii - our travels together. Her influence, however, was wide, even though she was frugal in footsteps.

My childhood inspiration, my Nonna, died on February 14th, 1921 - two days before my own 20th birthday. Her funeral procession was led by a long line of fancy carriages and service wagons, all pulled by teams of horses wearing lavish Pirone harnesses made by my grandfather, Don Carlos, and his sons. Finally came the black funeral carriage of glass and lacquer that carried Nonna. It had strutting horses that were also graced in Pirone harnesses. They said the sound of their clicking hooves echoed everywhere from the hills. I wish I were there to touch my Nonna's hand one last time. "Mia Bella Nonna."

Tragically also, less than a year later, her second youngest son, my Uncle Francesco, died as well. He had diabetes and a carbuncle inside his neck suddenly ruptured. The toxemia went into his body and poisoned him, just like the stab wound of the harness needle that killed his own father. All the old Pironi of Pratola Serra were now gone.

Uncle Francesco's wife, Filomena, sold everything of her life in Pratola Serra and moved to Venice, where one of her sons was living. She would spend the rest of her own life there - cloistered.

I get ahead of myself a bit. Now this notion of the courtship "dance."

Aunt Bernadina's sudden death in New York happened only a few months before Nonna Pirone died. This was a heavy burden for all of us, especially for my dear Uncle Antonio. He lost his wife, his young son, his mother and his brother all within a year. This poor man was devastated. For many years, he had been sending money for not only his mother and her store but also his brother Costantino's family who died of the influenza. Uncle Antonio was the third of the Pirone sons, yet with that came an acceptance of an unclaimed responsibility. Uncle Antonio sent money to his brother Francesco in Pratola Serra as a down payment to buy an estate for all the Pirone family to have and to live in the future. But Uncle Francesco spent all of that money on their mother's convalescence when she moved in with him.

Uncle Antonio was spiritually drained. This good, generous man thought only of his new business and of what was left of his family in the Bronx. So, soon after Nonna's death, Uncle Antonio wrote an urgent letter to my mother in Pratola Serra. He asked Mother for a favor in this letter: "'Please, Angelina,'" he wrote, "help me to find a wife from Pratola Serra? I trust no one else but you to do this. Please do what you can for me. I need a wife."

Uncle Antonio was now in the business of buying and distributing wholesale grapes. It required him and Fortuna to go to California often. In just one year of this speculation business, he had made lots of money. He was able to buy a big house in a better section of the Bronx for himself and all of his children. Now, they needed help; the children needed more care. Fortuna was traveling with him doing bookkeeping chores and had no time to control four demanding siblings.

So, after Nonna's death, Mother got a letter and set out with her duty to find a proper new wife for my Uncle Antonio in New York.

In Prata, the next village across the valley from Pratola Serra, the village of the Pisano and Giacomino Fabbo, she found a beautiful woman through a compare friend of hers. The woman's name was Marietta. I do not remember her family maiden name, for it was not to last long anyway.

Marietta was an old maid of forty-five, who had been jilted in courtship by her gigolo boyfriend when she was only eighteen. He had taken her virginity, but no child was to become of it. Still, there was a big scandal between families, and all of Prata seemed to have been embroiled in this everlasting betrayal.

Because of her undying love of this man, Marietta never thought of marriage but instead resigned herself to live alone the rest of her life. This submission was not good enough for her father, however. Dishonored and ashamed, he shot and badly wounded the young fellow. Marietta's lover survived, but he never wanted to fulfill his obligation to marry the beautiful Marietta, who had surrendered her honor to him. She carried this weight with her for years. Wherever she went in Prata, she was given the deference of respect.

Marietta's family, like the Pisano family of Prata, was one of the outstanding of that commune. She was always thought of as a poor victim of this local rogue who later married a much richer girl. Well, I think that the pity and sympathy my mother always felt for jilted young girls made her think of Marietta when she had to choose a wife for her brother-in-law, Uncle Antonio.

One day, Mother, along with my other widowed aunt, Peppina, went to visit this woman named Marietta in Prata. She greeted them patiently, having heard of their mission in advance. Mother and Aunt Peppina gracefully told Marietta about their brother-in-law, Antonio Pirone in America. They brought with them his picture and explained in detail to her his conditions and situations. "You will make a good wife for him, Marietta." "We would be pleased and honored if you will accept him."

Mother had an opportunity now to do a good deed. She went on, "The children of Antonio are left alone. Besides, why stay here all alone by yourself, now that all your brothers and sisters are married and far away from Prata? Our brother-in-law, Antonio, is a wealthy man with nice children and is very well-respected. Here! Look at this wonderful photograph of him. See?"

Marietta was thinking hard, I'm sure. Alone? Yes, but she had enough property left to her to be comfortable all the rest of her life. "But why be alone?" she must have thought. America has always attracted the paesani in one form or another, and she was attracted too.

Marietta accepted the offer to marry my Uncle Antonio's picture.

Marietta was then forty-five as I mentioned, tall and beautiful. Soon, after two months, she found herself on a boat sailing to America - not in steerage class of course, first-class. Uncle Antonio had arranged everything properly for his unseen bride-to-be.

Marietta came; they got married.

My Uncle Antonio right away gave Marietta a beautiful wedding. I wondered many times, knowing her, how this tall beautiful woman felt when she first saw my uncle - a rather fat, short and older man - much older than she. How did she feel when she found all those children at home? I think I would have died if I ever had to be in her place. Understandably, it turned out to be a challenging marriage.

For the Italians, early on, America had almost a dangerous attraction of security for them, a destination of easy harvest just for the taking. During that time, anyone in need of money, or who suffered loneliness, or needed relevance in their lives - any little excuse or half invitation, they would readily come to America. Italy was no help in its governance of her people either. The First Great War had dissolved Italy's resources and its influence in the world. Where could all these needs of the people be supplied easily and freely? America.

So, marriages between people who never met continued, not only between families and villages - but also between continents.

Chapter Nine

Destinies Converge

Another event of great importance happened to me during the Christmas holidays of 1920.

It all started with meeting a compare and associate of Chambelli's. He was a family doctor, and his name was "Dottore (Doctor) De Rosa." But his soon-to-be nickname in the North End was, "Pulcinella" - a comical name really. The theatrical character, Pulcinella, was a court jester with big baggy white pants, a black dour face mask, and a long, hooked nose. This fit our Dottore De Rosa's image exactly. *[Aside: Different references confirm that the fictitious character, "Pulcinella," was a buffoon/mime of 17th century theater who either played dumb, though he was very much aware of the situation, or acted as though he was the most intelligent and competent of anyone around, though he was woefully ignorant.]*

Dottore De Rosa came over from Naples in the summer of 1920 to America to make his fortune. That was his only plan - to make cash money and leave. He intended America to be his personal bank account - or so he thought. This doctor wanted to use every ounce of his effort to secure as much money as he could, as soon as he could, so that he could go back with it to Italy. Naturally, Dottore De Rosa gravitated and found a collaborator in this pursuit with the support of the notorious Chambelli. But, Chambelli had other plans for that money, as I will explain.

Dottore "Pulcinella" De Rosa wanted all this money, or so it was believed in order to return home to Naples and to be married to a Florentine Contessa there who demanded from him a palace and servants, etc. This little doctor soon became a poor paesano of Chambelli's - one of his minions.

Dottore De Rosa had been in the Great War before he came over from Naples. He just wanted to seek his fortune and to provide his own form of dowry for this Contessa. When he got to America, to Boston, the Pulcinella-Dottore had the support of an older brother who was a friend of a friend of Chambelli. Capisci? (understand?). So, Dottore De Rosa was to become an integral part of the Chambelli's larger "family."

Chambelli gathered all his charm, and he profusely bestowed it upon this doctor, as if he came down from heaven. Now Chambelli's big plan, I found out, involved his daughter and my dear friend, Annie Chambelli. Chambelli had in his mind a secret desire to marry Annie to Dr. "Pulcinella" De Rosa before he could run back to Italy with his new-found fortune. This way, Chambelli could advance his family's financial position in the competitive North End and still keep his daughter nearby. "Perfetto." And also, I think, he wanted to convince Dottore De Rosa that life would be much better for him if he stayed in Boston.

Of course, all the Napolitano paesani in the North End called upon and wanted the services of the new doctor who came from their region. "Oh, yes, he is just what we need! Bravo!" They loved him. He had them in his hand, and he well knew this.

Chambelli pushed out the other doctor who occupied the office on the street floor of our apartment building and the Pulcinella-Dottore De Rosa moved in right away. He used the office space for his own habitation as well; he slept in the back room. Dottore De Rosa also took most of his meals from then on with his new friend, Chambelli, at Chambelli's expense. Very frugal fellow, eh?

Chambelli also convinced Dottore De Rosa that in order to maintain his new office and practice, he would need some good help to do so, and at a good rate of course. "Dottore, I want you to consider my daughter, Annie, to do these tasks for you. She is experienced with doing small business, and she, of course, knows every one of your new patients by their first names. What do you say? Good idea, no?" How could the doctor not accept such a generous offer of support and sound reason?

Poor Annie - she became Dottore De Rosa's secretary and assistant. She had no choice in the matter. She even knew why her father secretly arranged this employment and yet did not object. She would work for the Pulcinella De Rosa - only her - alone. She made the appointments, cleaned the office, took care of the cash. She was forever around De Rosa. At least it gave her a chance to forget Frank Battone the pharmacist, thank heavens!

The doctor was so stingy, even his pennies were counted. All of his money, the paper bills, he had Annie iron them flat and then she gladly ran to the bank with his neat bundle, every week on Monday. Monday for him was bank day. I never knew anybody who was so mercenary. This situation went on and on until Christmas season arrived.

Chambelli's Christmas Party

"The" North End, Boston, Christmas, 1920

The Chambelli's

Christmas in the North End of Boston for me, my second Christmas, 1920, was my favorite Christmas for many reasons and for many, many, years after. I was free from most of the pressures to resettle and of immigration. I was working in a wonderful creative job and environment on a fashionable cosmopolitan street in Boston. I finally had quiet peace and freedom from incessant suitors. And, I felt I had a little time left to enjoy my own freedom, whatever that freedom might be.

Christmas that year in the North End is forever in my mind. All the sights, sounds and smells of Italy and America melded together for me in one place. Hanging Christmas banners spanned every street. As I walked, I took in everything. I reveled in the smells of open bakery doors, the buzzing of all the paesani running about with colorful packages and happy children alongside. On Salem Street, I walked passed butcher shop windows which were hanging full of cleaned birds, rabbits, sides of beef, lamb and pork - all ready for the table. The fish market on the corner that offered lobsters and live eels, swimming in stone tubs underneath hanging sheets of Baccalà (salt cod) strategically placed at the sidewalk entrance. Then there were the busy produce markets with their olives in oak barrels, hanging salami, dried herbs and aging orbits of aromatic cheese. Everywhere, was the sweet smell of wet sawdust on the marketplace floor - in every store. I remember the service wagons that passed by and how big flakes of snow fell and melted on the steaming haunches of the heavy old horses - the "clop, clop" of their hooves. This, plus Christmastime! It was like being in old Naples. All these images and the aromas of roasting coffee and sweet chestnuts spun around in my head until I was lost in the dizziness of it all.

There were many more types of Italians and Jews there in 1920, spread all over the North End, each celebrating Christmas in their own way - but truly celebrating. It was just the time to celebrate. The Jews celebrated Christmas too and their own religion at the same time. On the west side of the North End, Greeks had their settlement. There too, they cele-brated Christmas with Greek traditions and ardor. Everyone in the North End that season was friendly, charitable - all having a good time together like a colony of mixed-up paesani.

I was on a corner of Prince Street when a call came out to me, "Lena! Here! Lena!" It was Annie making her way up that street with bundles of her own under her arm. "Hello! Lena!" We joined arm-in-arm and together pushed through the big snowflakes ourselves - unafraid of fail-ure. "Come up to my house, Lena. I want you to meet my mother and my brother and sisters. We are planning a Chambelli Christmas party and you must help me." "I am invited?" "Of course, you are! Don't be silly. You are my special guest - my comare!" "Wonderful," I laughed. "Let's go!"

We crossed several streets to our destination - another Chambelli apartment building.

Well, we went upstairs to their apartment house overlooking all of the main street, Hanover Street. We climbed four stories until we got to their main door. Here, I must say something about most of the rich apartment houses of the Italian North End at that time; they were spacious, many almost palatial. These apartments, like my Aunt Alfonsina's, had bigger spaces in them than most full houses did back in Italy. They had four, sometimes five bedrooms, a dining room, a separate parlor and a full sit-ting kitchen. Succulent plants of all descriptions framed the windows and there was a perpetual retention of marina sauce or of roasted peppers in the air - that, mixed in with a thin veil of bleach.

Once inside, I met Mrs. Chambelli, a beautiful but over-dressed woman. She was rather plump and short with heavy legs. She was very nice though and down to earth, not like Chambelli at all. It was obvious that she was Chambelli's pride and joy however - his idol. To start with, the woman was a perfect cook. She was already assembling Christmas delicacies in their kitchen. I got the feeling that she liked me well enough, but after knowing her for some time, I do not think she liked anybody else really. She had not one close friend, but she was a good wife. What else mattered? She knew just how to please Chambelli. This ability made her a very wise woman indeed!

In the apartment, I met also Annie's brother and two sisters. I came to know them all well. Annie's younger sister was named Lydia (twelve). She would become my godchild in confirmation just two months later. In this case, there was no need to again climb Monte Vergine. For this I was grateful. Lydia was a perfect mixture of Chambelli and his wife. The girl was small for her age, stout, but alert, intelligent and studious. She was not so musical however, like her sister Annie. There was another older sister, whose name escapes me for a reason. This girl (about twenty-three) was just a stranger even among her own family, it seemed. She was stubborn and a constant complainer. The one detail I do remember most about her was that she wanted to marry a milkman to the horror of Chambelli. "What?! Marry a simple man? A milkman? Impossible! The answer is no, absolutely not!" There was also a son, Fabio, Chambelli's joy and expectant heir. Too much expectation for Fabio I guess because it all went against this simple but nice boy. Later in life, Chambelli's son had lots of involvements with a bad group - lots of trouble with the authorities and other parties. No one really talked openly about it - especially not Chambelli himself.

Chambelli arrived home a short time after and everyone in his family went hush. I never really ever spoke directly to this man - mostly only I listened of course. When he saw me, Chambelli made a big deal about me being there. "Michelina Pirone! How wonderful to see you, my child!" He held up one long spring of my curls and said to me in pure Italian, "What a beautiful paesana you are! What a fine example." I thanked him in pure Italian as well - without blushing. Chambelli's approval came as a quiet delight to Annie and also to her mother. He was first and always a proud Italian.

Chambelli sat in his special chair, crossed his big arms over his robust chest and smiling asked me, "So, how do you like America so far? Does it suit you? What do you think of this place, eh?" He was testing me, exploring my mind, I could tell. I thought carefully before answering. He had a tremendous presence about him, but I was not nervous. "I really can't say how much I like it here or not until I see the rest of America. I assume there is much more of it to see outside of the North End, no?" Chambelli boomed out another laugh. "Well," he said, "I love your manner. You remind me so much of where we come from." "Thank you, Sir, I am honored."

Annie then told her father that I was to help her plan the Christmas party. "Wonderful! The best one yet I think. Many guests. Right, Mamma?" Mrs. Chambelli only nodded. "I shall invite your boss, Dottore De Rosa, Annie, so you can introduce him to Michelina." Annie just stared at me without blinking. I know what she was thinking - we were comare after all.

After a nice visit, it was getting late. I told the Chambellis that I had to go and that I was sure that my father was waiting for me at home or looking for me at the Social Club. Annie and Chambelli both brought me downstairs to the street. There, we found my father at the front door - hat in hand - waiting. He wouldn't come up nor would he knock on Chambelli's door - it just was not done. Someone had, in fact, told Papa that they saw Annie take me upstairs to meet her family, so he waited all that time. And now I come down with Annie and Chambelli in happy conversation. My father stood very erect when he greeted the three of us.

There was a bit of posturing between the two men at first, but my father quickly deferred. Papa told Chambelli that he had heard his latest speech as president of the order, Sons of Italy's organization. And then, in the most proper and puristic Italian, my father congratulated him, adding that Chambelli was doing lots of good work uniting the Italians of Boston, promoting respect and fighting the discrimination that existed in Boston against the Italian people. I couldn't help but smile as my father rattled on and on with not a hint of dialect. I thought, "Pure Italian suits you well, Papa, when it finally suits you, eh?"

Chambelli was holding Papa's hand in his own as he was being complimented by my father. He embraced him. "I thank you, Mr. Pirone."

Then added with emphasis, "Please, next Sunday at two PM, I am giving a Christmas dinner and then a party after at my house for a few of my friends. Will you come to both with your daughter and your son - please? To dinner as well." My father readily accepted. "Good night, Mr. Chambelli." - again perfect diction. "Good night, Mr. Pirone, and to you, Michelina. You are a wonderful girl - a delight. Good night." Annie was so happy. She walked us to the corner. We hugged each other good night.

Ah, what a night. My father was smiling from ear to ear as the snow kept falling hard.

Then came the party - the Chambelli Christmas party that everyone was invited to - just a few dozen of Chambelli's closest friends.

The Party

I had made myself a very special dress and coat just for an occasion such as this. It was a style like a bohemian dancer would wear which I thought suited me well. Fun. Festive. I wanted the look of an artistic gypsy, a finely dressed gypsy. I designed this dress and blouse like a character in my wonderful cinema that I loved so much. In my design, I considered how I loved the free-spirited gypsies of Italy or Hungary and did not wither at the comparison. I was so happy to attend this Christmas party wearing something of my own design and making.

Chambelli had a reputation of doing many things and having wonderful social parties was one of the good ones. He loved to invite people to frequent dinner banquets held in his spacious and luxurious apartment house. This Christmas party was no exception.

Annie asked me to help decorate the main parlor with her and also to help organize the dining room for food tables and seating. It looked wonderful, in a style suited for both an American Christmas, with a decorated Christmas tree in one corner, and a traditional Italian Baroque Crèche and Nativity scene in another. The Crèche occupied one large heavily draped table all by itself which had many elaborate hand-carved figurines in it, all dressed in Renaissance Italian costumes. Even the little Jesus in his manger looked pleased with himself.

Annie and I made sure that the parlor arrangement featured the grand piano so that we could perform a recital together as we had practiced. We planned to sing some duets and also some traditional Italian songs of Christmastime. It was not uncommon for friends to perform at parties this way - a recital of sorts. We had practiced hard beforehand.

I couldn't wait for this Sunday to arrive. I put on my festive Gypsy-styled pleated dress, silk head-scarf, and best wool overcoat. Together, I walked arm-in-arm with Papa and Ralfo over to Chambelli's Sunday Christmas dinner and party. We sang the entire way, to many well-wishers.

At dinner, before eating, we met many people, one of them an august, old gentleman named, "Don" Filippo Assanti. He was tall, lean and looked well-scrubbed. Every hair on his head was neatly accounted for. Don Filippo was venerated by Chambelli, to be sure, and saw to his every comfort. I asked no questions of their association as Don Filippo spoke with only the hint of an ancient Neapolitan dialect. Don Filippo had delicate, waxy hands, the kind of hands that had never seen manual labor. He asked Chambelli for permission to change his seat at the table so that he could sit next to me. "Oh, how nice," I said. "Yes, of course, Maestro," boomed Chambelli.

I remember this Christmas dinner party as if it were yesterday. There must have been thirty people at Chambelli's long table, all speaking various forms of Italian dialect - but mostly Neapolitan. Don Filippo and I talked about lots of things together: about the Great War (WWI), the terms demanded of the Kaiser, librettos of opera, the influenza pestilence and its misery, etc. During these discussions, there came to us two courses of antipasti, wine, minestrone soup, pasta (three kinds with meat sauce), at least four roasted chickens, wine, two legs of lamb, roasted potatoes, sautéed greens in oil and garlic, wine, mixed salad, fresh fruit and several different cheeses for dessert, along with strong Italian coffee and finally, Mrs. Chambelli's ricotta pie, biscotti and port wine. Chambelli festivated like the noblest Romans he admired.

The dinner seemed to fly by even though I know it went on for hours. This was one Italian tradition, the long Sunday afternoon dinner, that I was glad is still observed in America.

After this very perfect dinner, Annie and her two sisters cleaned off the table. This made for lots of room, for the table had been extended out into the parlor to accommodate all the guests. Annie also helped to wash the dishes. She wanted me to stay with her in the kitchen, but not to do anything. At this point, as custom dictated, Mrs. Chambelli went to her room to rest leaving her daughters to clean. "Good order," I thought. I loved this system for doing things. Then, when everything was done, the kitchen organized, Annie changed her own dress, and Mrs. Chambelli came out of her chambers. More cordials were then served and after a while, conversation started again in earnest with black demitasse coffee and anisette.

People now kept coming and coming to Chambelli's door.

More people came knocking who did not attend the dinner part of Chambelli's Christmas party. He was giving his party in stages. Paesani came in and out. "I see," I said to Annie. "Your father is a man of planning - of staging things." "Yes, he has many friends he needs to see," she said. "Now comes act two of this opera, eh?" We both laughed at the continuing knocks at the door.

Annie went over and answered one knock. In came Dottore "Pulcinella" De Rosa who could not attend the dinner part. The doctor was accompanied by two tall, handsome and distinguished looking men. "Hello, Annie. I am late. I am sorry. Your father is here, yes?" "Yes, Dottore." "I brought with me two more paesani friends - patients. They know your father from the Sons of Italy." "Yes, come in, Sirs - please."

One of these men looked very familiar to me from a distance, but I could not be sure who he was. I kept up my conversation with the venerable Don Filippo as Annie took everyone's coat and pulled me over to the piano. The room was not yet hushed until Annie sat at the piano and Chambelli cleared his throat loudly. He then boomed an announcement that the recital was about to begin. All the paesani, drinks and small pastries in hand, entered the large parlor where the grand piano waited patiently for everyone to enter.

Annie looked very nice. She sat at the piano and sang - her voice was very cultivated and beautiful - a contralto. She sang folk songs and operatic arias. One of the arias was *"Tosca's, Vissi d'Arte,"* ("I Lived for Art") by Puccini. I think my brother Ralfo was in love. He just wore a dreamy smile on his face - the older woman problem again. I was seated near to Annie at the piano. I too was smitten by her singing. I honestly felt I had found a gem of a friend.

Mr. Chambelli then asked me, "Michelina, sing something too. Please. Did you ever learn any paesani songs in Italy?" "Yes," I said. "Can you sing, *'Oi, Marie, Oi, Marie?'*" "Yes, yes, of course." He asked Annie to accompany me on the piano. So, I sang, *"Oi, Marie."* Then I sang the latest song in Italy. I had learned it just before I came to America. It was called, *"San Tornate a Fiorire le Rose."* And finally, as we had practiced, Annie and I sat together and did many Christmas songs of our region - one now-famous called, *"Tu Scendi Dalle Stelle."* As we sang this, I noticed out of the corner of my eye that the Pulcinella-Dottore De Rosa was inching closer to us with his two tall friends.

Everyone liked my singing as well as Annie's who accompanied me as if we had practiced those songs for days - which of course we had. I was so pleased that they all liked us. Even my father beamed encouragements.

The dinner party and recital ended all too soon for me. I agreed to assist and to accompany Don Filippo down the four flights of stairs to the street level - arm-in-arm, he was beaming all the way down. Don Filippo was going home with his stomach and his heart filled with the season.

Halfway down the stairs, Don Filippo Assanti spoke, asking, "Your voice, Signorina, is beautiful. It has been trained, I can tell." I quietly answered that I sang for many years in the girl's church choir of our village back home. I smiled, thinking to myself that I had been basically kicked out from that church for speaking my mind and for my choice to start a book club for girls. We both smiled to ourselves all the way down.

At the landing entranceway, Don Filippo took my hand to say goodbye, and added, "Michelina. Did you not notice those two tall men looking at you as you sang?" "Only slightly," I said, "why?" "One of them is a State Senator of Massachusetts who helps Chambelli with his Italian cause and the other is the Senator's best friend - a successful barber from

Lynn." I waited patiently as Don Filippo now took both my hands. "I think this barber friend of De Rosa's came to see you specifically." "Me?" "Yes. I think he used his connections with De Rosa and the Senator to come today. He kept staring at you as you sang. He could not take his eyes from you. Did you not notice? I think he loves you." "What!? How do you know this, Don Filippo?" Don Filippo responded with an all-knowing smile. "Who is this man? Which one is which?" I asked. Don Filippo answered me with a sagacious look, "Go upstairs now, my child. Christmastime gives us many gifts, eh? Many blessings. Bless you."

After Don Filippo left, I was almost afraid to climb back up those four flight of stairs.

When I got back inside, I saw the two tall men still standing and chatting with the "Pulcinella" De Rosa as I went to find Annie. "Which one was Don Filippo referring too?" I thought. They were both well over six feet tall - almost equal in height. I decided to ignore this fantasy and I followed Annie into the kitchen. "Annie. You must help me."

I told her in confidence of my conversation with Don Filippo in the foyer of the building. "Which of these men do you think he was talking about? They are both tall. One is a Senator or something, and the other is a barber. But they are men!" "I know them both. They are patients of the Dottore, and they follow my father from the Sons of Italy." "But Don Filippo said the barber from Lynn came here to see me - I don't know any barber from Lynn." But before she could say more, in came one of the two men - the barber.

Annie smiled and excused herself leaving me alone with this tall "man." Yes, he was a man - not a boy. He had to be several years older than me, maybe by a dozen years. How many I couldn't tell. I just looked at him curiously as he walked up to me with a calm gentlemanly smile. "God. He does look so familiar," I thought. "Who is he?"

In pure Italian, he spoke to me.

"Signorina, Michelina? You know, your name has a rhyme to it?" I did not respond. He continued, "Do you believe in coincidences?" The expression on my face did not give my answer away, but I was a little worried at this question. "Oh, boy," I thought. I let him continue still more. He took my hand and slightly bowed with a smile, proclaiming, "I am

239

Luigi Pisano - You know my youngest sister, I am sure, Amaila Pisano - and also my baby brother Rezziero - 'Richie.'"

I was stunned and happy at the same time. "Oh, my God! No!" Another meeting of coincidences. They kept coming. "But do you remember 'me,' Signorina?" "No," I said in an easier way. He told me. "I was in your Nonna's store, in Pratola Serra many years ago, buying bullets for my bird gun with a priest - a friend of mine. You were just little then. You tried to take my rifle from me so I could not shoot birds! I held you up high to stop you. Do you remember this?" I blushed, "That was you!?" I said at the thought. "Yes. And I must tell you, that you have grown up very well since then. I don't think I would try that same thing again," he laughed.

I happily said, "Yes, of course! I remember!" and that I knew his brother and his sister very, very well. Amalia was my dearest friend back in Pratola Serra and also his brother Rezziero. "You look like your father," I said joking. Just then, Annie returned, but this time with the tall State Senator. He name was Anthony Garofano. He stated his pleasantries and then hastened Mr. Pisano. "Come, Luigi, or we will miss the boat back to Lynn." Both men left, with Luigi Pisano literally backing out of the kitchen with his hat and coat in hand and a big smile on his face. "Later perhaps," he said as he left with his friend. *[Aside: This first encounter with Luigi Pisano was not as coincidental as it seems. Even though the migration from Italy was large before, during and just after WWI, immigrants not only tended to resettle into dialectal pockets, they also had a propensity to resettle by regional villages as well. But in Luigi's case, it became family knowledge later on that the tall barber from Lynn, Massachusetts made a special trip to seek out meeting Michelina Fabrizio Pirone first-hand.]*

Annie could not wait to question me on this new coincidental story that was unfolding. I told her everything - of the Pisano family - Amalia being the brightest of our girl's book club and how her younger brother Rezziero was the "matchmaker" with Giacomino Fabbo and me. They were all from my village, yes, Pratola Serra, but they were also all from Prata, the commune across the alpine valley. I told Annie, "But if Don Filippo is correct, I think this man will return again - but he is an older man, Annie."

Annie became quiet. She leaned against the sink and told me, "There is a reason he wears all black, Lena - Luigi Pisano. He's a widower." "What do you mean?" I said very concerned. "It's a sad story. A few months ago, Luigi Pisano lost his wife - she died." "How?" "In childbirth, Lena. Both the mother and the baby died. There were no other children." I had no words. Annie continued, "You must be careful of this man and his intentions and feelings right now. You are much younger than he and not as advanced in the vulnerabilities of life."

I did not wish to hear anything further about Luigi Pisano. It was a sad story, yes, and I did not want to add to that narrative in any way. Still - there was something mysteriously dark and wonderful looking about this tall quiet barber from Lynn with his melancholy eyes. Mature but eloquent. I would also describe him as "cinematic," although that is not a description I would have used at that time - only now.

After that Christmas party, I only occasionally saw Luigi Pisano on Sundays or a Monday, downstairs, as I passed the office where Dottore De Rosa, the "Pulcinella," also lived. Louis Pisano was one of Pulcinella's regular patients. At those passing's, Mr. Pisano and I would exchange pleasantries. I would ask if he heard from his sister Amalia or brother, Reggerio, and he would simply nod "yes" and smile. As I left, he would always pause and follow me with those quiet eyes of his. I did the best I could to let that pass as well.

Luigi Pisano, 1920, aged thirty-four

Michelina in her Christmas "Gypsy" creation, Christmas, 1920 - 19 years of age.

*A portrait of Luigi Pisano - both circa Christmas, 1920 –
35 years of age.*

Chapter Ten

"To Be or Not to Be"

During the winter of 1921, Annie Chambelli and I would take the trolley and go at least twice a month to the exhibits at Boston's Museum of Fine Arts and also to the house of Isabella Stewart Gardner. The Gardner Museum was a museum modeled on the Renaissance palaces of Venice that Mrs. Gardener designed, drawing particular inspiration from the Venetian Palazzo Barbaro. She even brought pieces of a Venetian palace from Italy to incorporate into her home. Her museum of old masterpieces was like walking back in time for me and deeply reaffirmed my heart and my own Italian heritage. It challenged my dreams hard. Each museum kept Annie and me busy, both in thought and conversations.

One of those Sundays, Annie and I went to see Picasso's exhibition at the Museum of Fine Arts. Somehow, I didn't understand Picasso. It was to me like he couldn't make up his mind as to what direction to move his brush. He would start one way - stop - turn around, stop, and then go again with another color. Why? Picasso had me thinking.

We stayed for a long time in the Jean-François Millet room and in the Impressionist room. I had lots to learn. As we visited these new artists, Annie, of course, would often speak of her dilemma with love and of life. She was often discussing her father's plans for her to marry Dottore De Rosa and how she still had secret hopes of being together with the pharmacist, Frank Battone. I wanted to discuss, of course, what was happening in Picasso's head. "Lena. I've made up my mind. I will marry Dottore De Rosa if he asks me, but I still love Frank Battone." I stopped her quickly, "But you don't love the Pulcinella-Dottore, and he thinks only of ironing his paper money and returning to his Contessa - if there really is a Contessa. And Frank Battone makes no intentions toward you, and his snooty mother dislikes your family. That cannot work when the mother poisons her son's mind against you." We sat a long time in front of Van

Gough; "The Postman." After a thoughtful pause she said, "Perhaps you are right, Lena. You always are."

Now it was my turn for wishes. In front of this great troubled painter, Van Gogh, I told of my secret wish. I quietly told Annie of my own crazy dreams - how I did not want to marry but only wanted to advance my education - maybe even go back to Italy to a college or university and study art and music. "Really! Of course, you should," she said. "But that is only a dream for me, Annie. It could never happen," I told her. She turned to me, "Don't be silly. You can do this. I know even of a university of classics in Roma for women where I almost went just for what you describe. It is run by nuns who concentrate on doing the Arts for women - piano, painting, writing - everything. And the cost is only five thousand dollars for five years. I can help you apply to this school." "Oh, my God! Really? But I am not a good Catholic, Annie. I do not get along with nuns very much. I could not follow their order or codes. I would only be interested in the studies." "That is what they teach and also how to teach these subjects to others. You will come from there a school teacher, an artist - or maybe even a writer as you planned before. You told all these fellows to wait, yes? So, let them wait. Tell them Annie Chambelli said so." At this we both laughed - at everything in life.

We got up from our bench, said our goodbyes to Van Gogh, and continued down a narrow corridor of masterpieces. It was a good place to think about Annie's suggestion. We kept the conversation going. "Five thousand dollars? A thousand per year? I could not afford that." "But your father could do this - maybe just to get rid of your pestering him constantly." We laughed again at the thought. "If you like, Lena, later I will give you the brochure they sent to me."

So, my friend, Annie Chambelli, got the image of a college back in Roma put securely into my head. It was like a Picasso brush stroke that stayed in front of my eyes for days - going back and forth and changing color - then shooting off in the opposite direction.

I came out from the museum with two postcards, the first of my wide collection over the years. One by Monet and the other of Renoir. Every day, I paid homage to these two artists by looking at the cards continuously, remembering what I saw. It's impossible to describe how much these works of art affected me. It is still so, even now. I felt as if another door in my mind had just been opened, and into it came interminable images - an immensity of possible fields. The reality of the need to get busy and do something with myself made me again anxious. Thinking. I 'must' learn how to explore my mind, until I knew all of my potentials - or even if I had any.

To compound the turmoil in my mind, the first months of 1921 brought with it additional suitors - many out of nowhere. Perhaps it was the cold. Perhaps the dark - who knows. Anyway, a friend of a distant cousin of my Aunt Alfonsina came home with my father one Saturday afternoon to join us for dinner. He came unannounced with Papa. I had never met him. Papa had expectations for this one. Why not? Nothing. "No, thank you."

Then, I was shopping in the North End one day when I met my old friend, Gianni Lotto. He was off from the coat factory. He asked me very politely if we could talk? "Yes, of course," I said. He took the bundle from my hands, and we went to my house. Papa was of course home, but went to his room, mumbling something to himself. He was also still on daughter maintenance.

Gianni nervously sat down and calmly declared to me, "Michelina Pirone - may I ask your father to marry you?" "Uh, what did you ask?" "To marry. I want to ask your father's permission to marry you. I love you, Michelina." "Oh, my God. Another one. Gianni now?" I thought. I sat back and smiled to him. "My good friend. This is madness." I said this to him in a manner very careful not to hurt his feelings. I added, "Gianni, I love you like a brother." He laughed, "I do not need a sister." "And I, dear friend, don't need a husband - capice? And you are good friends with Eugenio Mettola besides, no? Impossible." I think I saw a smile of relief at my remark. He sat there like a sad puppy holding my hand. "Come on," I said. "I have so much trouble here with my father and mother. I need a confidant. Please. Let's be friends." Relieved, Gianni understood. We talked like we used to do. Now I felt in my heart that I had a very good friend - a male friend. A very rare species of animal indeed.

Later, I got to thinking, even my old co-worker at the men's coat factory, Gianni, wanted to ask to my father for permission to court me with intentions of marriage. What was the basis of this story? Was I a farm animal? I was feeling like two persons and one of me was hanging in the corner window of the butcher shop.

The Breakup

Early spring, a few weeks later, Mettola came at lunchtime to the Parisian Dress Shoppe. He came unannounced also and was adamant but polite in his invitation to going somewhere together - quietly. I reluctantly accepted the offer. As we left, the girls all smiled at each other with various convictions of outcome, I'm sure.

It was obvious that Mettola had something on his mind, and I knew what it must be. Another proposal of some sort. Maybe a "goodbye?" I did not know for sure. I knew he still had some vague idea conveyed by his mother that I would hold my love and wait for him until he gained his citizenship and found better employment to take care of his mother and his mentally dependent brother - and also maybe a wife - me.

I wanted this lunch meeting if for no other reason than to get a resolution to our situation which had been on my mind in many forms since my last conversation with Mettola's mother. I cared for this handsome Neapolitan with the bright teeth, black curly hair and deep baritone speech. Still, it was left that his mother wanted me to wait for her son, to bide my time in purity of heart, and to then join his family. But Mettola never made that plan known to me - not in person anyway. Not so directly. Now I figured was his moment of opportunity. Yes, his mother often spoke of this future for him, and now was the time to hear his position once and for all. A part of me welcomed it.

The day was a perfect day - a beautiful spring day. We went to our old spot in the Public Garden which was at its best with early blooms and promises - a cool myriad of colors. Mettola had a small sack of fresh fruit, bread and cheeses which he quickly opened to share. For a long time, we sat quietly and ate.

Eugenio smiled at my good mood. He also looked so handsome just like the flowers full of colors. I was happy in that moment. He asked me, "You feel better, eh?" I answered, "I haven't been sick. I am fine. Why do you ask?" "You have disappeared from our relationship. You haven't been yourself lately."

Remembering all my heavy thoughts, a bad mood grabbed me. I answered him shortly, "Myself? How do you know what 'myself' is?" He did not respond. I continued, "Perhaps it is your fault." "My fault? How is it my fault? What did I do wrong?" I became enraged, "That's it, you didn't do anything wrong because you don't do anything at all. Then you assume things are as you see it and keep going." A very confused look came over Mettola's face. I added, "You just do nothing. Your mother plans your life for you. She even plans my life for me. Everyone plans my life for me. I need to plan my own life! No assumptions!" Oh, boy, I was mad.

Mettola looked deeply hurt which set me back a bit. I had taken a hard approach for the last several months of being pressed upon to wait for something I didn't want to wait for had built up to a bursting point in me. Poor Mettola got the brunt of it. But I still had a sense of freedom to finally say these things openly to him. I ended my tirade by saying to him, "I need more time to straighten out my own complicated problems - alone." "But that is why we agreed to wait, Lena." I just stared at him. He was not following my thinking. "I agreed to wait for what? To postpone your mother's proposal of marriage? I'll wait forever on that."

Mettola then suggested, "Why don't you come to my house after work today? My mother would love to have you. We can talk more about this there." This remark made all my tormentous thoughts come back. I jumped up and interrupted. "Your mother? Your mother?! Were you not listening?!" I began to walk back in the direction of Newbury Street. Mettola caught up to me and stopped me by the arm. He was so confused.

"Wait, Michelina! Please. Let's have some coffee first. Start again. I will listen. I promise you. I want to understand."

We walked without a word to the café across from the Shoppe. This was good, for there was not much time left for lunch, and there would also be little opportunity to speak disruptively in a crowd with any loud conversation. Mettola brought two espressos to the table and sat with a beaming smile. He became the handsome fellow again whom I first saw smiling and talking with the sultry Neapolitan dialect.

Mettola wanted to know just now how and where to start our conversation. He said I was to decide this. He sat back calmly and smiled, sipping his coffee. Then he got serious and spoke first of course, "I don't think you love me, Lena. Am I right?" "Yes and no," I said. He continued, "I do not pay much attention to our relationship. You are saying this. Am I right?" "Yes and no," I said. He went on again. "You resent me because my mother spoke for me, but you had agreed with her to wait for me until I get my citizenship and to make more money, didn't you?" "No. I did not agree. I listened to her but agreed to nothing. I told her that she was lucky to have a son such as you." Mettola sat more erect at this remark. "Yes, well," he went on. "Do you love somebody else, Lena?" "No." "Are you sorry you promised to wait for me?" "No, because I did not promise to wait. You do not listen, Eugenio. I promised your mother to be friends and to support you while you are finding your way." In almost a whisper he asked, "Are you sure that I love you?" "No," I said, "I am not sure of that either."

Mettola leaned back to consider my words. He could not make a scene, so he thought hard. He did succeed in putting me in the mood to further explain. I started. "It was nice of your mother to express your difficult situation, but I wished that you had done that yourself." He said, "What is the difference?" I added, "And there you are. Eugenio, your mother expects me to marry you, but insists I wait. Your mother! You have no time to spend with me. I like you, yes, but I do not know you. I need long discussions, seeing you, to learn who you really are. I think it is not enough just to like your looks, your good manners or what you represent." Now he looked even more puzzled. I continued, "I also think that you do not know me. Me, Michelina Pirone." He was so surprised, he had no words at all to add.

After a pause he said, "Then what will you do - what will 'we' do? "I wish first to be your friend," I said. "I wish to get to know you better, Eugenio. Perhaps in time - who knows. I have maybe a plan also to study somewhere. That will take time as well." "Study! Study what?" I told Mettola of my hope to go away to art school if my father would give me the money and to become a writer. I told him that my friend, Annie Chambelli, inspired these thoughts in me. "Go to Roma? To study? How long would that be?" He asked, almost too loudly. "Five years," I said. "When I come out of there, we could see where we both are. Either way, it's a wait, isn't it? Having an education of that sort, I could do anything." He was surprised and amazed. Mettola stood up slowly from his chair which signaled the end of the conversation for him. "That is an awful idea," he said. "Five years away! Back to Italy? Now I know that you do not care at all about us. I thought you would be faithful to our agreement."

I got up angrily now. "There was no 'agreement!'" He became red in the face. "You expect me to continue while you study back in Italy for five years more? You cannot afford this anyway. Your father will never pay for you! It is a ridiculous idea in your head." Now my turn came, "What about you, don't you think you expect too much from me? Just pulling the needle for God knows how many years of waiting? Besides, I must fill my own time and measure my own mind." He didn't answer anymore. Mettola and I left the café without another word.

Mettola walked me across the street to the Parisian Dress Shoppe, and I turned to him without expression. He tried in his heart to smile before saying cordially, "Okay. We will go slow and think about it. Thank you for taking lunch with me, Michelina." I went quietly inside.

A few times after that, Mettola came during the lunch hours. If he didn't find me there, he would look around Newbury Street for me. We made up from our fight, but it had taken its toll. Mettola's mother might have had some conversations about it with him as well. He did try further, but there still was an awful evidence on my part - a hesitation. Also, the argument revealed the strong desire in me, no matter how "ridiculous," of going to art school in Roma. Mettola had the chain of his mother's expectations to carry around his neck, and I was not in a position or of a mind to upset her plans. Finally, he was getting my message. It depressed me greatly, but I had made up my mind.

I did not see Eugenio Mettola again.

Chapter Eleven

Papa's Glands

Papa got sick, or so he thought.

Prophetically, just around the Ides of March 1921, my father woke up with a hollering that sent my brother Ralfo immediately down four flights of stairs to fetch Dottore De Rosa. I heard him stumble about two flights down. The Pulcinella-Dottore eventually made his way back up the stairs with his little doctor's bag and my breathless brother alongside him. This was one good thing about living in a Chambelli apartment house and in the North End - nothing was ever too far away.

By the time they came up, I had Papa sitting at the kitchen table, and I was plying him with a large cup of strong black tea and lemon. All the time, as Papa drank with one hand, he kept rubbing his other hand up and down his throat area, coughing and massaging. He really looked scared which scared me.

I must say here that as long as I have known my father, he has always been a bit of a hypochondriac. He never once had an operation for any reason, and he was always taking some sort of home remedy for various ailments - real or imagined. But this session of discomfort had me worried. "What is it, Papa?" "My glands! My glands are so swollen. I can't breathe!" The Pulcinella-Dottore jumped into the kitchen with an opened bag and sat next to my father. He pushed Papa's hand down from his throat and examined the tonsil area and lower neck. He told Papa to hold his hands back in the air as he examined his heart. A tap on the shoulder released them. He then took a pulse. "Okay, Giuseppe. I see now what it is."

Dottore De Rosa stood and repacked his bag, quickly looking at his pocket watch to see how much time was spent with this patient. "What is it, Dottore?" asked my father. "You have swollen lymph glands." Silence. "And?" "And it may be only an allergy to something in your house or in your work - or even just stress." My father still looked worried and said,

"Or?" "Or it could be something more serious which we will have to keep an eye on." Ralfo then asked, "What do you suggest for swollen lymph glands, Dottore?" "Rest. Even better, Giuseppe. A change of surroundings - less stress and allergies, maybe from your work. Take a change of location." "Where?" Papa cried out. "Italy. I recommend that you go back there and rest for a while. See your wife and the rest of your family. No stress. Better air. That will cure you, I think." And without another word, the Pulcinella left back for his office downstairs along with my brother to settle the details of the bill.

"Oh, my God," Papa said out loud and stunned, still rubbing his throat. "Oh, my God," I thought silently, "What next?"

"Have some more tea, Papa."

Emergency Immigration Act

Just at this time, spring, 1921, came a troubling Proclamation from the American Congress. The first one of its kind - ever. We had heard rumblings after the Great War, WWI, but now it was information. This Proclamation was supposed to be temporary, three months only, but it lasted for almost half a century more - almost to the time as I write this letter. It was removed only in 1965.

The American government voted to make a quota of immigration and to diminish and reduce the number of immigrants coming to America - mostly from the eastern and southern parts. They made a law that immigrants from these two regions of the world were "undesirable" and that they were diluting American culture. They argued that southern Europeans were competing too much with traditional American labor and way of life and that 15,000,000 immigrants were waiting now to migrate from that part of the world. Most of the immigrants who were here, they said, were not blending well in America, so the Proclamation was made to curtail any more of these southern Europeans from coming in.

This all happened on a Thursday, May 19th, 1921. It was called "The Emergency Immigration Act." Mostly, it was a strict quota. But who's "emergency" was it? If we like you, you can come in - if we don't like you, then you cannot. In this new Proclamation, they "liked" the English, the Irish, the Germans, the Swedish and anyone from northern Europe and allowed them greater numbers of entry - no problem. Come in. But southern European regions? No. Asian peoples were not allowed into America at all. None. They did not restrict, however, migrations from Central and South America. They could come in without questions.

None of this made any sense to me. How can one dilute a culture without first blending? No Asian people at all to come in? Why? And did the American government not know that the majority of Central and South America was occupied mostly by Spanish, Portuguese and Italians? No quota on them? The word "undesirable" became a misdirected dogma in my mind.

It was all the talk of the North End that spring, in every newspaper, on every corner and in every café. This entire section of Boston, the North End, was one hundred percent populated by those named as "undesirables" by this new law - the Jews, the Greeks and the Italians all were named and targeted to be reduced in number by means of a quota.

Naturally, I worried now about any back and forth travel to Italy that my father might have or how to get my entire family here from Pratola Serra. How will Mother come now? My siblings? They would only permit 3% a year of the number of immigrants who were already here from any one country. They used the census of 1910 to determine this entry 3% quota. Most of America obviously immigrated from northern Europe, England, etc. It was a convenient formula for them. More of the northern group came originally.

Another big issue they said was that the Italians were not assimilating into the American fabric. What they forgot to say was that in many ways, tens of thousands of Italians already helped to build that American fabric. All the city bridges, roads, buildings, canals - and art - were touched by Italian hands. All of them. Yes, more than half of the paesani returned to Italy with the money they made; the others stayed and sent money back. Melded? How could one tell the number of Italians who did eventually

255

"meld" into America's fabric when a simple dropping of a vowel would accommodate that purpose? But what advantage would there be to meld in this manner?

Anyway, I remembered the deep discussions with my cousin Fortuna when I first arrived about how the Italians came to America to preserve their heritage because of the failings of the Italian government at that time. In their own way, the paesani came to preserve two thousand years of art, music and heritage that was temporarily obfuscated by war and unholy governments, but never, never was Italy to be forgotten or to be abandoned. Ultimately, that was the cultural contribution that the Italians made to the American fabric - to share these cherished gifts. They also left a few magnificent monuments behind in the process.

I had to do more than just worry alone about this in my head. The Emergency Immigration Act became an emergency for me and my family as well. I thought to call upon Annie to help me. I wanted to get her help to write an article in the Italian newspaper about these concerns. Even just a letter to the editor. I was adamant and had resolve in this purpose.

What happened next was even better. My first publication submission and acceptance on the subject of injustices. There would be many, many more.

I met Annie several days later on Hanover Street in the large pharmacy where Frank Battone had his place of business selling medications. They also had a small seated café inside where we could sit and talk and where Annie could keep a vigil on her wishful intentions. He of course, hardly noticed our presence.

I deliberately ordered a rose water soda because Michelangelo used to drink rose water with his tea every day when he needed to think. I discussed with Annie this vile new law put upon the paesani by America's Congress. What to do? I handed her a ten-page letter, in perfect Italian, going over point-by-point the law's injustices and the false reasoning of it. She read it carefully while I kept an eye on Battone trying not to be noticed. "Lena! This is wonderful! We must get this to the papers - the

Italian papers." "It's only a long letter to the editor - too long maybe," I said. "No. It will be an article. My father will call the editor himself and get it placed for you. It's much like his pro-Italian speeches he makes at the Sons of Italy meetings. It's brilliant!"

For a moment, I thought; then I said to Annie, "But it should be typed. I cannot type. It is in longhand." "Beautiful longhand, too," she said. "I'll type it for you. This must be published."

We sat there and discussed the points that I made in countermeasure. The law was a quota rule, yes, but aliens like my father, who go back and forth and who are "skilled workers" can come and go with impunity. Certainly, Papa is skilled. But was I skilled? Could I go and come back unimpeded? This was the question we discussed. No one knew just how this law worked yet.

Annie mentioned professionals, like the Pulcinella-Dottore De Rosa, could go back and forth. She could, too, because she was born in America and was a citizen. Even domestic servants could come and go - no problem. But I said, "No paesani I know comes to America to be a domestic servant. Unless they come to help another paesani." We both laughed at the thought. I then said, "I just worry for my mother and my siblings being stuck in Italy. Another excuse for Papa not to bring them here - or just to go back and forth as he alone wishes."

Annie sat back and said with a quiet smile, "I will type this, and it will be published."

She did, and it was.

For many weeks, I was stopped and complimented on the street for my article by those who knew that I wrote it. It is true that the pen is mightier than the sword, eh? "Brava, Michelina! Brava, Signorina!" I got two dollars sent to me in the mail by the paper and afterward, I think I bought one dollar's worth of newspapers with it. That was a lot of papers. My brother, Ralfo, was now calling me, "Dante-Nella," (little Dante). The newspaper, *The Weekly Italian News*, gave to me the author credit - "M. Pirone."

My friend Annie's misgivings in courtship, however, were getting no better as these weeks went on. The pressure on her by her father, Chambelli, to have her marry Dottore De Rosa was more and more evident. The pressure was also on Chambelli as well to make this plan of his happen. He was getting impatient - even with the Dottore. This situation was not good for anyone.

We at the Parisian Dress Shoppe made all of Annie's suits, coats and dresses - all of them. Mrs. Chambelli was even helping in this scheme to force a union between her daughter and the Pulcinella-Dottore. She was constantly ordering new clothes for her daughter. Poor Annie. Yes, she was a well-dressed girl, but the Dottore never looked either at Annie or to the dresses she was wearing. His mind was only on making money and going back to his little contessa in Italy. Annie collected all of Dottore De Rosa's mail for him at the post office, and never once was there a letter from any Contessa, nor did the Pulcinella even send any letters out with such a name as a Contessa in the address. What then was the real story? I could imagine.

I never disliked anybody as much as I did this man, this Pulcinella. He could feel my disdain, too. Once, he met me passing in the street. I tried to avoid him. I coldly said, "Hello," but kept on walking. He boldly followed me and stopped me by stepping in front of my pace. He wanted to talk to me. "Okay, what?" Dottore De Rosa looked at me with a very skinny smile on his face and openly said, "You don't like me. Am I right?" I didn't know what to say. I paused, then answered, "I never said that. How do you know what I think?" He continued, "Lena, I am a doctor, and I studied psychology. Believe me, I can tell." I didn't say anything, but he would not let the subject go. He abruptly persisted, "Answer me. You don' t like me."

I firmly answered him back, "Yes. True. I do not care for you or your actions." "And why is that?" "You could be a little less mercenary," I said. "Oh, yes? Well..." "Oh please," I interrupted, "let's stop this nonsensical talk." "No," he said, "Wait. I know you want me to pay attention to Annie as well. Like everyone does. I am right?" "No. You are wrong. I hope she never will think of you - she is too good for you." Dottore De Rosa just looked at me - smug and pleased with himself. I felt so indignant. "My, my, what a temper," he smiled back. "Temper?" I retorted, "I didn't say enough. Goodbye." And I left. After this confrontation with the little Pulcinella, he made some trouble for me with Annie's mother, Mrs. Chambelli - but I didn't care. Two weeks later, Annie confided in me a new secret plan of hers - a plan that shocked me and included me at the same time.

Annie and I sat again at the café inside Frank Battone's pharmacy. "Lena, look!" Annie placed in front of me a filled-out application to the five-year school for women of the Arts in Roma, Italy. "I'm going to leave here," she said. "I will go to Italy to study in the Arts as I described. I don't want any more worries about that fellow over there, Frank Battone, and I don't want anything to do with the Pulcinella Dottore either. I will quit him and the job in his office. I will go to Italy, Lena! I will!"

"Oh, my God! This is wonderful. And your father will pay? He agrees?" "Yes. He will, once he sees there is no future with the Dottore. I think he is close to seeing this now, and my sister is giving him other problems with her milkman comare."

I had to sit back on this revelation. I was both sad and happy for my dear friend because I knew that once she put her mind to it, especially an old dream that never died, that she would go through with it. Then she grabbed my hand and said, "Lena. Let me apply for you as well. I know you will get in. I will send to them your brilliant news article and explain that you want to continue as a writer and to study the Arts. I know you will be accepted. I will apply for you - Okay? What harm is there? And your father? Who knows. I think you will drive him as crazy as my own father has become with me."

How could I argue? "Papa will not pay. I'm sure, even though he can afford it," I said. Annie smiled, "Look at it this way, Lena. Your dowry will cost less for him the way you are going." We both laughed. Annie knew by my not answering that she had my permission to try.

A month later came the reply for us both. "Signorina Annie Chambelli and Signorina Michelina Pirone, you are both accepted into the women's college of classical and applied Arts in Roma, Italy." You could hear our shouts of joy across the entire North End of Boston.

When I was walking back to my apartment, I could only think of the wonderful possibilities that going to this five-year Art school for women would open for me. But Papa? Would he listen to this argument? Were his swollen glands now to become a financial burden for the family as well? Would Mother and my siblings be allowed to come to America under the law? Could I leave for college and still come back? Would I be forced to marry if I was made to stay in America? Or was the American government, with its new quota law, preparing to make it a burden for all of us anyway? So many questions at this time in my life. At least my dear friend, Annie, had some answers.

Now to confront Papa with the news.

Giuseppe "Peppino" Pirone, Master harness-maker,
1922 at age forty-four.

Chapter Twelve

Onslaught - Suitors Beg the Question

My father, after my refusing several offers in marriage, the poor man really got worried. "Will she never marry?" This question was constantly on his mind. What could he do to hurry me up? First, he told everybody he knew how sick he was - how he had orders by his doctor to go back to Italy for a health cure. He had swollen glands after all. This proclamation was what he did first. Then second, Papa gave nearly every potential suitor permission to ask for my hand in marriage - many of whom I had never met before. He gave permission to these fellows to come into our house while he was there and to talk to me personally about marrying them. It was a steady line of young men holding their hats in their hands. Literally. A stream! I am serious about these words. One of them named Hamleto Guarini, a very handsome, educated fellow of Charleston, also a young friend of my Aunt Alfonsina, came up freely. Even when Papa wasn't home. I did not let him in on those occasions, of course. He was so refined. At first, I had no heart to be rude with him. I listened and listened, but he was deaf about any refusal. Then a common theme entered his dance step when my reluctance persisted, a defensive position that suitors make against feeling rejected. It is the worse feeling in this situation for either of the combatants.

This friend of my aunt went on by arguing my father's own plea for help in this situation saying, "Your father intends to go back to Italy for his cure, no? What will you do here alone? A girl as yourself - alone." Patiently, I answered him. "I will stay here with my brother." He continued, "Well, how long will your brother suffer to maintain you with your extravaganzas? He is only seventeen years old." This was a really bad thing to say to me. "What!?" "Yes," he said, "you know you spend all you make on yourself." "Listen here," I retorted, "I make all of my own clothes, and, if I have to cut out on other things to live here, I can do that easily. Please let's stop talking about me. I am busy. I wish you would go. Goodbye." So, that day as well, another petitioning potential husband left with his hat. Alone, finally, I thought, "The nerve of him. Oh, what a world." I was so irritated.

———————

Another random candidate for consideration was a friend of my brother, Ralfo's. I don't even remember his name at this point. He was a shortish Calabrian. A very nice but intense young man who was a tailor with his own shop in the North End down from the Social Center. Every time I passed his shop, he would make it a policy, if he saw me, to stop anything he was doing, even with a customer, to jump outside to the sidewalk and to greet me.

This one was certainly dedicated to his matrimonial cause on his own behalf. He was truly in earnest to the point of comedy. He danced with the pigeons. He would take my hand, look up with big blinking eyelids and say, "I will be your slave, Michelina. Forever! Even your brother Ralfo I perorate for!" Oh, boy. I felt constantly set upon and abused, thanks to my father's swollen glands and his tireless mission to marry me off. I was very indignant. My father, how wrong he was. But how to reach him? He kept on complaining about his swollen glands and kept on offering up potential husbands.

Glands or not, I felt I was on sale. Papa considered me an old maid. I was 20 years old! Was I an old maid? He is so very wrong I thought. I became very serious, almost morbid as a result of this misconception. When I met with my old friend and co-worker, Gianni, after, I was silent and morose. He too was rejected months earlier but got over the issue. He was of such sound character as I wrote before, that he could still be my friend. How rare was this? A very special rarity. But even Gianni was confused by my morbidity. He thought that he bored me. I did not bother to explain much, so I let my friend down a bit in this regard. I feel sorry about that now. I should have told him my feelings of being constantly set upon.

Then the most disturbing happenstance for me - a ghost from the past.

———————

A Surprise Landing

One late Sunday afternoon, there came a knock on the door to my apartment. I heard a man's voice from the other side of the door say, "Hello?" I thought, "I know this voice. Mettola? Gianni?" When I slowly opened the door to see - there stood Giacomino Fabbo. My heart went straight to my throat. "Oh, my God!" I thought. Thankfully, Papa was home on that Sunday.

Giacomino pushed past me with his distinctive limp due to the missing toes on his right foot. The first thing he said was in an irritating way, "Michelina! I am here! Why did you not answer my letters?" He stood there, arms crossed, taking ownership of the kitchen area where we stood until my father came in. Papa was carrying his Sunday newspaper and wearing only his long-john underwear. "Mr. Pirone. Signore. I sent to you letters, as well. I have spoken many times with your wife too - in Pratola Serra. So, you know me and you know that Michelina and I are sworn and engaged to each other." Papa just stood there surprised, but a slow careful smile slowly filled his face. When I saw this, I felt like screaming at him.

Looking at Giacomino now standing there inside the kitchen doorway where so many others had recently crossed, I was forced to analyze him again - comparing him with the others. I knew right then and there that I did not like him at all. I left the kitchen, and I went into the parlor and sat on the couch. I could hear them both but not clearly. Giacomino talked to my father for a long time. Then, he broke out in a voice that everyone could hear in the building.

Giacomino started hollering like mad, "She has ruined my life! I came here to Boston because I want to marry her as we planned in Italy! We are engaged. I came all the way from Italy! Ask her yourself. She said 'yes' to me!" The surprise response from my father came. Was it finally paternal protection? Or was it that he saw in Giacomino what I saw - nothing.

My father told Giacomino that that all happened a long time ago and that things are different now. He would have to stand with the others. "Thank you, Papa - finally you speak for me," I thought.

Then Giacomino pushed past my father and came into the parlor where I sat. Papa followed him. Giacomino stood over me and said menacingly, "You shall pay for this, Michelina." I said, "Pay for what?" "You should leave now," said Papa in a way that left no interpretations. And Giacomino did.

Word came to me that Giacomino had first stayed for two days with cousins of his in the North End before even coming to my apartment - it was not spontaneous. And, after leaving my house, he then went down to New York. I found out later that Giacomino did not come all the way from Italy to find me - he came all the way from New York where he was working for many months. Only now did he come up to Boston. Paesani friends also told me that Giacomino found work in an Italian café, the Café Ferrari, in the worst part of the Italian section of New York. A dangerous place. It fit Giacomino well I thought.

Soon after this incident, Giacomino's pleading letters again returned - this time from New York. I put them in a box, unopened. Of course, I did not answer them. I felt no guilt because I didn't encourage him to come to this country - at least, I told myself that. But looking back on it now, I did accept his kiss on the forehead and we did make hypothetical plans to open a gift shop together in Avellino. But that was nearly two years in the past - a century ago to my mind. And I was only a child back then.

Days later, as I went past Dottore Pulcinella's door, I met again the tall widower from Lynn, Luigi Pisano. I slowly was going upstairs to my apartment and he was coming out from Dottore De Rosa's office. We both looked stunned at the sudden meeting - but grateful. Luigi stood politely in the hallway. He looked different to me. What was it? He had removed his black necktie. He had on a fitted blue suit, not black, and a white t-shirt only, no dress shirt with collar. He also looked - beautiful. This time he actually spoke. Quietly, he asked me how I was. I said, "Just a little tired now. I have to go up to rest. It was nice to see you again." "Oh," he said. "I thought I could speak to you. May I?" "Not just now," I said, "I'm sorry - I need a rest. Have a good night." Mr. Pisano gave no response at all after that. No pushing after or objecting. No interrupting my step. He was definitely a gentleman and an older man. I think because of this, it offered a quiet respect to my wishes. A different sort of fellow indeed.

Now to end this fateful day, as I entered our apartment on the fourth floor, Papa was waiting for me, again sitting at the kitchen table and rubbing his throat. "Mamma Mia, what now?" I thought. "Michelina," he said. "Sit down. I have something to say to you." He was holding a letter in his hand. "This letter is from your mother - to you. I did not open it, but I know what it will say. She wrote to me as well. And - we both think the same way." "And what way is that, Papa?" "You must stay in America and you must marry - someone - please!!! It is becoming a burden on us. A burden to the entire family."

Oh, boy. That was it. I stood and gave him a horrible argument. I was livid. "A burden to you and Mother!? How awful of you to dictate the rest of my life to me, just to make your own plans work! I do not want to marry! I am not ready!" Papa jumped up. I thought he was going to slap me. "Michelina! What do you want? You are killing me!"

I stood my ground with him, like I did in front of Aunt Alfonsina. I was not afraid. It was my life we argued over. "I want to go to college. In Italy. I have been accepted. I told you this!" "And you said five thousand dollars for you to do this?" Papa was looking at me as if I was asking him for his life. He continued, "You want to ruin me, eh? How can a sick man give you so much, just to satisfy your crazy ideas? You have a job now. You have qualified husbands coming to our door - every day! What is wrong with you?!" I stopped him there. "Enough! Tonight, you will make your own supper, Papa."

I stormed out from the apartment. I had never been so bold or so rude to my father. In olden days, for a daughter to do just that was a sin beyond sins, I know. But this wasn't the olden days, and the weight of any sin is measurable.

I walked for almost an hour on the streets but became uncomfortable doing that alone. When I got back to the apartment, Papa was in his bedroom asleep. On the kitchen table was Mother's unopened letter to me. It had no stamp on it, so I thought she just put it inside a letter to my father. She must have mentioned the contents to him in her letter to him like he said.

I sat there thinking of my plight. Where was I to go? How could I afford to stay if Papa went back to Italy? Was his concern for my placement in marriage not sound? Wouldn't I be cared for properly? Was I being selfish? These questions never stopped coming.

I took out from my pocketbook the two postcards that were well worn now from the Museum of Fine Arts. One by Millet and the other of Renoir. I studied them hard, still holding my mother's unopened letter to me. I thought of Annie Chambelli and how she would be going to Italy to study the Arts and how her father would champion her in those dreams of hers. But why only Annie? Why was she so fortunate? Why not me? I had been accepted as well to this college, but I had no support from my own father even though he could afford it. He was no Chambelli.

My brother, Ralfo, came in just then and was going to bed. I told him what had happened - everything. He sat very patiently. He was such a good brother, but definitely his father's son in his loyalties - almost to a fault. Still, I sought his counsel as my brother and valued his considerations and quiet attention.

I asked Ralfo solemnly, "If father goes to Italy, would you stay here with me in this apartment? Would you? We can manage together. I know we can." He had already been brainwashed on this subject from father. He said, "No, I don't know what I will do when Papa goes away. I am only seventeen years old. I may go back, as well. I would be left at work without him. We work together, side-by-side." I felt so sorry, but not for myself, but for Ralfo. He was so helpless - and yes, so young. Papa always instructed him what to do. There never was a question in his mind. This approach is what made my brother so happy. He would just quietly follow the right path - behind, in his father's footsteps.

I loved my brother so much, but he had fallen to the powerful condition so prevalent in our family - in most Italian families. Paternal order. Our relationship had always been not only fraternal but also friendly. Anyway, I half believed that in case I was left alone, Ralfo would stay - that we would find a way together. But in my heart, I feared otherwise.

I said no more to Ralfo, and then he too went to bed. I made myself a cup of tea and thought some more. Maybe I could stay with my Aunt Alfonsina perhaps, but then she had so many of her own children and I already had an earlier obligation to her when I first came to America. "I cannot go backwards," I thought. That would be too much for me to ask of her. And, she would probably think of many reasons why I am not married by now to one of her suggested suitors. She would push harder, like Papa. My mother's brother, Uncle Ferdinando, offered for me to stay in Lynn with him. As much as I loved him, I said no. Uncle Antonio, too, was from Lynn and was my father's best friend. Lynn seemed like another country to me - a faraway country. Anyway, I could not bring myself to live with either of my mother's brothers as they both also thought of me as a potential old maid.

I had to be independent. My father? My brother? They could do what they pleased. I would find a way by myself. Yes, my father was right in one thing; I was getting old. "Well then, I will act old from now on," I thought. "No more worries - no more pre-arranged plans." I still felt this way when I finally opened the letter from Mother. It turned out that she was afraid that I was going to come back to Italy with my father unmarried and that her fate of remaining in Italy would then be sealed. This was her strange way of saying, "Stay in America. Find a husband - now! We are trapped here. Only in this way can we come from Italy." But in her clever ingenuity to see me married immediately, she wrote instead:

"Dearest Darling Daughter

You also must acknowledge the fact that the old woman, Dame Simonetta, the one who you shamed at your Nonna's store when you showed her to lie, she has a vendetta on you. Remember her? You challenged the old woman because she said the soul's penitent came from their graves in the cemetery at midnight, and then you told everyone what she was, a liar. Well, she put a curse on you. She said to me that what you said about her to others in the village, that she shall get revenge. She told me just wait to see what will happen on your daughter if she comes back alone, without a husband.

This, I fear very much. Child of my heart, do not do this to me. Stay in America, marry. Then you can come back home.

Mother

267

"Mother." Angelina Fabrizio Pirone: 1908 at age thirty.

Chapter Thirteen

A visit to Lynn with my Uncle Ferdinando

As I wrote before, my mother's two brothers had both immigrated to Lynn, Massachusetts from our village in Italy. They both were master shoemakers, and Lynn was heralded as "the shoe-making capital of the world." So, where else would these two brothers go to in America, eh? And, I became more and more confident that the newly formed immigration law considered them "skilled workers," which of course they were. They would need little validation on that measure.

Uncle Antonio, Mother's older brother, was my father's best friend since they were boys making mischief together in Pratola Serra. He gave Papa no grief when it came to family matters. Mostly, he stayed out of any issue my father might have with his sister.

Mother's younger brother, however, Uncle Ferdinando, considered himself the master shoemaker of the Fabrizio family. He was also the emotional and hot-tempered one, and he let everyone know it too. I was in America for two whole months before Uncle Ferdinando was told I was here. He found out only by a stranger that I was in Boston. Well, he was enraged at this lack of respect. He blamed Papa for this snubbing, of course.

When he heard the news, my hot-tempered uncle came right to Aunt Alfonsina's house and really had an argument with my father. It was just like the time Uncle Ferdinando threw the shoes he made for Nonno, Don Carlos, back in his face. That episode still festered in my father's heart as well. Uncle Ferdinando wanted to know, why was he not told of my arrival? Why was he so disrespected? But after the argument, my uncle and my father forgave the world of its faults and embraced each other dearly. For a while, the peace lasted.

I loved Uncle Ferdinando right away. I vaguely remembered him from his fainting spells and courtship walks he took with his intended,

Margherita, and with me as a child in Pratola Serra. He had something about him that I liked. Uncle Ferdinando was studious and audacious, with a deep sense of humor. He was also a beautiful, wonderful man.

Ever since I arrived, almost two years earlier, Uncle Ferdinando kept constant pressure on Papa to perform his family obligations. He reminded everyone that, even though he was a Fabrizio and not a Pirone and also the youngest brother, he still considered himself the "guardian" of the family and its interest - my mother's interests especially. Who ruled? What "male" held the family paternal reins? Well, the reluctant harness-maker, of course, Papa. This peeved my Uncle Ferdinando to no end. The umbrage he inwardly took with Papa turned into delight and extra attention he placed upon me - his only sister's oldest child.

One Sunday morning, after my own big argument with my father, my Uncle Ferdinando came to Boston to take me to his house in Lynn for a Sunday dinner with his family and an overnight stay. I welcomed the invitation openly. I left Papa a note on the kitchen table. Both he and Ralfo were asleep, for it was not either of their habits to wander out on a Sunday morning. Church was never observed unless there was a funeral of a paesani.

It was a beautiful spring day, and I needed a refuge. Perfect timing. I had on one of my most comfortable and tasteful creations and joined this proud uncle of mine, arm-in-arm, down to Boston Harbor.

The city of Lynn was less than an hour's ferryboat ride north of Boston. A smooth passage across Boston Harbor with its many dotted islands made of rugged stone. Good opportunities were available for happy conversations between my uncle and myself on this short ocean voyage.

When we got to his house in Lynn, I was happily met by all his family and his wife, my Aunt Margherita, still beautiful of course. Well, we had a good dinner. More American in style, I think, than I was expecting, and I noticed with a little dismay that my uncle's family had very limited order. Aunt Margherita was a bit too easy-going with her children. I didn't think she knew how to manage them. It certainly wasn't a ritualistic Italiana like the Chambelli table. And, like Papa, Uncle Ferdinando was not an easy father to get along with either. But this was his family, and so it was mine as well.

We talked for hours during and after dinner and had a good conversation. Gratefully, none of the discussions were of my getting married or about the suitors who were paraded in front of me by Papa. We talked of Pratola Serra and the old country. And of course, Papa's swollen glands. I did discuss with my aunt and uncle the possibility of going back to Italy, to the Art school in Roma taught by nuns. I told them that I had been accepted there. My uncle stopped me with a laugh and said, "You? In a college taught only by nuns? I think you would not come out alive." "Oh, no, dear Uncle," I said smiling, "I would come out very much alive."

The evening went by quickly, and I said goodbye to Aunt Margherita and my cousins in the morning after a short breakfast. Uncle Ferdinando couldn't part, and I couldn't either. He was a lot like my mother, very sentimental, and I loved him in everything. I found myself always laughing when we were together. Dear, dear, man.

Uncle then walked me back down to the ferryboat in Lynn Harbor. It was a chilly Monday morning, lots of wind I remember, but invigorating, as well.

As we were going toward the main square, Central Square, we had to pass a busy street called Market Street, which, as it was called, was the business and market area of Lynn. My uncle pointed out the shoe mill where he supervised his workers to make the latest designs in shoes.

As we crossed over the square, we had to pass Summer Street. Then a voice came out over the traffic sound, "Michelina! Michelina! Here!!!" Mr. Luigi Pisano had seen us from his barber shop window from across the street as we were passing. He jumped out of his shop and crossed the busy street. He was wearing a vest, tie, suit pants - and a big smile. He came up to us quickly, like an old lost friend.

Mr. Pisano held my hand with full emotion and said, "Hello! Michelina!" He ignored my uncle entirely. I don't think he even saw him. He was talking rapidly, explaining that it was Monday, his day off, and how he came to clean his barber shop, pointing across the street. "How nice," I said. He continued to talk until Uncle Ferdinando abruptly interrupted him. With his adorable roughish manners, my uncle said to him, "Eh, eh, you. I am here, too! What is the matter with you? Where are your manners?" Mr. Pisano only half acknowledged the puffing of my uncle. Uncle continued, "I guess you never talked so much in your life. Let's go, Michelina."

It was classic Italian positioning - by the men. Mr. Pisano came back with a conciliatory smile but no words. We said our goodbyes and left.

A few blocks later, just before Lynn Harbor, my uncle explained rather gruffly, "This Pisano fellow. He is a stern character - a solo individual. He doesn't even say hello to anybody. People here in Lynn call him the 'Hermit.' All of a sudden, now he finds so much to say? He is shy, too. He never joined any of our Italian community activities." I interrupted now with a smile, "Uncle, you talk too much yourself, eh?" "Like hell," he said. "I am not through yet. Oh, I think he has his eyes on you. Do not pay attention to him. He is a widower and much older than you are. You deserve better." I reminded my dear uncle what Mother told me when they arranged her own wedding, when he himself stormed out of the house saying to my mother, "This man, Guiseppe Pirone, will never make you happy! You deserve better! If she had listened to you, dear Uncle, I would not be here today." It had him thinking a bit and kept Uncle Ferdinando quiet for the rest of the walk to the ferryboat.

Shifting Influences - the North End

That same year, matters of influence in the North End took a downward turn for the paesani - at least the paesani I knew. In the spring of 1921, "Don" Filippo Assanti suddenly died in his sleep. This distinguished and unchallenged community leader, with few words, was gone in an instant. You could almost feel the windows of the apartment houses closing quietly behind him. This death would bring us unseen ramifications, not only to the Assanti family, but also send deep reverberations to our carved-out sanctuary of the North End. And it would take on deeper meaning with our mutual friend, Mr. Franco Chambelli. There was a sense of broken order - of a stability suddenly unpinned.

I got the news from Annie Chambelli. She came to me desperately right after they found Don Filippo dead in his bed, and she made me promise that I would stay close to her at the funeral. She was afraid. "Of what?" I asked. "I'm just afraid, Lena. Please!" "Yes. Of course."

Don Filippo's funeral got everyone's attention in the North End - even Papa forgot about his swollen glands. No one knew exactly how Don Filippo died. Yes, they said he died in his sleep, but he was a healthy man by sight, and he was only in his late sixties. Dottore De Rosa said little if anything about it. He just fretted about here and there in tight little circles.

There were whispers of course. How much of the rumors were true or not was questionable. "The Black Hand." "The underworld." "Mafia." These words on face-value are hollow. They hide in the seams of gossip, superstitions and myths. They scare those who wish to be scared. They are thrown about loosely by those who claim to know - but do not. The Black Hand was, in derivation, a political manifestation which began in the 1800's as much as a modern cultural one. And, I was not a believer of cultural bias and superstitions. Religion and politics can kill you - curses cannot. Did I believe in the "malocchio" (evil eye) either? No, of course not. Just like I didn't believe finally, as a girl, that the souls penitent came from their graves in the cemetery of our village and walked in a line to church at midnight like Dame Simonetta claimed they did. The Black Hand? No. Still, I did believe in our family gnome, Matzo Mauriello. But he was different. We knew he actually existed. We had proof of it.

Don Filippo was loved by everybody in the North End. It was a sunny Saturday morning. When the line of funeral cars passed down Hanover Street, all the storekeepers were at their front doors, saying goodbye to the grand old man. Still, there was a quiet uneasiness to this procession, and not just because of the dark Catholic mist that hung over Don Filippo's hearse. I rode several cars back with Annie Chambelli and her mother and sisters. Chambelli himself was nowhere to be seen. I asked about his absence and, of course, Annie just nodded, "not to worry."

As I promised, I stayed very close to my dear friend as we squeezed ourselves into St. Leonard's Church on Hanover Street along with a dark sea of paesani, politicians and onlookers. Everyone was very well-dressed in ceremonial mourning. And, as tradition, there were even some "professional" mourners hired by the family. Old women. Why? I did not know. It was a custom steeped in tradition and superstition along with all the others. The mourners were certainly not needed and probably would have been cast away by Don Filippo himself.

All the men held their hats in their hands and nervously kept from bumping each other while all the women kept their heads and eyes low. It was very macabre. Everything seemed to me in slow motion. Such a strange ending tribute to such a revered man. It was like everyone was measuring themselves in context to this man's life. A natural thing to do, yes, but this was different. In my young life, I have never experienced anything like it before or since.

I don't remember much of the priest's eulogy, but when he completed it, the silence in this massive cathedral weighed heavily on my shoulders. At this moment, Annie leaned into my ear closely and whispered, "Lena. I can't breathe. I must go away from here." We were toward the rear side aisle, and we slipped out past the shadows of the massive confessionals. I did remember the smell of heavy incense as it trailed us in swirls out into the bright light of day. Was this the smell of death or of what was to come?

Annie and I made our way back up Hanover Street, and yes, we ended up yet again in the café of the pharmacy owned by Frank Battone - he, thankfully was still at the church.

Annie and I ordered large espressos to compose ourselves. "Where is your father?" I heard myself ask. "I didn't see him." "He is about somewhere. I think he felt it best to stay in low profile right now," she said. There was a long pause before she continued, "Lena. Things will be changing now in the North End because of Don Filippo's death - for us I mean. He had a lot of power and influence in the community and in City Hall and my father was his closest ally. Now there will be some other "influences" who will try to come and fill the hole left by Don Filippo. It's only natural."

Annie sat quietly in place. "Who told you this?" I asked. "My father. It's all politics - and money, of course." She took a long pause, and I shall never forget what she said next. "I fear that my father's influence will be challenged in a bad way. He could lose everything. Everything. He wishes me now to give up any thought of marrying either Frank Battone or even the Dottore Pulcinella. My father wants me to leave here."

For a long time, we sat together without speaking another word. I was thinking hard about Annie's words. "What will you do? Where will you go?" I asked. Then she said, "To the School of Art for women - in Roma. I will leave in a few weeks." I was shocked. "What?! That is good news! How could it not be? But will your family be okay?"

Annie made a small nod of her head in a gesture of hope. "Yes. Of course. They will survive. The Chambellis have resources. But my father said it would be easier for him to see me safe and content, following my own dreams. One less worry. He sees me now marrying some noble Italian, I think - in Roma."

The happy look on my face must have given Annie confidence, and she added, "Please, Lena. Come with me, too! You are my dearest friend. We both were accepted. Together we could rule the world - or Roma at least anyway, eh?" We both laughed at the thought.

I had no other reaction. What else could I say? I knew it was only a dream for me. I knew that it would not be possible. My father would never finance a formal education for me, his oldest child who carried no namesake. He once kicked me as a child for even thinking of such a thing. I sank into my seat a bit, and Annie knew her suggestion was doomed. Still, we took comfort in the vision of it all. "Annie. You know my father will never do this, even though we are accepted together at this school of Art. Perhaps next year I can join you. Perhaps I can save enough on my own to do this." "Yes. Yes," she said hoping for the best. I held up my cup of strong coffee to offer her a toast. "Let us pledge then, together as sisters, that we will always be in touch with letters and we will unite - no matter what - somewhere - someday - and conquer the world as we have planned." We clinked cups loudly with a laugh. "Done!" she said, and then she finished solemnly, "Lena. Say a prayer for my family - and for my father especially. Please. Okay?" "Yes. Of course, dear friend."

<hr />

Three weeks later, just before Memorial Day, 1921, I met Annie and her family at the train platform in Boston as she was about to board for New York and then go by steamship to Italy. It was all chaotic and sad - and happy too. Mr. Chambelli hugged us both. He looked tired and grieved but still gave his daughter the best farewell hug a father could give a daughter. My embrace with Annie came last, and we reaffirmed our pledge to each other to reunite again and to rule the world some-day. It was all over in a blast of steam from the train's engine.

Annie was gone. My best friend. Yes, we wrote to each other, monthly at first, then every so often. But we never stopped. Ever. It would be decades before I saw her again. My dear sweet Annie.

Michelina and Annie Chambelli, Spring, 1921

Chapter Fourteen

A Summer Time Out?

New York Revisited

Soon after the farewell to my dear friend Annie Chambelli, I accepted afternoon tea with my Aunt Alfonsina at her apartment house on Salem Street. I was despondent of course that I was not able to join my best friend at the School of Art in Roma - especially knowing the fact that we were both accepted at the same time. I really had no other place to find solace or comfort.

It was my aunt's house where I stayed when I first came to America, so the tea session she offered me that day was soothing and resettling, even though I feared her bringing up the marriage issue again. I needed to be there anyway.

We sat together alone in her expansive parlor at a small inlaid mahogany table covered with the most delicate embroidered lace that she had woven herself. She brought the tea and biscuits in on a silver tray. The set was of the finest porcelain with shiny mother-of-pearl handles and the cups rimmed in gold. We sat sipping for many minutes with hardly a word between us. Then my aunt observed, "You are far away, Michelina. What is the problem?" I boldly told her of my constant battles with my father, of his unending complaining of his swollen glands and of the feeling that he simply wanted to marry me off to get rid of me. I thought at first that Aunt Alfonsina would support him - but she didn't. I saw a new side to her - my Nonna Pirone's younger sister. The two were now indistinguishable in my eyes.

My aunt continued with, "You have been fathering your own father - and your mother, too, to some extent. He cares about you, but not as to any further obligation. You have come of age. You are born first - yes. But to your family, not the Pirone. Your Uncle Antonio heads the family now, even though he is younger than your father. Your father doesn't care to be head of the Pironi." I interrupted, "And you, Auntie. You, too, head the family." "Only in relevance of age," she said with a smile. She poured more tea and said, "Even though you are the oldest in your family, you are not a namesake, my dear Michelina; you are a girl." I answered back, "I am well aware of this manifestation, Auntie. I live with this affliction daily." She then said, "Being a woman is not an affliction, being unmarried is." This assertion set me back a bit. My aunt then said, "Once a woman is inside her own family and inside her own home, with her own husband and children, then will she become realized as a woman. That is where you will rule, Michelina. Not on your own, forever searching for hidden meanings. If you never marry, then you can never have children - and you will always regret being childless. All women who chose never to become mothers, always suffer remorse at the end of their lives. The family gives true meaning." My Aunt Alfonsia was never more insightful or caring in manner, even though I still had doubts about her reasoning. She meant well even though, inside, I felt differently.

Regardless, Aunt Alfonsina truly was concerned for my well-being. I think her efforts to have me married off was dictating a renewed under-standing and justification of her own life. She opened her heart to me on the subject - this time by considering me and my plight specifically. I think she was handling it as her own obligation to the family - as a figurehead by her admission and as a strong Catholic.

At this point, my aunt thought a bit then got up and started to clear the table of our tea and biscuits. This action signified to me that the conver-sation was coming to an end but I sensed there was something more that she was about to divulge to me. I spoke first to extricate it. "I don't want a family yet, please understand." "I do, darling, niece - I do. Your father also never wanted the responsibility for a large family or the obligation to my sister as a son or the obligations of his own gifts as a harness-maker. Too much burden for too little a man." I was taken aback at my aunt's candor. I followed her to the kitchen with the rest of the tea setting.

"You are father to your father like I said, Michelina." "What can I do then?" I asked. My aunt considered, then looked me squarely in my eyes. "Why don't you go to New York for a while? See your Uncle Antonio and his family. They've invited you, no?" "Yes! I was invited many times by him and Fortuna. Both!" "Go then. Make your way there. Your cousin Paulo and his wife will go to New York themselves on a vacation - for the Fourth of July. I will ask if you could join them on the trip there. He would also like to see his Uncle Antonio, as well. Would you like that?" I paced around the kitchen thinking of the possibilities. "Yes - oh, yes! But I must plan then. I must contact Uncle Antonio - talk with my bosses and Papa - and it is already June." Aunt Alfonsina had me thinking. We gave each other big hugs, and I then helped my dear aunt finish with the domesticities before I left her home. I had come to respect her now more than ever.

I could not wait to get back to my apartment. No one was there, so I sat quietly by myself to reflect everything I had talked to Aunt Alfonsina about. I read Mother's letter again. "Don't come back to Italy without a husband." Those words from Mother repeated and repeated in my ear. I couldn't believe what I was reading. I thought of our Pirone gnome, "Oh, sweet Matzo Mauriello, what has happened to you, dear friend? Did you yourself die with Nonna?" I wrote down a plan and a schedule, and I found Uncle Antonio's letter to me of invitation. I will do this.

Then the apartment door opened, and in came father, fresh from losing another small fortune playing cards with his adoring and grateful paesani. He was obviously frustrated. All I could think was how his condition verified Aunt Alfonsia's words about him and our fragile relationship. How much more gambling loss would it be for him? Couldn't he instead gamble on me to help the family and to further my education?

We started an argument almost immediately on the same old subject. My father said everyone thinks as he did that I should be married by now and how others supported this view about me. "Not everyone!" I said, thinking of Aunt Alfonsina's words. So, I gave Father a good lecture. I told him not to influence everyone against me, adding, "I can take care of myself if you just stop worrying about me! Tell your people that so they will stop bothering me. I am tired of your endless parade of husbands before me. Go ahead! Go to Italy. Forget your glands and your duplicity with Dottore De Rosa. I do not believe that you have anything wrong with you. All you have is money that is lining your pockets to spend in Italy or to lose at cards. Go! Goodbye! Leave me alone! Go!"

Well, Papa said nothing and went out. He came back later and told me that he was making his passage and filing for his passport. "Good," I said. "I will stay the summer in New York with your brother and cousin, Fortuna. Uncle Antonio wrote me a letter inviting me. They support me on this. He will be glad to have me stay with them and get away from these constant pressures of yours." My father did not openly object to this plan. He then said, "What happens after summertime, if I'm not here? If I go to Italy?" "Go then. We will see about that at that time. Uncle Antonio will see to my coming back properly before they go to California for the grape season. I don't need you to ask him." Again, my father did not object. Why would he? "Good," he barked back. I stood my ground. "All I have to do now is to call him. I will go with cousin Paulo and his wife for the Fourth of July. I need a change badly. It will do me good to get out of here." He agreed, "Okay." That was it. Papa left me standing with no other words. Inside I was boiling. One less obligation on his part. Aunt Alfonsina's words came back to me. "You have been fathering your own father."

What a night! How could I sleep after so much emotion? I thought I really needed a rest from everything and everybody. I had another thing to do. I had to ask my bosses, Rosa and Agnes at the Parisian Dress Shoppe if I could take the rest of the summer off. Would they let me? I had to contact cousin Paulo also about the trip and I had to call Uncle Antonio as well. I could not sleep - but first things first.

The next morning, during my walk to work on Newbury Street, I had plenty of things going on in my head. Will my bosses understand? Not knowing why, I felt the two sisters would not object. Still, I did not want to lose my position or the best job I had ever had. What if they said, "no?" What would I do then? I was wondering this as I requested to talk with them during lunch break. Well - no problem! No problem at all. Rosa and Agnes were so wonderful and gracious. Not only would they give to me two week's pay for my vacation, but they also gave me permission to have a leave of service for two months. In the summertime, there wasn't too much to do anyway. Still, I had a nagging feeling - a premonition

- that maybe I would never work there again - why? As usual, my vivid dreams and my premonitions were telling me this would happen - almost as a certainty.

The last day of work, a Friday, Rosa and Agnes gave me a little going-away party with all the girls happily joining in. We ate at the big table, all together. Rosa and Agnes brought lots of food. They came out with cordials, and they made black coffee in our little coffee corner. It was all so wonderful. They knew nothing at all of what was going on in my heart, which made the joy they showered on me even more appreciative. I hid the intensity of my aching mind the best that I could. I bathed in the feeling of joy they shared for me and of the love that we felt for each other. I returned to them fully what they felt toward me.

But deep, deep in the back of my mind, was a little demon voice saying, "Goodbye you wonderful, wonderful ladies. Goodbye, beautiful Parisian dressmaking room. Goodbye, Newbury Street. Goodbye, North End. Goodbye, all." I felt just like the night I stood on the back deck of the steamship *America* as the lights of Naples slowly disappeared behind me. Goodbye, Italy. Goodbye, Pratola Serra. The feeling was hidden, but it was the same and it was there.

When I kissed them all goodbye, the voice in my head was saying, "Just say goodbye. Smile. Just say goodbye." None of them suspected that that was perhaps my last day at the Parisian Dress Shoppe. Or perhaps they did suspect it. Was it? No one really knew.

I actually ran home that afternoon. I said nothing to anyone who greeted me on the street. It was as if I were running through a desert. I didn't even hear any street noise or voices - nothing. I knew that my life had taken a big turn - what was it? To where? Oh, Matzo Maurellio, where are you, little friend?

———————

My Uncle Antonio was shouting happiness of joy over the telephone at my coming to visit for the summer. (What a wonderful new device of mankind - the telephone. It was invented in 1871 by an Italian immigrant, Antonio Meucci, of New York. A point to argue later.) Anyway, Uncle

Antonio would have everything ready for me. I did have a pleasant fare-well with both Papa and my brother, Ralfo, as well. It was all better that way. They both were genuinely in favor of this trip of mine. The apart-ment got a third larger. No protestations. Good. The summertime is less burdensome in the Northeast of America than other times of the year. The people are always on vacation during this time it seems - even if they are not.

My cousin Paulo was a chef - a very good one. He and his wife, Raffaella, would welcome me to join them on their trip to New York, just as Aunt Alfonsina predicted. So, I did. I went with them by boat. Going by boat was a little bit of a surprise to me because I had thought we would all go by train. But we didn't. Part of my cousin's plans was to make a party all the way to New York - both ways. There was dining and music on the boat to New York, so this was his vacation plan. I had no objections. How could I?

We left Boston Harbor at dinnertime, Friday, July 1st. The seas were calm, but the old feeling of crossing the Atlantic soon influenced my stomach. This time it was, however, more controllable, because I knew that the trip would be short, and I put my mind elsewhere. I tried to any-way. I had brought the best sea-sickness pills, as well, something I did not have on the steamship *America*.

My cousin's wife, Raffaella, was a very funny person - about my age. She was dark, stoic and shorter than me, with a dark sense of humor. They had been married for three years, but still no children. After dinner, she and I wanted to move about the boat and to digest. Paola, on the other hand, was tired and decided he would go to his cabin. Perhaps his stomach was not cooperating with his party plans. Anyway, he went to bed early and Raffaella and I went all over the place. We found the sec-tion of the boat where people had gathered to sing and dance - yes! First came, "La Tarantella." The record filled the air. Everyone danced and partied as if they were paesani. But they weren't all Italians. They were all Americans from different backgrounds. Everyone shared cultural dance music, except our queasy co-traveler, Paulo. I doubted that any train trip would have had such delight of sound and activity.

We then joined some Irish people singing, "My Irish Rose" and "Too-Ra-Loo-Ra-Loo-Ral." I really forgot everything and completely became immersed in the communal effort of everyone making happy music together. It reminded me how much I missed singing in a choir. I liked the group American dancing and singing as well. This was all new to me. A truly American experience. At three o'clock in the morning, Raffaella and I finally went to bed.

My cabin was next to my cousin and his wife. After Raffaella got undressed, she knocked at the wall between us with beats of, "La Tarantella." I returned the same. I tucked myself into bed but could not sleep at all. The demon voice of uncertainty again came to haunt me. Like a heavy shadow, it obfuscated all the joy I felt that night. I shouted out loud, "Oh, God! Give me some peace." I felt inside like I was being thrown about, here and there, like this boat rocking and rocking - all controlled by men and by the elements. Then I heard myself say, "Lena, keep quiet and go to sleep."

Did I sleep? No.

The morning after, right on time, at 8 o'clock, we steamed into New York. Lovely Fortuna was waiting for us at the dock, just like she had done two years earlier when I came from Italy. Oh, the joy of seeing her lovely face again!

We embraced, and all of us young cousins got into Fortuna's car - her car. It was very nice to hear her voice again also - so smart, so efficient with her quick talk and perfect Italian. I loved her. I was thinking how she had lost both a mother and a brother since I last saw her. Outwardly, the deaths didn't affect her. Paulo, Fortuna and I carried on simultaneous conversations in two different languages as we rolled along with Raffaella laughing at each loud breath we took.

We were about to arrive at the Pirone house in the Bronx when something else went through my mind. I never met my new aunt, Aunt Marietta. She was the old maid of forty-five whom my mother found in Prata for my widowed uncle to marry - sight unseen. I remembered that she accepted the proposal only by seeing a picture of him before their arranged marriage. They have been together for only one year. "This will be interesting," I thought.

Well, Uncle Antonio and his new wife were on the front porch, waiting. I had a sneaky desire to see these two together. There they were! Smiling - waving to us. Aunt Marietta was tall, slim, beautiful and self-assured. I felt a little guilty, for I expected her to possibly be a kind of monstrosity. I don't know why. My Uncle Antonio, of course, was still handsome with his blondish-gray curls, blue eyes and red cheeks. He was, however, a little stout, but jolly. The visual that caught my eye first was that when Marietta stood, she was more than a head taller than my uncle, who did not seem affected by the discrepancy. In reality, they looked nice together. She, very calm and dignified - he, full of a contentment of a man who was well-to-do and who wanted you to know it.

All my Pirone first cousins then came out and surrounded us. There was Flora (12), Maria (10), Tammi (8), Francesco (7) and little Venera (4). Mikele (6), had died the year before from losing his mother. I was most happy to see how my little cousin Flora had grown in two years. A beautiful little lady of twelve now. Her youngest sister, Venera, was a plump version of her father and just as jolly. It was evident that all of my cousins were well taken care of. As Aunt Alfonsina said, Uncle Antonio was living as the new "Don" of the Pirone family.

I could not help but to think that my Nonno, Don Carlos, would have been proud of his third oldest son and the bountiful life he made for himself in America. I also wondered if these things might be the same way if my uncle and his brothers hadn't left Pratola Serra in the first place. Who would they be now? It crushed Don Carlos when two of his three oldest sons left the family harness business for America. Would they have succeeded as well if they had stayed in our village? Was this the root also of my father's own unrest with himself and why he kept going back and forth? Later, I would read and study these concepts of psychology - nature versus nurture. I say it's almost all nature. Good Pirone genes, yes, but Don Carlos' upbringing of his sons, the nurturing of them, was dictated by his instincts which, of course, were genetic, inextricably forged by thousands of years of "nurturing." There was no question about one thing, however, Pratola Serra's loss was America's gain.

The house was large and in a magnificent section of the Bronx. It had a full porch out front with lots of outdoor furniture. The large yard had formal gardens on both sides of the house, and a large vegetable garden in the backyard with also fig and pear trees. Inside, there were many formal rooms filled with beautiful ornate furniture and large windows framed with hanging Venetian drapery. It was stupendous.

Fortuna helped me with my suitcases and took me upstairs. Almost immediately, however, she quietly pulled me aside while showing me the bedrooms. She could not wait to tell me about Marietta - her new stepmother. I was a little shocked at her immediate negative comments about her. In a whisper of secrecy, Fortuna confided, "Nobody calls her 'Mother,' Michelina." She went on, "Marietta seems good, but do not believe her. She is only for herself. She says 'yes, yes,' but she does as she pleases. It's a good thing that I am here so I can balance Father." I was surprised to hear such negativity from my otherwise cheerful cousin. "I am the business head," she said, "I made lots of money for my father. Without me, he would be lost right now." I asked her, "Why do you tell me these bad feelings about your stepmother? Are you missing your own mother? I would think so." "No, I say this because she might influence you too, Michelina, like she does the children. Be careful." I then said, "I am glad the children like her, but for the love of God, do not try to poison me against her right away. Give me a chance to see for myself about everything." Fortuna answered quickly, "All right. All right. I told you also because my father loves you like he loves me. He wants the best for us." I responded as tactfully as I could, "Please. I don't want to be upset right away about this. Why don't we just enjoy the family and let things run naturally? Let's see what will happen. I have just arrived here." Fortuna calmed herself, "Okay. Okay. Don't be upset."

We walked along the upstairs corridor. There were five bedrooms, two baths and lots of closet space. I asked, "Where will I sleep?" Fortuna told me, "Any one of the girl's rooms, but please stay with me, Michelina. The room after the master bedroom. I have a very big bed, so we will fit."

"Okay, yes," I said, smiling, "as long as we do not stay up all night talking family business, eh?" "I promise," she said returning a laugh.

As I unpacked my suitcase, I was thinking of how quickly family turmoil and uncertainty can boil up when new blood is added. I could not compare myself in any way to my cousin Fortuna at this point. Secretly, I envied her. My cousin was lucky to come to America when she did as a very young girl. Now, she was an American citizen. The year before, like all American women, she acquired the right to vote. She had her own car, and she helped to run her father's large business. And because of America, Fortuna could remain single and choose to be her own namesake without repercussion. She was the firstborn grandchild of Don Carlos, and when her own mother died, she became the open ruler of her father's family. It was easy to see how a new wife who came to replace an old one would certainly challenge this dynamic. To my mind, her stepmother, Marietta, was at a disadvantage from the start.

Monday, July 4th, 1921

Well, Cousin Paolo and his wife, Raffaella, were staying with us too, of course. And the two days after we arrived, we planned our celebrating the Fourth of July out on Long Island with another cousin of ours - cousin Pasquale Pirone and his family. Cousin Pasquale was the eldest son of the eldest Pirone son, Raffaele, who chose not to come. That was his general sour manner. Anyway, we had the weekend to plan and to festivate America's birthday.

Cousin Paolo got up before dawn on Monday and took care of all the cooking. Uncle Antonio made a special request of him and his cooking specialties. Uncle wanted Paolo to make a baked timballo macaroni. The timballo is a baked macaroni pie with a golden crust and inside is mezzani pasta (macaroni), mozzarella, provolone cheeses, ricotta cheese and tomato gravy of course. It is finished with grated Romano cheese and some soft spices. Poalo was making one to perfection.

I asked Uncle, "Why make a timballo? The timballo is almost like lasagna." He interrupted me saying, "Ah, but we can eat it with our hands, like a sandwich. We are going to the cottage of cousin Pasquale in Long Island, near the beach. He never had anything like a timballo. It will be fun, and a good surprise for him." My dear uncle was always ready to eat fun food and to share in the joy of it.

Cousin Paolo was so attentive to his chosen duty. He was to cook for everyone many of his Italian specialties. Meanwhile, Aunt Marietta was putting drinks in a basket, also too, bread, cheese, wine and other stuff just as the timballo pie came nice and hot out of the oven. Paolo covered the golden beauty in a cloth and placed it on a wooden slab. All ready.

Everyone went out to the cars. We needed, of course, two cars for the trip - Fortuna's car and the family car. I, Cousin Paolo and his wife, Raffaella, rode with Fortuna and the bounty of food prepared by Paolo. My uncle and aunt took all the children into the family car. Both cars were fully loaded - one happy group of happy Italian gypsies.

A few hours later, we reached the beach cottage. I met my first cousin Pasquale and his large family for the very first time. It was another joyous family reunion of sorts - a nice bunch of congregating Pironi. The glorious part was that even though we had never met before, we all resembled each other either in physicality or in mannerism. Bravo Nonno Don Carlos and Nonna Pirone! If you could see this now. This was a wonderful start to my "get away" vacation from all of my woes.

The beach cottage was right in front of the ocean. The first thing we did after arriving was we took our shoes off and splashed our feet in the surf. Cherubic little Venera had to be helped out of the car I remember. Her big sister Flora was teasing her. "Oh, oh. I told you, you got to lose weight, baby. No timballo for you today." Venera yelled back, "You are not the boss! Marietta gives me anything I want." "Oh, dear," I thought. "Here they go on again."

The Fourth of July was celebrated with hilarity and fun. Cousin Pasquale provided everyone with firecrackers and beach towels - all used to exhaustion. We had good food and excellent company. Kids ran everywhere. It reminded me of the fiestas we put on in Pratola Serra. Even Fortuna was caught in the feeling of joy, and we festivated all that day and into the evening. We sang, bathed, drank and dined away in simultaneous noisy chatter. We didn't arrive back into the Bronx until the early hours of Tuesday morning. Happy birthday, America!

———————

Three days after, cousin Paolo and his wife, Raffaella, left on their return ocean voyage back to Boston. A wonderful end to their own vacation.

Those early vacation days for me in New York were restful. I began really to feel at ease. In the morning, I was the first one to get up - ahead of the children. I bathed and went into the peaceful backyard garden. There was a hammock in the yard where I read, and I felt calm and relaxed. Not one petulant thought dared to enter my head. It was wonderful.

On one of those mornings, Uncle Antonio joined me, and I knew he wanted to talk to me. He took up a chair and sat next to me with his morning cappuccino. Without hesitance, he said, "Michelina, I wish you would remain here with us, when your father goes to Italy. We will have your brother, Ralfo, here too if he likes. I would love for you to stay and to live with us." I answered, "But, why Uncle? I can take care of myself in Boston, even without Papa. I was just thinking of these things myself." With conviction, he said, "Why? Don't ask me why - I don't know. I guess it is that you are a good influence on my children perhaps. You fit in this family. You are family." I said to him, "How about me? I have to work and make something of myself." He interrupted, "I will give you everything you want, Michelina - here in New York. You should stay here with us. Please. We have plenty of room." "I thank you, but no, dear Uncle. I will have to go back to Boston at the end of the summer. I have plans of my own. You are too kind. I shall help here as much as I can while I visit you. But I must find my own way, even if my father returns to Italy."

My uncle said nothing more. I knew his heart was in the right place - yes, a concern for my well-being, but also a concern for his own immediate family as well. Echoes of my conversation with Fortuna came to me. How sure was the marriage between Uncle Antonio and Aunt Marietta? Fortuna was leading the family business. Who would be there for Uncle Antonio and all the children if Marietta left for any reason? Not Fortuna.

She was a young businesswoman. Now, these thoughts came into my head. Not a very pleasant thought either.

Also, there was a deep sense of duty that my uncle conveyed during our conversation. Not just for the immediate concerns of his family, but also the strong influences of his father, Don Carlos, who always wanted family to stay together - to build a large Pirone compound where all the Pironi lived, worked and prospered. Was Uncle Antonio, being the new head of the family, just fulfilling the commands of his late father? Perhaps it was a little of both. My father's own plight was conspicuously absent in this conversation, outside of his glands.

My Uncle Antonio was so generous; he always had been, but he knew little of how proud and ambitious I was. Then a doubt occurred in my mind. Perhaps he himself wasn't sure of Marietta either - their future together. Was it Fortuna's influence on him to perhaps feel this way? I had to wait many years to find out the real roots of my uncle's offer to me to live with them. I did, however, after that meeting in the garden, commit myself to being even more attentive to Uncle Antonio's family, his needs and to be as helpful as I could to maintain whatever form of harmony existed in his large and fragile household.

My twelve-year-old cousin, Flora, and I were inseparable that entire summer. We loved each other's company. Fortuna was mostly working now at the Pirone wholesale grape business. Flora and I went to movies in downtown New York City or right there in the Bronx, with my uncle's permission of course. We also went to the Metropolitan Museum of Fine Art, where I really left my heart. It was a reaffirmation of my inner desire to learn more and more - of how much there was still to learn. Systematically, for two wonderful weeks, we did just fine.

Until...

One day in late July, Fortuna and Uncle Antonio came home from work together, and they brought with them, Giacomino Fabbo. I was shocked beyond belief to see him when they all came into the kitchen. My uncle beamed, "Michelina! Look who I found! Your fiancé." Giacomino just stood between my uncle and Fortuna with his hat in his hand and a sheepish grin on his face. I could not take it. I got furious and said angrily, "Where did you find 'him'?" My uncle looked confused and did not answer. I got up, pushed past them, and ran upstairs to the bedroom.

After a while, Fortuna came up. I was sitting on the edge of the bed with my arms crossed firmly. I spoke angrily, "How did this man find me? Find us? How did he know I was in New York, and why was I not told first?" Fortuna sat next to me and said, "I don't know. He came to the office. It has our Pirone name to it. Maybe a paesano told him." I said, "Why did you bring him here?" "Giacomino said he was your longtime fiancé and wanted a chance to appease you. He was sure that a surprise visit would renew your happiness in seeing him. He was very sincere and persuasive." "Well, I am not renewed, and he obviously persuaded you." This was a response that my cousin was not prepared for. She thought she was part of something that would have pleased me. It didn't.

Fortuna got up and paced a bit. She realized how upset I was at the sudden appearance of the surprise guest downstairs. She offered a sound question - to her anyway. "Giacomino told father in the office that he was your fiancé from Prata, and together you promised to marry here in America. This is why he came from Italy. Is this true?" I couldn't respond. I was so angry. Fortuna continued, "He also told Father that your Uncle Francesco, in Pratola Serra, gave you permission to be his fiancée." Still I said nothing. Fortuna continued, "When Giacomino came in the office, he talked and talked - we felt so sorry for him." I spoke back, "So you brought him home?" "We believed him when he said that you would be happy to see him, Lena."

I kept quiet marveling at the audacity of the man. Fortuna finished with, "We were sure that you must love him too - that there must be some misunderstanding. After all, you made him come to America; you promised to marry him, didn't you?" I jumped up at this last comment. "Stop, stop!" I said. "I can't stand it. Tomorrow I shall go to back to Boston." Fortuna now was shocked at my tone and resolve. I think she might have also felt that she somehow might have made a bad mistake in her evaluation of the situation - that it was not a good thing when she and my uncle brought Giacomino back with them.

I was searching for my suitcases just as Uncle Antonio finally came up to the bedroom. He pleaded softly, "Please, Michelina, do come downstairs. I feel sorry for the poor fellow. An educated man with such polite manners, etc.," adding, "He is in love with you. It is obvious." I retorted, "Please Uncle, enough! I shall take care of this." I went downstairs into the parlor with Fortuna and my uncle following slowly behind me.

I faced Giacomino with indignation in my expression. He stood politely. My uncle took the room and told Giacomino, "I don't know why she is mad at you. Did you tell me the truth, Sir?" Giacomino still sheepishly holding his hat answered, "Please, Mr. Pirone, ask her yourself, Sir. Please." My uncle turned towards me. He wanted just one answer from me. "Michelina, did you promise this man to marry you here in America and then go back to Italy together?" I hesitated and lowered my voice. I heard myself say almost in a whisper, "Yes - but it was long ago and things are different now." My uncle took a deep breath and I could feel Fortuna sliding backward behind me. My uncle said nothing, but he was shaking his head as if I had done an injustice to this nice, innocent fellow. He quietly left the room with Fortuna in tow, saying nothing more.

Left alone with Giacomino, I kept the fire and indignation in my eye. I told him angrily, "You big bluff! You know that you are lying, don't you? My Uncle Francesco only gave permission for you to come into my house! Never did he give you permission to marry me. You didn't mention my father said there is no engagement either, did you?" Giacomino pressed closer with the eyes of a doe, pleading, "Please, please, Michelina, do not spoil everything! It was so hard for me to find you and to be listened to by your uncle. Can I help it if I love you so much?"

I stood my ground. "How did you know I was in New York? How did you find me?" Giacomino said that the cousin he stayed with in Boston was a patient of Dottore De Rosa. He almost bragged the information, "Your father told Dottore De Rosa about your visiting his brother in the Bronx, and the Dottore told my cousin. My cousin wrote to me and I found your uncle's business. Easy."

For a moment, I was again speechless at the audacity of Giacomino Fabbo. How to get rid of this man? He was flypaper. I thought to myself, "Papa you fool. You could not keep your mouth closed." He came to me and took my hand with both of his - pleading, "Michelina. I am so sorry. I just had to see you again - to make good on my sincerity to you." I took my hand away and sat on the couch, thinking. He sat next to me and spoke quickly, convincingly. "I have been out of work for weeks looking for you. I lost my job over finding you. I passed your uncle's business many times without going in until I found him alone. We had a good long talk - man to man. Then your cousin came in. They like me. He even offered me a job, to work for him!" "He offered you a job? Doing what?" "I will receive and record the railcars of grapes that come from California, to dispense to his salesman." I added, "In other words, he offered you a job as a mediator, am I right?" "Yes, yes," he answered happily. "Your uncle is a successful businessman. He sees the worth in people."

I could only stare back at Giacomino in disbelief. I removed my hand from his. I hadn't even noticed that he had gotten a hold of it again. I simply got up and left, numbed by this last confession. Giacomino called after, "I will call on you again, my love! You are the moon and stars!"

I remained quiet and reclusive for days. I said not a word nor committed to any outward emotion even when Giacomino kept showing up at the house. He kept on coming to dinner at the invitation of his future boss, my Uncle Antonio. The job offer remained in place, and so did Giacomino. My uncle just enjoyed the man's company. I was squeezed in between their laughter which slowed into an echo in my head.

That night, I remember having one of my prophetic dreams. I was being chased and pushed down to the ground by men, my father included. I struggled but could not get up. I dreamt of my two best friends Amalia Pisano back in Italy who was forced to marry the choice of her father, the man in the hat, and also of Annie Chambelli who barely escaped with her life. So many other girls like them flashed by. I dreamt of my new Aunt Marietta who married a photograph and I dreamt also of my Aunt Alfonsia's words to me, "Being a woman is not an affliction - being unmarried is." And also, my mother's letter came to me, "Don't come back to Italy without a husband - you are already cursed."

I woke from this horrible dream in a sweat. I was convinced that I saw my own future. There was no hope for me to dream of anything otherwise. What was the use?

Giacomino, of course, charmed everybody with his stories about Italy and his experiences while he was in the military and the Great War. He told why he limped and how he lost his toes in service to Italy to the vocal sympathy of his large captive audience. My uncle and his family absolutely loved him. The chatter around the dinner table was always light and happy. Giacomino had them all eating out of his hand - literally.

Every evening, Uncle Antonio and Marietta waited supper for Giacomino. Once, I caught myself smiling at one of his ridiculous but funny stories. This smile did not go unnoticed by my cousin, Fortuna, who shrugged and smiled back in my direction.

Little by little, as usual, this poor fool Michelina relaxed. I understood that my uncle and Fortuna needed Giacomino in their business, that he was an able man and had acquired skills over the years that they could use. I, too, found myself being sorry for him. Perhaps it was good that he lost his job at Café Ferrari because of searching for me. The job at the café was a horrible situation in the worst neighborhood, amongst all the worst Italian elements. So, I tried again to listen to and tolerate Giacomino's declaration of love. I relented, yes. I dared to be receptive one more time - at least to listen. I caved in under the assault, an assault of purported love and affection - but still an assault.

After these many dinners, Giacomino would go to the piano in the parlor where he sang all the old Italian folk songs and operatic arias. He had a wonderful singing voice. All anyone had to do was ask him. The children quickly gathered around Giacomino and would gleefully accompany him. Even I, who loved to sing, joined in.

Giacomino and I were often left alone on the front porch of my uncle's house after the children went to bed. There was no such thing as a chaperone or any guardian surveillances. This was not Italy. Giacomino and I talked peacefully, and we even laughed together. He was a charmer forever, this man. Perhaps it was this - perhaps the summer night on the front porch in the Bronx, who knew, but Giacomino said in the calmest and nicest of all faces, "Michelina Pirone. May I ask your father's permission now to marry you? I shall make you happy forever." I took a moment before answering him. I quietly nodded and said, "Yes." I immediately almost retracted it, but I couldn't. I just couldn't take it back. It was too late.

Giacomino jumped completely in the air and took my hand. He shook it vigorously like someone would a long-lost friend. It almost came off. He then bent down and kissed me on the forehead, exactly like he had done two years earlier, the time I left him behind in Italy.

The next curious thing Giacomino did was to run down the stairs of the porch and happily wish me goodnight. That was it. I was left alone on my uncle's front porch newly engaged to a crazy person. I had no understanding of how I got myself into that position.

I went upstairs and cried myself to sleep.

Giacomino immediately wrote to my father:

Dear Signore Mr. Pirone, Sir,

I have been visiting Michelina at your brother Antonio's house for some many days now and I write to you this letter to formally request again your daughter's hand in marriage. We have made up our differences with the consent of Uncle Antonio. She has agreed to marry with your permission, Sir. You can ask her yourself. We asked your brother if we could marry in New York in the near future. Your brother will

confirm this who was present and also has put his blessing to our union.
He has even welcomed me into the family by giving me a position in his
grape transport company.

I hope and pray that you will consummate the final approval for this
longtime engagement.

I thank you Sir and respectfully remain,

Giacomino Fabbo.

My father wrote immediately back, "Oh, yes, yes, of course. You have my blessings."

Giacomino showed the letter to my Uncle Antonio and to Fortuna before he even showed it to me. They gave us a surprise party. Was it a surprise? Yes. Was I happy about it? No. At this party, Giacomino gave me an engagement ring - a small diamond ring. He tried to kiss me on the lips. I offered my hand to kiss instead.

Everyone after that day was happy. Not me. I often took the ring off. I didn't know if I was doing the right thing. But every time doubts filled my head, Giacomino would always succeed in pulling me back by charming me with his anecdotes or his knowledge of opera and music of all kinds. He would endlessly charm me with reviews of the books he had studied in his three years at the university and other books he had read. He would do all these things with an accompaniment of his baritone voice. Giacomino wasn't shy like my past main suitor, Eugenio Mettola. All to the contrary, Giacomino had more nerves than brains. I was charmed, yes, but sadly, I still did not love him.

Then a paesano came to the house one Sunday morning, a worker friend of my uncle who knew Giacomino personally. Oh, boy, the news he brought. Well, this man claimed Giacomino was not out of work as he had said, that he was still a bartender in the Sicilian section of New York in the old and decrepit Café Ferrari. The paesano also told us in mock whispers that Giacomino had many girls at his disposal where he worked and that he was a Don Juan. Nobody believed my uncle's friend - except me. They thought the man was a little jealous. But he got me thinking.

Naturally, Giacomino kept showing up - just in time for dinner. He was the same as he had been in Italy during these visits, demanding all of my time. He went on and on about the planning of our marriage every chance he spoke. Even my well-meaning uncle suggested that Giacomino and I live together with him until Giacomino made some money to buy or rent a home nearby. I could never win with those two stubborn men at the table. Through it all, my cousin Fortuna kept quiet. Marriage was never a topic she joined in on. Giocomino was confident now that everything was settled.

One night, after dinner, Giacomino wanted to go for a walk. This time, I insisted that my twelve-year-old cousin Flora join us. An Italian tradition I wanted to maintain. Giacomino thought it a bit strange, but relented. He had a bigger audience for himself he thought, I'm sure.

We went to a nearby square that was a miniature park. It was a beautiful night. The Bronx was full of these small park squares. Every street seemed to have one of them. This park, because of the quality of the area, was heavily cultivated. It had beautiful Italian style bushes, and lots of trees - even an Italian style fountain in the middle. Giacomino tried desperately to impress us with his baritone voice - which he did.

Being such a babble, Giacomino narrated to Flora and me all of his escapades before coming over to America. Very braggadocio. He let slip that he lived in Paris for a while. I said to him, "What? Where did you get the money to live in Paris?" I caught Giacomino checking himself quickly, like he said something wrong. "Oh," he answered, "I always had money. Don't forget that I was the manager in my father's business." Something was not right about this story of his. I stopped and pressed further. "Wait. If you managed your father's business, why did he permit you to go to Paris? And why did you go there?" I asked.

For the first time in many hours, nothing but silence came out of Giacomino's open mouth. Then he candidly said, "No, my father didn't even know where I went. I just left." I insisted further, "You didn't answer me, Giacomino - why did you go to Paris?" He hesitated. "Come on - tell me." A pathetic expression came over his face. He shrugged out the next words of his, "Well, you had stopped writing to me and all that silence made me feel hurt and abandoned. I was a man - left there in Prata - alone." That response was not complete enough and the expression on my face told him so. Flora nervously stood back at the rising tension between Giacomino and me. He choked out, "I thought I fell in love with a beautiful singer. She went to Paris. And - I followed her. It was a short interlude, Michelina. Please believe me! She became impossible. She had so many other lovers. I had to leave Paris because I had no more money left." I repeated, "No more money, eh?" Then I shouted. "You hypocrite! You will do it again and again. Never! Never again to me - capisce!? You will never see me again!" I took the ring off my finger and put it in his pocket. "Flora you heard him. Let's go!" Giacomino quickly held my arm. "Wait! I thought you knew! Oh, my God, everybody in our two towns knew this. Michelina, be reasonable." I pulled away, and Flora pushed him off. We ran home.

When we got back to the house, I ran hard up the stairs while Flora told her father all the details in what had happened in the park - the entire conversation. She was old enough to fully understand all of the ramifications.

A little bit later, my uncle and aunt both came up to talk to me. At first, they tried to excuse Giacomino. "Men are like that, etc., etc." I said, "Please Uncle, sit near me." I embraced him dearly. "Uncle, you are too good. You always have been the angel of our family. You have been helping everyone, even when you had limited earnings. But you are not able to look into my heart. I can't marry a man like him. He runs after actresses and takes money from his trusting father and disappears. He uses his charm and not his honesty to win over good people like yourself. I can't marry a man such as this. I can't, and I won't."

My uncle got up and kissed me on the cheek saying, "Well, what do you think - that I will make you suffer? I will command him to keep away from here and that is that." "I thank you, dear Uncle." And so, it was done. The third and final ending of any engagement with Giacomino Fabbo. But it was not as easy as that.

Giacomino called by phone incessantly, to talk to my uncle or to my Aunt Marietta. Nobody listened to him. He even dared to come to the house one afternoon, at dinnertime. He reached the porch door, but my uncle calmly took him out of the yard. What he said to him or what he did, I never knew. Eventually, Giacomino stopped bothering us in person, but he kept sending menacing letters to me and to my uncle at his business. Not a smart move on his part.

I couldn't forgive Giacomino. He spoiled my summer in New York. I spent the rest of the time I had left cooking with Marietta the dishes that Nonna Pirone taught me. I knew that that would please my uncle. This cooking took my mind off of the situation and allowed me to focus on my New York family. I also made a timballo like our cousin Paolo did. The children were always around me. Uncle was right, all the children loved me. And I loved them in return.

At this time, my dear cousin Fortuna was my undying inspiration. I told her, "Perhaps you and I will be old maids together, eh? We are not interested in marriage anyway." She laughed. "I guess not. I am in love with my business and with making money. You are in love with your books and culture." We laughed together about it. I shared also with my cousin the lovely, long letter I got from Italy - from my dear friend Annie Chambelli, who, too, was exploring her own independence and the wonders of life.

One night, Fortuna took me to a play in Broadway. Uncle Antonio brought us there, then came to take us home. I think he was afraid we would meet trouble - meaning Giacomino or other bad elements of the city.

The play was by George Bernard Shaw, "The Doctor's Dilemma." A very interesting play, it could even be applied to today about the ignorance of some doctors and the virtuosity of others. Dottore Pulcinella's own ignorance came to my mind. I could understand the dialogue of the play easily because the roots of almost all English and Italian was Latin and because of my longtime studies, I could read and speak Latin easily. My English was continuing to grow in my ear, thanks to Cousin Fortuna, who plied it to me often. But, I was prideful in my diction of it and guarded in the usage of the English language itself. Why? I wanted it to be perfect - nothing less. So, I listened and studied the sound of it. I would not be comfortable until I could speak in a fluid, uninterrupted English narrative. It had to be perfect, like the Italian I embraced. It wasn't just yet. I wanted always to have no dialect - no accent - in any language. My Pirone pride? Perhaps so.

Another evening we went to the Opera to see La Boheme of Puccini, of course, that was in Italian. That music rested in my mind for days and days afterwards. Both nights, I had the balm I needed for my turbulent mind, for I again felt persecuted. I felt I lacked something that was near, but I was unable to grasp what it was. I didn't know yet. I consoled myself, thinking, "I need time." I remember, "Did I have time?" This stuff called time was running away from me. I couldn't find space in it to quietly plan my future. My first vacation was spoiled, all my good intentions were poisoned by vengeful letters, marital demands of my family and many incidents. I was thankful to Fortuna, however, in treating me with what I loved the most. She was smart, perhaps too smart. She had brains, but she also was tortured by what she wanted in her own life against what she had. Was anybody happy, really, at peace with themselves and with the world?

I saw Fortuna at work with the few men involved in the grape business - none of them were open suitors. I was amazed at the capacity she had. She gave orders to these men of how to go about selling and what she expected from them, etc. My Uncle Antonio would always nod his head in approval. It was a revelation to me. Yes, I had to agree that she was running the business almost by herself. Did Nonno Pirone know her potential - this firstborn Pirone, a girl, when he held her in his arms - Don Carlos' dearest little girl? Did he inculcate in her the confidence she had in herself now? Would I find the same confidence?

A few days later, there started another battle which brought new confusion and revelations - all involving my supposedly ailing father. While I was away from Boston, Dottore Pulcinella De Rosa took a meeting with

Luigi Pisano, the widowed barber from Lynn, who requested that the Dottore set up a meeting with my father. At that meeting, Luigi Pisano asked my father for permission to court me with intentions of marriage. But my father had to answer him, "I am sorry, Mr. Pisano. I sent a letter to her fiancé, Giacomino Fabbo, giving him permission to take Michelina's hand in marriage. I also sent a letter to my brother in New York, who also accepted Giacomino's proposal. Giacomino is from your same home village - Prata. They will be married soon, and I will go back to Italy for my health - you can ask the Dottore about this if you like." Luigi Pisano left with his hat in his hand - another disappointed suitor, I am sure.

But now, when Papa found out from Uncle Antonio that again the engagement was off and that he had thrown Giacomino out of the door, Papa immediately ran downstairs and told this story to Dottore the Pulcinella. All of the particular details were expounded upon, nothing spared, especially about the threatening letters and confrontations made by Giacomino. What happened next? The Pulcinella-Dottore immediately went and told Luigi Pisano of course.

Mamma Mia!

As I later found out, the very next day, Luigi Pisano took a train to New York City and went directly to the Italian district. He asked the paesani where he could find the Italian café called the Café Ferrari? Luigi Pisano went straight inside and found Giacomino in this miserable decrepit bar and pulled him outside. He gave him such a fiery talk and forbade him to ever to write me again or to bother me or my family in any way. When Giacomino strongly objected, Luigi Pisano beat him up badly and left him on the street bleeding from his ear. I didn't know anything about this incident until later. No more letters came. "Oh," I thought, "this man finally understands." But I didn't know the real reason why.

The rest of the summer went quickly - too quickly. I got a letter from father saying that he was booked to leave for Italy in October and that I was to make arrangements with either my Aunt Alfonsina or one of my mother brothers in Lynn to live with them. Or, he wrote, I could stay in New York. I had no choice. I wanted to go home to the North End. Perhaps I could convince everyone before October that I could live on my own - with my brother Ralfo. Poor, poor Ralfo. The pressures I put him through.

I left by train back to Boston the third week of August. Tears were openly given and shared between me and my dear New York family. I shall never forget that summer of 1921.

Chapter Fifteen

Biting the Final Bullet

After I arrived back home in Boston, I found myself exhausted beyond reason. I was so very emotionally drained from my trip to New York that I slept for two days. This for me was not a depression; it was exhaustion. Yes, I needed rest, time to be by myself and alone, but our apartment was always full with my father's and brother's friends, so it was difficult to be truly alone. In reality though, one can't be alone in Boston in the North End even if he or she tried. If I opened the window, I could hear the vendors calling out their offerings, the echoes of children's shouting, the clopping of horse hooves, etc. Still, I missed the solitude and beauty of my uncle's garden in New York, and I had it seriously in my head that I might move back there as my Uncle Antonio had offered. I also missed the mountain circumstant and the hills that surrounded my village in Italy - Pratola Serra, itself so calm, so silent. But, just being alone those mornings in Boston was equally comforting and special.

Soon, I started to get moving again, to shop, to cook for my father and brother, to walk and to socialize. I had forgotten how many friends I had in the North End just by walking on the sidewalks. If I went out evenings, it was with my Aunt Alfonsina, my many cousins or to the picture show with my brother, Ralfo. And, if I stayed home, my brother and his political friends were always wonderful company in debate. Still, the clock was in my head. I had to plan for when my father would leave for Italy in October. I just pushed that out of my mind - for now.

At the very end of August, I called my boss Rosa at the Parisian Dress Shoppe and explained that I wasn't ready to report to work yet and I wasn't feeling just right adding, "Many incidents had occurred that made me upset. I still need to clear my head." Rosa assured me that nothing was more important than my well-being. "You will come back when you can," she said. "I thank you, Rosa. You are an angel. Goodbye."

A few mornings, I went to the Boston Public Library in Back Bay on Copley Square to read books, mostly Latin and operatic libretti (books) that were in Italian. It was a glorious ambiance. I stayed there until the afternoon. The library was very near to my Parisian Dress Shoppe on Newbury Street, but I avoided passing by that address if I could. I didn't feel like going in or making my presence known yet. Instead, I read in solitude in that grand library.

To get to Copley Square from the North End, I avoided Newbury Street altogether. I would walk around it through the West End and down Beacon Street which crossed the primarily Jewish section in Boston. The Jews dominated this area with stores of all kinds and buildings with apartments that were close together - almost touching each other. Often, the Jewish women would converse through their open windows across these busy streets and alleys. Noisy, yes - annoying, no. I loved these chatterbox people. They let out all their troubles with such a deep sense of suffering, but after this catharsis, they would laugh about it. A beautiful people.

When I got back home, my father was still complaining about his health. I asked him, "Why don't you go to see another Dottore instead of Dottore De Rosa? Perhaps another Dottore will give you a cure that can help you now - here in America. I don't trust the Pulcinella." Papa bristled, "Oh, no, no! I can't be cured here. I need my country's air - Italian air. I am suffering. You know this. Nobody in America knows how to cure me. I can't be cured here. I must go back to Italy and no use talking about. I am going." Every angle I took to keep my father in America was not working - even the rational ones.

Just while my father and I were arguing that evening, two of my mother's cousins suddenly came up and knocked on our door. They had just arrived from Italy and could not wait to meet us. Their arrival into our kitchen put a fresh joy back into the air. Gabriele and Peppo Fabrizio, two very delightful young brothers in their thirties, twins, with a contagious sense of humor and zest for life. These two wore constant smiles and went about slapping everyone on their backs. The Fabrizio brothers were clean looking and handsome - both of them. And, the two of them looked just alike, so much so, that they had to keep repeating their own names in front of us as to which one was which. Gabriele would brag loudly, "Easy. I am the tall one!" and Peppo would yell back, "No, I am taller! See," pushing himself up into his brother's laughing face. It was impossible to tell them apart.

The brothers were in business together back in Italy - in the large city of Avellino. First as furniture makers, but later, when the demand for fine furniture became scarce in Italy, they changed their business to building coffins. There was far more demand for that eternal piece of cabinetry.

The twins had voyaged to America in hopes of finding renewed work as furniture-makers or to start their own business, much like my father and his own two brothers had done as harness-makers years earlier. Fortunately, these Fabrizio fellows did not get rejected to come by America's new Emergency Immigration Act. They had valuable skills and came to America not without resources. They also knew that they could rely on their backup craft of building coffins. People die in every part of the world.

Of course, we set extra plates for the table, and I added more pasta to the water on the stove. I had also made a big roasted chicken in white wine that night, so there was plenty of good food for everyone. At dinner, my brother, Ralfo, was beside himself with questions of Italy and the troubling social conditions there. Talking politics and world events during long dinners was always an Italian tradition. This one was no different. Ralfo was now very much exploring the cause of the Socialist Workers' movement worldwide and in America. He was a Marxist and hungry for information - especially coming directly from central Europe and Italy.

The first thing the twins told my father was that my mother and the children were all just fine and that they were anxiously waiting for him to go back. Nonno Fabrizio, their uncle, was still the warhorse and protector, but everyone wanted my father to come home and to bring them back to America. This did not help my own cause any, but I felt my family's desires back in Italy.

Then my brother interjected, "How are the workers doing now? What is their situation? I heard it is bad." Peppo said to him, "The present conditions of Italy are disastrous - as bad as they have ever been." Reflecting, he said, "And Italy is still so overpopulated, that the paesani keep leaving to America." Gabriele then said, "We are here because the situation is unbearable. We have skills that would die if we stayed in Italy. Or we would die first." "And the workers?" my brother again asked. Peppo told him, "Big industries of war are closing or are closed. The workers have been let go. These industries have passed on their failures to the banks that had subsidized them. Now, nothing." Gabriele finished with, "Also, these things ruined people with their small capital and small businesses - like ours. The lire changes value, lower every day. Talented workers are out of work. They are desperate and uneasy. They protest openly." Ralfo said, "I read there was a big strike in Avellino." "No, not a strike," said, Peppo, "we always have strikes. This one was a revolt." Everyone sat for a moment to consider. The previous look of curiosity on Ralfo's face soon went to remorse.

I listened intently to this argument and figured that I would add my own opinion of the subject - why not? After all, I had been studying these issues as well as anyone - even my brother. I pointed out that The Treaty of Versailles had been disingenuous to Italy, robbing her of materials with which to build and recover. And with no raw materials, there is no market. The other winning nations got more after the Great War. The Treaty left Italy with no colonies either with which to exchange. This agreement was biased against Italy and narrowed her possibility of expanding or to occupy her people's talents. Italy was even bigger in size than Great Britain but did not profit in victory. As I finished, there was a great deal of vocal support of my opinion. I felt vindicated that I was allowed to express them at the table. Even Ralfo beamed.

Then my father climbed into the conversation saying, "Well, these things do not affect me. I left Italy long ago because of these reasons. I will go back a better man than when I left." I thought, "Not so, dear father - not so." Gabriele and Peppo then tried to discourage my father about going to Italy. "Yes. Go back, but not now, Guiseppe." "Maybe it would be best to wait a bit," said the other twin. "Oh, no!" Papa objected, "My health can no longer wait on the lire to recover." I quickly changed the subject by offering, "It is an awful picture you two paint. Hearing it from you directly seems more veritable though." Silence. "I shall get everyone strong coffee and cake, eh?" At that announcement, the Fabrizio twins again returned to their happy boisterousness.

***

"La Forza del Destino" (The Force of Destiny).

My Notations of Fate

Here, I must again restate my beliefs of fate versus destiny. It truly came into focus for me one late summer morning at the Boston Public Library when I was studying my books during those many solitary hours. I took out the Italian libretto (storybook) of Verdi's opera, "*La Forza del Destino,*" "The Force of Destiny." A wonderful, but tragic opera that Verdi wrote in 1869, composed to the libretto written by Antonio Ghislanzoni. The story and the music I knew, but fate brought us all together one summer's morning. I happened to hear on record the night before, the big aria of this opera, "*Pace, pace, mio Dio.*" I could not help but to see this as a signal of fate when I most needed it. "A message - yes," I thought out loud. Many nights I woke up with these words in my troubled head - "pace, pace, mio Dio." Now I heard them sung - "Peace, peace, dear God!" I was struck by the coincidence of it, another coincidence in my life that needed looking into.

Simply, the opera is about two lovers, a girl of royalty, the daughter of a Marquis, and the man, a nobleman from South America. These two lovers are forced to elope because her father does not approve of the match and he refuses to allow the marriage. In their attempt to elope, however, the Marquis catches them and by accident, the nobleman's gun goes off and kills the Marquis, the father. Now comes a duel between the nobleman and the girl's brother, who is also killed. The story ends in the declaration that destiny would never allow their union, so they both commit suicide instead of eloping. All this drama to Verdi's music. You can imagine the power of it. It was hopeless for the two lovers. They believed their fate was also their destiny, and so they killed themselves. The girl sang the same aria I had been singing, "pace, pace, mio Dio." Ah, but I came to realize then that she and Verdi were wrong!

Why? Because during these sessions in solitude, I also studied in great detail the writings of the ancient Greeks. There was Plato, Homer, Plutarch and Euripides and others - their various plays and mythologies. And the answer came to me like a thunderbolt as if thrown by Zeus himself from Mount Olympus. I would combine together these ancient writers with their plays and also with Verdi and his opera. I thought and thought and thought about this - fate versus destiny. I had my answer - an answer for me that I still believe now to this day.

My belief was compliant with the styles of Greek mythology where the gods controlled the day to day events in our lives over which we ourselves have no control. These forces play with our immediate situations, rather than with the idea of a future "destiny." "Fate" is the present tense in this form, and destiny would be both the past and future tenses. I believe we can only be destined to be "who" we are and not "where" we are on any given day. There is no changing the "who." Fate puts situations in front of us, whether it is influenced by a deity or deities or by simple chance, it doesn't really matter. That is just fate. Destiny is more infused in our souls - in us. Destiny, in itself, is our soul. We can only be destined to be who we are. We have no say in it. Whether we are fated to die in childhood or crumble away in old age, there are other influences on those occurrences. No matter what age we die, we die the same soul. My destiny? In my heart, I believe, starting back then, that I was destined only to be Michelina Pirone. I was already my own destiny at that point, and at every other point of my life, it would be the same. I had no say in that part of it. That was predestined. Prophetic dreams and coincidences? They happen only when two or more destinies collide.

But, it's the gods and fate that brings the actual knock to your door. It just happens.

The second week of September in Boston was beautiful. The air was sharp on the edges and bucolic. There came a knock on the kitchen door. It was a Monday. When I opened it, there stood my father. "Why are you knocking on the door, Papa?" I asked him. He smiled slightly and stepping aside; in came Mr. Luigi Pisano - hat in hand. Mr. Pisano smiled slightly himself with just a polite nod. No words - no pretense. "Michelina," boomed my father, "I wish you to please welcome to my house, Mr. Pisano. I think you already know him."

There was something about Luigi Pisano that now impressed me as completely different than any of the other fellows my father brought home with him to meet me. He was quiet in manner without sudden moves like most of the others had, especially Giacomino. He was just the opposite of Giacomino. When Mr. Pisano walked in, he never turned his back to me and he left a hint of barber's shave lotion as he passed. He was very neat, very clean, very tall and very, very handsome. He was also, to me, a very much older man. "Yes. I remember. Hello, Mr. Pisano," I said. "Please," he said, "Call me, Luigi."

All this was so much more formal than my other brief meetings that I had had previously with Mr. Pisano. I remembered thinking that my Uncle Ferdinando had taken a dislike to him. Still, I did not formally object.

That afternoon, the three of us sat together for a short period in our parlor. Mr. Pisano still had his hat in his hand, and my father was going on and on about the healing powers of Italian mountain air. There was also some talk about our two adjoining villages, Pratola Serra and Prata. Of course, I was thinking, "Oh, my God. Prata is Giacomino's village too." Mr. Pisano smiled and just kept nodding politely in my direction. He won my father over completely when he said, with a slight intentional Neapolitan dialect, "Signore, Pirone. Often, I remember, when I lived in Prata, going into your mother's store in Pratola Serra and buying supplies from her. She was a wonderful Signora. I remember Michelina there, too. Only, she was a very young girl. She was tending and helping her grandmother in the most professional manner." "I know - the bossy one," said my father almost with pride. Mr. Pisano did not go into the details of how he pulled me away from his rifle by my curls and how he held me up in the air with teasing laughter. But we both looked at each other and shared the same memory in thought. I shook my head and smiled.

As permitted by both my father and myself, Luigi Pisano returned almost every afternoon after that - always with the same quiet knocks on the kitchen door. Tap, tap, tap - tap. Always. I did not object seeing him because I actually liked his manner and calmness. The adventures I had suffered with Giacomino left me numb to any similar style of person. The age difference of sixteen years was still a concern, but only as an afterthought. He was thirty-six and I was twenty. No one mentioned it to us in our company, nor did we mention the discrepancy to each other either. My father was happy that someone got at least past two visits.

Mr. Pisano came up to the apartment freely and talked to me like a friend. Yes, I was still protecting my independence, but not to the point of sequestering myself. I let that part go. There were many occasions that Luigi Pisano took a visit with his doctor-friend, the Pulcinella-Dottore. One afternoon, after one such visit, Mr. Pisano came up and asked if I wanted to go to a movie with him. I told him, "I am sorry, but tonight I am going with my brother to see a movie about Beethoven." He laughed, "A silent movie? About Beethoven? This will be interesting to hear. He was deaf anyway you know." I laughed at that obvious point. He added, "Can the three of us go together? I love to 'watch' Beethoven." Ralfo came in just at this point and I introduced him to Mr. Pisano. I said, "Ralfo, do you mind if Mr. Pisano comes with us to the movies tonight?" My brother beamed a smile, "Of course not. Yes. That would be nice." Ralfo was only seventeen but acted like a man in his role as my attending guardian.

Mr. Pisano paid for the tickets of 25 cents - worth about $4.00 now. The silent movie of Beethoven was comical for the three of us. No matter how we tried, it was impossible not to laugh. I loved Beethoven so much, but the pianist could not keep up with the flipping cards on the screen or the visuals that told the story. She couldn't play piano that well either. Everyone in the theatre was hysterical with laughter, except the pianist who tried hard to keep up, but she was only a piano player.

After the movie, Mr. Pisano took my brother and me to a café to have coffee and pastry and to laugh at what we just witnessed - and heard - on the movie screen.

Ralfo went off later with friends, and Mr. Pisano escorted me home. On the front stoop in front on my building, he furtively kissed me, saying, "I love you," and ran away.

Soon after, by invitation, Luigi Pisano went to my Aunt Alfonsia's house on Salem Street to have tea. It was for sure an interview by this great aunt of mine and great lady. Some of my cousins came in thereafter and set upon the poor man - an inquisition of the first order that Mr. Pisano received with easy manners. He met all of my family groups, friends, and acquaintances - the ones that I had left in the North End. Everyone seemed to like him, especially my brother, Ralfo, who praised him continuously. Luigi Pisano was making good impressions on everybody, except, of course, my Uncle Ferdinando in Lynn.

A few days later came a letter directly to me. The letter was from Mr. Pisano - not Luigi, but from his father, Domenico Pisano, still living in Pratola Serra. Luigi wrote his father and told him of his intentions to marry me and that a letter of encouragement from him to me would be helpful to his cause. Luigi Pisano knew how much I cared for his sister, Amalia, who was my best friend back home, and how much I loved his family when I was myself in Pratola Serra. I opened the long formal letter and read the tight penmanship:

My Dearest, Michelina,

I write to you this letter representing my family, the "Pisano." My wonderful daughter, Amalia, still talks of you and like myself, loves you dearly. My youngest son, Rezziero, sends his good wishes and reminds you that he was the most faithful chaperone both to you and his sister.

He will come to America soon and stay in Lynn with his oldest sister, Maria, and to be with his brother, my wonderful oldest son, Luigi.

Now as to why I send you this letter. I thank you. Luigi tells me that he has asked your father permission to marry you, and your father has accepted his proposal. Of course, you have the final word in this matter and I hope that you know how much we love you. I know that you will love my son. I encourage him to be good and to do the right things.

Dear girl, please marry Luigi. All the family would be honored to have you as one of us. Remember how you called my wife, Mother Caterina? She loves you too. It is destined my child. Luigi will make you happy - he was always a good boy. He was a man even before he reached puberty.

I love you, everybody loves you,

"Papa" Domenico Pisano

I showed the letter to my brother and said, "What do you think?" He made a little light of it by saying, "Mr. Pisano writes very small." "No, please, Ralfo. What do you think?" "Ah, well," he said. "It's up to you whether you marry him or not. Do you love him?" "Not yet." "Well, that would help you if you did." I took a deep breath and looked at the letter again. "Why don't you just relax about it, Lena," he said. "See what happens. I like the fellow, actually. He seems like a good man to me - a good fit for you. No matter what, you will always be my sister." My dear brother then hugged me and said, "Piano, piano, eh?" (Slowly, slowly). I smiled and cried and hugged him back.

Punctual as ever, Luigi came the next day - Monday afternoon, his day off. Together, we walked over Beacon Hill, across the Public Garden and went downtown to the picture show at the Colonial Theatre on busy Boylston Street. The theatre was cavernous and gilded, like a monolithic

314

cathedral. Almost two thousand seats it held. This theatre was also used as a theatrical stage for weekend matinees. We were a bit early, and, of course, Luigi found us just the best seats for viewing. We sat quietly as the movie theatre slowly filled with patrons.

Luigi offered me a cigarette. "No. No, thank you." He lit his cigarette and said, "My father wrote to me and said he sent you a letter. Did you receive it?" "Yes. I read it." Luigi then turned and leaned closely toward me in his seat. The theatre was still very empty, so he felt he could speak freely, "What do you think?" he asked. "About what?" "Michelina, my family loves you and your family likes me as well. I guess it is destiny that you must be my wife." I told him, "I do not believe that marriage is my 'destiny.' It may eventually be my fate, but not my destiny. And, I 'must' do nothing about anything." He considered and smiled, "I feel sure that you will consider me as someone who loves you more than life itself - since I saw you at Chambelli's Christmas party - remember?" "Yes, I remember," I said. He reached over and took my hand. I let him. "I cannot stop think-ing of you. Nobody, really, nobody ever affected me like you do. You are in my mind constantly, night and day." At this moment, the theater organ drowned out our conversation with the introduction to the movie. To this day, I have no memory of what that movie was.

That night, when we got back to my apartment, Ralfo was on his way out and told us that he would be right back. This was my brother's way of assuring his responsibility of not leaving us alone - not for long anyway. Mr. Pisano and I went to the parlor and sat - he on a chair and I on the couch. Suddenly, like a strong tempestuous impulse, he got up, sat next to me, and started hugging me tightly and kissing me. This had never happened to me before. I was stunned. I cringed and struggled to push him off, but it was impossible, he was just too strong and too stubborn. He then placed his head on my shoulder and for a long time he told me, close to my ear, how much he loved me. I finally pushed him off and said firmly, "You shall never again grab me like that. No, no." He laughed and then holding my hand said, "Tell me, suppose I had asked you if I could kiss you. Would you have permitted me to?" He continued laughing, "No, of course, you wouldn't. So, I kissed you first because I know you like me. You do - don't you?" I pushed him again, toward his chair and said, "Go sit down. I will never be alone with you again. You can only come in if

315

I am in company." "Ah," he said, "All right fine. I shall go now. But you admitted just now that I can come see you again - yes?" "Yes. Okay. You can. Now go." At that, Mr. Pisano took his hat and made a bow to me and left, humming a song.

———————

Yes, I unconsciously invited Luigi Pisano to come back, and he did, the very next day, Luigi closed his shop in Lynn and took me out again. We walked everywhere, close together, He tried to kiss me - less aggressively, furtively. Once or twice, I let him. We found a French restaurant. "Enough with Italian food," he said. "I make better food myself than I can get anywhere. Let's go in here. French, I don't cook French." I had forgotten that this man was a widower for more than a year and lived all alone. I pushed that from my mind.

It was a wonderful candlelit dinner. Mr. Pisano took care of everything with the waiter in the most commanding English - and even in some French. He was so very happy that night. He looked very, very handsome. I forgot any doubt that I might have had about him. I didn't care anymore about the difference of age or about his being a widower. At that dinner, I remembered what my old friend Don Filippo said to me going downstairs from Chambelli's party, "That tall fellow loves you, Michelina. I can tell. He kept looking at you all the time." I also remember when Don Fillippo told both Annie and me, "My darlings, marry a nice-looking fellow and you will always have beautiful children. And Annie, if you marry this Dottore De Rosa - do not have any children." It's funny what comes back to your mind in such situations. Then I asked myself, "Why do you think of these things now? Is fate about to declare itself?"

Coming back from dinner, Luigi took me up the stairs to my apartment. My brother was faithfully waiting for us because Father was still out playing cards with his friends. Then, in front of Ralfo, Luigi kissed me good night and left. Ralfo looked at me with a questioning eye. "Yes," I said, "Mr. Pisano has been kissing me all afternoon. I couldn't fight with him anymore." "Oh yes. You like him then?" "I guess so," I answered.

My brother and I sat at the kitchen table. This time it was he who made the coffee. We talked. My dear brother, Ralfo, summed up a lot of things, but always kept me in his heart first. "Lena. I have always liked this man, Luigi Pisano - even right from the start. And I just found out something that happened." "What happened?" I asked. "Dottore De Rosa told me that Mr. Pisano went to New York and found Giacomino Fabbo." "What?! What's this about Giacomino?" "Yes. Mr. Pisano went down there on the train, to the bad section of Little Italy, and found your old fiancé - Giacomino - and told him to stop bothering you." "What?" "Yes. When this fellow Fabbo refused to listen, Mr. Pisano gave him a good beating, and he left him with a scar." Oh, my God," I said, "did he really?" "Yes," said Ralfo. "Oh, Santo Dio," I exclaimed. "That is why he stopped pestering us. Good! Just fine. He needed somebody stronger in character. Bravo Luigi Pisano," I said.

My brother brought me some more coffee as I put in my head the images of Mr. Pisano beating up Giacomino Fabbo. It was not an unpleasant image. Ralfo sat and said, "Personally, I think you love Luigi. I think finally your heart is waking up." I took my brother's hand in mine and said, "Love? I don't know, Ralfo. Love between a man and a woman is different than any other love I have ever known." "Then how will you 'know'?" he asked. "I may never know." "Then you must open your heart a little more and not be afraid of it. Do you have any feelings for this man? It is obvious that he loves 'you'." "I like him better than any other fellows I know. I feel secure with him." "Then give yourself a chance - give him a chance. Sometimes we are meant to gradually fall in love with someone - over time. This situation is not uncommon. You and this man to me seem a good fit - if given a chance."

Of course, my dear brother was right. I loved him so much. I repeated to him what Don Filippo said to me going down the stairs of the Chambelli house and his comments about how to have good-looking children and that a handsome man like Luigi Pisano would guarantee it. We laughed about that. Ralfo and I kept on talking until late into the night.

I would open my heart. I would give it a chance.

"My Dear, I am he who serves you…… Luigi." 1921

Luigi Pisano and I saw each other almost daily for the next several weeks. Then, while sitting in the churchyard gardens of St. Leonard's Church on Hanover Street, Luigi took out a large diamond ring and meekly asked of me, "Do you love me?" Spontaneously, I embraced him and said, "Oh yes, I love you!" And then I, Michelina Pirone, kissed him. He asked like an innocent child, "Why do you love me?" "Because you are so very honest and because you love me so much." Without exaggeration, he almost cried. He kept repeating to me, "See! I told you. I told you that you would find love for me. You kissed 'me' just now! Me!" I said, "Yes. You had the first kiss. I never have kissed any other fellow before in my life." For a long time, he couldn't believe that I spontaneously had kissed him. Luigi put the ring on my finger and I, with my own will, kissed him a second time. He kissed me back.

Well, when we got back upstairs to my apartment, we showed the ring to Papa and Ralfo and told them that we were engaged to be married. "Oh, Yes! Of course!" shouted my father. "I knew this all along! Of course! Yes!" Ralfo just smiled broadly, gave me a long hug and shook Luigi's hand solidly.

Papa, Ralfo and Luigi then went off into the parlor to plan the wedding. They planned the marriage for a Sunday, the 27th of November - just two months away. That date was almost two years to the day that I arrived in America.

That gave me plenty of time to prepare my trousseau, to build my own wedding gown, etc. Papa then changed his October plans and would now leave for Italy immediately after the wedding.

It seemed as if those two months went by in an instant. I was very busy, constantly with my Zia Alfonsina and Papa - preparing. Changing my marital status, I would have to accumulate a trousseau. My Aunt Alfonsina took it as her utmost responsibility to see to every detail of it. She gave to me a hand-carved wooden hope chest that she already saved for just such an occasion. This made my father only partially happy - yes because the chest was free, but it was also very large and had to be filled. We would have to buy bridal accessories, jewelry, lingerie, toiletries, makeup, bed linens, bath towels, curtains, drapes and even kitchenware to use in the place wherever I would end up after the wedding. I kept remembering my dear friend Annie's comment about how it would have been cheaper for my father to send me to the school of Art in Roma than to supply the contents of such a dowry chest. Too late now - for both of us, but not Annie.

My aunt would order my father to sit in the corner of all the shops we went into with the strict instructions not to move and to have his money ready. The poor fellow did not even think to challenge such an imposing order as that. Yes, Papa waited, very reluctantly, but he did. For three Saturday afternoons in a row and several mornings, we did all the shopping needed. When the hope chest that Aunt Alfonsina gave to me filled up to capacity, we bought another, just as grand. We filled that one with linen, silk spreads, tablecloths and dinner settings.

With one of Luigi's Mondays off, he took me over to the Parisian Dress Shoppe on Newbury Street. They were all so wonderfully excited to see me and Luigi come up the stairs together. I think the sisters already suspected something. We shared many paesani together. The two sisters happily welcomed us and the girls in the shop who I worked with had their hands on everything we were about.

Luigi bought two dozen long-stem roses and brought them with us to the shop and handed them to Rosa and Agnes with a gentleman's salute. We told the two sisters and the girls that I was through working and that I was getting married. I invited them all to the wedding. Rosa took the roses and hugged them to her breast. "How wonderful! What a beautiful gesture!" Agnes hugged me, and right there she hugged Luigi, too. She scolded him with a finger and a smile, "You will take good care of this child, Monsieur." "Yes. Madame. I will." The girls around me were admiring my ring and the new suit that I recently had made for myself. It was a beautiful, bright and even "romantic" afternoon. One of the girls whispered in my ear, "Lena, he is even better-looking than Mettola." Rosa then insisted in front of everyone on making my wedding dress. "My dear girl, it's bad luck to make your own gown. We will make it for you if you would accept it as our gift to you. Please." "Yes, Oh, yes!" She made me a very dandy wedding gown with a long removable train and veil. I was then small, 110 pounds. I really made a nice bride, and so the sisters said.

Luigi kept coming almost every evening after his work was done in Lynn - punctually, exactly at 6 o'clock. We would walk and walk down the familiar North End streets and sit together for coffee. I asked him, "How about furniture? Do we need something? My cousins, the twins, want to make for us a gift." Luigi laughed. "Wonderful! Maybe end-tables if they like - 'identical' of course." We both laughed. He then said, "Next Monday, we will go to buy the bedroom, all the other things I already have. Everything is new." I was so happy. Luigi was so generous. Every time he came to the North End to see me, he brought me a present. I was so thankful. He was so loving, so protecting, so very handsome. I loved to touch his face. He would always smile with no words.

One week before the wedding, my mother's brother, Ferdinando, came to the house telling me how offended he was nobody consulted him before decisions were made about the wedding. He was still not a big supporter of "Mr. Pisano," nor even of his sister's marriage to my father. Still, my uncle meant well. I calmed him down saying, "Please Uncle. You know I always seek your advice - separately. And I always will." He quieted down and said, "Well, anyway. I am glad that you are going to be moving to Lynn. I will get to see you more often." He smiled and then presented to me my first wedding gift - a set of beautiful hand-cut crystal glasses from Murano, Italy.

My Uncle Antonio Pirone and Fortuna were in California for grape season when I wrote them and told them of the news of my pending marriage. Right away, my dear uncle sent me 500 dollars, not only as a gift but also as his contribution to my dowry. He was after all - the new "Don" - the declared leader of the Pironi, with absolutely no objections from his older brother, my father. The day of the wedding, Uncle Antonio and Fortuna were still in California on business and could not attend, but they sent to me telegrams with their felicitations. *(Aside: $500.00 in 1921 was worth $1,750.00 at the time Michelina wrote her letter. That wedding gift would be worth about $6,300.00 today. Even with a large trousseau, this was a small dowry. Michelina does not mention any other family cash contribution to her dowry. This dowry gift to Michelina was an important offering as she later relates.)*

Thursday, November 24th, just three days before the wedding, Luigi and I went to make arrangements at St. Leonard's Church on Hanover Street. This was the same church where my friend Don Filippo Assanti was eulogized and where, in its courtyard, Luigi had proposed to me and presented a diamond ring.

Well, a ceremonial and obligated meeting with the priest of this church brought the first bad omen along with it. Luigi's enormous pride and obstinacy came to the forefront for the first time. Luigi, like me, was not a practicing Catholic. However, he was prepared to go through these matrimonial rituals because of his fixed commitment to Italian tradition and cultural integrity. His commitment to everything and anything Italian was fanatical. But, like me and my father and brother, Luigi Pisano rarely went to the messa. He went to this meeting, but the smile soon left his face as soon as he entered the actual church. He looked aggravated, almost angry, for the first time.

We entered the vestry/sacristy precisely at four o'clock. It was a dark sanctuary with the scent of stale incense buried in the corners. All too familiar for me. The priest who received us, Father Don Ernesto, knew me from my association with the Chambelli family. However, he did not know of my views on life, nor of my views on religion or the church. I was sure that he suspected I was as innocent as the child unborn. Luigi and I sat in two small chairs across from the priest - a portly, baldish man in black layers of cloth. He had Luigi squirming in his seat with questions of his faith and his views on the Holy Trinity, God, the devil, etc. Luigi nodded a lot and deferred to me to answer most of these questions. Many times, we stopped talking about religion and its function and concentrated on a man's obligation to his wife but mainly a wife's obligation to the husband: fidelity, the obligation to have many children, to remain faithful to the church, never to divorce, etc., etc.

About one hour into this inquisition, the priest abruptly stopped questioning Luigi. Obviously, he had taken a dislike to him. The priest looked me seriously in the eye and asked abruptly, "Does your father permit you to marry a man so much older than you?" Oh, boy. Here we go now. Luigi sternly answered for me. "I don't think that part should concern you." The priest sat more erect and said, "Everything concerns me when it comes to marrying innocent young girls." I interjected calmly, "Father, I want to marry this man. Please keep our booking for us this Sunday. I think it's unfair for you to try to discourage me." This brought a thin smile to Luigi's face, which he focused upon the holy father. The priest blinked at my nerve, but defended, "All right. It will remain three o'clock on Sunday. But I will speak with your father first before I speak to God." Luigi stood at that remark and told the priest, "Speak to whomever you want, Monsignor - as long as you keep your hands in your pockets." "Dio, Mio," I thought. I got myself involved with another rebel and again I'm in trouble with the church.

Luigi took my hand, and we left the priest in the sanctuary of his plush high-back chair.

Chapter Sixteen

Till Death Do Us Part

Sunday, November 27th, 1921.

The big day came.

It was a regular November day - Boston grey and a little on the cool side. I woke in a daze. I hardly believed that it was "me" who was getting married that day, but I was calm. I slept soundly the night before and had not seen Luigi for twenty-four hours before the wedding. He was out celebrating with his best man and other fellows, as was custom. Luigi's youngest brother, Rezzerio (Richie) Pisano, arrived from Italy just in time for the wedding and was part of the ceremonies. The Pisano men were happy.

That Sunday morning, they had to wake me up. It was already ten in the morning, and it was no use calling me. I never heard either Ralfo nor Papa call, "Lena, get up!" I was lost to the outside world under my blankets. Ralfo finally came into my bedroom and sat on the edge of my bed and touched my face with his two hands. "Lena, wake up. You can help me with breakfast. Papa and I are waiting for you." "Waiting? Why waiting?" Ralfo didn't answer me. "Oh yes! This is the last breakfast we will have together here in the house, isn't it?" Ralfo went out into the kitchen, and I made myself roll to the edge of the bed.

I got up and went into the kitchen. There was father making coffee, and Ralfo was putting something on the table. I was still in my pajamas, and I was cold. Without asking, Papa got me my bathrobe. Papa never had been so attentive at breakfast. I drank the coffee - he poured some more. Ralfo pushed some biscuits and eggs on my plate and I finally became fully awakened. The two of them just kept staring at me as I ate.

I looked at my brother, and I saw a deep emotion in his eyes. There was love, affection, friendship, all combined in a profound concern. I said to him, "Why do you look so disturbed? Who is getting married? Me or you?" "You are," he answered quickly and then added, "I am busy today.

I want to get started." "Oh, yes," I said, "you are the one who will take care of the refreshments - I remember. Thank you." "Yes," said Ralfo, "and the Fabrizio twins are coming soon to remove the furniture." I just looked at him incongruently. Father added, "Yes, we have to eat now and be ready to arrange everything." I said not a word and finished what was put in front of me. When I got up from the table, Ralfo kissed me on the forehead and directed me off toward the bath.

My Fabrizio twin cousins came in and, along with Ralfo, energetically started to remove furniture from our fourth-floor apartment. My young brother took complete charge. They took all the furniture away, leaving only chairs and tables. Papa was left to rearrange what they left in the place. Where they took the furniture, I do not know. I wasn't even thinking about it; I was just automatically preparing my hair and thinking of the day ahead. Then, the twins and Ralfo brought in more tables and lots of folding chairs - then out again. Papa placed those chairs all around the room. It was a noisy and busy operation.

In came even more cousins and hired paesani friends. After one hour, I was surprised at the amount of food that was brought up. The apartment transformed into a reception area of surprisingly good size. There were all kinds of sandwiches, salads, antipasti, Italian pastries, and biscuits, etc. In one corner of the kitchen, they stacked up box upon box of soft drinks. I came out of the bath, and I watched them as they brought in the stuff. I was amazed at the speed and the quantities and the variety of food. When I went into my bedroom, Papa had half-filled it up with folding chairs. Where to dress for my wedding? Mama Mia! (As I write this, I am reminded that in 1921, fifty-eight years ago, wedding receptions were usually done at home - so it was with mine. Yes, there were banquets and catered affairs in reception halls or restaurants outside of the home, but not very often - and not very many. Wedding receptions and wakes were usually done at home.)

Later, the Fabrizio twins arrived back to the apartment along with my Pirone cousins, Paolo and his wife, Raffaella. Raffaella was chosen to be my maid of honor by everyone - including me. I wanted my cousin Fortuna to be my maid of honor, but she, true to her destiny, was dealing in big business in California. Also, during that time, it was not an easy

326

affair to go back and forth across the entire country. It was long, expensive and difficult to do.

Raffaella carried up with her the maid of honor gown which I had made for her. We took it past the men and into the semi-seclusion of my bedroom. We closed the door. Not even Papa was allowed to interrupt us with requests of freeing up more chairs. Raffaella admired my wedding gown which hung alone in the closet. I had only a suit left hanging for after the wedding. All of my other clothes were sent to Luigi's house in Lynn. His sister, Maria, was there preparing the post-reception.

Raffaella made me sit down, and we fussed a little more about my hair. Then, more excitement came from outside my bedroom door. Into the apartment came Rosa and Agnes with small wedding gifts - even more than the gift of the gown they made for me. I loved those two sisters. Ralfo brought all gifts down to Alviti's Photography Studio, downstairs, on the street level to our building. This prevented confusion, and it left room free - convenient and organized thanks to Ralfo. Signore Alviti would handle the wedding photos and final farewells.

Luigi's brother-in-law came up, made his salutes and stayed close to Papa. Luigi's sister, Maria, sent the husband to the wedding and remanded herself to wait and to attend the bride once I arrived in Lynn. She lived on the floor below Louis. So, there she dutifully waited.

At two o'clock, my dear Aunt Alfonsina arrived and took charge of everything from there - bridal-wise. She brought into my bedroom, Rosa, Agnes and two of the girls from the Parisian Shoppe. It got crowded quickly. All together, they attended the dressing of both Raffaella and me. Chatter, chatter, pinch, tuck, chatter, pinch. Aunt Alfonsina, like an older sister, dressed me herself - I let her. Rosa, Agnes and the two girls from the shop were buzzing all around the bedroom. I didn't move an inch. I was joking with all of them - especially with Rosa, who just stood back smiling and admired the ritual which she witnessed and had attended many, many times before. I said to her, "It must be painful for you not to dress me up, isn't it? She laughed and added, "Our friend here is doing a very good job."

Zia Alfonsina, all dressed up in a blue-lace gown, looked adorable as she primed me. My great-aunt played the part of my mother, but also reminded me so much of my dear Nonna Pirone. Suddenly, out started to come soft tears with the thought of Nonna, my mother and all of my siblings I left behind. I remember the last time I saw all of them in Pratola Serra two years ago - Nonna now gone. I remember as Mother and the children were grouped together in front of my house when I said good-bye. I quietly murmured each of their names as tears came to my face and slowly went down. Rosa saw this and ordered me, "Stop, Lena. Stop, now, dear." She wiped my face and asked for powder to help her to make up my face again. An uneasiness was growing in the pit of my stomach.

People kept on coming. My two Uncle Fabrizio's arrived from Lynn with their families. The house now was full to capacity. Then, at 2:45 pm, exactly, we heard a loud commotion, laughter and clapping outside from my bedroom. Luigi came with the best man, Antony Garofano. When the commotion died down, only then did I come out of the bedroom. All of the ladies came out with me. More applause, laughter and cheers. It seemed as if the building would come down around us.

Luigi looked so elegant in his trim three-piece black suit, silk vest, gloves, pocket watch and belt medallion. As soon as he saw me, Luigi stopped talking and looked at me. He came immediately over and said, "My, what a beautiful doll." He kissed me on my forehead and so very gently touched my crown of orange flowers and my veil. He looked deeply into my face with calm and resolve. He was so amazingly handsome.

Luigi then introduced me again to his best man, Anthony Garofano, whom I had not seen since Chambelli's Christmas party that he attended with Luigi. Anthony took my hand and kissed the back of it and made a curtsy gesture to the delight of all the ladies in attendance - including myself. Anthony was a wonderful gentleman - tall, like Luigi, and very distinguished looking. He was a Massachusetts State Representative - very elegant and very proper. Luigi then interrupted with mock concern, "Hey, hey, there, Sir. Find your own sweetheart! This one is mine." Anthony stepped back with a smile and offered me to Luigi with an outstretched arm. Luigi then placed around my neck a three-diamond pendant. It was very dainty and appropriate for the cut of the gown. The two gentlemen looked wonderful, and so did my maid of honor, Raffaella.

The bride's group presented our bouquets of flowers. I wore lily of the valley, and Raffaella had pinkish roses for her compliment. Aunt Alfonsina received a blue corsage to match her gown. Papa then boomed out a command over the crowd while holding his pocket watch up, "Tutti! Okay. It's time now! Let us begin! Everyone!"

We left the fourth-floor apartment, and all of us went down the stairs to the street level. A limousine was waiting there for the bridal party - the four of us: me, Raffaella, Anthony, and Luigi. The rest of the group walked. What was so beautiful about our location in the North End was that the church, Saint Leonard's Cathedral, was only a short walk down Hanover Street, a few blocks from the apartment house. Perfect for everyone concerned.

My Pironi tribe filled almost half of the large space of this beautiful church. Many paesani were also waiting inside, who did not come up to the reception. When we entered the church directly from the limousine, exactly at 3:00 pm, the organ began playing, "Here Comes the Bride" precisely on time, but there was no priest waiting at the main altar. The wedding party, the four of us, went down the aisle all-together and stood quietly at the head altar with hands folded in front of us waiting for the priest. No priest. What was this about? Luigi leaned over to me, clutching his gloves tightly in his hand and said to me, "I think the Monsignor, Don Ernesto, overslept his duties this Sunday." I looked back toward the gathering. The lingering scent of incense in the chilled air hit me solidly.

My nervous father quickly sent my brother, Ralfo, to the back of the church, to the sacristy house, to see where the priest was. A few unsteady minutes later, Ralfo came back with a young priest who was quickly making adjustments to his ceremonial vestments. This new priest we had never seen before - he was not Father Don Ernesto, the priest who interviewed us. Luigi looked at me with a smile and winked at me, "This is better for us. This child priest looks innocent - closer to God I would think." "Yes," I whispered, "Don Ernesto did this switch. He didn't like me." Luigi smiled and said, "Forget the Monsignor. He is not God. He only thinks he is."

The girl at the organ started to play and to sing "Ave Maria," by Shubert. Her voice was beautiful, but not powerful enough to carry past the massive organ she was commanding. When this happened, most of my family and all the paesani knew they needed to help the poor lady out. So, they began to assist her in singing this famous aria in such a way as only the Italians, en masse, know how to do - full and harmoniously. Oh, so beautiful a sound. Then all went silent. I felt as if I had been standing for hours instead of just long minutes. In these moments, challises were raised, the incense ambula was shaken in place, statues looked down from their high perches of piety, vestments were adjusted, candles were lighted, pages of the massive Bible were turned and silence was maintained.

I found myself at the altar saying, "I will, yes. Yes, I do. Yes, I will. Yes." Luigi did the same. We kissed and immediately were pronounced man and wife who were "joined together in the presence of God, to have and to hold from this day forward, for better, for worse, for richer, for poorer, in sickness and health - until death do us part."

We started to go back out to the limousine which was waiting in front of the church. As we were going out, all the family and the paesani stood, clapped and shouted well-wishes. We returned the salutes and smiles. It was all a bright blur in a large dark space. Among the crowd, I only saw my brother, Ralfo, and my Uncle Ferdinando - the latter was crying. I threw a kiss to them both.

As we got to the limousine, there was someone to greet us on the curb in an elegant top hat, cane and overcoat. It was my compare and friend, Annie's father, Franco Chambelli. As soon as Luigi and Anthony saw Chambelli, they froze in place and respectfully stepped aside without saying any hello. They gave Chambelli clear access to me. You could tell these three men had a complicated and unspoken history together. Chambelli took off his hat and said to me, "What a beautiful, beautiful bride. Like my own daughter would be. We all miss you, Michelina. Please, take this with our respects." Chambelli gave to me an envelope, which I handed to my brother who was standing nearby. I gave Chambelli a kiss on his cheek, and he left us with a tear in his eye. My father hadn't noticed that Chambelli was even in the crowd.

We shook the hands of everyone that we could before entering the limousine. Aunt Alfonsina was like the military commander, stepping in front of my father with her style of crowd control. All of them wanted to kiss the bride, but my aunt handled everything, demanding, "Do not kiss her. Just shake her hand. Do not spoil her toilette!"

We went back to the house. Before going upstairs, the wedding party stopped inside to Alviti's Photography Studio downstairs, where we took some pictures. As I mentioned before, taking a photograph in this era was a big deal - only professionals made them, and they were meant to last forever. Our gifted photographer, Signore Alviti, showed Luigi and me the side room of gifts he would put in Anthony's car afterwards. Anthony would be driving us to Lynn. We then took some splendid photographs, and, finally, we went upstairs to the reception.

They seated Luigi and me in the middle of a long table with Aunt Alfonsina, her husband and Papa across from us. My aunt looked just like my Nonna Pirone in this setting. Every time I looked at her across the table, she sensed my thought and signaled to me, "No more crying, child, no more crying." "Yes, dear Auntie, no more crying - I promise."

For a brief moment in all of this, I thought of how I attended my first wedding ever as a child back in my village of Pratola Serra. It was the wedding of my dear departed Uncle Costantino, the youngest Pirone son, and his bride, Peppina. I was so young and impressionable back then. I thought, just like now, how we all walked from the church across the village square and into my Nonno Don Carlos' house where there was also a long table for everyone to rejoice - where everyone sat by rank. I remember everything about that wedding and how similar my own wedding was to it, to Uncle Costantino's, in this far away village called the North End. Have we Pironi evolved? No. I remembered how I fell asleep to the sweet tenor voice of my father and how I resented my new aunt for marrying my uncle and taking him away from me. No resentments now - or at least I hoped not. All so long ago.

Some paesani came up and played the accordion, mandolin and guitar. The Fabrizio twins harmonized together with such wonderful folk songs, that they had everyone in tears of joy. Mama Mia could they sing - freely. Even my father brought out his special gifts as a stellar tenor - still with the perfect high notes! Everyone shouted encouragements to him with his nickname, "Bravo, Peppino! Bravo!!!" No note was beyond his reach!

My brother and his friends, Alfonso Donadio and Charles Nobilio, passed food and drinks around. No one was wanting. They waited on everyone like expert maître-ds. It was such beautifully organized confusion. So much wonderful energy, food and song. Eating, music, dancing, singing and cavorting had everyone spinning. Luigi, my husband, not to overdo it, smiled and quietly enjoyed everything he surveyed.

Hours later, my new brother-in-law, Richie Pisano, the matchmaker who once chaperoned me himself, wanted to dance with me. I begged him, "Please, Richie, I can't. You will get me all dizzy!" Richie went off and danced with Ralfo instead. People were leaving, but others were coming in. Anytime I gave a glance around, it was a different crowd. Paesani everywhere. I did miss and think of dear Annie. I wished her father, Chambelli, had come.

Finally, Luigi and I were ready to go to my new home in Lynn, Massachusetts. My father came to me, kissed me and brought me aside. The music was still in the air. Papa held my face closely in both of his hands and said to me, "Bless you, Michelina. You have kept everyone strong and honest in this family. I thank you. You have been the inspiration and force for everyone - even me. You are a gift to us. Bless you." He started to cry, and then I felt such remorse at how badly I had treated him since coming to America - this dear father of mine. Now, I am gone, and I felt that I had let him down badly. I should have done better - for him and for Mother who still awaits him. My, the plagues of a heart that never rests.

Ralfo came and took Papa into the other room. I think finally my father openly felt love for me. How many years had I tried for this? I loved my father dearly - with all my heart.

In the bathroom, I got out of my gown and changed into my travel suit with the help of Rosa - just the two of us. Neither of us spoke. She expertly extricated me from my presentation. I gave my old boss the gown in a cloth garment bag to keep separately for me - a future connection? The corner of her eyes teared a bit, but she remained steady. Rosa was thinking perhaps of her own beginnings. Always, will I remember what she said to me almost without emotion, "Lena. Never forget your gifts, my dear. You are a talented designer and builder. Never forget this, eh?"

I cried and nodded to her, "Yes," as an assurance that I would not forget. Rosa simply turned and left with the gown that she had designed and built for me. Not another word was needed.

I said goodbye to all who were still left in the house. Looking back now, fifty-eight years later, I don't remember much of it. I remember Zia Alfonsina kissing me goodbye. I remember hugging goodbye to my maid of honor, Raffaella. I remember Anthony Garofano, the best man, also hugging me with a promised guarantee of the future, and I remember Papa's kisses of apology and devotion which he put upon my cheek. Ralfo, too, of course. But I don't remember any other goodbyes - only that I almost ran away.

In Anthony's car, I sat in the back with Luigi, who quietly held my hand and smoked a cigarette. Anthony drove us in the chilled darkness in another direction, north to Lynn. Luigi's brother, Richie, talking incessantly like the Mad Hatter, sat in the front. Where was I going? Who was I going with? What have I left behind? Goodbye, Boston. Goodbye, North End. Goodbye, my little Naples in America, Goodbye, Parisian Dress Shoppe, Goodbye, Michelina? I did not know. But I was secure in the knowledge that I always had my God-given destiny inside of me and that, no matter what happened next, I was determined to be in control of my own fate.

We drove North in the deepening shadows of November. I looked out the window of this fine car. In the darkness outside, everything was close yet distant at the same time.

Did I love this tall, handsome, older man named Luigi Pisano? Yes. I took my vows with him that day, and I meant them. How much did I love him? I did not know. I knew only that I loved him as much as any man that I had ever met - but still - not as much as life itself.

Luigi Pisano and best man (Mass. State Senator)
Anthony Garofano - circa 1920

Michelina Pirone Pisano and maid of honor, Raffaella Pirone,
November 27, 1921

Michelina and Louis Pisano, November 27ᵗʰ, 1921 (Alviti Studios)

"The Wedding Party, Louis and Michelina's Wedding. Nov. 27ᵗʰ, 1921

ACT THREE

Chapter One

Lena and Louis

Post-Marital Bliss

As a further *[Aside: Michelina restructured her identity in more ways than one when she married. She changed her maiden name from Pirone to Pisano, but she also changed her given name. As a child, she was called, Michelinella ("little Michelina"), as a young woman, she was called, "Michelina," but after her marriage to Luigi Pisano, she went exclusively and only by the name, "Lena." My grandfather Anglicized his own given name as well and went by the name, "Louis."]*

We arrived to Louis' house on Church Street in Lynn about nine o'clock. It was the second floor of a two-level house with his sister, Maria, living below him on the first floor. Anthony Garofano helped us up the stairs with some of our wedding gifts as Richie Pisano finished off the task by running back and forth until the car was empty. I must add here that the day after my wedding, my father went to New York and two days after that, he embarked for Italy. Ralfo gave up the apartment in the North End and went to live with our cousin Paolo and his wife, my maid of honor, Raffaella.

Louis' sister Maria greeted us when we got upstairs. She was six years younger than Louis, making her still ten years older than me. Maria was tall like all the Pisanos - about six feet. She stood there blondish, very beautiful with refined manners. She was also very intelligent and chose her words with deliberateness. Maria looked at me with an adoring expression and said to her brother in a curious way, "Luigi, I hope you will deserve her." Her comment had a tinge of foreboding about it. Richie was laughing, saying, "Maria, hold your tongue." I took my jacket off. My georgette blouse was another cause of admiration by Maria. "Oh, my Dear, that blue makes you look even younger!" She kept on repeating, "How lucky can you be, Luigi?"

Richie left us to our privacy. Maria made a nice supper and set a beautiful table. Louis thanked her. Well, our best man, Mr. Garofano, decided to make it a three-way dinner with the bride and groom. He stayed for the entire supper, boasting confidently, "I can eat Italian food without hesitation - anytime." As Anthony attacked his servings, Louis almost fed me himself by hand. I had eaten nothing at the wedding. I was too busy kissing people and shaking hands. Louis reminded me of this as he carefully offered me strands of pasta on a fork, "Eat now, Lena. You must be starving." So, he almost forced some delicious bites upon me, feeding me like a mother would a child. Anthony and Louis then drank some white wine while Maria and I had some coffee. We left the men sitting in the dining room, and Maria took me around to show me my new second-floor apartment.

There was the kitchen with a sink and two stoves - one black coal stove and another stove of gas - all like I had had in Boston. There was a large bathroom with a deep enamel, cast-iron bathtub, pedestal sink and water-closet. My bedroom was very nice. I had chosen that rich cherry-color furniture myself with Louis only weeks before. The room had a large bed and two separate bureaus with end tables - yes, expertly made by my twin Fabrizio cousins as a wedding gift. The dining room was complete with a nice table that the men were at and a floor to ceiling mahogany china-chest filled with many collections Louis already had in his life. In the parlor, there was a surprise for me. Louis had commissioned from Alviti Studio's, a large portrait photograph of me wearing the gypsy dress I built for Chambelli's Christmas party where we first met. The portrait hung squarely on the wall in the middle of the parlor. It was really nice, for it dominated the parlor. On another part of the wall, was a portrait of Louis when he was about twenty-four or so. We looked wonderful together. In those pictures, we were only four-years difference in age.

Maria and Anthony left. I was exhausted. I laid down on the couch in the parlor and fell asleep. Louis took my shoes off, put a blanket on me, and I slept until morning. *[Aside: Curiously, Michelina did not divulge in any detail the consummation of her vows committing her to her husband on her wedding night. "As tradition would have it," one can only imagine. I can say, however, that I am glad that my grandmother left it up to her reader's imagination as to what transpired (and when) during that conjugal union between her and Luigi. Her cultural bent and sense of decorum throughout her life had her mute on the subject, but the actions to follow this night hinted their own implications. Suffice to say, I'm glad my grandmother spared me, as well, from this particular narrative in her letter.]*

Stay Home Honeymoon

We didn't go anywhere for our honeymoon. I was very ignorant about where to go. I had only been in America for two years and was not aware of any options other than Boston or New York City. Louis suggested that we go to New Jersey to his younger brother Alfonso's house. Alfonso came first from Italy and was also an established barber. I thought it would be better to meet Alfonso later, after we had settled from the wedding. So, we celebrated in place.

Louis didn't go to work for three days. We barely made it out of the house - just to buy groceries. We had lots of company at this time - many paesani, Louis' friends from Lynn and my friends and relatives from the North End. During these weeks, we were very happy together. Louis was kind, gentle and considerate - nothing abrupt in manner or demand. At times, he couldn't part from me to go to work - he wouldn't part from me.

One Saturday, Louis came home for lunch and I started to tell him the story of Scheherazade - the story of the *One Thousand and One Nights*. I was a babble, and of course, I didn't stop being one, even with him. He kept quiet and hung on every word I spoke. I carried on and on with enthusiasm of the tales of Ali Baba, Aladdin and the magic cave. I kept Louis very interested in revealing the slowly unfolding story and he was so interested in my telling of it, that he stayed home, forgetting to go to the barbershop which was only a five-minute walk from the house. Many hours later, at nine at night, he jumped up saying, "Oh, my God! What time is it?" Louis had forgotten to pay his three-man help because he was so caught up in my storytelling. He ran to his shop just before they closed the place.

Louis and his Barbershop

[Aside: According to the "List or Manifest of Alien Passengers for the U.S. Immigration Officer at Port of Arrival," Luigi Pisano came to America as a "steerage passenger" on the S. S. Moltke, sailing from Naples, Italy, January 5th, 1907. He

arrived at Ellis Island, New York, January 18th, 1907. According to this Manifest, Luigi Pisano was twenty-two years of age on arrival. He was from the village of Prata. He was single and his occupation was listed as "barber." The ship manifest goes on to designate him as "literate" and his "Race" as "Italian, South." Also, he paid for his own ticket and arrived in this country with twenty dollars American in his pocket. His younger brother, Alfonso, of New Jersey, signed him in. Luigi's destination was, "Boston, Massachusetts." The rest of his mandatory information was filled out as follows: "Ever arrested?" No. "Polygamist?" No. "Anarchist?" No. "Suspect of Espionage?" No. "Mental Health?" Good. "Deformities?" No. "Complexion?" Light. "Eyes-Hair?" Pale-brown. Each passenger on the S.S. Moltke had to answer the same list of questions. Now, what I know: Luigi came to America wearing a formal hat and coat, a three-piece tailored suit, and carried with him, a solid gold comb, a gold pair of haircutting sheers and $20 American money. Within a month, he left Boston and settled near his sister, Maria, in Lynn, Massachusetts and immediately went to work by setting up his own shop as a barber. Luigi Pisano changed his given name to Louis, quickly learned English by serving his diversified customers, and never once worked for anyone in his entire life. Now that is coming to America.]

Louis' barbershop was on Summer Street, in a very prosperous and busy section of the city. Summer Street had many separate kinds of stores around the barbershop. There were produce, clothing, furniture, fruit, meat, poultry and fish stores all around his shop, and most of them were owned by Jews and Italians. It was not the North End, however, for the neighborhood was more of a mixture of opposing and crisscrossing cultures which I will describe later.

Louis kept this same location for his barbershop until many decades later when urban renewal after World War II went to work tearing down that part of the city - building by building. When that change occurred, Louis' barbershop was in the last holdout building on a vacant city block. But at that time, Summer Street was a busy street, more like Washington Street of Boston.

Louis's barbershop was one of the best in all of Lynn. It was very clean with classic black and white checkered tile floors, a full wall of mirrors, four hydraulic barber chairs, and in the middle was a large fan attached to the ceiling that never stopped spinning, even in winter. There also was a big "mother-in-law-tongue" plant in the full street window. Louis rightly was very proud of his place, and everyone in the city of Lynn knew of its location.

There were no beauty parlors back then for girls to have their hair cut or styled. That was always done at home, usually with girlfriends assisting. Hairstyling was a new vogue after the First Great War. Because of this change, Louis was very much in demand and made a good deal of money as what is now called a "stylist" - both for men and women. Now, they would call his shop a "salon." But Louis was given to more than that. One might even call it an obsession. Personal grooming was his one singular passion - almost to a fault. He always wore a starched white shirt and tie and was always, always, extremely well-groomed himself. He also took pride in wearing the latest style in men's shoes. Shiny shoes and fashionable - the best shoes made in Lynn - the shoe capital of the world. He even claimed, by request, to have designed the first "seamless men's shoe" with no threads around the toe. Louis was impeccable. And this passion, I will confess was what we found most in common, I being just as fastidious and a builder of my own fashioned wardrobe.

Many times, Louis would walk around our house on Sunday or Monday with a shirt and tie on. Grooming was his calling to life. He took it judgmentally with almost everyone he met by first measuring them, up and down, in assessment. And all the fancy people of Lynn came to him for just that special "look" he gave to them. He was a master at preening others. Always, men and women would ask for his attention and would be regular visitors to his shop. Many of them, including the mayor and the owner of the city newspaper, became good friends of his, just like the State Senator, Anthony Garofano. They all wanted Louis' special attention.

Louis brought home the profits of his barbershop every Saturday night after paying the salaries of his three barbers. I asked him, "How much did you make this week, Louis?" "One hundred dollars - maybe more," he said with pride. At that time, that was lots of money. *[Aside: $100 in 1921 is worth about $1,250 today.]*

That very first week we were married, Louis gave me an allowance for food and household things - all the other house bills, he paid himself. It was exactly the same arrangement that my father had implemented for me when I took care of him and my brother Ralfo in the North End. I bristled at this arrangement at first but made myself keep quiet about it. It did make sense of sorts, and I was no longer working for myself, so now my income was entirely dependent on my husband. This situation, knowing me, would soon need some adjustments however.

The allowance came to me as a little savings book. When Louis handed it to me, he told me, "Here. This is for the house things. I will deposit something in it every week. Try to save on expenses, Lena. If you make a surplus at the end of the week in this book, then you can deposit the extra money in your own bankbook." Well, I already had deposited the 500 dollars in my own bankbook from the wedding present my Uncle Antonio gave me. That was the starting system for us in our marriage. I tried hard to save at least a dollar a week from my household allowance.

I knew this system could not go on indefinitely for me if I were to still keep my sanity.

1921

"Temporary" Emergency Immigration Act,

Extended - Indefinitely

Everywhere, the world was problematic for me and my family, as well - both sides of the ocean. I was tucked away safe in a marriage in Lynn, Massachusetts, yes, but not safe in the world. No one I knew was safe. The Emergency Immigration Act of 1921 was an extension of the same administered in 1920 only it increased the percentage allowed in from 2% of original 1910 migrants to 3% that number in each ethnic group. Not a lot of hope. The "temporary" part of it was extended we were told - indefinitely. I was also shocked to find out that at this date if you were already an American citizen, you could not marry an Asian person. That was verboten. If you did, you would automatically lose your citizenship in America. No Asian people at all were allowed in either. How insecure and unjust a law was this? *[Aside: My grandmother again remembered correctly, only she called it the "Immigration Act," not the "Quota Act." This, taken from American-Historama notes: "The Emergency Quota Act restricted the number of immigrants to 357,000 per year, and also set down an immigration quota by which only 3 percent of the total population of any ethnic group already in the USA in 1910, could be admitted to America after 1921. The Emergency Quota Act was intended to be a temporary measure, but the National Origins Formula continued until 1965."]*

As for Italy, on the 28th of October 1922, organized military squads of the Fascist Party moved toward Roma, the famous March to Rome, to change the government and to seize power. King Vittorio Emanuele III, maybe being timid and afraid of more social disorders, moved also with faith in the new party. The King fired the old ministers and gave Benito Mussolini the power to form a new government - a Fascist government. The Fascist remained in power from 1922 until 1943, uninterrupted, guided by Mussolini, who gave himself the name, "Il Duce," meaning, "The Leader." Many awful things happened in those 21 years of Fascist power and it was not limited to Italy alone. *[Aside: Again, my grandmother's historical memory holds true. In cross-referencing her dates from various resources, she was off by a day - or perhaps they were.]*

Chapter Two

Unveilings

My sister-in-law, Maria, downstairs had the good idea to bang on the ceiling with a cane right under my kitchen whenever she saw her brother walking up the street for lunch - a forewarning of sorts. It was like her saying with her tapping, "Here comes Louis. Do you have his lunch ready?"

One day I overslept badly and didn't even hear Maria's warning thumps from below. Louis was coming home from the shop for lunch and when he got upstairs, he found the door locked. I didn't even hear Maria's continued knocking below. I woke up, just in time when Louis was about to force the door open. I was so ashamed, no lunch ready, nothing. I opened the door just as Maria came up. Louis grabbed me up in his arms in front of his sister and laughed, spinning me around, "Oh my Darling, you are so young, so beautiful!" He carried me into the parlor where he sat us down on the sofa, rocking me like a baby. I said to him, "Please don't rock me. I might fall asleep again." Laughing he said, "Okay. I know how I can really wake you up." He went to the phonograph machine and winded and winded it up, and then the voice of Caruso was heard. Bravo!

I made a nice, quick lunch for Louis, and he left back to work, but Maria stayed, still sipping coffee. I knew there was something on her mind, and she eventually brought it up.

First, she told me that Louis hated her and her husband because they eloped to get married. "He never forgave us for this," she said. I told her, "Louis hates nobody. The man is full of love. He is so honest." I tried to talk about happy occurrences, but Maria brought up the subject of Louis's first wife, Tina.

Maria said, "She died in this same apartment - in your bedroom - the baby, too. All the furniture in this house before you came, the utensils, even the forks and spoons, were in her trousseau, her dowry." I sat there shocked at these things that Maria was saying to me. Why? This woman was the sister of my husband and also my best surviving friend, Amalia, in Pratola Serra. Why was she being so cruel? I could barely speak. "Oh, please," I interrupted. "No, I don't want to know." But she ignored me. She went on and on. She told me of some of the pictures on the walls were friends of Tina's. She pointed to one picture, "That one there. That's Tammy, Tina's very best friend. She's Jewish. They were together constantly."

Then I realized why Louis didn't like Maria; she had a mean streak in her. Richie was something like that, too, but not as bad. How did I feel with all those distorted thoughts with the presence of Louis' first wife in my house? I was thinking of my husband's first wife dying with their only child in my bed. Something right away went out of me after this conversation. I could barely swallow. I felt very insecure - afraid to be afraid.

I said nothing to my husband for days.

Louis soon realized that something was wrong and that I was hurt about something. I cried out my frustration and fear, "I can't stand it any longer. I must tell you. You have not been sincere with me. You didn't really respect my worth. I was a young, naive girl believing that everything was new here in this house - that you prepared it new just for me - for us! I believed you when you said to me, 'It is a new life now. I shall never think of anybody but you.'" Louis remained quiet - somber. I continued, "Everything around here is about your other wife. Maria told me everything. Why didn't you tell me she died with a stillborn child in our bed? Why are pictures of your friends together with her still on the wall? The only difference is that I am the live replacement - is that what all this means?" I then reminded him how he brought me to Tammy's' house right after we settled in, saying that she was a faithful client, but he didn't tell me that she was Tina's best friend. "You made me invite her to this house, and she came many times. She knew, your sister knew and you knew - everyone knew this secret - except me. How long did you expect to live this charade?" Louis had no response. He just went back to the barbershop. I cried all afternoon on the couch in the parlor under our separate portraits.

Reality Sets In

I became insecure. I had been so careless about so much. Was I stupid as to what was really going on around me? Everybody knew everything about everybody, except me.

For many days, Louis said nothing, and Maria was always busy elsewhere. I think she knew that her meddling information was now out in the open. When Louis got upset - all through our marriage together - he would retire to his one comfortable chair in the parlor and hide behind a newspaper - for hours - sometimes never turning a page. The silence in the house at that time was deafening.

Tensions finally eased, and life returned to normal, of sorts, but the seed was planted and could never be uprooted. In some ways, my husband and I were now on level ground together. I was growing in this regard quickly - very quickly. He was beginning to realize that I was not the innocent "little doll" with no brain or resolve. But he, of course, was not changing at all.

During our disputes, I suspect Louis spent those first solitary hours behind his newspaper contemplating to himself as to just what he had gotten himself into - what did he marry? Good. Still, I pressed forward - dutifully. I was able to put all thoughts of his deceased wife and child behind me. I truly did. There was no changing that episode in his life, so I focused on self-determining my own fate.

The Challenges of Change

One afternoon, Louis showed me his personal bankbook. It was quite a pile of cash savings - all in his name. I began to act grown up - more responsible. I said to him, "Louis, why don't you put my name on your bank book?" He didn't answer and never did. But it spoke words to me about many things that would trouble our marriage for years.

Earlier here in my letter, I described the "dance" - that of the expectations of courtship. Well, there is a "marriage dance," as well. In those earlier times, many people didn't get to know each other well until after the marriage consummated - not before. Unlike today, so many marriages back then were prearranged, and each person was insulated before taking their vows. The people involved rarely had the chance to really know the other person prior to the union. Marriage and time would have to solve that issue. Marrying for love only was not the common reason. The thing was that the song and this dance of marriage was never ending and the dancers were never allowed by the Catholic Church or Italian custom to change partners. The only escape sometimes used was simple desertion. But because there were always so many personal possessions involved, that route was almost always futile to attempt.

I began taking stock of my position as a wife. "Yes," I told myself. "I am his wife, but I am not his doll. I want most of all, respect." I also wanted to get away from his sister, Maria, on the first floor. I thought hard about it for days.

One lunchtime, I said to him, "Louis. Let us buy a house." He quickly said back to me, "We will need a thousand dollars down. I don't have that ability right now." All I could think about was having seen his bank book and the large savings it contained. "Was he another penny-pincher, like his friend the Dottore Pulcinella De Rosa?" I said to him calmly, "Louis, I will give you my $500 that my Uncle Antonio gave to me for my wedding. It's a lot of money and that will be enough for half a down payment. I just have to move away from here." "No, no, no," he said. "We cannot split the cost of a house. That is not for a woman to do. It's the man's responsibility, and I am not ready to leave here." "Why?" I asked, knowing full well of the house's history. "Because I am not ready. Remember, you are a woman. I shall do all the business in this family."

I got up from the table and took my dish to the sink. The utensils from it made a loud noise on the bottom which visibly startled Louis. I said in a demanding way, "What you just said is an insult to me and my trust I had in you. I don't need a supervisor or a father - one was bad enough." That got him up out of his chair. "Look," he said apologetically, "I work, not you - Okay? I will bring in the money and pay all the bills for both of us. I want you not to worry of such things. Please do not change. I don't want to spoil you. Please stay as you were. Please, Lena - obey your husband." Louis said no more and went back to the barbershop.

I called my Aunt Alfonsina in Boston. It was a long-distance call, but we still talked and talked. Her conclusion was a predictable one, but one I needed to hear anyway. My aunt told me that I could do nothing. It was too late. I should have asked him all that he expected of me before the wedding. Before I hung up the phone, she finished with, "He is your husband now, Michelina. Luigi is a bit old-fashioned, but he means well. Listen to what he says now. When you have children, you do as you please." Again, I found myself spending the afternoon crying on the couch.

At that time, a woman didn't count for much. My husband gave me love, sincere love, but business affairs or spending money was his worry not mine. I was so stupid. I thought I lost confidence in myself. I didn't believe in divorce, and he knew it. I was married forever. I also wrote before, "Once committed to a marriage - that was it. It really wasn't an option later on in my life either. We Italians put such demands on ourselves to be right the first time."

Was fate cruel to me? Did I believe the condition I was in to be a detriment to my marriage? Not really. Pandora let hope fly out of her trunk, too, and that hope was around me as well. I ignored all the evils of Pandora's trunk and stayed with the winged hope aspect of the story. I began to try different ways to approach things - different methods - to adjust to my problems. But nothing helped. Having children, according to my Aunt Alfonsina, would solve these problems? Change everything? Really?

The big argument happened one night when Louis came to me repeating, "Please, Lena, do not change. I love you too much to spoil you with the burden of finance and large bills. I wish to protect you. You shall be my precious doll forever. Let me take care of you - please." "Yes," I answered in anger. "Your precious 'dumb' doll! Don't ever call me that ever again! I need more respect than you have shown so far." I left the room and went to bed. For a few days, I hardly spoke to him. He kept on reading his paper as if he didn't care. Then I started to read my books, and sometimes I stayed up in the kitchen reading all night. I wish I never started along these lines, but I could not help it. I was answering an old voice inside of me. Always - reading was my salvation. Louis began to hate my "old books" as he called them.

What of Papa and Ralfo? (1921 - 1922)

As I mentioned, after my wedding, Papa took his troubled glands and went immediately back to Italy. That was December 1921. My brother, Ralfo, left the apartment in the North End and moved in with our Cousin Paolo and Raffaella. Cousin Paolo was living in Orient Heights next to the city of Revere. When Italians moved away from the North End, they would mostly go to East Boston and a little further out to Orient Heights. Ralfo stopped working the harness shop in the Coleman Truck and Carriage Company. Without Papa being there to mentor him, my brother sought something different - more in line with our Cousin Paolo's work as a chef.

In the summer of 1922, Ralfo took what savings he had and opened a food stand on a busy boardwalk in Revere Beach. He sold frankfurters and hamburgers. It was Ralfo's first attempt at his own independence, and I felt compassion for his efforts. Also, Cousin Paolo needed help in his own restaurant, and, ever since my father had gone to Italy, Ralfo helped Cousin Paolo all he could.

Finally, that summer, my brother Ralfo came to stay with us a day or two in Lynn. We all had a wonderful time together. It was a healing situation for me; old times appeared right in front of me. A wonderful visit. I loved my brother dearly.

Louis and I convinced Ralfo that he should take a small apartment next to us on Summer Street. He did. This move did two things for me. It gave me solace that my brother was again near me with his easy manner and understanding ways. And, Louis also loved my brother, and he had no problem with the suggestion to move to Lynn. He saw Ralfo coming to live next door as a positive thing, for many reasons. Our Cousin Paolo was happily working on his own family now and could also use the extra room. So, Ralfo would commute from Lynn to assist Paolo in the restaurant. I was ecstatic when Ralfo moved next door.

<hr/>

A First Christmas with Louis and my Twenty-First Birthday

During Christmas week of 1921, we had a little Christmas party. We had been married now for only a month. Our Christmas party was not as expansive as the one Franco Chambelli would have thrown, but a good one all the same. My two Fabrizio Uncles came with their families. I had many cousins now. Cousin Paolo and his wife Raffaella were there, so too was Ralfo and his Socialist friend, Alfonso Donadio. My darling Uncle Ferdinando, with that beautiful sense of humor of his, was the life of the party, as always. My Aunt Margherita was her usual quiet and condescending self but never belligerent. The table was set with many Italian delicacies that everyone either brought or that I had made myself. It was a mixed family discourse from the beginning.

My Uncle Ferdinando and I debated intensely about Mussolini's declarations in Italy about the conditions of this country and on other matters. Ralfo and his friend, Alfonso, took the Socialist workers position on everything, which was contrary to what both my Uncle Ferdinando and my husband believed; they were both for Mussolini's Fascist government. Finally, a common ground between my Uncle Ferdinando and Louis. It was a revelation to both of them - and to me. Louis wanted only to talk about current events. He was our newspaper man - no history. I worked in the subjects of art and humanity - throughout history.

<hr/>

North End Friends Visit. New Years, 1922

My crowd from Boston came to see me during New Year's. They came with all the news of the North End, of course. They asked if I had a letter from Annie Chambelli and I said, "No. It has been awhile, but I know one will come soon." When Dottore De Rosa's name came up, I was all ears. "What about the Pulcinella?" I asked. Well, it came to be that Dottore De Rosa proved to be what he really was - just a miserly Italian carpetbagger. He quickly fell into disfavor with Franco Chambelli after Don Filippo passed away. As soon as Chambelli saw no signs of marriage between Annie and the Pulcinella, he lost all interest in Dottore De Rosa. When this happened, it became a signal. The paesani of the North End began to go to other doctors, not to the Pulcinella. Everybody stopped seeing him, even Louis stopped going to him. But, it didn't matter by this time. The Pulcinella had already taken the pressing iron to many bank notes. After a while, the Pulcinella Dottore went back to Italy with his pocket full of money. Did he marry his mysterious Contessa? We never knew.

As for our dear compare, Chambelli? He, too, lost much of his power and position in the North End after Don Filippo's death. Once or twice, however, Chambelli happened to come to Lynn for some festivities of the Sons of Italy. Louis was very active in this group, as well as his good friend the State Senator, Anthony Garofano. On these occasions, Louis would give Chambelli special attention with hair and moustache cuts and afterwards, Chambelli would graciously stop by for supper along with Anthony. Louis never charged Chambelli for these groomings. At these last dinner meetings, we all noticed that Chambelli was changed, for he was very sick. All the power in his eyes and in his presence had dimmed to a great extent. All I could do was to have great sympathy in my heart, and I was thinking if my dear friend, Annie Chambelli, knew of her father's condition. I suspected not. Still, I couldn't help but to love this once robust and upstart leader of men who helped all of my family become adjusted to America. He was still dignified and refined - only slower in his movements. When he left dinner, he took my hand saying, "You have been a good friend to Annie, Michelina. And - you write so very well. Do not ever stop. We Italians need you, eh?"

A few months after this, during the summer of 1922, the great Chambelli died.

My 21st Birthday, February 17th, 1922

I buried the hatchet with my husband. "What is the use?" I thought. "I can't stay mad with anybody." So, I read less in front of him, played the records that he liked when he came home and we made up. We promised each other never to argue again, no matter what.

The day of my twenty-first birthday, Louis came home with twenty-one long stemmed roses of the deepest red. They were fresh and beautiful, especially rare for the month of February. It was a Friday, I remember. I made my first cake with the help of Louis' sister Maria downstairs. We shared it quietly in the glow of candlelight and long-stemmed roses.

A Buyer's Bias

I must relate now of my uprooting and moving to Lynn, Massachusetts. Being in Lynn was so "foreign" to me - literally. I felt far away from the North End and its images and fragrancies of Italy. I could have been in a separate country altogether. Very seldom did I meet anyone in Lynn from Boston's North End. It was just too far away and might as well have been in another part of the world. When I took long walks in Lynn, I saw the same faces every day. I would roam the streets looking for different stores that would have cloth materials or books, or just would keep walking. There was always an explorer in my heart. When I came to signs in windows or on the street, I would repeat them aloud to hear the English words to myself. I read these signs to advance my knowledge of this very complicated language. I learned that nothing is phonetic about English. Italian is different. In Italy, there are no such things as spelling bees. There is no need for them. On the ear, Italian is exactly as it is written. Not so for English - but as I mentioned, Italy was far, far away now.

It was at this time in my life, walking the many streets of Lynn, that I began to notice the differences of how the Jews, Italians and other minorities in America were treated by the larger, more populous public. I was not sure about the rest of the country, but I was not living in the rest of the country. Many times, Italians, Jews and negroes were treated as subhuman creatures - even the children. *[Aside: In 1979 when this letter was written, the common vernacular for "Black" people was "negroes." In the African American Registry, they write: "From the 18th century to the mid-20th century, "negro" (later capitalized) was considered the correct and proper term for African Americans. It fell out of favor by the 1970s in the United States." I did not abridge my grandmother's description of this era in her descriptions of ethnicities and her nomenclatures. In her mind, these terminologies were as good as endearments.]*

Once, to do my food shopping near Louis' barbershop, I stopped into a meat and produce market called "Blood's." What a name for a market that also sold meat. Can you imagine? But true. Blood's Market. I walked up, and carefully I asked the store clerk for tomatoes - in English. I was careful with the pronunciation for I still didn't speak the language comfortably enough to be assertive with it. He didn't answer at first. I asked the clerk again, "Excuse me. To-mah-toes?" "What?!" He shouted back as if he couldn't hear me from three feet away. I repeated the darn word, "To-mah-toes. Where please?" The helper was tall, with a fresh look on his insipid face. He smiled and pretended that he didn't understand me. "What?!" He barked again loudly, "Did you say, 'po-tah-toes'?" He had me confused, to his delight.

Just then, an older man, the floor manager, came up from where the tomatoes and potatoes were sitting together a little distance away on a counter. The manager said in English to the clerk, "What is the problem? What is it that she wants?" The clerk mockingly responded, "I don't know if she said, 'to-mah-toes' or 'po-tah-toes'?" The manager, seeing that I was visibly upset, got angry himself and responded to the clerk, "Get the hell out of here, you idiot. I will serve her."

I became amused at the confrontation. I knew that much English anyway. Such a fuss and so nonsensical. I pointed to what I wanted, "Yes, please. I want 'tomatoes'," this time choosing the alternate pronunciation. The manager brought me over to the counter and helped me fill a paper sack of tomatoes. The clerk was still nearby smirking at me with his broom. The manager said to me in careful English, "Don't mind him - that beast. He teases to flirt with you. He also hates Italians and Jews."

Oh, boy. When the clerk heard what the manager said to me, he threw down his broom and came running up to challenge the manager directly to his face yelling, "Yes. I am a beast! And you are a dirty Jew!" I do not know what happened after that because I ran out of the store, without tomatoes or potatoes.

After a few days, I gained courage and went back there purposefully to confront them. The younger man wasn't there anymore, but my Jewish friend, the manager, was. After that, whenever I went in, he specifically ran up to me and always greeted me with a smile. This man was tall, dark skinned, and he looked either Italian or Jewish. It was hard to tell. Then one afternoon, I stopped into Louis' barbershop, and there he was - sitting in Louis' chair with his face half covered in shaving soap. Louis introduced him to me. "Jerry," he said, "this young girl is my wife, Lena." The man jumped right out of the chair with a towel still around his neck and gave me a hug. "Really, Louis! She is my friend! The 'to-mah-toe' girl." Louis didn't get the joke, but he laughed anyway. I always got first-class service at Blood's Market after that.

Well, that little episode in the market made me notice other distinctions that separated the Jews and the Italians from other races in Lynn. It was a constant struggle between all of the races and many times out in the open as well. Where I worked in Boston, on Newbury Street, it was all different, refined, a little cosmopolitan sanctuary unto itself. On Newbury Street, the Italians were loved there, yes. I realized that the Bostonians on that street had style, culture, and understanding of all people. They reflected that. What a terrible difference than in Lynn.

The Italians in Lynn did not help themselves either. They did not dress well. They were loud, and they often fought openly with one another, like they did in Mr. Pietro's men's jacket factory in Boston's garment district. I had been spoiled by the North End where the paesani loved each other. I mistakenly thought all the people of America were happy people - but not true. I was relocated to an industrial city of shoe-making and I didn't like it much.

On one walk, I saw near my house a spiteful battle between two Italian women and a Jewish woman all screaming at each other for something one of their children had done or said. I shut myself away from this noise in shame. I thought of this and the episode at Blood's Market for a long time. Why the differences and animosities? Was it locality alone that determines the civilities of those around us? The answer, I found, was that in the North End, the confidence the paesani had with one another kept them happy and civil. They were loud, yes, but seldom belligerent. I never heard an angry word from any Italian against the Jews in my old neighborhood. The Jews were like our own paesani; that's all. I felt I was in a different world in Lynn. Was this America? Another evil creature had escaped from Pandora's trunk.

A Measure of Freedom - English

There were lots of Jews in Lynn, and I loved all of them I met. Still, I also noticed how they hated the negroes - and, at that time, I had a problem myself. I seldom had seen a black person in my entire twenty years of life - ever. Even in the area in which I lived and worked in Boston, I seldom came across negroes in the streets or in stores. They just weren't around.

In Lynn and vicinity, there were many negroes. They kept to themselves in grouped apartments and neighborhoods of all black. I said I had a problem; yes, at first I did. I had no understanding of this race of people. I needed more information about them and other race groups in Lynn.

I came soon to realize that I could no longer just get by with my fluency in Latin, pure Italian and only some basic English. Not being fluent in English was hindering my development in this new country and in this new city I found myself living in. I can literally remember the hour and day I decided to focus solely on becoming truly bi-lingual in speech and reading ability. It was the day after my twenty-first birthday - exactly two years after my arrival in America. They say it takes six years to learn to speak a language fluently and that is only if you live in the country that has the language you wish to speak. But I wanted more than just to "speak" English. Two years was not enough for what I wanted - I wanted to master it as a writer. My desire always was to be a writer and writing only in Italian in America would not credit me.

Because of these incidents I write about, I needed now to read the local papers to know and to understand more about what went on in Lynn and why. Louis, of course, was fluent in English. He came many years earlier to this country, and his constant contact as a barber with many groups of people made him conversant both in manner and speech.

Louis was extremely supportive in my quest. He bought me a third-grade school book and taught me to read it. No problem. I then bought a "True Story" confession magazine which had very simple language in it and peppy stories. I could read and understand whatever was on the pages with speed. I told my husband not to bring me any more candies or flowers but to spend the money on books - English books instead. Louis did his best but without understanding my objective the books he bought for me were not what I wanted. I needed books about things that I could "almost" read. That was a hard concept for Louis to grasp, so I went all by myself to the Lynn Public Library to get myself a library card. Oh, how I loved that building. It is still today just as it was in 1922, a little gem of Gothic architecture that echoes.

I got my adult library card, and most every day on my walks through the city, I would stop there. The main reading room was every bit as inviting to me as the Boston Public Library was. There, with diligence, I ingested the free newspapers and magazines - all in English. I would whisper quietly to myself, as I read, to hear each word come out of my mouth. I wrote down any word that I didn't understand and crossed it with my knowledge of Latin first. If unsuccessful, I put the word and the slip of paper in my pocketbook for later.

One afternoon, I saw a black man was checking in his late books and was handing some coins to the librarian. I was a distance away, but I saw that the librarian had a disgusted look on her face. She had to give the black man back some change. When she did, she made sure she didn't come near to touching him. It was obvious. "Oh, boy," I thought. "Maybe I am the same way. Would I not want to touch his hand, as well?" I became confused and hurt, against myself.

In truth, inside, I felt the same as the librarian in some ways. I could not deny it. "Well, Lena," I said to myself, "do not blame the librarian. You are made of the same cloth." Then I reasoned that I was brought up with all the same types of people, civilized Caucasians. Even in all the books I read, I never thought of any other people of the world. My horizon was very narrow. Yes, I had read about the people of Italy, France, Germany, England, all about the Russians, because of their revolution, and still, I didn't know much about other races. I studied nothing about Asia, Africa or South America - nothing about racial differences. I felt so ashamed of myself at this incident in the library. I was so ignorant of human conditions and of why bias of race was so unkind and dominant in the world. I said to myself, "Lena, you will have to change. But how?" I acted fast.

I approached the same librarian. I said, "Please, could you suggest to me a book that has a story of American negroes." "Yes dear," she said politely, "wait here." She came back with Harriet Beecher Stowe's book, *Uncle Tom's Cabin,* which was written in 1852. "I thank you," I said to her and signed out the book.

At home, I had a dictionary of English and Italian. When I opened the book, I had two immediate thoughts on my mind; first, this was a novel written in English during the last century by a woman. And second, I wanted the same distinction to be a writer myself. I knew I had a big, big job of translating on my hands, not just of meaning but of significance.

Well, with the help of my husband, I read the novel. Now, when I look back, Louis helped me a lot. He really taught me how to read English, and he helped me to speak it. He was so patient. Even from the beginning of our marriage, he spoke English almost all the time with me. He knew how much I wanted to be fluent. *Uncle Tom's Cabin,* this serious historic book, was my treasure. I had to buy it and read it again and again. At times, I cried along with the characters.

A Social Conscience Blooms in my Heart

One day while I was shopping in Lynn, I saw a black woman pushing a carriage. I looked at the beautiful baby she was strolling. A beautiful baby with black eyes, black intelligent face, and I felt genuine love for him. But I also felt remorse that this little bit of humanity perhaps will be crucified by a horrible society of ignorant people like myself. This feeling gave me lots to talk about with Ralfo. He agreed with me that society was cruel, but also that discrimination was an excuse to deviate the people away from the real issue that was at hand. To my brother's mind, the injustice that was continually done to the working people was the real culprit.

Another day, something very significant happened in front of me while I was inside Woolworths, the five and ten cents store on Market Street. At that time, all the items in this store actually cost only a nickel or ten cents. A little black boy was scuffling with a store clerk who was holding him roughly. On his way out of the store, the boy had stolen a ten-cent toy and was caught. The sales girl was pulling him back and forth - shaking him hard. I couldn't stand it. I took the toy away from her and threw it on a counter. I gave the girl a push and embraced the boy with protection. He was crying. I said to him while I was holding him, "Listen. Don't do it again. Promise, yes?" "Yes," he said, and then he quickly ran away. The sales girl said to me, "He is no good. He will come and steal again." I didn't answer her. I had won something for myself. Since then, I loved every other race somehow. I felt to be a citizen of the world. It was a good healthy feeling. One never touches a person he or she doesn't like. After that, I could touch, kiss and embrace anyone of the world - I was liberated. I was made whole.

Reminders of Ellis Island - the Sisters

Then came an episode that reminded me of my passage on the steamship *America* and the two little sisters, Stefania and Pina, whom I thought would be orphaned until their father miraculously found them.

I was waiting in the barbershop for Louis to get through working so we could go home together. It was the first week of March 1922, when one of the workers of my husband named Enrico came in with two little girls at his side - one about eight and the other about five. The father looked sick. He excused himself for not reporting to work that day adding, "I'm sorry, Mr. Pisano about today. My wife left me flat last night. She is gone for good this time. She left me with my two daughters. I'm trying to place them in homes." Louis and I were speechless as we looked at these girls. He continued, "I found lodging with an old friend for Adele, the oldest one here, but, my friend can't take care of two. I am sorry to be a problem in the shop."

While this man was talking, I kept looking at Louis, asking him silently with my eyes, "Please read my mind, dear husband. Please, read my mind." I soon caught Louis' attention and, comprehending, he asked me, "What do you want to tell me?" I didn't answer him; instead, I looked at the smaller, scared girl and hugged her. She hung on me and then looking at her father said, "Daddy. Can I stay with this lady? Please?" Louis smiled. The father, awkward and confused said, "No dear. They have no room. You will go to another home somewhere like your sister." I looked again at Louis questioningly. He understood my silent message and said to his worker, "Yes. We have room. She can sleep on our couch in the parlor. We will make room for her, won't we, Lena?" I was so happy, I kissed him. It all brought visions back to me of my two little friends, Pina and Stefania, who at the same age, were nearly lost to their father in the chaos that was Ellis Island.

We had that little girl with us for three months. Her name was Gabriella. I called her "Gabby" in English - because like me - she was. She called me, "Mamma Lena." I loved her so much. She was instantly like my own child.

Gabby was my obedient, little companion and so very handy with everything in the house. Never a complaint - just a beautiful child. Together we went almost every day to the public library. I brought her to the children's section and while I looked for books about mythology or biblical stories to tell her about, I sat her down next to a black boy at the reading table. Gabby immediately looked alarmed. She moved away. I said nothing. I found a book and sat near the boy myself. I opened the book and showed him the picture of Hercules, how strong he was, etc. The boy was a darling little thing, so well behaved. His mother was around elsewhere, looking for books herself. After a while, Gabby sat at the other side of the boy and the three of us were looking at the other pictures in the book. Again, I felt I had gained some unity with the world.

Louis and I loved Gabby. In the three months she stayed with us, we made her feel free from her fear of not being wanted and her fear of being abandoned. She was serene, never mentioning her mother. She had gained weight and she looked beautiful. She was a listening sponge to my many stories and observances.

But then we found out that Enrico's story was not exactly as he had told us.

One Sunday, we took Gabby to Revere Beach for the amusements and saw her father, Enrico, arm-in-arm with a young woman on the board-walk. When he saw us, he quickly stepped inside a souvenir store. Louis went alone inside to follow him. There he confronted his worker, "Why are you hiding from us?" Louis demanded. Enrico said back, "I didn't want Gabriella to see me." Louis got angry, "You could have come to spend a Sunday or a Monday with your child once in a while - to take her here to the beach yourself. Never did you come. I could be alone with my wife just once." Enrico had nothing he could say in return. Louis left the store, and so did we - immediately back to Lynn. I knew my husband's moods well by now. When he was peeved at somebody he was mad with everybody - so I kept quiet.

Soon after, we found out that the woman on Enrico's arm was his wife's sister who he was having an affair with and that was the reason his wife had left him. When Louis found this out, that was the end of Enrico - he was fired from the barbershop. I knew that Gabby would want to stay with us, and there was the problem. She couldn't. What will happen to this child? The Children's Aid Society was the early answer to foster care. It was possible that she and her sister would end up there. I was horrified at this thought. Louis would not discuss the matter. He just wouldn't. Gabby had to go.

On Tuesday, Louis was at the shop, and Enrico came up to get Gabby to take her away. He hardly spoke a word to me or his daughter. He just gathered her and her things and left. The poor child was in tears the entire time, and I could do nothing other than to hold back my own. Where he took her after that, I didn't know.

Louis' brother, Richie, found out for me. That was his calling in life - a sleuth. Richie came up one evening and told me that he had found out through paesani friends that the two girls went back to their mother. I was so happy to hear this. "But how? Tell me!" He said Enrico had received a letter from his wife asking for the girls to come back and to stay with her. So, he brought them to her. "Oh, good," I thought. Richie continued, "My friends tell me that Enrico's wife is in Boston, ready to divorce him for his affair with her sister and is petitioning the church to sanction this divorce due to his sin against God. But, when she found out about what he did, she went herself to have an affair and is living with another man. The church doesn't know about this though. So, maybe the girls will stay with the mother. Maybe not. That's all I know." "Mama Mia!" I thought. I asked him, "Why would someone spite someone by doing the same misdeeds? Who is worse - the father or the mother?" Richie then said, "The woman is not as bad as he claims her to be. I think they will go with the mother - and the church." I replied, "It is all so sad. These poor little girls are being tossed back and forth between broken homes. But in this case, even the mother is better than the father for keeping the girl secured, eh?" Richie shrugged and said, "I guess so." And then left me to my thoughts.

This family, all of them, have completely disappeared from the area. Now perhaps, little Gabby is a happy mature woman somewhere. I pray this to be true. I sometimes wonder if she made it in life to find someone true in his own heart - faithful only to her. I wonder also if ever she remembers her gabby Mamma Lena?

Chapter Three

The Stork of Fate Knocks on My Door

Louis had a strong personality, strong desires. He loved me deeply. He also knew my character. I was also strong in opinion, strong about catching some education and with all my heart, I loved him for many reasons. Sometimes these two strong, opinionated people had confrontations and problems which needed to be ironed out. But as I discovered in life, one small confrontation is a more powerful dye than hundreds of happy moments given away to abstract memory.

I was a very dutiful wife, and so was Louis as a husband. I was learning cooking as if it were a science. I learned a system for maintaining a very clean home and began to feel a little more confident of myself.

It was in June 1922, that I first felt a joy was growing inside of me. I wasn't too sure, but Pandora's "hope" was still on the wing flying around me. It was a joy that I didn't want to share with anybody else but my husband. I was very, very cautious as was my temperament. I had to be certain myself.

One Monday evening, after supper, Louis offered to take me to the movies as we usually did. I refused to go this time. He became very concerned. "Lena," he said, "you don't want to miss this one. It is a cowboy Western. You would love it." "Louis," I said gravely, "let's sit down in the parlor. I have something to tell you." First, he became worried, then scared, saying, "All right." I followed him. When he got to the parlor, he tried to ease the conversation by talking more about the movie. I ignored everything that he was saying and interrupted him, "Louis. I am pregnant." "What?!" He yelled out. I quietly said, "Yes. I am." He grabbed me by my waist and pulled me close to him as if to dance. "Yes! Yes!" He shouted. "Repeat it please." "It's true. I am sure that I am pregnant." "Yes!" He shouted again. "Oh, my God. I heard it!"

Louis then lifted me up and carried me all over the room spinning. I thought we would fall together to the floor. "You are crazy, Louis," I shouted. "Put me down! I'm getting dizzy." "Oh, yes," He said. He seated me next to him on the couch, kissing me rapidly on my hands and face. "Stop, Louis. Let's talk." Finally, he calmed down. I told him not to say anything to anybody until I would show. He promised. Then he asked me why? "I don't know," I told him. "I am afraid I would get too many questions. Or, I just like to share this joy with you for now." "Okay," he said as he started to joyously kiss me again.

Yes, we stayed home that Monday evening. We had a little party of our own. I had made some new types of cookies. We brewed some black coffee and stayed huddled close together. We didn't even play any records or did we think about anything else. I remember what he said quietly to me. "For this, I am eternally grateful to you, Lena. Having a large family means so much to me." I asked in alarm. "A large family?" He continued, "Well for a while, I thought that you couldn't have any children." He was counting the months we had been married. "Well, Dear," I said, "I only want three children. Remember, they must be educated, and it costs money to have a home, doctors, or for whatever they are inclined to do in life. Three only. No matter what. Okay?" He made up his mind not to disagree with me. Everything I said to him was approved immediately without question. Louis started to light up a cigarette. He was going to offer one to me as he usually did after dinner, but then he retreated the package and said smiling, "Oh no, not you."

I shall always remember Luigi Pisano like he was that night. My memory of our shared joy and hope together was neither abstract - nor lost.

Nurturing Walks

Summer was approaching. Louis and I frequently went to Lynn beach and walked most of the three-mile dunes barefooted, looking for shells. There was no talk of pollution then. The beach was clean and beautiful.

On most Mondays during this summer, we would go to the seashore and relax with some compare friends - but mostly we went alone.

As was custom, sometimes we got all dressed up and went to the beach where we listened to the band and promenaded with others. It was the roaring twenties after all. Happy? Yes. I was with child and with the most handsome man anywhere, even in the movies. It was heaven.

"Me and Louis at the Beach, 1922"

Making a Nest

I was doing very well with my pregnancy. I began to feel my baby moving. It was a boy I knew that - I felt that. Only another mother could explain this premonition or understand this feeling with no solid basis. One just knew. It was all a mystery of life, mostly when a young mother didn't understand the functions of all that growth that is going on inside. The how and why for so many things. How was this new life moving and growing so fast inside of me? What true forces brought it all together from nothing? How much was mine? How much was Louis? How much was brand new? Why was it so difficult for some people to conceive and why so easily for others like my mother? I had in front of me so many issues of ignorance to solve. I wished more with each day that I had my own mother to guide me.

So, I scheduled my weekdays like a soldier; reading and studying one hour of heavy subjects every morning; learning four new English words to memory every day; resting in the afternoon one hour and then shopping for two hours and allowing two hours more for cooking supper. After supper, I would converse for a while with Louis, clean up, read for two more hours in bed, either newspapers or some key books. A regular schedule for a serious expectant mother. Of course, I could not keep up that schedule every day because weekends brought company and other distractions which took my time away. Every day, however, when I learned those four new words in English, I would repeat them aloud to the growing child inside me.

Goodbye Maria

My sister-in-law Maria and her husband moved away from Lynn that summer. Richie stayed. Maria decided to join her other Sister, Generosa, in Saint Louis, Missouri. Generosa was the oldest Pisano child, just ahead of Louis. Generosa had been in that place for a long time but had recently lost her husband. So, she called for Maria to come join her and to make a new life in the prosperous American city of Saint Louis. A lot of Italians had settled in that part of the country after building America's railroads along with the Irish. So, the move was an important one for Maria and her husband to consider. Louis and I were both happy and sad to see her go.

We said our simple goodbyes with no other conversation allowed. I almost felt glad. Maybe the company of her older sister and her growing family would fill up the void of Maria's mind and inspire her to think more constructively. And in time, it did. Maria had two excellent children of her own who grew up in Saint Louis, both of whom became very prominent. One of her sons, Richard Renna, was a famous bandleader and also co-founded a union called the AF of M - the American Federation of Musicians - a big deal.

I think now that Maria's resentment of how her brothers Richie and Louis treated her, made her a little sour and contentious. For in the end, after she moved to Saint Lewis, Maria regained her composure, grace, and intelligence - a Pisano forever.

Invitation from Another "Generosa."

General Pisano

One afternoon, Louis came home for his lunch with excitement. With him, he brought a large letter that contained a photograph. It was a theatre invitation with tickets. The invitation was for us to go to New York City and to see his first cousin perform his act on the Vaudeville stage there. I remembered this incident as I write about Louis' sister, Generosa, in Saint Louis. Generosa and Generoso are two very popular Pisano names. There are many of them in Louis' home village of Prata, Italy. Even the mayor of Prata was named, Generoso Pisano III.

All the Pisano men had expert prowess with guns and liked to shoot. That is how I first met Louis, in my Nonna's store, when he was buying bullets. Louis' father, Domenico however, as I wrote before, was not as proficient. He lost his left arm up to his elbow after his own rifle exploded in his hands with bad powder. He was lucky he was not killed. Anyway, this other Pisano cousin of Louis', Generoso Pisano, came to America and put his gun skills to good use. He didn't kill anybody; that was not his temperament - but he was a showman. So instead, Generoso put an act together and went on stage as a "sharpshooter." Of course, he used the stage name, "General Pisano." He and Louis grew up together in Prata, same age, almost like identical twins. No one could tell them apart as boys because the two first cousins were almost the same as twin brothers. Why? Two Pisano brothers married two sisters from the same village, so the cousins were related more than cousins but less than brothers, if that is clear. This was Louis and Generoso's close connection.

Louis told me of one story of how when he and his cousin, Generoso, first came to New York in 1907, they looked so much alike, they would fool all of the paesani by causing a big fuss in two different places at the same time. They had great fun with this ploy. But they almost did not escape Ellis Island because of the confusion they made with the officials. It was fun to listen to this story.

In his stage act, General Pisano used an assistant who would hold a cigarette between her teeth and from across the stage, he would use a .22 rifle and shoot the cigarette out of her mouth without having her lose her smile. Also, he played a stand-up piano by rapidly shooting the keys to play popular songs on it. He was a really good shot and got lots of write-ups in the New York papers.

Louis and I, of course, could not go to New York, or anywhere else of great distance in my condition, but the fact that Louis got a personal invitation to be at his cousin's opening performance in Vaudeville made Louis glow like a lightbulb for a week. He was so very proud. He put the invitation and picture up on his barbershop mirror and talked about it to all his customers, should any of them happen to find themselves in New York City.

Later, Generoso "General" Pisano retired from the Vaudeville stage, married his assistant, who had a full set of her own teeth, as far as we knew, and opened up a very expensive wine and liquor store in Manhattan. Perhaps to calm his and her nerves, eh?

Generoso "General" Pisano as a Vaudevillian Sharpshooter, Circa 1925

Chapter Four

Louis' Surprise Birthday Party

It was 1922, November. Louis's birthday was on the 5th - almost one year since our marriage. My child was giving me constant proof of existence - moving in me, sometimes kicking. I often talked to him. "Eh, big boy. Do not be so fresh, and do not be so anxious, eh? We have to wait another three months. And don't you dare come any earlier. You will be born in February. The month of your mother's birthday. I feel you will be just like me, Capsci?"

I kept dutiful and busy as ever, but at Louis's birthday, I was magnificent. I wanted to make for him a very special surprise party. Oh, what confidence I had! I remember this so clearly. I made a big beautiful three-layer cake with three kinds of cream. It was a sponge cake of Italian style (pane di Spagna ricetta) - soft and tall. Well, I cut the cake into three layers and bathed each layer with a savory rum. Then, I added chocolate cream, lemon cream, and coffee cream. On the top, I covered it with heavy whipped cream. I also made three kinds of cookies, some with special almonds, two inches long and one inch wide. The other cookies were lemon zest rounds covered with confectionary sugar and the third bunch were old fashioned Roman cookies, round and high, like little donuts. They were boiled first, then baked and last, I rolled them in a sugar syrup. Everything was just the way I wanted. I hid everything downstairs in the ice chest in Ralfo's apartment. I worked all this in when Louis wasn't around. It took me one week to make all the preparations.

It was a Sunday, and everyone sneaked up the back stairs right after church - those who went to masse. The usual family crowd, except my Aunt Alfonsina. My brother, Ralfo, was my co-conspirator for he kept Louis downstairs in his apartment and away from the secret.

I prepared a beautiful table setting in our dining room. My mother earlier sent me all the work I did in embroidery while learning the art by

373

the nuns. Also, she sent to me a silk spread and a spread of Venetian lace that I made on which I arranged all our goodies. I placed the cake in the middle with thirty-seven little candles. The cake was big enough for the people I invited. Around the cake, I placed short-stemmed flowers, the cookies, finger sandwiches, juices and wine with crystal glasses. For my first time, it was a great achievement for me. Everyone patted me with whispers of congratulations. I think I surprised everyone.

I shut the sliding door between the dining room and the kitchen, dimmed the lights and lit the candles just when Ralfo brought Louis upstairs. I opened the door of the dining room. Oh, the surprise! We all sang, "Happy birthday to you, dear Louis!"

I was very proud because I did everything all by myself. Louis was so surprised and happy. He kissed me over and over again. He felt honored. Louis then said to everyone, almost in tears, "I have no words. Never have I ever had a birthday party - in my whole life. I am so happy. Thank you, everyone. I love you 'too much,' Lena." That "too much" was funny, and everybody laughed. I said to him, "After this, love can never be too much." More laughs and congratulations. My Uncle Ferdinando at each bite of the cake said to me, "Yes my dear - you are a woman, a complete woman!" I was not offended.

Well, now it is almost nothing for me to prepare a complete birthday party. But believe me, at that time, it was a hard task. I was so anxious to learn the art of cooking modernly. It was so different growing up beneath the mountain circumstant of Italy. Back then, we had no gas stove to do justice to cakes or cookies. Coal-fired ovens are indifferent - they are mostly for heat. The secret of really good cooking is not just the amount of the heat used, but the subtle control and timing of it. I experienced so much preparing Louis' birthday party that, after that big effort, it was nothing for me to cook anything. In Italy now, as it is here, there is no difference. But growing up in Pratola Serra, the Roman way of cooking was the only way.

Another Premonition - my Son Appears in a Dream

At this time, my son continued to move, and I continued to talk to him. Yes, I was certain it was going to be a boy. Why? I always dreamt of him while I was pregnant. The same dream persisted, and there was no denying it. My Great Uncle Costantino was always in these dreams, as well, and with him was a little boy looking almost like him - cherubic with dark curly hair. When I dream things to happen, I dream the same exact dream for many nights - and they always come true. So, it was this time. The child holding my late uncle's hand in my dreams was a beautiful little boy. I knew this child already - even before he was born.

Well, I got everything he needed ready. I made many little boy's jumpers, with embroidery etc. I bought swaddling bands to band him with after he was born, like an Egyptian mummy, to keep the legs and arms straight. These bands were sold in all the European stores. It seems impossible now to hear about these old-fashioned methods, but we did them then. There are many paintings of mother's swathing their babies in bands in an earlier period than even of the time I write about. Paintings of babies up to three months old were rolled up in these mummy-like bands. It seems hard to understand now why we did this practice. I would say ignorance, and perhaps even that old customs die hard.

In this time in Europe, and in some parts of America, there were lots of babies with bowlegs due certainly to malnutrition of the mother - circumstances like the lack of calcium and other minerals in their diet must have caused this malady. Today, I never see anybody with bowlegs. I did at this date, however, 1922 or so. Some black people who came from the South were bowlegged. Even some Slavic farmers in America who sold all the milk and cheese to others from their farms, but for their own necessities, they ate badly. They only ate bread. They thought eating only bread was enough. As long as their bellies were full, that was all that was necessary. The idea of nutrition played havoc with a newborn baby's health as a result. So, I prepared properly for my own child - even the swaddling bands.

Papa Returns from Italy

In 1922, across the ocean in Pratola Serra, Papa was constantly preparing to return to America. He was doing this almost as soon as he arrived back there. The commitment of family, the haunting memories of his mother and father, and the general conditions of Italy, all gave him more concerns than his glands which somehow miraculously healed. My father had now been in Italy for a year with my mother. He had spent almost all of his money that he made in America, much I would suspect on gambling. Only one good thing came out of it. Papa moved Mother and my siblings out of Nonno Fabrizio's stone farmhouse, and he built for them a home of eight large rooms with full bath and modern commodities on a new street in Pratola Serra. Why didn't he reopen a harness factory again? Why? I don't know. There still was lots of work for him along this line. There were plenty of horses in Italy still, especially in that country region, and the government troubles were far away. But, Papa didn't work at all. Nothing. In one year, he went through what is now forty thousand dollars of what he brought back with him. It was a lot of money and I'm sure the village of Pratola Serra appreciated it greatly. *[Aside: My grandmother obviously estimated the inflation rate from 1921 to 1979 when her letter was written. Projecting forward until today, the rate is 3.49136%. That would mean the $40,000 my grandmother estimated her father to have brought back with him to Italy would be worth something near $150,000.00 today.]*

Many times, Ralfo and I worried about whether Father would be able to return or not with Mother and our siblings. The fear was that they would not be able to return because of quotas being set for Italians in the Emergency Immigration Act of 1921. Maybe he would be stuck back there in Pratola Serra with Mother and the rest of the children forever. The immigration details were still uncertain, and we figured that one of Father's fears was that he might have to stay in Italy - a place that he had been trying to flee much of his adult life.

After the new house was built and a year had passed, Papa decided he would test the "skilled labor" exemption of the Quota Law, and he made travel plans again to come back to America - alone. He was cleared.

In the fall of 1922, my father came back directly to Lynn where his two oldest children were living and his soon to be new grandchild. My father, Guiseppe Pirone, would finally be a "Nonno" himself. Also in Lynn, were both of his brothers-in-law, one being his best friend.

Papa moved immediately into the small apartment Ralfo had next to us. When he did, several things happened. It was no time at all that Mother's brother, Uncle Ferdinando, helped Papa get work as a leather-smith in the top shoe factory of Lynn. Of course, Ralfo dutifully joined him at his side. But most important to my mind was that upon his return, my father made immediate plans to finally become an American citizen - a commitment that would open the gates wide and bring all of the family from Pratola Serra - one by one they started to come to America.

One year later, 1923, with Ralfo in tow, Papa left the shoe-making business and would move back to an apartment in the North End, near Aunt Alfonsina, where he opened his own harness shop.

Bravo, ancora, Papa!

Christmas/New Years: 1922 - 1923

Brother Mikele Arrives

After Papa became a citizen of the United States, we created for him a big Christmas party at my house. Everyone came - everyone. I thanked God that I had so much help for I was swollen with child. Everyone who came brought wonderful food, gifts, and a helping hand. I did nothing except to happily cheer for my father's new status in the world. It was the most wonderful Christmas gift shared at the party. There was a sense of peace on Papa's face.

Papa, as he had promised, made immediate passport papers and travel arrangements to get my brother Mikele over to America next. Now that

Papa was a citizen of America, he could bring his family over unimpeded without questions. Mikele was first, even though our sister Allisandra, was the third born after me and Ralfo. She was helping Mother with the other children, of course. The plight of the next daughter in line.

Mikele was just out of high school. Our other brother, Constantino, who was older than Mikele, stayed behind until he finished college in Benevento, Italy. Constantino was studying business and accounting. We had beautiful letters from him as well and how he soon wanted to join Mikele in America. I mentioned earlier, after my brother Constantino came to America, he added an extra "N" to his given name, Costantino, and made it "Constantino" so as not to confuse people in the family from his late uncle. But there was no confusing my loquacious brother "Connie," however - with anyone.

So, my brother Mikele came first from this group, in January 1923, all by himself. He was only fifteen years of age. A big test for the family and for Papa's new status as an American citizen and the Emergency Immigration Act of 1922. We were all holding our breath and what it all would mean if there was any difficulty. Thankfully, we had no problem for Mikele getting in.

My father kept Mikele's arrival time a surprise. He and Ralfo went to get him off the boat in Boston Harbor and quietly brought him back to Lynn without our knowledge. Ralfo made Mikele knock on the kitchen door. I said, "Come in." And there he was! My baby brother, Mikele - all grown up. "Oh, my God!" I yelled. "I have not seen you in four years! You are so big!" Mikele embraced me, then he put his hand on my stomach, "Oh, tu aspetti?" ("You are waiting?") "Si, si, io Aspetto." ("Yes, yes. I am waiting.") It was another celebration for us. What a beautiful young man.

Mikele stayed with Louis and me for several days, and I loved cooking for them both and listening to my young brother's puristic Italian - beautiful. Louis loved all my family and loved to be around them. They loved him back. After dinner, Louis would go out and buy some sweet pastry, and we would be joined by Ralfo and Papa for strong coffee and conversation. Papa would usually just go to sleep in the parlor. The topic was always about one thing - the politics of Italy!

I was surprised at how far apart my two brothers were in ideology. It started as a conversation about Mussolini. My brother, Mikele, to my surprise, was a true Fascist and strong of opinion and, like Louis, was a supporter of Mussolini. Mikele claimed that the educational system is now unified and inclusive, and Ralfo countered that he hated dictators because all that advancement was on the backs and exploitation of the workers. Ralfo was infused with Socialism. I would bridge the two sides with the commonality of art and music, how art was the true spirit and soul of the Italians - not politics. Hours would go by. It was wonderful. A few weeks later, it all wouldn't matter.

Pains of Labor

The pain started. Toward evening, other signals appeared. The pain became very strong, as strong a pain as I ever imagined could exist. I made them worse by moaning about them. I knew no better. I was so lost and helpless. I cried out as the pains got more frequent and even stronger. Foolishly, I lost all my strength that way. I had no prenatal care or preparations. I was completely ignorant and mad at myself.

They brought me to the hospital. I had pains all through the night. The following morning, the doctor came into my room three times. "Not ready yet, Lena," he said. "Bear the waves of pain for when they come, they also must go." Ten more hours of labor happened. I thought, "If these pains continue like this, my baby will die. Oh, God, now I really need you!"

When they finally brought me down in the delivery room, my husband was waiting in the corridor. He was not permitted to come in. A nurse was helping me and she tried to give me some juice to drink - orange or something. I couldn't drink it. I had to cry with my pains.

February 9th, 1923

Birth

Finally, the doctor came again and decided to force the baby out. They gave me ether, and I felt like if my mind was separate from my body. I never had had ether before. Little by little, I got far, far away to nowhere. No dreams were allowed where I went. No safety for my mind to hold onto. Nothing.

Then after a while, I heard a baby's cry - my baby's cry. A nurse was busy fussing with my empty stomach. I was stunned and confused - then another cry. "What happened? Where am I?" I asked. The doctor told me smiling, "Congratulations, Lena. You have a beautiful baby boy! Eight pounds and two ounces." "Oh, yes, the baby!" I shouted. "Let me see him, does he have any births marks? Any defects? Let me see him!" The doctor then said, "He is perfect, Lena. A perfect baby boy."

They were cleaning my baby behind me at the back of my head. I tried to get up to see, but the nurse pushed me back down. The doctor finally showed him to me. I cannot describe the feeling. This little boy was mine? How beautiful he was. He had a face like a doll, round - a perfect head. I said to the doctor, "Let me touch him, come closer, let me touch him, perhaps he will stop crying." "No, no, you can't touch him yet," said the doctor. They then gave me a pill, to quiet me down for I had after-pains. Pains again? I was again dazed and stunned.

When my husband came in. I hardly heard him. I remember the Doctor saying to Louis, "He is a perfect big boy, and the mother is fine. We had to force the birth. Her pelvis refused to open naturally, but she is all right." My husband bent over and kissed me and then said very emotionally, "I thank you, I thank you, Lena, for giving me a beautiful son." Even as stunned as I was, I forced myself to answer him. Weakly, but audible enough, because the nurse and the doctor laughed at my answer. "He is also my baby - not completely yours, eh?" Louis laughed, "Yes. Of course."

All in the Name

The second day, my baby was brought to me dressed up with hospital clothes and wrapped up in a blanket. He was as hungry as a bear. They placed him at my side. I couldn't believe how warm and perfect he was. I had seen other new-born babies before - my brothers, my sister and even my brother, Luigi, as he was coming out of my mother. And also, I saw many babies of strangers. They all had elongated heads at first, and they had reddish skin and other spots on them. But my baby was perfect. He even had lots of hair, blondish, light skin and straight legs with strong beautiful hands. I loved how much I loved him. When I touched him, something divine ran all through my being. Instantly, I became a better Christian. I thanked God. I had to thank somebody. "I thank you, God - I thank you for giving me this little creature!"

The baby laid in my arms for a long time. Then the nurse came in again, washed my breast and he was fed. The breastfeeding of the baby gave me more joy than I ever felt in my entire life. This job was accompanied with a whispered promise, "For you, my child, I will suffer if I have to. I will endure any pain, anything, and through you, I will love life more. I shall be a perfect mother."

When my husband came in, first he saw how this little fellow was sucking for dear life. Louis laughed. "My, what a hungry man you have there." When the baby finally stopped, he turned his face toward me, satisfied. I wiped his mouth clean, and then facing his father, he fell asleep.

Louis saw the tears in my eyes and asked me, "You are sad? Why?" I answered, "No, not sad, not at all. Don't you know that tears of happiness are rare and very precious? I am happy, that is why I cry." Louis just adored the baby and gave him a smile as wide as I have ever seen him wear. Louis wanted to pick him up. I said, "No, no, wait for the nurse."

"Well," he said, "what we will we call him?" "Ah! Yes, 'Reno,'" I said. "Why Reno?" Louis asked. "I don't know, it seems to fit him. Just listen to the name - 'Reno.' It has a strong melody with some mysterious significance." "I guess so," Louis said, not totally convinced. Then he offered, "Reno Vittorio." "Why Vittorio?" "Victory for Italy," he said, with braggadocio. "Mussolini will make Italy big." "Stop it," I exclaimed. "Okay," he said, "Then Vittorio after the King. Same thing." I sat up a bit to consider. "Yes. I like Vittorio too, but because it is the name of Victoria Columbia - Michelangelo's love - a poetess. I like the contrast."

We agreed. And so, it was registered at City Hall of Lynn, Massachusetts. Reno Vittorio Pisano, born Feb. 8, 1923 - at 12 noon.

I began to eat more steadily. They had to band my breast because I produced too much milk; it was leaking out. So, my baby was well provided for. After one week, I went home with Reno in my arms.

Reno Grows

When Reno was three months old, we took a picture together - "mother and child." I still have it here with me now, hanging in my bedroom. In this picture, Reno looks as if he is trying to tell everyone just how happy he is. The picture features him naked after his bath. I had a scarf around my hair and I held him up on my lap, but I felt he could already sit straight enough by himself. The baby was so satisfied, so healthy, so very beautiful.

My husband and I used to talk to the baby to catch his attention. This was easy to do. Anytime Louis and I said, "Reno," the baby would babble his baby's babble. Louis and I would laugh and laugh.

I nursed Reno for almost nine months. Since I was a heavy sleeper, when he cried at night, I never heard him. Louis would get up and change him, and then he placed the baby at my side and nudge me awake. "Lena. Here is your boy."

At six months, when Reno was through with one side of feeding, he would cross over me to get to the other side. We jokingly called him, little "Mangiare-Mangione" (little glutton eater.)

At eight months, Reno began to eat solid foods. I used to shred the meat very fine and strain vegetables and fruits. He loved pastina with butter. He also loved cow's milk at nine months, so I stopped nursing him.

These early months of nursing and influencing went by so quickly, but I promised myself that I would concentrate and enjoy each and every day as it came, and I did. I spent every moment fulfilling my promise to be the best mother I could to my child even though I started that journey as an ignorant child myself. But when I saw in front of me the little boy who appeared in my dreams, I was plenty prepared.

Was I giving up any other part of my dreams - of my hopes and desire to be a more complete person - to be an accomplished writer or to be a woman of influence? No. Never!

"Mother and Child," April 1923.

Chapter Five

Grapes of Wrath

In that same year, in August of 1923, my Uncle Antonio and Fortuna came up to Lynn from the Bronx, New York. With them also came Fortuna's brother, Frank, and two other men - all from my uncle's wholesale grape business. Uncle Antonio, my husband, and Fortuna were collaborating together on an investment in the grape business - Louis as a silent partner. And, I think at this time my husband wanted to do something more than just to have a successful barbershop in Lynn because he was a new father. Louis also felt he had the resources now saved up to do something important in life and that the time and situation was right. Louis was forever full of demanding pride, to a fault.

Everyone from New York stayed at the Hotel Edison in Lynn and had their dinners with us. They came to Lynn to sign Louis and another man, a friend of Louis', Mr. Joe Saverino, to a purchase arrangement in the wholesale grape business. Mr. Saverino was a bank associate of Louis' on Summer Street. All day, inside the backroom of the bank, everyone discussed the investment, the arrangement and the procedure. Louis and Mr. Saverino agreed to invest five thousand dollars each to purchase California grapes with my Uncle Antonio's company being the purchase agent of the sale. It was agreed that Louis would go to California to oversee the details of the purchase and to ship the grapes back East. He would then return to sell the grapes from the Boston Railroad Yard to winemakers in the area. The profits from this sale would be shared evenly by Mr. Saverino and Louis alone. *[Aside: The $5,000 invested in wholesale grapes in 1923 would be worth approximately $72,000.00 today.]*

After the backroom deal was consummated, then the visitations commenced.

My Uncle Antonio came up the stairs with a big box under his arm and a generous smile on his face in anticipation of the effect the gift was about to have. Uncle was immediately overjoyed at seeing his new grand-nephew, Reno, for the first time. "Oh!" he exclaimed, "He is so nice-looking! Like the Pironi, yes, and also strong like the Pisano."

Reno, six months old now, was seated in his high chair. He was playing with some little toys with long strings that went up and down. Whenever he reached for the moving strings, he laughed and babbled his baby talk. He was adorable. When Reno saw my uncle, however, he stopped playing and just stared at Uncle Antonio, not knowing what to make of him. The child just stared and stared quietly. It was funny how he concentrated only on my uncle. Then Reno gave a funny sound as if he had noticed something funny. My uncle looked at him and pointed to the other people around and said, "Look at him! He loves me! He is so smart."

Uncle Antonio then went to Reno, picked him up, and told me to open the box. I did. Inside the careful wrapping was a beautiful baby's coat of pink silk lined with same color, also of silk. It was the best silk I had ever seen. There was a pink wool sweater, just of the same colors to match. Two pairs of silk pink stocking and six pairs of toddler underwear. Two pink rompers, and a pair of white shoes. I'm thinking, of course, that perhaps blue would have been a better boy's color choice, but I was not going to mention anything. The clothes were exceptionally well made and beautiful - even for a boy.

Later, I found out that my cousin, Fortuna, evidently was in love with one of the gentlemen, an aid to my uncle named, Dominic. This love interest of hers was a short, stout man and from the start, I didn't like his demeanor much. I just couldn't see them together. They didn't fit the eye. Was I skeptically protective? Perhaps. Her fellow had something in his movements and expression as someone who would stop at nothing to win. He was about forty years old. The other fellow was very nice, courteous and about fifty years of age. His name was Mr. Ciolino. This man was very dignified, with tall, graceful manners. I could visualize him with my cousin Fortuna, except that he was too old for her. But that was what people had also said about Louis and me.

Fortuna, nevertheless, was extremely happy with the fat man, Dominic. We separated off into the kitchen because I felt Fortuna had something she wanted to confide in me. I could not hide the obvious, and I said to her, "Fortuna - Dear. What in the world do you see in him? You are brilliant and nice-looking. Can't you wait until you find a better man?" "Please, Lena." she refuted, "I will never be able to explain to you why I love him. You love people for different reasons than I do. He is good for me. He knows the way to make money." "Okay." I said, "let's change the subject before I tell you what I think about money." "Tell me," she said.

I looked at my cousin and said, "Money? It destroys all reason." It was a sensitive topic that we abandoned after that, and we rejoined the group of men.

During that entire visit, I surprised my dear uncle with all my new recipes that I had learned of Italian and American cuisine. He was his usual happy, hungry self.

Uncle Antonio put Reno on the kitchen table and tried the coat on without objections from the child who sat patiently. He looked adorable. Reno, as if he understood what all the fuss was about, looked at the coat then up to his great-uncle. Everybody laughed. My Uncle said, "This son-of-a gun, he likes everything. Smart boy! Good for you." We had fun that night. I noticed the love which my uncle continued to have for me. I loved him, as well.

California or Bust

Well, Louis went out to California the first of September 1923, and worked very hard there. I received letters almost every day. Love letters. My husband was lonesome. But he also wrote, "How is Reno? How is my brother, Richie, doing with the assistants," etc. Richie was left in charge of the barbershop and payroll while Louis was away, and he gave me some money every week for my expenses. Just what my husband left him orders to do.

Louis came back at the end of October, and after two months, he couldn't believe how our son had grown. Reno was a healthy, active baby and was crawling all over the house and even getting up holding onto chairs. He was so happy - we were so happy - as a family.

Louis came home looking dark, tanned and healthy himself. He had been out under the California sun for the entire time. It truly suited him.

Thinking back now, maybe that was the only real vacation he ever had in his whole life - a working vacation. Yes, Louis had to work and to save. There was no reason ever for him not to do otherwise. That was Louis. But this different change of work for him was very restful. You could see that he needed it, but Louis would never ever seek such an experience again.

Unfortunately, through no one's fault, the wholesale grape business didn't command as high a price as expected when the grapes arrived for sale at the Boston Railroad Yard. The first lot was sold at only a small margin. Many times, Louis would not be able to go to the yard to help sell them, and the remaining grapes in waiting became spoiled and were wasted.

With his investment gone, Louis couldn't pay his three helpers. He had to let them go. I lent Louis four hundred dollars to help make his back expenses. I had another four hundred dollars left from my savings. We managed to get by those last months of 1923.

Louis concentrated on his own business after that and to build his resources back up. He never discussed grapes again nor did he take any animosities to my Uncle Antonio or his business. I think it solidified Louis' resolve to do what he did best, to run a successful barbershop alone - without help - without letup. To his credit, he did.

Chapter Six

My Miscarriage - My Misgivings

The new year came, 1924. On the 15th of January, I had a miscarriage. I was not certain what was going on that Tuesday morning after Louis left for work. The pain was sharp and felt again as if I were in labor. Too soon! It can't be. By phone, I managed to call Louis back from work, and he immediately brought with him the doctor and his nurse. Everyone was concerned - even the doctor. When the doctor and the nurse began to quickly give explicit instructions, all my husband could do was to shrink away into the other room with pallor on his face. Now I was terrified. All I could think about was that this was not normal and that I might die. Was I to die in the same bed as Louis' first wife, Tina? In the same manner? In stillbirth?

God, help me.

In this scene, I remembered my dream of the last three nights. I dreamt of a little girl, sickly, looking like my old Great-Nonna, Maria. The doctor gave me a shot of something, and I fell back into a horrible sense of emptiness. I vaguely saw the doctor with gloves pick up and remove something from me and my bed. He handed it to the nurse, and I went unconscious.

When I became awake and groggy, I could only think that this might be in the life after - death. Was I still alive? The room was dark and empty. Silent. The nurse came back first - the doctor soon after. They were both sympathetic and consoling to me. I was not dead. The doctor explained to me, which I heard vaguely, "I'm sorry, Mrs. Pisano. You lost the fetus. It was three months - a girl - too bad." I felt terrible and cried only in mild resistance, "Oh, God, again fate punishes me, why?"

The nurse took the fetus and remains away - where? I don't know. I was told later that it was rolled up it in soft paper, then in a newspaper, and then thrown away in the garbage.

Only much later, when I was alone in my bed, curled in remorse, did my husband come in. He could say nothing. Nothing at all. He only held my hand, and together we both cried.

A girl child. Lost. Would I ever see another? Could I ever now justify my belief of fate versus destiny? Was it my fate to lose this child, and was it her destiny not to see this world? Was she even destined a soul at all?

"Dio, aiutami a." (God, help me.)

My Dear Sister Allessandra Arrives!

As the winter passed, Mother now was nagging Papa that Allessandra should be the next child of theirs to come to America. But what Mother really wanted was for Papa to bring everyone. Letter after letter kept coming. In the back of my mother's heart, she still didn't trust father's resolve. She persisted to unite the family in America once and for all. I kept the subject alive as well. At this time especially, I was thankful to my husband for his generosity to all my family. He became another brother and perhaps even a father to Ralfo and all the others. Louis opened his door wide to them all and they each loved him in return.

Spring came again, and in 1924 my father finally decided to have the third born, Allesandra, come here to America. Even with Papa being a citizen, that year there was some trouble for us with immigration. The quota when Allesandra came was more heavily guarded, so we had to use some influence through our best man, State Senator, Anthony Garofano. Bravo, Anthony!

Allesandra came alone, like our brother Mikele did earlier. She was twenty years of age, same age as me when I came. We welcomed her to our house with tears and open arms. It was such a blessing to see my dear little sister again. [Aside: According to public access records, Louis Pisano's best man, "Tony A. Garofano, was an American politician and barber who served in the Massachusetts House of Representatives in 1920 and from 1923 to 1935. After

390

leaving the legislature, he served as the chairman of the Board of Registration of Barbers and was an employee in the State Department of Public Works."]

Allesandra related to us a story of interest. Because she was so petite in stature and not assertive at all in her manner, the officials at Ellis Island gave her little notice and almost overlooked her completely. I mentioned before, her nickname in our family was "Fregolina," ("Small Crumb.") Well, when they finally processed her papers, she had to have an interpreter. She told us that the guard on duty was not sympathetic at all to Italians. As he filled out her form, he coldly asked what my sister's name was? The interpreter responded, "Allesandra Fabrizio Pirone." He looked at my sister unimpressed, and said, "A big name for such a little person. She's in America now. I cannot spell that name. Tell her, her name in American is 'Alice.' I will mark her down with that name." So, the first hours in America, Allesandra lost her given name and was given another. She would be called "Alice" for the rest of her life.

My beautiful little sister, Alice, was quite a lady now, well poised and intelligent. Oh, how she had grown. Too bad I missed the joy of watching her develop. It reminded me how Mother and Papa made so many beautiful and gifted children. This feat was one thing they could do well together. Eight of us! Four of us now in America - four still left in Pratola Serra.

Alice wanted to remain with me for a while instead of moving in right away with Papa in the North End. She couldn't part from Reno. I remember Reno following her everywhere, babbling continuously. When he couldn't find the proper words in English, he made up noises, babbling something and moving his hands for emphasis. My sister said to me, "Lena. You should teach him Italian." I said, "Okay. You try." She did try. Alice showed baby Reno some bread. She said, "Reno. Look. Say, 'pane.'" Reno answered, "No, bread." How funny they were together. Two little, beautiful people, babbling away together.

Alice stayed with Louis and me for a mouth. I made her some dresses and a spring coat. She looked very nice. After that, Alice moved to the North End and kept house for Papa and our two brothers in their large apartment. Her turn, eh? She did, however, make Mikele help her with all the house chores. Alice also went to work in a nice tailor shop for men right in the North End. She did very well for herself from the start.

I introduced Alice to all my friends in the North End - the ones I left behind. We all embraced and told Alice of our old times that we had together, even though I had left only two years earlier. It was old times for me anyway. My life was so different than what it had been in Boston. I was loaded down now with duties and daily menial tasks. The freedom of thought and deed had vanished for me in being a wife and a mother. I had been living in the most glorious part of Boston with a wonderful career, all of which had been scrawled away with my signature on the marriage papers. Well, so it goes.

Alice promised, "Anytime you like to take a day off from home, do not hesitate to leave Reno with me, and you go on as you please. You have a sister here now." How wonderful it felt. I joked back with her, "But to go as I pleased? Not possible. I have to ask permission from my husband first." We laughed about that obvious piece of reality.

Another Stork Comes Knocking

Spring 1924

I was again pregnant and coming along beautifully with my third child. I already knew what to expect, but I still got awfully tired. I carried on. All summer, every Sunday and Monday afternoons, Louis and I would take Reno to Lynn beach. I couldn't bathe in the beautiful ocean, but Louis and Reno did eagerly. At these moments, watching Louis and little Reno splash about, I could only think of my miscarriage and the unborn child whom I lost at the same stage of pregnancy. Was I worried? I was daydreaming about it anyway.

Soon after, my constant night dreams returned. Night after night. Am I exaggerating when I say I knew it was another boy? No. I must say again that dreams for me are prophecies, not premonitions. I wanted to somehow force these dreams to be one of health and happiness for my new son which I knew instinctively was growing inside of me. I wanted to see him completely grown, not like the little girl I miscarried and was thrown away. Every night I patted my stomach. "Please little one, be good. I want to see you whole and beautiful."

If I only could remember all of my dreams, but I push most of them aside. I do not want to know what it is coming. But when I was excepting, yes, that was a big reason to remember them in every detail. It was easier, of course, when they came every night.

In these new dreams, I dreamt there was this beautiful boy, about one-year-old, walking around my bed. The child would pick up toys, sit on the kitchen floor and break them. He then would put them back together. Other times, I dreamt that he was pointing at me that something was burning on the top of the stove. A serious child, almost like an old man. "Oh, dear me. Please God, make my dream come true."

I can't pray as others do; I was always that way. But I prayed now. I was praying that the new baby in my dreams was the baby that I carried in my body. "Please God. I want him just as he looks as you show him to me each night in my dreams."

Then came another Tuesday that I remember well.

It was the morning of the 25th of November when the birthing pains came. I couldn't get up from the bed. Louis decided to stay home and not go to work because of my suffering. He came into the bedroom with Reno in his arms. He said to me, "Lena. I am going to call the doctor to take you to the hospital - and Alice to take Reno to Boston." "Oh, my, yes. Reno has to go, of course." When the baby heard this, he said, "No! I stay here with Mommy." Thousands of fears came to my mind, "Will he be all right there at Papa's house? Will Alice have too much to handle?" Etc. Louis placed Reno at my side and went into the dining room to telephone. Reno was talking real sentences now, "Mommy sick." "I know, yes, Darling." "No, no," he continued. "You get up now, yes?" He was so cute. I tried not to neglect his concern, but I thought of his brother who again was knocking to be born.

I refrained from crying and told Louis to take Reno away. The pain came every five minutes with additional signs of readiness. The doctor arrived, and he drove me immediately to the hospital himself. He drove very quickly because he also thought that the baby was coming for sure. After a few more pains - they stopped.

When we got to the hospital, all the pains stopped completely and stayed that way for the rest of the day. No more pains. The doctor came later to my room and told the nurse, "If there's no more pain in four more hours, she can go back home."

The hours past, and the nurse came back with my clothes. I dressed up, but while walking out the door, the severe pain returned. "Oh!" I stiffened and reached for a chair near-by. The nurse said, "You have a capricious baby coming. He is teasing you. Let's go back to your room." The pains came again and again - quicker - the big sign. The doctor came, and he examined me. "Not ready." "Oh, God," I cried.

All evening and all night, I experienced terrible, insufferable pain, and at times I fainted. No sedatives or drugs were allowed at that point. I thought through my tears, "Dear Mother! How did you do this alone at home? How, how did you ever deliver eight of us children with just Signora Lida, the midwife?"

Finally, at four o'clock in the morning, the doctor came again, and he examined me and determined that he had to use instruments to force the little one out.

They at last gave me ether, and I went away into space unknown. Then - I heard the baby cry behind me. I asked in a daze, "Please, let me see him." "How do you know it's a 'he?'" laughed the doctor. The nurse brought the baby over, very close to me. He was already cleaned up. The nurse said, "Beautiful, he's perfect. How did you know your baby was a boy?" she asked. I said nothing but to smile. When the baby was given to me, I saw two marks bleeding on his forehead. I said in alarm, "Will these marks heal?" "Oh, yes," said the doctor. "They will be all right after a while. They will dissolve into his hairline."

My baby was beautiful and perfect as the nurse had said. Small head like Reno's. Ears close to his temple - just wonderful. He was small, only 7 pounds, and he had wrinkles all over his legs and arms. He looked like a little old man with a long torso. The after-pains were not so severe as the first time. But I was tired. I finally was put to sleep with some sedatives that they gave me. I welcomed it.

Louis was called, and he came about six o'clock in the morning. I was still asleep. Louis had already delivered Reno to my sister, Alice. They told him I was asleep, so he went to see the baby in the baby nursery. When I finally woke, my husband again had a tearing smile on his face, "My, what luck! Another boy - just as beautiful as the other." I told him about the marks on the baby's forehead. "Will they be scars?" Louis asked. "No, no. The doctor told me that they will disappear as he grows, and they will not show." Louis was jubilant. He continued, "Two boys! Oh, that is just a gift from heaven!" That left me thinking about the child I lost. I said nothing, of course. I was surprised that Louis didn't even ask me how I was doing - not a word of what I went through. I reminded him that there would be only three babies for me in my life. When he questioned my arithmetic, I shook my head saying, "No. I have had three children, Louis - and you know this." I told him just like that, and he said nothing more.

What's in a Name?

I went home from the hospital and after a week, my baby still had no name. I was left with a pressure on both of my sides and couldn't raise up anything heavy. I was tired and I didn't feel good at all. Alice came to Lynn with Papa and Reno. Tears were cast about everywhere. "Oh, Reno, look!" I said, "Mommy brought you a baby brother home." The baby was in the crib - Reno's little old crib. Reno was curious and happy to be home again but still curious about all the commotion. We rolled his old crib into the bright light of the kitchen and showed Reno his little brother. He first looked at the baby and then to me. Meekly, he raised his hand straight up high and asked, "Mummy. Can I touch the baby?" "Yes," I said. "Softly. You can touch softly." Reno placed his chubby hand on his brother's face and then laughed. "Nice, Mommy, nice." I had to be very careful. I followed Angelo Prado's column, and he advised not to make the older child jealous. Make him part of the "little stranger" (as he called the newcomers). After this homecoming, Reno was around anytime I nursed his little brother. He would sit patiently next to my side and talk to him, waiting for a response. He would say, "I will take care of you. But, you must behave as I do. Mummy will love you, too."

Almost a month passed before we named the baby. We named him, Adolfo Luigino Pisano. A big name. Why? Louis admired what Adolf Hitler was writing in Germany, and the interest Hitler had in Italy and Mussolini's Fascists' beliefs. Always, Louis thought of the advancement of Italy first. He often said that if these two men got together, they could bring harmony and peace all over the world. Little was known back then, in 1924, as to what each man would eventually become fifteen years later. And the name "Luigino?" That was what everybody called Louis, "Luigino," when he was a young man in Prata, Italy. I remember when Louis came into my Nonna Pirone's store to buy bullets along with Prata's village priest. My Nonna called him, "Luigino." Even Louis' own father continued to call him Luigino after Louis came to America.

So, when my sister Alice came to bring Reno back, she suggested to shorten the baby's name - she was experienced in this matter. She said, "Lena. Why don't you call him, 'Geno?' Then you will have a 'Reno' and a 'Geno.'" My sister always made the most of her common sense. "Okay! Yes." I said. Louis lamented for a bit, but finally agreed.

The name went on to city hall of Lynn. There it was registered as: "Adolfo Geno Pisano born, November 26, 1924." We forever after that called him, "Geno."

A Mother's Calling for Me?

I was left alone with two small children and very much in need of help, so Papa told my sister, Alice, it would be okay to come stay with me and help for the first two months. I was so glad that she did because I had strange pains continuing unabated on my side, even though the doctor said I was fine. I kept on doing everything as a wife and mother, but even with Alice's help, I was still exhausted.

After a month of good nutrition of mother's milk and a little boiled warm water, Geno had no wrinkles on his legs or arms at all. He filled out quickly, gaining weight and looking beautiful. All through this time, I could not concentrate on anything other than my two babies. To nourish them yes, but not just of body - but of soul. My validation of life now came through them, directly to me as a mother. Would it be like this for the rest of my life? Was Aunt Alfonsina right that I was now at the pinnacle of existence as a woman? Would this be the end of my journey into independent discovery and self-awareness? My constant obsession to need to know? I would have to worry about these questions later.

Louis and I went out to buy some records with the purpose of entertaining the babies and helping them go to sleep. To do this, he and I flipped coins to see what record to buy Reno and what record to buy Geno. With Reno, heads came for me to choose Reno's record. I bought Johannes Brahms,' "The Cradle Song." We tossed the coin again. This time, the coin came to Louis as heads, and he chose Geno's record. He chose "Giovinezza," written for Italian youth. It was the official hymn of Mussolini's Italian National Fascist Party.

We played these records in our parlor while I cuddled both children in the rocking chair. Louis put on the records, lit his cigarette and read the paper as I rocked the babies to sleep with the records. This occurrence was nightly because we did not yet have Marconi's radio transmissions. Other times, I would sing to them. When I stopped singing, the babies would lament until I started up again. This routine lasted for months, and I was not in discontent.

Christmas 1924

December, again. We made a Christmas tree for the children that year - our very first. It was a beautiful tree which had a few toys under it for Reno to play with. When he first saw it, Reno wanted to show to his baby brother the beauty of the tree. "Mommy, bring the baby into the parlor! I want to show him. A tree is growing in there!" I was nursing Geno when I brought him into the parlor with the new tree in full splendor. Immediately, Geno stopped his suckling and brought his full gaze toward the tree. The little baby was only one month old. He stared and stared. Sometimes he would suckle again and then stop and place all of his attention back on what he saw. He knew something different was there. I was thrilled. At that moment, I felt I had given birth to two of the best children there were. This question of assertion and proper guidance has been in my mind ever since then. I never felt I did enough, or that I was a mother they should have had. They always were my superior. I still believe that to this day.

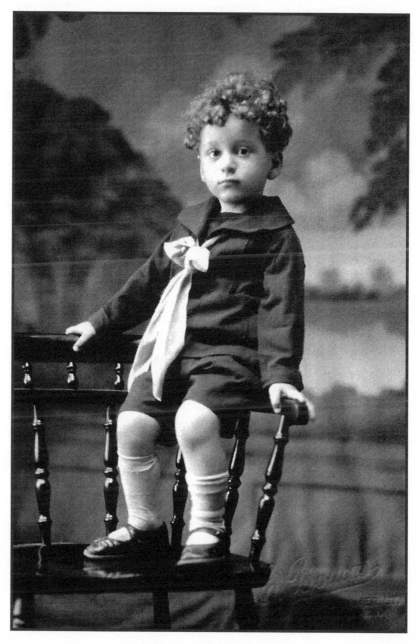

Reno at almost Three.

Chapter Seven

1925

Love Thy Neighbor

Finally, because we needed five rooms, Louis decided it was time to move from Church Street into a bigger house. I said goodbye to Louis' old house, where, like it is said, I went in as a lion, but came out as a lamb. We moved to the first floor of 62 Lawton Avenue, into a two-story tenement house about one mile from Louis' shop so most days he had to take the trolley car to work. The large apartment had a parlor, a dining room, a beautiful large kitchen, a hallway between the two large bedrooms and a large bathroom. It was open, bright and sunny. We had gardens on each side of the house and a large garden in the back. In its day, it was heaven.

What was wonderful about this new neighborhood was that there was a great ethnic communion about it - almost everyone around us were immigrant families from different parts of Europe. I made many new friends, and some of them even owned automobiles. Around us were Jews, Greeks, Italians, and Polish - quite amazing when now I reflect on it. Only a few were American citizens and English was the second language on our street. Many different flavors filled the air during dinnertime.

Louis, of course, was the self-declared breadwinner, and I was the stay at home wife. With two little children, I had plenty to do. However, I took this opportunity to delve back into my concentration on becoming more proficient in the English language. During the morning and afternoon naps for the boys, I would study the newspaper that Louis left me from the day before from cover to cover. Current affairs kept me thinking hard. Imagine, in this new, diverse neighborhood, this multi-cultured harmony, I was reading about the discontent of the rest of America in its struggles to identify her own people.

Yes, reading the papers brought to my attention lots of disturbances. At this time, the awful society of the Klux Klux Klan was in full exploitation and given so much power. The country was in a cruel state of being, and this secret society was no longer secret. It was openly permitted to do as it pleased. The KKK was terrorizing the Negroes of the South. Since after the Civil War, there existed different secret societies of this sort. But the Klan had now grown politically, so strong in fact, that it governed legislators in many states and also politicians in Washington. Even judges were members of this horrible society of the KKK. The lawmakers were indifferent, and the Klan's immunity to the law continued. At night, they flogged people to death right under a burning cross with their hooded masks and white robes or did other horrible crimes like lynching Negroes and burning their homes. My God, why? Wherever this society existed, intolerance and crime happened. The cruel injustice of it all was that they were protected by the men in political and legal power, many of whom were also members of this growing terror.

In the summer of the year 1925, a monster procession occurred in Washington that really was the climax of that society calling for the "burning of the cross," etc. The newspapers had pictures of that procession. There were spectacles of 50,000 Ku Klux Klan marching along Pennsylvania Avenue, dressed in their white robes, hooded, like the inquisitors of old Spain. Imagine this beautiful land with the best Constitution written for justice, freedom and for peace, permitting such infamy to receive this mob as its own. This tremendous tearing apart of American ideals and of the idea that this government should follow the way of the burning cross. In my heart, I knew the KKK wanted to steal this country for themselves and leave those of us who came later to perish under their boots. Was this why the authors of the Emergency Immigration Act called it an "emergency" in the first place? I had read America's Constitution. I studied it. The words "immigrant" or "emergency" do not appear on any of its pages. This conflict was all in front of me to postulate.

Were my family, my paesani friends and my neighbors from different lands supposed to ignore or forcefully give up those beautiful words, "… liberty and justice for all?" No. This country was based on universal laws - this I knew - and also based on Roman laws. These evil forces would, by reason, succumb.

The flogging and killing went on for a long time after this date, until all the world was laughing at the complacency of America and to permit such an evil society. Even the Italian newspapers had two pages of the parade in Washington with many pictures describing the inhumanity to man this group represented. Eventually, the KKK was again driven below ground, but still, it festered with support of a few powerful men. What were these people thinking? What an evil and arrogant god they worshipped.

Now my Brother Constantino Arrives!

Also, in that year, 1925, my dear brother Constantino, now nineteen, came from Italy. He had been graduated from the College of Benevento, Italy where he studied accounting. It was helpful for him that he had a skill.

"Connie" was tall, handsome, and an incessant babbler like his sister, Lena. He never took a breath except to smile his big smile. It was wonderful to see him. He had a contagious laugh, and again I must say that I loved my family, and I cried tears of happiness every time one of them came from Italy to America. Now Mother was left with only three children back in Pratola Serra: Josephine, Francesco, and Luigi. The rest of us were here in America with Papa now.

One by one, my siblings brought the addition of joy to my house. Louis was like a father to them all. Until the end, all my brothers loved him. They came often to Lynn to see us and to seek Louis' advice.

My brother, Constantino, had been in Roma when, on the 28th of October 1922, Mussolini called for every man in Italy to march on Rome - another march on a capital city by zealot men, eh? Mostly young men, no women at all. My brother Connie did happily march - for himself, for the excitement of it and for what he thought was for the good of Italy. Connie, like our brother Mikele, was all for Mussolini - another "Fascista" (Fascist.) A Nationalist. They both had my husband's ear on the subject, as well. Ralfo and I countered. We could see how Connie and Mikele had

403

been brainwashed. Louis, too, was a Fascist in his own manner of patriotism for his homeland.

After the march on Roma, King Vittorio Emanuele III elevated Mussolini to be the Prime Minister and his Fascist government was made. The people, mostly the young, all of my young cousins in Italy, for instance, were Fascists. Connie described how after Mussolini's government had taken control of everything, it had promoted big industry to function again in Italy. He also boasted that Mussolini had flooded the dried-up Pontine Marshes in the Lazio Region of central Italy, making the land fertile again. An opulence of grain was the result. Connie then told us that both farmers and workers were finally occupied again, so they had no reason to strike or to cause a rebellion anymore. But Ralfo and I argued, "How long would this bonanza last? The workers are not allowed to strike, are they? With this kind of totalitarian power comes unlimited control and intolerance to dissent."

Connie had to agree with us that the workers were prohibited to strike, and the writers in the press were also not permitted to write anything about the many abusive ways of the new Italian government. Writers, even musicians, had to write what Mussolini would personally approve in advance. Well, I loved my brother Connie. He was intelligent, yes, and an avid reader - but he had no retort on this argument.

[Aside: This seems to be a common thread throughout Michelina's letter where ever-changing historical events played a significant role in her day-to-day life. Mussolini at this time, 1925, was still fifteen years away from aligning himself, and Italy, with Adolf Hitler against the Allied Forces in World War II. After reading these observations of hers, it seems World War I never really ended.]

On back of photo: "Brother Constantino "Connie" Pirone, (age 20), 1926."

The Burning of Books

Connie took his own apartment together with Ralfo near Papa in the North End. Right away, he started to work at small jobs while also going to school in the evenings at Bentley School of Accounting. Connie had to restart his whole schooling in accounting because much of his college studies in Italy were not considered valid in the same subjects. Connie just laughed and said, "So what? It just makes my classes at Bentley a lot easier. I can sleep through them because I know them anyway. Easy. They speak in numbers not big English."

When my brother came to America, he had already learned "big" English in college. That was my brother, Connie.

Connie also loved psychology, and he bought many used books about practical psychology just to freshen his own mind and his thirst for language and science. After he was finished with them, he would give these books to me, and I cherished them greatly. He even bought me some other books just for me, so I expanded my collection. The few times I was able to visit my family in Boston, I would also try to buy used books on many subjects. My collection, however frayed, was growing like Nonno Don Carlos', and I was reading them all.

But soon I misplaced some of them - or so I thought. I couldn't find many of the used books that Connie had given me. I lost them somewhere - I just couldn't find them. I honestly think now that Louis took them away and burned them one-by-one because they looked bad in the parlor. He never answered my questions as to where they might be. But many books disappeared this way. I think to Louis they looked too old and shabby. I got around this obstacle by promising him I will not buy or receive any books unless they are in good condition. I will only ask for or buy "new" books from that point on so as not to hurt his eyes. They would be in good shape. I then told my family, "Please. If anyone wants to give me a present, buy me books. New ones. I can't go to the library as I used to." And they all did.

After Connie, the first new unspoiled book I received as a present was from my brother, Mikele. He gave me a big Italian Dictionary by Robert C. Melzi. It was wonderful - very concise information both scientific and literary. My Uncle Ferdinando followed this direction by giving me a big English dictionary. Ralfo next. As a Marxist-Socialist, he was interested in the situation of workers in factories and their class struggle. Ralfo had no formal education other than pre-high school in Pratola Serra. However, he was a true intellectual - a brilliant thinker. When visiting us, Ralfo and his friends were forever expounding about political economics, a subject that I found arid and hard to like, but repetition has power of penetration. I began to listen to these young anarchists and they made lots of common sense. When they went back to Boston, Ralfo left me new books on social economics and on Karl Marx. Louis, however, gave me no books at all as a gift. But at least he stopped burning the old ones. I kept count on this.

Chapter Eight

Death of an old Warrior - my Nonno Fabrizio

Letters came from Mother. First to Papa and Ralfo and then a separate one to me. Her father, Luigi Fabrizio, my Nonno, had died alone, quietly, in his sleep. Mother's note said:

———————

"Michelina,

I am sorry and in grief my child. Your poor Nonno is now with God. I am lost and unable to say how much my heart is broken. He died peacefully in his sleep. I cannot pray anymore through my tears. I cry constantly. There is nothing left for us here now. Nothing. I am lost for new prayers and to ease the pain I have inside of me. They do not come. My Papa, your Nonno, is gone. Pray for us, my child.

Pray. Mother."

———————

The first thing I thought about was my poor Uncle Ferdinando in Lynn. How he would also suffer with this bad news. His brother, Uncle Antonio, as well. The venerable old Nonno, the old soldier, the last of my Nonni (grandparents), had passed away. I sank hard in my chair as I read Mother's letter.

Nonno Fabrizio had never been sick, except during the influenza pestilence, but that was no problem for him. He had never been even to a doctor for advice. He was a rock. But the old soldier and rebel ceased fighting when there was no battle left to fight - literally. It was the only way my Nonno could possibly have died. Like Great-Grandmother, Maria,

Nonno Fabrizio didn't die of any cause. He just stopped. He was not of this time.

My grandfather was truly the vestige of a Roman Centurion, like his namesake ancestor, Fabricius, and the other principled Fabrician generals who followed him and who championed Rome.

I would miss my Nonno Fabrizio forever. He was born in 1842 and died on the 12th of March 1926. He was 84 years old and never traveled far beyond our village of Pratola Serra. He had been true to his honest nature and the love he had for his little jail-keepers daughter who passed away a dozen years earlier. How he loved his "tiny angel" - right up to the end.

Mother Sells the House and Loses the Money

The death of Nonno Fabrizio and the desperate sounding letters coming from my mother hastened my father's plan to bring the rest of our family over from Italy. No more "one-by-one." Mother and the youngest three children were the only ones left. Papa suggested to Mother that she sell the house that he had built for her in Pratola Serra and put the money in a bank in Avellino. She was to come immediately to America with the profits of the sale for everyone's passage and other expenses. The rest would later be transferred to an American bank from the Italian bank.

Pronto, my mother sold the house. Eight thousand dollars in American money came clear to her. [Aside: That would be equivalent to $108,000.00 today].

After the sale, Mother asked my father in law, Mr. Domenico Pisano, to escort her to the proper bank in Avellino. Louis' father was still living near to her in Pratola Serra. "Yes, of course," he said. "I will escort you. We will go tomorrow by carriage." Well, they rode half a day, all the way to Avellino with cash money in Mother's pocket. For some reason, when they got there, the bank was closed, so they had to turn around and go back. Mother and Louis' father got halfway back up the mountain and stopped in a nearby town called Arcella, Italy. It just so happened that was where one of Louis' cousins lived. His name was Eduardo Pisano and he ran a theatre company in that village. My father-in-law stopped the carriage in Arcella and introduced Mother to his nephew, Louis' cousin.

I don't know how Eduardo Pisano happened to be to around, but he was. He was having trouble at this time, financial troubles, with the theatre he was running. No one knew this of course. In a gentlemanly manner, Eduardo advised Mother to leave the eight thousand dollars with him. He would deposit it in the bank in Avellino in her name the day after. She did, but he didn't.

Days later, when Mother finally went to the bank in Avellino on her own, the money had not been deposited at all. In a panic, she stopped in Arcella on the way home, but Eduardo was not there either. He was gone - nowhere to be found. My father-in-law failed my mother. He should never have let her trust his nephew. He should have been more wary of the situation. He was embarrassed and thunderstruck but more hurt for the Pisano name. He knew that he failed in his mission and had no extra resources to cover Mother's loss. So, he too quietly disappeared from sight.

When Papa found out about the horrible news, he blamed both my mother and my father-in-law. But my mother never should have given anybody the money to hold, and neither should she have needed an escort to deposit it.

When I found out about this story, I was livid. I was caught up in the middle with my father getting palpitations and my husband refusing to either acknowledge the theft or to discuss it with me. Louis could not admit to himself or anyone else that a "Pisano" would do such a thing, or that his father could have been so negligent - so he admitted nothing, and he said nothing. I wanted Louis to write to his cousin and to make him pay my mother back. He was dead to my plea. I was so disturbed about the matter and so unrelenting in my objections that my husband finally forbade me to talk about it at all.

The only money now for Mother and the children to live on was what Father could send. Luckily, there was some money for the Sale of Nonno Fabrizio's stone farmhouse, but that would have to be split three ways, Mother thought. However, her two brothers refused their share, and she kept all the money. Not nearly the same amount, but enough to live on. She kept the cash hidden the old-fashioned way - inside her mattress. Even in death, Nonno Fabrizio took care of his family.

Mother's Final Demand - She was Coming to America

My mother now expressed even more of an urgency and demanded to my father that she come with the children and live here in America, "for better or for worse" - that was the way she wrote it.

Well, Father didn't have enough money to set up a big home for her after the stolen money event and also not enough money to send her for their tickets, etc. But Papa knew I still had some money left in my savings. He asked me to lend him whatever I had to help. How could I refuse? I gave all that I had - one hundred dollars. Just enough to buy everyone's ticket in steerage class. It cleaned me out. Obviously, my husband could not object to this loan because he refused to discuss whatever happened to the money that was stolen in the first place.

Finally, Mother Comes to America

September 1926

Mother and the children temporarily stayed with our Pironi cousins in the village as they made ready for their passports and to be in line with the quotas of the Immigration Act. After a few months of waiting for passports, Mother and the children finally came to America. Ellis Island again saw my Pironi clan - four more of them. They were running out of ledgers.

Mother and the children had choices as to where to live. Papa found them a large six-room apartment in Orient Heights - a nice section near the beach and near cousin Paolo. Alice and all of our brothers fitted out the apartment and made it perfectly ready. Inside, they put everything Mother could want. The apartment was not in the North End - a bit away because they could not find enough space for a family of seven for a good price. Seven, yes. Ralfo and Connie already were living together separately, and I, of course, was married. So, Papa, Ralfo, Mikele and Connie stayed in two different apartments in the North End while Mother, Alice, Josephine, and brothers Francesco and Luigi moved into Orient Heights as soon as they arrived. It was also easy for everyone to go back and forth to the North End.

My God - we all made it to America! Perfetto!

"The Last Four 'Pironi' Arrive Through Ellis Island."
Mother, and Michelina's siblings, Francesco (Frank), Josephine and Louis.
September 1926.

Chapter Nine

Coming to America - Family Reunion Complete

I shall never forget this scene. The apartment in Orient Heights for Mother and the children was ready before they arrived. My brother, Connie, brought them by cab. I was there patiently waiting in the apartment with Alice, Reno, Geno, and Louis. When I heard everyone excitedly climbing up to the second floor, my heart was skipping hard. I could not breathe. All those Pironi steps coming up gave me such a thrill, their voices, their clambering up, up. As soon as I saw my mother - I fainted. I did, really. I thought I was stronger than that, but I lost control of my emotions. All the children were hugging me and Mother was holding my head close to her breast. "Figlia, Mia," ("My daughter") she cried, stroking my hair. I became awake after a little, but I still couldn't speak. I looked at my mother through my tears. She was still beautiful, but she had undeniably aged. Then everyone dashed about and caressed and touched Reno and Geno - like a mob. My own children were excited from so much attention, by all these strange uncles and aunts dancing about them everywhere. "A grandmother?" Shouted my mother, joyously, with her hands in the air. "I am a Nonna! Dio mio!!!"

Sister Josephine, now fourteen years of age, was beautiful, precocious and full of devilish ways. My pre-teen brother Francesco, (Frank, 12) was a serious treasure - a nice looking young man with the classic tight Pirone curls. Little brother Louis, (8), the youngest of us, had a beautiful crop of fine auburn hair. He was a sweet boy, and he looked just like Reno who was only four years younger than him. Together, my baby brother and my son made quite an impression - as child uncle and nephew.

After work, later came the rest of our family for dinner. Mama Mia - what energy - what a crowd! They could have heard us shouting all the way back to Italy. We opened the big table in the dining-room and enjoyed an excellent supper which Alice and I prepared with Josephine's assistance. Mother sat like the queen that she was and watched the entire procession through quiet tears of joy. Mother, Papa, all their children, Louis and my children - we made a table of thirteen. At last! We were all together and united again.

The following Sunday, Mother's first Sunday in America, was like a gathering of a society. Louis and I came again with the children. We were driven there by Uncle Ferdinando in his new automobile. All the Pironi came, also many paesani, Aunt Alfonsina, cousins and the families of Mother's two brothers as well. All wonderful people. I was exhausted at the end of this day. It was like Christmas, Easter and a family reunion all wrapped into one. After, Uncle Ferdinando took me, Louis and our boys back to Lynn in his car. In the automobile, I drifted off in a staring daze, all the way home, much like I did during my wedding night heading in that same direction. I slept so soundly that night as well - just like old times.

Subtle Changes

After Mother's arrival with the children, things changed in my own house - a subtle change at first. My husband was still very much in love with me, but somehow there came a change. We had been married for five years. At first, I reasoned, the change in him to be natural. Why not? We had a complete family now with other interests interwoven in. But I would often now remember how ardently Louis would openly love me, from the first day he saw me. I was his idol - his little "doll." I even admonished him about it. At the time, perhaps that was silly of me to do. Perhaps all women wanted to be openly loved and fawned upon for eternity by the men they love. I knew my mother wanted this from Papa, and I also knew my father was equally incapable to respond. Was this a universal condition? The main reason I married Louis was because he loved me and declared it to the world, and also because he was so beautiful and so attentive. But, it was not for me to be protected. Aunt Alfonsina was right. I came to love him more and more, and he began to openly respond less and less.

The children had first place in our lives. And together Louis and I had agreed - no more children. Was this the issue? Was this only why people marry? Children? I naturally felt this, to put our children first. How could I not help but to think that? Louis and I were both a good mother and father, but I hadn't changed my manner towards him. I felt the same growing love. I loved to be with my husband, to talk about what interested me most, even gossip a little like we used to do, laughing about private things. But Louis developed a complacency. He became taciturn. When he came home after work, he read his paper, talked with the children some, ate, and then went to bed. It became a universal occurrence - the same, every day. Sundays, we also no longer walked together. If I had something to say to him during dinner, he only half listened. Louis had changed.

At the end of 1926, December, Louis studied, took the exam, and became a citizen of the United States of America.

A Christmas Card from Annie

Christmas, 1926, also brought with it a beautiful Christmas card and letter from Roma. It was from my dearest friend, Annie Chambelli. I couldn't wait to open it up. It read:

My Dearest heart, Lena,

Buon Natale da Roma, la mia cara amica! (Merry Christmas from Rome, my dear friend!).

Soon, I will write more of what is happening here in the "Eternal City," but first, I wish to send to you great love and inspirations at this most cherished time of the year, the birth of the Son of God and the sacred Holy Trinty. Buon Natale!

I must confide to you, dearest Lena, that I think of you often. Always, you are in my daily prayers. How I often wish we were able to come here to Roma together, to this wonderful Academy of Art for Women as we so often talked about and had planned. You for writing, me in music. I know, however, that you are so very happy in your life as a wife and mother. As I also know your talents as a writer will never abate. Brava!

But now, I am graduated! Thanks to the Sisters of the Academy, I am a complete music teacher now and have promised myself also to marry God. Finally, a marriage, a divine marriage. Yes - I am so happy about this news. I am now also a nun, Lena. Yes! I carry out the teachings of both God and Mozart - almost the same, eh? What could be better? Since my Papa died, I have had plenty of time to think of how to dedicate my life in serving humanity. What better way than to teach musical arts and to serve God? I am so blessed, Lena.

Someday you will come to Italy again, and we will still explore this wonderful world of art and music together, just as we used to do in our little museum sanctuaries in Boston.

Così ancora, una volta come la vostra sorella e cara amica, saluti! (So once again, your sister and dear friend salutes you).

Sister Annie Chambelli

Natale, (Christmas), 1926

Louis Battles an Ulcer

I began to notice that Louis' mood changes were becoming more prevalent and revolved around his struggles with his nervous stomach. They were intertwined. When he wore his tailored dress shirt, he would tug at the collar almost constantly - he would never loosen it. It came to light that most of his inner worries were about himself and money. I was so worried about his emotions that I offered to move yet again. I said to him, "Louis, if your brother Alfonso still wishes to team with you in New Jersey as barbers, I won't mind leaving my family here in Boston. I will go with you wherever you want to go." He said, "What gives you the idea that I want to leave Lynn?" "No idea at all," I said. "But I noticed when your brother writes you and invites you to join him in his success, you get morose." Well, he got straight up and went out of the house with not a word.

Louis came back at one o'clock in the morning in a talkative mood. I asked calmly, "Where have you been?" He answered respectfully this time, "I went to the new Italian-American Club on Market Street. I played cards with your uncle and some clients of mine." I was glad that he had relaxed. Because of my father's addiction, I didn't like cards, but I knew Louis only played for pennies and nickels, sometimes just free games. I didn't worry. If this calmed him, then good.

Louis knew how I felt about card playing, and I said nothing more. He knew I would never approve of him playing with my father and his friends. Those men were professionals, and the stakes were always high. They were blindly and continuously playing the game. I was desperately trying to find a way to settle my husband down from his nervous worries. Losing at cards was not therapeutic to my mind. In Louis' case, I was hopeful, perhaps this comradery with men-friends would bring back his better disposition. But he soon regressed again. He went to play cards every evening and came back late. He was nervous now for lack of enough sleep. There was something wrong, and he was not telling me. I was afraid to complain, but his stomach began to bother him greatly again, and he refused to spend the money to go to a doctor.

I didn't yet confide in Mother with my marital problems or Louis' mood changes. She was newly arrived, and I didn't want to give her any reason to worry herself or to be involved in a negative situation. She had enough of her own worries to think about in coming to America, so I relied on my next best adviser to help me - my Great Aunt Alfonsina.

Over the phone, Aunt Alfonsina and I had one of our long talks, she advising and I listening as if I were waiting a sentencing in front of a judge. My Aunt encouraged, "Accept Louis' mood changes, Lena, because all men, when children come, have more responsibilities, and they worry for their own futures. Their interests drift. I am certain that is why he took up his citizenship papers, my Dear." Then she opened my mind to something really wise. She said, "Lena, do not forget that he is sixteen years older than you. When you are his age, you too will lose some of this tremendous enthusiasm of yours. You will worry more about life as well." "Oh, Auntie, I worry plenty," I said. "I will never change. I also want to love him forever. I shall find a way to bring his attention to me, wait and you will see!"

Did I? Perhaps a little. How? I made a choice to accept his moods as they came. I was less openly spiritual with him around. I acted a little more "oldish." I avoided bringing up things that would bother him. I tried everything that was humanly possible. I gave myself up. But I was afraid to ask of myself, "for how long will you do this?"

After a while, Louis was a little better. But anytime he had letters from his brother, Alfonso, writing about his immense success in business, he fell more and more into a deep depression. My conscious peace of mind helped me more than ever now with my husband. As I said before, he was still sick, stubborn and would not go to any doctor. I didn't feel well either, partly because his irritability and bad moods were contagious. I wished I could go away myself somewhere, but Louis never ever thought of a vacation or going out even for a dinner. At best, we just went to the local movie theatre - if he was in the mood.

Two weeks later, just after supper, Louis started to spit up blood and was in great pain. Uncle Ferdinando came rushing over with his car and immediately took him to the hospital. I waited in panic until my uncle called me with news. "Louis is okay now, Lena. A peptic ulcer. It burst. They had to remove half of his stomach." "Oh, my God," I cried. "No, no," my uncle said, "Don't cry. He is out of danger. They told me. I will come to you when I know more."

Uncle Ferdinando came directly at six in the morning - tired and disheveled. At once he said to me, "I need coffee." Uncle Ferdinando told me that Louis had almost died and that he would need a long, recovery from this operation. It was complicated because Louis had let his condition go too long and so full recovery was not hopeful. This news sank me to my knees. My uncle and I sat in silence for God knows how long as my two boys slept safely in their beds.

Louis survived. He came back from the hospital after two weeks of healing, but he was gaunt, ashen and uneasy on his feet. Still, he slowly stiffened within his prideful self. His operation was expensive, and we had not enough in the bank to pay for it. But Louis was alive.

The doctors sent him away with only a 50/50 chance of living five more years with half a stomach. That was all Louis Pisano needed to hear as his challenge. He recovered fully - at least in his mind. Louis went back to work within a month against the doctor's orders and put enough cash aside each week to eventually pay for all of his medical expenses. Yes, he still worried, fretted, and remained ever moody - but he managed it better and lived many more decades - just to spite his doctors.

1927 - a Year of Healing – Growing

Mother got adjusted quickly and very nicely to America. She made lots of friends with her neighbors who were mostly paesani, and she was constantly out and about connecting with them as she had done in Pratola Serra. My husband absolutely adored her. Mother's sense of humor was like that of her brother Ferdinando's, and she was so easy-going like her other brother Antonio, my father's eternal and equal friend. This move to America for her and her entire family rejuvenated my mother and made

419

her bright-eyed in appearance again. This for a woman in her late-forties, with eight children, each delivered by a village midwife - or alone.

Father's new harness shop in the North End was doing very well, too. His clients were mostly horse-drawn firetrucks, milk and ice trucks delivering goods all over Boston. There were still plenty of horses around in this year. The "Golden Needle" was again producing beautiful work. He had new inspiration it seemed. He also was happy to have his oldest son Ralfo, directly at his side again as he himself had been with his own father, Don Carlos. Ralfo now partnered with Papa in cutting leather patterns, stitching and building harnesses to perfection. Papa also had enough work to hire two other assistants. He could walk to work each day from his large, beautifully furnished apartment of five rooms - a house large enough to host his own Sunday gatherings with Mother and all of their children. Old Pratola Serra, that little village tucked away in the mountains beyond Naples, had transported itself to America.

My Brother, Francesco

My brother Francesco, "Frank" as we all called him after he came to America, was born July 29th, 1914, and was only eleven years older than Reno. Frank was a natural student and learned English more quickly than anyone I can remember. Like me, his questions about everything were insatiable. He spoke English almost immediately. No hesitancy - easy for him.

At first, Frank had to go into a grade at school that was two years behind his own age, but soon he graduated into a grade one year past his own age. My young brother was so smart. One of his teachers took a strong interest in him and she even came up to the house to give Frank extra English lessons. Later, my brother would eventually transfer his high grades and attend the prestigious Boston Latin High School.

I must write a side message here. In the years that followed, our entire family had to make a choice. We were so big a family and we had so many children of promise within it, we had to make a collective decision as to what child of our Pirone family would go to full-time college in America? We didn't have the money to send everyone - only one. We all agreed to work, to save extra and to send "one" child to college. Connie was already finished at Bentley night school, Ralfo was assisting Papa as a skilled harness-maker, I was married off and Alice and Josephine were girls. Mikele had no interest in college, so that left only Frank and baby brother Louis.

The family chose Frank as the one to "go as far as his own mind and talents would allow" - no financial hindrances. So, Frank was the chosen one out of all of us. I was not resentful, although I perhaps had good reason to be as the firstborn. Yes, my brother and I had the same passion for books, art, science, reason and the betterment of humanity. But in those times, males took on that role of influence, and I had resigned myself - it was now too late for me. Later in life, my youngest brother, Louis, would resent the family for choosing Frank to be the one to succeed, and he would have some justification for his resentment. But Louis was only eight at the time of this decision making. And he could still look ahead to possible success as yet another Pirone male.

Well, my brother, Frank, took many odd jobs during his college career and with financial help from all the family, including me and my husband, he graduated from Harvard University with honors and went on to graduate from Tufts Medical School. Frank Pirone became a respected physician in Lynn with its largest practice and also an epidemiologist and medical examiner for the State of Massachusetts. All the Italian immigrants came to him - they even came from Boston. He was to become, "il Dottore di paesani" - (the doctor of the people). My amazing brother was no "Pulcinella."

More Sibling Side Messages – 1927

Sister Josephine (15) went to regular school as well. She was not forced to study domesticity alone as I had been forced to do with the nuns. The little devil was so cute, stubborn, and we teased her and treated her as a Sicilian girl. The family was well-established by the time she turned marrying age. No pressures on her. Later in life, my sister Josephine would marry well, follow her husband to San Francisco and raise a large family. Josephine also competed and became a champion in cake decorating - a "Master" baker. She too had captured the guiding hand of our family gnome - Matzo Mauriello.

Sister Alice (23) was not pressured as much as I was to be married off. She was not a burden to the family and was given amnesty. Both Papa and Mother would lose a valuable asset if she were to marry right away. This was because she was not considered a financial burden. Just the opposite. Now Alice could help everyone, including herself while living at home and assisting our mother. No talk of being an "old maid" for her - no. She was a second mother, as I had been in Italy, to the younger children. Alice worked hard as a seamstress in a clothing factory and became really the strongest help of all the family who needed something. She worked hard in the house and in the factory, giving all she made to the family and a little for herself to get along. Eventually, Alice would marry the first man who courted her - Alfonso Donadio - the Socialist best friend of our brother Ralfo.

Together, Alice and Alfonso lived their entire lives in Somerville, Massachusetts where she continued as a seamstress, he as a salesman of Ford automobiles. They had no children and finally divorced after fifty-five years of marriage, but only after the death of Alfonso's domineering mother, so as not to upset the old woman in her dying years.

Brother Mikele (19), after coming to America, skipped high school and went immediately to work as a sous chef for our cousin Paolo in Boston. Mikele was more like Papa than any of his sons. He wanted no responsibility and was very content on getting by day-to-day so long as he was near the family for his support. My brother had a beautiful baritone voice and aspired to be in the opera. So, while assisting cousin Paolo in the restaurant, Mikele took singing lessons in Boston, auditioned for and got into the New England Conservatory of Music in 1927. But Mikele could only get a partial scholarship, so, like Papa, took the easy road and went directly elsewhere. He would sing only for family, friends and customers in Paolo's restaurant. The need of money to secure a singing degree in music and to further his fame were not his interests after that. Mikele would forever remain in the restaurant business - and a wonderful singer.

Also, in 1927, Brother Louis (8) was a very handsome boy - very refined and obedient - our baby. Louis was just wonderful to watch growing up. He also went to regular school and did very well. Later, after finishing high school, he followed our Uncle Ferdinando into the shoe-making business and moved to Lynn, near us. Brother Louis soon married a lovely American girl named Jenny, also from Lynn. After the Second Great War, he moved with her to Portland, Maine to raise a family of his own and to escape the Pironi clan. My brother maintained a resentment underneath for what I'm sure he thought was abandonment. Louis Pirone returned his perceived non-attention by remaining silent with the family for the rest of his life.

<hr />

And Now "My" Family at This Time

Every Sunday afternoon, Louis, the boys and I had dinner with the Pironi clan. Every Sunday. Mostly the dinners would be at my house in Lynn because of my children. Everyone would bring something. Papa, just himself, or sometimes a ricotta pie. Other times, the dinners would be at Mother's house in Orient Heights and rarely at Papa's house in the North End. When we went to Boston, it usually was with my Uncle Ferdinando in his car - just him, and my family. I brought my food there, and we all ate together staying all day. If any company suddenly showed up, then they joined the family meal. Ralfo, Mikele, and Connie brought their own friends. Imagine the crowd, but we loved it immensely. We had plenty of meat gravy, so we just put on more pasta, broke more bread and poured more wine.

Louis was better at this point. He had gained his weight back and also his good disposition. Everybody in my family respected and loved him, and being around such a young crowd did my husband lots of good.

Reno, now four years old, went to kindergarten. This was so invigorating for me. In the beginning, I brought Reno to his school down the street every morning - it was within view of our abode. Later, he went alone all by himself out the door. I can still see him now, with a pretty suit and new coat walking away down the street like a little man of purpose. He looked scrubbed, clean and beautiful. Before Reno left for school, his father always combed his hair, trying to part it properly to one side. Well, the curls always interfered with the parting, so Louis would fuss with his comb and apply a little hair tonic to make the hair behave.

I would watch Reno running off to school - meeting with other boys along the way. Before entering the building, knowing that I was looking through the window, he would turn and wave - sometimes he would throw a kiss. A very beautiful event happened for Louis and me at this time. I pleaded with Louis to wait before going to work and to watch through the window to see Reno wave to us before going inside the school. He did. Geno was in his arms and waved to his brother too. Louis put Geno down and he hugged and kissed me. "Oh, Lena, you made me the happiest man on earth with these two perfect boys." I placed Geno in his carriage and we walked together, the three of us, to the trolley which Louis took to work. Geno and I then waved goodbye to him as well, going to work - happy as he could be.

Geno's Third Birthday "Toast."

In November 1927, we had a grand feast at Geno's third birthday party. I had plenty of practice on the preparations of such a celebration. All the Pironi children and adults came to our house to celebrate this little old wise man's birthday. Beforehand, Reno had to instruct his little brother of what to expect and how to act. "You are three years old, Sir. You must act big now and not be scared to speak." So, Geno made a speech at cutting his cake. "Ladies and Gentlemen. My mother makes the best cake that you can buy. Everyone - eat! Enjoy! And do not make too much noise."

Another dear remembrance I have of Geno is when he was about four. I was dressing him up, standing him on a chair. He was fidgety, going back and forth and he was swaying with the music from the phonograph.

I insisted to him, "Stay still, Geno! Keep quiet now." He opened his hands straight out and said, "Mamma. Me no speak nothing."

Another time I came into the kitchen and he was smothering mounds of fresh butter on both sides of his toast. I called to him, "Geno! What are you doing with that butter putting it on both sides of your toast?" He looked at the toast, took a bite and said without hesitation, "Mamma, can't you see? I am eating both sides of this toast." He was so cute.

Geno at Four and Reno at Six, Fall, 1928

Chapter Ten

Spiritual Alignment

1928

Dear Amalia Pisano Dies, Suddenly

While we were still living on Sheppard Street, we had three bad news from Italy - all within months of each other. My sister-in-law, her son, and my mother-in-law, each had died.

Amalia Pisano, my dear, dear beautiful friend, and sister-in-law, had died of an infection on her kidneys. She left three children and a husband. She was only a year older than me - 28 years old. Amalia became not only my sister-in-law, she was also my "sister" from the beginning. As I wrote earlier, she was one of my two best friends growing up in Pratola Serra and the smartest girl in our girl's book club. Amalia and I alone stood up to defy and challenge the sanctimonious village priest, the "Archiprete" ("the Bishop"). Just the two of us. But I was the one who was able to escape - not she. She was forced to marry the little man in the hat that her father chose for her and to bear three of his children. Was she happy? I did not hear otherwise. Amalia always knew how to make her own happiness. She made the most of her situation - always. This was a spirit and kindness in her own heart. There is no doubt in my mind that she was a wonderful mother, a giving wife and dutiful daughter to her own mother. Now she, her young son and her mother were all gone. The news stunned us. We couldn't believe it. How could this be?

Around this time, I would awake in sweats and see vague figures at the foot of my bed - just standing in front of me. All sorts of penitent figures would appear in front of me and then dissolve away, but I never connected any of them with Amalia. Never. It seemed impossible that a girl of such vitality, of such love for life and conquest, was no more. Where did this light go? What was the meaning of her life if she would not live long enough to fulfill it? She was only my age and had the same number of children - I losing one to miscarriage. Was that it?

I remembered all of the enlightenment Amalia and I had shared together as the last holdouts of our girl's book club in Pratola Serra. The pilgrimage hike we took with the other girls guided by my dear Uncle Costantino up Mount Vergine. I reflected upon how we were essentially banished from both the church and also our village. What tormented me the most was that I could still hear her inside my heart so clearly - the resonance of her beautiful invoking voice as she read out loud to all us girls in our club. Our leader.

Growing up, Amalia and I both had plans to escape the dogma of our village and of the church - if only through books. I fled and kept searching - Amalia remained and persevered. Until the end, I must say that Amalia was one of the most naturally beautiful women I have ever seen. Tall - elegant - striking. A Botticelli painting in motion. Now gone in her youth.

The shame of it was that Louis hardly remembered his sister. He had left Italy in 1907 when she was only a child of seven years, but he felt mostly sorry for his parents when she died. We had only a few pictures sent to us. After three months, the last child born to Amalia, a boy, Reno's age, died with the same kidney trouble as his mother. There was no hope at that time in either country to save people from this form of disease.

Amalia's youngest boy, Stephano, survived and was a beautiful person, like his little sister, Angelina. Much later, however, he too would die, but as a hero in Cephalonia, in the Second World War while fighting with the Italian resistance against Germany. It was called the Cephalonia Massacre which was a mass execution of the men of the Italian 33rd Acqui Infantry Division by German occupation on the island of Cephalonia, Greece, in September 1943. This happened following the Italian armistice. The Germans killed Amalia's son, Stephano, after a truce to negotiate was agreed to. It was all so tragic - so German.

Louis' mother, Caterina, couldn't take the loss of her daughter. She herself got sick and died after two months in bed calling to her daughter's name in heaven. Only Amalia's daughter, Angelina, would be left of Amalia's children. My dear father-in-law, Domenico, loved Angelina as if her mother Amalia lived inside of her. I, too, would carry this loss for my dear Amalia for a long time, much more than her own brother did who hardly remembered her.

Louis pensively focused on the loss of his mother whom he had not seen in twenty years. But he never spoke of his pain openly to me - never confiding. Instead, he carried on with his own private grief, adding it to his already burdensome cache of remorse.

Amalia Pisano Marano (20) and Mother Caterina (62) 1920
(eight years before both their deaths)

A Heart to Heart, with Me

It was just past my 27th birthday, February of 1928, that I remember one night that would solidify my spiritual mind for the rest of my life - truly. In the complete darkness of my parlor, I thought and thought. More than thinking - a self-searching meditation occurred. But it certainly was not a prayer. The room was as quiet as in my childhood nights in Pratola Serra.

First, I reflected on Annie Chambelli's Christmas card, now a year old, saying that she was giving her life to God, to the Catholic Church and also to teaching. My dear Annie. I then thought of what I had gone through having nearly lost my husband to stomach surgery and the total demand of raising two strong, intelligent young boys. Then came images of my dear Amalia who had just passed away - at my own age. My questioning heart again became empty as to "why?" I became all of a sudden scared - at nothing. Was this all there was to life? Was this it for me? I knew that I would have no more children to raise, and I was still struggling with the need to accomplish something besides being a good mother and wife - a happy and lifelong dedication for most other women. And now I lost the two closest friends in my life to God, and he nearly took my husband as well.

"What if?" I thought. What if I had gone to the Academy of Art for Women in Roma with Annie Chambelli after we were both accepted. Would I have become a nun like her? No. I could never see that happening to me. That is a calling of destiny for someone, not a calling of fate. I must say that the Christmas letter I got from Annie set the tone for my thoughts completely. I could not get the question out of my mind as to why she chose to become both a Catholic nun and virtuoso piano teacher. Why did she do this? Did she suddenly discover something that I had missed? Was she sour on marriage? Men? The death of her father? Why did she not just marry well and still teach? What was this draw for her to be married to the church - forever? All these questions I had that night in the parlor - that, and where was dear Amalia?

I knew that I couldn't find answers in Annie's letters alone, so I resigned myself to settling this in my spiritual mind. A challenge was made. I would challenge my spiritual self and study to be a better Catholic - or not to be one at all. But I would at least try. I would study the Catholic religion like a nun would to see if I was missing something. Was there such a thing as marrying "God," and would it all make sense to me? It had to be reasonable. So, in keeping as I did as a young girl, I dove into books, religious books of all kinds - especially the Bible in all its many forms - first, books of the Latin Vulgate. I did not forsake, however, the books I had already studied in Greek mythology or modern sociology. Yes. More books to procure then. More old books to hide from my husband.

As I sought to add to this solo book club of mine, I thought back of how we girls of Pratola Serra were ostracized and suffered at the hands of the village priest - the "Archiprete." What would this intractable man think now of my studying the Bible, searching for answers and other spiritual books of Christianity? He would find some objection to it, I was sure.

For months, I studied religion and spirituality hard and in seclusion.

Debating a Future Archbishop

One Monday, I had been visiting my mother who was ill and bed-ridden. I took a late train back home to Lynn. Louis was watching the children. Both Reno and Geno were baptized at Saint Mary's Cathedral in Lynn, so I went there directly from the train to seek solace, to pray for my mother and to reflect - alone. I, of course, genuflected first, then took a seat in the very back pew so that I could feel the ambiance of the entire empty Cathedral. It was moving. Yes. Especially the artistic radiance and fragrance of it. I had to admit, it was comforting. Even the votive candles of offering seemed to echo. I said my prayer for my mother's recovery and I just - "meditated." I opened one of my new old books and studied it.

A priest suddenly came up from behind and stood next to me in the aisles where I was seated. The priest recognized me from having done the baptism for both of my sons. He seemed pleased to see me and just stood there as if he wanted to talk. I quietly closed my book and looked up at him.

"What are you reading, Mrs. Pisano?" he asked. I showed him the cover. It was Giovanni Papini's, "Storia di Cristo," ("The Story of Christ"). "Good," he said, "keep up the good work." I wasn't sure if the priest ever read Papini's work, for it was arguing for a new and radical transformation of the Catholic Church. I said nothing. The priest continued, "But we never see you in church anymore. Are you well?" "Father," I said, "I am a bad Catholic, I know. I always was." He was curious, "Why?" He asked. "I just don't know why, but I do not believe all that is said at the altar - about dogmas and rules and regulation of Catholicism. It makes no sense to me." He had a confused look on his face. I continued, "I just finished reading Tolstoy, 'My Confession' and also Thomas Paine's, 'The Age of Reason.' They made more sense." He first looked appalled, but after seeing my firm belief, he sat down in the pew in front of me and leaned back over his resting arm and said, "Why then did you have your children baptized? You were coming to church before, etc." "Yes," I said quickly, "because once in a while I feel this guilt. I tried many times to come here and to be a good Catholic, but I always fall back again to this awful dubious question I have of what to really believe."

We talked for a long time, mostly he listened patiently to my protestations. Then the priest said, "Not believing completely or following the Word of God could result in eternal hell. This judgment faces all of us. Is this what you want?" His words set me with indignation. "Impossible," I argued. "I can't believe in the punishment of an inferno, purgatory, etc. God is the merciful creator of all life," I said. "I feel Him in all my being. He couldn't punish me in such a horrible way - to burn me for eternity in fire? No. For what? Because I question? God is everywhere, and I am part of Him." This was a bad thing to say at that moment perhaps, in that setting. The priest was visibly upset and said, "Oh. No. Stop. You would condemn me as well as the church for recognizing there is a hell as certain as there is a heaven?" "Condemn you?" I challenged. "Yes, me," he said with almost disdain in his voice. I stayed convicted and said firmly, "Are you

God, Father?" "No, certainly I am not," he said. "But I am consecrated as his servant." I looked at him and said, "Then you do not serve God if you intimidate me with fears like burning in hell forever if I challenge your canons. God is merciful. He is with me. You tried just now to push God away from me with fear of punishment, with your sense of sanctimony and superiority." Thinking back, I should have been more diplomatic with the priest in his sacred church, but I had struggled my entire life with this question to the point of misery, and I was now demanding answers. This was as good as any time to challenge.

The priest reflected my words and then calmly said to me, "Mrs. Pisano, this is not the place to debate such things. We will get nowhere like this. We need more time to discuss this subject a little further. Please. Would you come to the rectory some evening? This is all very interesting to me. Please." "All right," I said. He finished with, "How about one week from tonight - next Monday, at seven p.m.?" "All right," I said. "I will."

Finally - My Spiritual Alignment Verified

On that date with the priest, I didn't know just what to expect. I told Louis about my debate with the priest inside Saint Mary's Cathedral, and he laughed saying, "Oh, my, Lena, you are a genius at getting into arguments - now with a priest inside the church!" He was not helpful in setting any confidence in me, but I was determined to confront the subject straight on. We got a babysitter to watch the boys because Louis didn't want me to walk the several blocks to Saint Mary's alone at night. Neither of us said a word the entire way. I think my husband was afraid to start the debate going before I got there. All week, I became more and more reluctant to having this meeting with the priest because I didn't want it to seem like I was making a form of confession. Finally, I had decided instead to settle myself into the convictions of my questioning mind and go from there. All the way, I kept remembering the confrontation I had with our village priest, "Archiprete," and how it all ended up badly because of my obstinacy. "But I will do this," I thought as we walked.

When we got to the rectory, Louis lit a cigarette and waited outside the front portal on the steps. It would take over an hour - how much, I couldn't say.

Well, the priest was an Irishman. I would mention his name here, but I better not for many reasons. The most important one is that this man did not remain a simple priest for much longer after this time. He later became an Archbishop - a real "Archiprete."

The priest and I sat together in two large chairs which faced each other, I with my hands folded politely. The priest first asked me, "Were you born into a Catholic family, Mrs. Pisano? Were you baptized?" I nodded, "Yes." "Why then do you have this terrible doubt about the church?" I answered resolutely, "Father, just because I was born into a family that believed a certain way does not mean that I have to follow them. If we all kept doing what older people have been doing, then there would have been no progress in the world at all." And then I added, "You say I have a 'terrible' doubt. My doubt isn't terrible, Father, no, because doubt is a common human occurrence. Questions cannot be honestly answered without doubt." A funny smile came to the priest's face. He said to me, "For me, doubts are answered by faith - even if there are no immediate answers." I answered him, "I need more than to stand by and wait for blind faith to answer my questions. I have been waiting all my life, Father." He reflected, and I continued. "For me, it is terrible to see many things that the church could do even now, but it remains indifferent." "Give me an example," he said. "Well, there is hunger right here in America, a rich country. I read about how mendicants wait outside churches for alms, here and in other Catholic countries too." He then asked, "Don't you think the church has helped civilization? All through history?" "Yes, of course," I said, "but not now. Religion, in the time of the Roman Empire, helped to bring freedom from slavery, freed the individual, because they were real Christians back then." "What do you mean by 'real' Christians?"

I sat up more erect to gain my composure. Never had I such a mental challenge from someone outside my family and with such lofty authority. "Let's start again please," I said. "During Roman times, the Christians were like Christ himself was. They aspired to emulate him

434

- the loving and 'destitute' son of God. They lived in a commune - they shared everything together - they helped each other - they sacrificed everything and abandoned material things in their lives and rejected things like wealth, property and big cathedrals. Do Christians live that way now? No. Just the opposite." He answered, "Well, times have changed since the beginning of Christianity. Needs have changed. It is a different time, Mrs. Pisano. There are many more Catholics now who must be accommodated. We are forced to act according to modern conditions and situations to preserve our faith." "Yes - a compromise," I said. He ignored even this. He paused for a bit then he asked me another question, "What made you so contrary to religion?" "I am not contrary to religion," I said quickly. "I just can't believe what you preach." "And what is that?" He asked. "Well, you preach of damnation in a forever inferno and how the judgment will be made upon us in purgatory. When you pray to the people, Father, you have to read your prayers. And we must repeat them back to you - exactly. Always to repeat them. I am not contrary as you say. I just have a need to be myself, to do or say what I really feel - especially in the presence of God." The priest then said, "That kind of denial and rejection of church practice and sacred canons is a bad way to feel." I replied, "Father, would a good father punish his own children with eternal fire no matter what egregious thing they did? Would he burn them alive forever?"

The priest did not respond. Instead, he stood and walked around behind his chair. He turned to me and said, "But punishment for sin is a must. We have the will to be good, but we abuse it. Punishment tempers temptation." I asked then, "Is it not God who gives us the will to be good? If God wanted us not to sin, he should have also given us a functioning will not to sin. But he didn't, and he is God after all." The priest stopped me. "Wait, God doesn't direct people to be involved with vice. The devil does." "But God doesn't stop people either," I retorted. "Why? If he were the God you say who creates all good, then why wouldn't he be the same God to prevent all sin."

The priest came back to his chair and stood behind it. He was appalled. "You my dear, do not believe in God at all." "Father, I never said that, did I? I feel God in me. I must find him elsewhere and not from rigid church creeds. God is in me, and I am part of Him. You stand at the altar and you tell us that, 'God is all,' and I repeat those exact words back to you. If he is 'all,' then I, this small atom, am also part of Him. But this is not what the church preaches."

The priest looked solemn and finally asked, "These books you told me about last week. I am familiar with them." I did not respond, so he continued, "What are you reading now?" "I am reading two novels by Eugène Sue - 'The Wandering Jew' and also, 'The Mystery of Paris." Oh, boy. Before I could tell him what I had learned from Eugène Sue, he became visibly upset - perhaps more frustrated - as if I had committed a real crime.

The priest sat back down and leaning in toward me said, "These books are not recommended by the Catholic Church, Mrs. Pisano." "I've heard this before," I said. "Why not? They make lots of sense. What would you do, burn them like the priest Savonarola did who burned beautiful paintings, and noble books, and anything that was against the church?"

This caused the man great pause. He gave up speaking for a moment. He just stopped. Then, I boldly brought up the work of Agostino Steuco, the fifteenth century Counter-Reformation polemicist and antiquarian in Italy who made the Latin term, "philosophia perennis," which means, "perennial philosophy" where there is a common root of love and brotherhood to all of God's great religions. I told the priest of how all religions point to the same truth of love of humanity and a single connection of what created everyone and everything. I babbled away, of course, then I finished with, "I believe in this perennial philosophy of man - and woman, Father. I respect all religions, and I will always think that they help to build a better consciousness - only they must adhere to new ideas, they must respect science and not fight it until by persuasion and conditions, their religiosity goes through evolution, until all the world is liberated from fears, superstitions and belief in God as the Universe - to believe that we are all one - to break the boundaries of lands, ideals, and greed." I was out of breath at this point and a bit lightheaded.

The expression on the priest's face could write another book to read.

I finally told the priest of my setting up a girl's book club in my village back in Italy and how the village priest, the "Archiprete," tried also to banish our books and how he threatened to kick us out of the church, his church, entirely. I told him how I was forced to study only domesticities by punitive nuns who were my teachers and punished me if I defied their regime. I told him how I learned to read on my own at the age of four and went on and on about the indignity of how only a few of us girls in our book club escaped to America - the rest, like my dear friend Amalia Pisano, were absorbed and then woven into the fabric of church dogma. I must have gone on for several minutes without any further objections or signs of life from the priest. I had perhaps worn the poor fellow out.

I could have gone on and on, but the priest finally acknowledged my adamant declarations and said with a smile, "Mrs. Pisano. You have amazed me. You are the daughter of Galileo." "Yes," I said, smiling back. "Perhaps. He too is part of everyone and everything - even you, Father."

The Priest again got up out of his plush chair and went over to the bookcase behind his massive desk. He scanned the shelves looking for some books and said to me, "Okay. Books. I will give you two books to read. Promise me that you will read them? Yes?" "Yes," I said, "But only if you read some of mine too." He laughed. Then I sheepishly asked, "Father, tell me something, please. Do you really think that I am a bad person because I believe in God in my own way?" He looked back at me and said, "No. Not at all, Mrs. Pisano." That "no" for me was so firm and beautiful. The most wonderful "no" I ever heard. I felt exonerated.

The priest returned with two books in his hand. I read the covers. "The Catholic Church and History," and "The New Testament." "Father," I mused, "I have already a complete Bible at home, and I have studied all twenty-seven books of the New Testament. I have even copies in Latin. I shall read them again if you like. Now, as for the 'history' of the Catholic Church? Do you want me to point out here about the Borgia family? Or, the four Medici Popes and other Popes that made financial business from the church? Not 'that' history, do you?" "No, no," he replied again with a smile.

I stood up and took the two books the priest held out. He took my hand in his before I left - a very gracious expression - genuine. "Thank you Father for letting me talk with you. Believe it or not, I found my answer tonight - a validation that I was always searching for. I am sure that you have had other discussions with people contrary to your own ideas." "Yes," he said, "but few of them have ever tried to persuade me with the same arguments or tenacity." "Yes, well," I said. Then I remembered my husband outside. "Oh, my God!" I almost shouted. "Father - I have left a husband out on the front steps all this time!" We both laughed.

Before I got to the door, I said to him, "I hope that I did not offend you tonight with my strong convictions." He answered me, "Not at all, Mrs. Pisano. And let me add that I respect your beliefs as you respect mine and also of this church - the perennial philosophy as you call it. There is solid truth in that." Then he added, "If ever you need to strengthen your feelings or anything moral that bothers you, I am 'your' priest and also your 'friend.' Please never forget that." The priest and I again shook hands, and I went out.

By this time, Louis was pacing up and down the sidewalk. When I came out, he ran up to me half frozen. He said, "My God, Lena. I thought you would never come out of there!"

The priest came a few times to my house, but we remained adamantly set in our separate arguments and positions - all crossed referenced, of course. However, I never felt insecure again about my guilty conscience because of this priest and his benevolent tolerance of everything that I held close as to my own identity and spirituality. He freed me. He made his own miracle with me. I was free, yes, but still connected to the church. Was I Catholic? Yes. But, I also belonged to all the other religious philosophies that celebrated the goodness and oneness of God. In some small way, I think I also helped this priest realize that all of his parishioners may not just be a sea of blank repetitive faces. And perhaps he remembered our debates to some extent as he went on to be a famous leader of the archdiocese.

For the rest of my given life, and from that point on, I was truly one with God - one with mankind. I knew what I knew. I filtered and collected what I fervently studied - that I was a good woman and that was all that mattered. From that year on, I would freely go into any church, any synagogue or denomination. They were all one with God for me, as was I. I felt whole. I owed this to my friend the priest of Saint Mary's who patiently debated me and tried to make me into a strong Catholic, but who instead finally awakened me and made me see what I really was - a spiritualist and a perennial philosopher. I can never thank him enough. I also knew that I would never burn forever in hell - why? Because my friend the priest and I both knew - that no such place exists.

EPILOGUES, PASSAGES, AND ASIDES

by Victor R. Pisano, Grandson.

Essentially, Michelina finished writing this section of her Letter as a "soft ending" of sorts. When my grandmother sent me her six-hundred-page, handwritten letter, I noticed that more than half of it covered the first twenty-seven years of her life - hence the assigned sub-title: *"Ellis Island Émigré - 1st Person - Present Tense."* To this day, it scares the hell out of me to think what might have happened had this letter been lost in the mail. It was written in longhand cursive, fastened together with sewing needles and hemming pins - and there were no copies. Thankfully, the original survives as mailed and the original pages comprise the background for the back cover and introduction of this book. My grandmother sent this handwritten letter, cross-country in 1979 when she was seventy-eight years of age. She lived until her mid-nineties.

439

ACT I and ACT II were set up by Michelina chronologically, as linear anecdotes and timelines. ACT III was more like recounted "nuggets" of isolated events. Vignettes. We remained true to this structure. The difference is subtle, but it is there. It's akin to her favorite Beethoven Symphony, his Ninth Symphony, where the Fourth and final Movement, the "*Ode to Joy*," is so markedly different from the first three Movements. Same hand - same mind - same piece - different stroke. Beethoven just suddenly turned his pen and took his arpeggios off in a different direction - Picasso-esque.

So, the rest of Michelina's Letter will be comprised of three separate epilogues. The first being her life from this point on until 1979; the second being her own epilogue contained within the Letter; and the last, my epilogue of the remainder of her long life that filled the gap from 1979 until her passing in 1995.

Chapter Eleven

Ascending Epilogue

Uncle Antonio's Plight

Remembering Passages

I must go a little back on the date of my story to describe the fall of a good man in my family. At Christmas time, December of 1928, I received a letter from my Uncle Antonio of New York excusing himself by writing that he couldn't send any more money to me as gifts, either for my birthday or for Christmas. Uncle Antonio said that Fortuna had married that awful Domenic fellow who came with them to Lynn and with whom Louis lost investment money. My uncle informed me that this man divorced his first wife in order to marry Fortuna and that he demanded control of the family business soon after. He did all this and insisted on cutting everyone out, including my poor, now sick uncle who was suffering from acute diabetes. Fortuna wanted to continue together with her father as partner, but no, her new husband Domenic wanted the grape business and Fortuna all for himself. The most generous of the Pirone brothers was suddenly a poor, broken man.

I felt so sorry for my poor, generous uncle. His letter sounded desperate, and he couldn't do anything now without help. He became very sick. I guess it was more from a sense of failure. He was one-time way, way up, with profit, but now he lost control of the business he created and was forced to sell his beautiful large house and to buy another in a different and less expensive part of the Bronx.

At the end of my Uncle Antonio's life, my cousin Fortuna's reign as a woman of independent control ultimately fell to the dogma of the marital customs of Italy - and now of America. A few short years later, during the depression, the grape distribution business collapsed under her husband's incompetent rule, and he left her. They eventually divorced.

Fortuna never had children and never married again. During the Second Great War, she became a school teacher like her sisters. She taught mathematics. Don Carlos' firstborn grandchild, a girl, fell back in place. We are still in touch by letter, even to this day.

Earlier in my story, I mentioned how I thought one of the reasons my Uncle Antonio wanted me to come live with him in the Bronx when I was not yet married, was he probably saw all of this coming. After the death of his first wife, Bernadina, and their young son, I'm sure my uncle thought that he could rely on me because he knew I had the instincts of his father, Don Carlos, the patriarch. He wanted to keep me nearby to help him with what he ultimately knew would come. He needed some insurance. Was this why he always gave such wonderful gifts to me and then to my children - why he always confided in me with what was in his heart? It was something I had to consider. It started the first time he requested that I move in and become a member of his own family after I arrived in America. Mostly, I think it was this and how much I reminded him of his own youth, his father and of growing up in our ancient mountain village - Pratola Serra. As Aunt Alfonsina attested, my Uncle Antonio was the new "Don" of the family. Would he have been better off following his father's wishes and not being the first to come to America? Yes - and no. Both success and diabetes know no nationality. But for the kind of man my uncle was, being so competitive, so free-spirited and industrious - I think only in America could he find all these things in the right combination to challenge him and his aching, guilty heart.

Not many years later, my Uncle Antonio died in his sleep at the same age as his father Don Carlos - sixty-nine.

Passages

And, as life goes in endless cycles, so too at this time did I lose my dear Aunt Alfonsina, Nonna Pirone's youngest sister - the last of the Pirone elders. She was my guiding light coming to America and who made my transition complete, almost by herself. There was naturally a big funeral in the North End with all the familiar faces and in all the dark iconic passages. Both my Nonna Pirone and my Aunt Alfonsina went off to another place with glory and with pomp - true matriarchs - true "women" of their time I might add.

We come and then we go. Is it important that anyone remember us? I say, yes and no. Sooner or later, everyone forgets everyone. It is only worthy enough that we were here to begin with and that we contributed to this fabric of life in a good way while we were here - to give positive influence while we are alive by deed and manner. In my heart, I know that once we exist - we never cease to exist - somewhere. Somewhere it all repeats itself, again and again...

So, Addio, Uncle Antonio - Addio, Uncle Costantino - Addio, Aunt Bernadina - Addio, Aunt Alfonsina - Addio, Nonna Pirone - Addio, Nonno "Don Carlos" Pirone - Addio, Nonno Fabrizio - Addio, "Don" Filippo Assanti - Addio, Franco Chambelli - Addio, Mama Caterina Pisano - Addio, dear, sweet Amalia and all of her children save one, Addio, my unborn child...

Addio tutti.

Chapter Twelve

Marital Disharmony

By 1932, it came to a point where I was having a hard time finding common interests with my husband. After eleven years of marriage, our discord with each other was widening, and I didn't know why or what else to do about it. Louis covered this all up by being so good with my family who sided with him on any issue or dispute we might have. Many times, I felt like I was fighting alone.

I had already noticed my husband suffered from jealousy. I couldn't even say a "hello" to any man. I carefully avoided talking about anything that would disturb his way of interpreting things. He used to get upset for the least little things with me. When I needed more help with the house allowance I was given, he would go over every cent that I spent and wanted to know about the accounting of it. When people talked with him, they were trained and ready to accept his immediate contradictions. And it wasn't only with me - it was with everybody.

My Pironi clan, being of gentle manners, conformed easily with him. They based their good attitude in the kindness he showed them, and they respected him for it. No challenges by them - no. Only me. When he got upset or insistent, they always let him have his way. If they had need for a clarification, they didn't ask - they would quietly defer with a shrug. No wonder they got along with him. Many times, I noticed whenever Louis said anything that I knew was contrary to what Ralfo or Connie or even my father believed to be true, they just changed the subject. In a way that wasn't indifference or ignoring Louis, they just diluted the essence of what they were saying in order to keep Louis happy. I couldn't go that far. I was his wife and I had a different relationship with him than they had. I needed to talk about what I was deeply interested in with him.

I said before that I tried everything possible and even suffered some public humiliation when he got nervous or irritated. He even raised his hand to me many times in private. My family adapted to his ways and accepted anything. He was the husband - and I was the wife. So markedly old Italian. They sympathized with me, yes, but they never got involved. So, my husband and I always had this secret, difficult little war.

Still, I had a deep sympathy for my husband. I knew how stubborn and proud he was. He was using all the money he had to keep his position in life, and he never would change. When he said, "No," that no was as big as the sun for him. I also decided at this point that I would never be a burden on him - financially or otherwise. I started to work again, and I would never stop from that day forward. I took work in at first.

I made myself independent for my own personal needs. Not to be spiteful or resentful, no - just to avoid Louis' financial dictates and to alleviate my monastic conditions. Even the boys went to work. They worked after school and on Saturdays. Reno sold newspapers for one year. One afternoon while he was delivering the newspapers, he found some money. I think it was about twenty dollars, a lot of money then, especially in the Depression. He went to the police station and gave them the money he had found. After six months, nobody claimed the money and it came back to him. Young Geno helped me with the work I took in. Every day, he went to the laundry outlet on Summer Street near Louis' barbershop and collected shirts that needed to be repaired. I turned collars on shirts for ten cents each. Geno went to get them at the laundry and then he returned them after I was finished. Turning collars was a long way from the Parisian Dress Shoppe on Newbury Street in Boston. I was not designing and building exclusive clothing for fashionable clients - I was turning frayed collars. That part of my life seemed an eternity ago. We all did the best that we could do - the very best.

I had to take anything, any burden. I promised the boys that I would do this when they were born. I succeeded for many years in living in harmony with their father because I had to. Divorce was never an option for me.

After a while, Louis questioned my devotion. He said to me, "Lena, you have changed. What caused this apathy in you?" "Apathy?" I repeated. "Not apathy. It's resignation. I know that you love me, Louis, but I understand you a little better now. You are not who I thought you were in the beginning." "What?" he asked. I continued, "Yes. You want to be left alone all the time. You are a jealous husband and a stubborn one. You even go against yourself - your pride too, it consumes you. I didn't see it in you before; you were my loving heart. I saw you in a different color. I loved you for the love and attention you once gave to me. And because you are a very capable person who can take care of anything." Wait, wait," he interrupted. "I am different now!" "Oh, yes, yes you are." He just stood there stunned.

Louis said very little to me after this for many days. I was sorry that I went that far. After all, perhaps my husband was discontented with me as well. I know that he needed a different kind of woman for a wife. I wondered. How much was I to blame in the loss of so much of his own promise he had made to himself? I was miserable.

The Costume - the Play

I jump ahead in time a bit with my plight.

One afternoon, sometime during the middle of the Great Depression, my mother's brother, Uncle Ferdinando, came to visit me for tea. He was very excited. The Italian American club he was president of was about to do a play. They did one every year. My uncle was to direct and to perform in it. There was also a drama club in Lynn, and my uncle was their best actor. Uncle Ferdinando insisted in the worst way to have me be the female lead in his new play. The play was about a Bishop who had a niece in his trust (I forgot the title). The roles were for a benevolent uncle as a Bishop and his precocious niece. I was to be the niece with lots of chatty dialogue. Perfect for "us," he thought. My husband agreed to let me do it. The first thing I did was to run out and buy material for my costume - a period piece, almost like the gypsy girl ensemble I had made for the Chambelli Christmas party.

Well, every rehearsal awakened me further, and it was fun. I got many compliments, especially about my acting on stage. Louis came to many rehearsals, and he would embrace me after each one, even kissing me. He was so good. We were all doing just wonderfully, until a week before the play opened. My husband suddenly gave strict orders not to let me act. Oh, my God! What to do now? Why the impulsive, "No."

My Uncle Ferdinando was really out of sorts about all of this. He came to my house saying, "Oh, my God, Lena. What a terrible and unfair man you married." He was the first of my family to make such a challenge about Louis. And he had good reason. He and my husband never did fully get along. Now my uncle was debating whether or not he could go on with the play at all. My understudy was not fully prepared, and she hardly could speak Italian. But I went every day to work with her to better train her for the part. I even refitted my costume that I built so it would fit onto her frame perfectly. With consistency, every day for a week, we worked, and my replacement succeeded to do a good job.

My uncle was visibly hurt throughout. He couldn't be as free to direct or to act with this girl as he had been with me during rehearsals. He let me know about it, too. Opening night, my uncle said to me, "Your husband cheated me of the best drama I ever dreamt of - with the best actress! I shall never forget how good we were acting together." I said nothing, of course.

During Play Rehearsal. Photo credit: "Ferdinando Fabrizio, director."

The Slap Across the Face

A few weeks later, at 8:30 in the morning, my Uncle Ferdinando came up to my house. I was delighted to see him at the door. But when he came in, he was very sad and his eyes were red. "What is the matter, dear?" I asked when he came in. He hugged me and told me while still holding me, "Your husband, last night, he slapped my face in front of all the friends at the men's club." "What?!" I said. "Yes. We were partners together at cards, and just because I said he made the wrong move - he played the wrong card - he got up from the table and slapped me!"

I was so hurt for my uncle, "How dare he do this to you?" Like a hurt child, he said, "Yes, he did!" Then he got irritated and said, "By God, he shall pay for this insult. I didn't mean to suggest that he was a bad player. One gets excited in the game and says something once in a while. He got up, slapped me, and went out." I consoled my uncle as best I could.

"What can I do? I was just thinking of how to adjust myself to his moods, now this insult. How, dear God, can I do anything but experience one humiliation after another? How?"

My uncle now got concerned about me and began asking me lots of questions. I told him what I was trying to do to tolerate Louis' fluctuating moods and how I was trying to keep my family together. He said, "No, no. Leave him. He will destroy your spirit - what you have left." I insisted that my uncle listen to me. I described the children, how promised they were, the awakening of my awareness, the understanding of what I wanted and of what I had. The adjustment I was making to survive mentally - the distance I had already come. He listened, then he said, "Now, it is me who is sorry. I came up here this morning and added to your burden." He continued, "Please, Lena, make believe that you do not know anything about this and this way he won't get upset with you and hit you like he... he..." My uncle didn't finish his sentence. He just got up, kissed me in a hurry and went out. I cried and cried.

Well, after supper that evening, I went immediately to bed. I couldn't read - I just thought and planned for "patience." I became a stoic. What happened to my uncle made me prove to myself that I could withstand anything. I never talked about this with anybody not even with Louis or Mother. It was too painful, but it made me stronger in my desires. Yes, my husband was a nervous man. He had an uncontrollable temper, mostly with the people he loved. I had to prepare myself to take even more, perhaps later.

After a while, Louis met my uncle, and they talked. Just quiet talk at first. Louis made some effort though to show how sorry he was about the slap. My uncle told me later, "I forgave him. Yes, because of you, I forgave him." And because of me, my uncle would have done anything - and I knew it.

These episodes made me almost afraid of my husband. What would he do next? I had to get my confidence back - I was never vindictive to him, but I never again gave him the chance to push me away from him just because he was in a bad mood. He had to kiss me first before dismissing me. From that point on, I never showed my husband how much I wanted him to talk to me. After a while, he noticed my indifference, and he became a little better. Because of this, we went to the movies again, and we visited friends. It helped and I felt better. But the Great Depression was now deeply upon us. Not a good situation for anyone's mood.

Louis' work suffered a lot during the Depression, and he lost lots of customers. People were out of work everywhere. They let their hair grow long before they went to a barber - they shaved themselves and so on. Strikes and more strikers.

I got lost in this subject - I am sorry. As I said, I understood my position at home and made the best of it. My boys gave us no trouble at all. Good in school, good at home. They were a joy and they helped me keep my sanity. I still can see them with their friends seated on the floor of the parlor talking like old people. When Reno got his first long pants, Geno demanded long pants, too. But Geno had to wait. So, Reno got his pair and strutted in front of his brother with an air of manhood. Geno resented that and stayed away from his brother in mock contempt. It was funny. We had lots of laughter together.

This all came to us in the middle of the Depression.

"During Play Rehearsal, with Geno (Short Pants) and Reno (Long Pants).
Photo Credit: Ferdinando Fabrizio, director."

Articulation

My Writing Career Restarted

By this time, in the mid-1930's, I now had full confidence in my English. When I first came to America over a dozen years earlier, I spoke very little English on purpose because I couldn't be perfect at it, and I did not want to be judged accordingly. I promised myself that I would conquer this new language that I inherited without vocal or grammatical hesitation. Naturally, no one moves to a foreign country without retaining some vestiges of their mother tongue dangling out from their speech. But I had promised myself a good effort and to a large extent, I succeeded.

Now, I could converse fluently with only a slight hint of an Italian inflection with my command of words. Thanks to all my books and the public library, I had solidified my understanding of even the most in-depth subjects of the English language. I spoke only English now to Louis, my children and to my girlfriends. With my Pironi family, I spoke mostly Italian with the older ones and only Italian with Papa and my mother. Sometimes, long conversations around the Sunday dinner table with all my clan would have dozens of words in both languages flying above our heads like a comic Rossini opera. But for everyday existence? I spoke and wrote English for communications and spoke and wrote Italian solely for the love of it. This bi-lingual command was truly comforting to me, and it furthered my self-confidence immeasurably.

A Writing Job Out of the Blue

It was at this time that Louis inadvertently restarted my career as a writer. Louis had an older Jewish man for a client named Mr. Salomon Gluck. Over the years, they became very good friends. Mr. Gluck was meticulous about his grooming, and he would not let anyone in Lynn do the job except Louis. Mr. Gluck would come faithfully every Friday afternoon for a shave and his haircut. Well, Mr. Gluck became sick and semi-invalid. Louis did not want to lose such a good regular customer so he found a solution to this problem. Every Sunday morning, Louis would go directly to Mr. Gluck's house and give him his shave and a cut there. Soon, Louis became one of the family and a friend to every one of the Gluck children. The oldest son was named Freddy, and he was one of the editors of the city paper - *The Lynn Telegram and News*. When this paper later failed, Freddie became a lawyer. Even now, he is still my good friend and lawyer.

When Freddy got married, we went to his wedding. It was nice, mostly because I had never seen a Jewish wedding before. My newfound trust in perennial beliefs held true. There was a feeling of "oneness" with Freddie, his new wife, Sally, and all their families in the Synagogue. A moving ceremony.

During the wedding, I sat right next to my friend, Mr. David, who was also my egg man. Every week, Mr. David would come in his little black truck and bring a dozen fresh eggs and a chicken to the house. He always left with some of my biscotti in his hand. Oh, such a wonderful and easy time it was back then. Dear people why did it all disappear? Why did you all run away? Why does life have to be made so complicated?

As I said, early during this time, Freddy Gluck was editor of the *Lynn Telegram and News*. He often came over to our house for coffee, pastry, and good discussions. It was always in-depth and he would sometime challenge my sources, but he would always lose the argument. All good discourse and in good fun. Even Louis was there sometimes in conversation. On one such visit, I was telling Freddy of my Uncle Ferdinando's theatre group and Freddy became very interested. From these discussions and because of my discourse with him in the Arts, Freddy offered me to write a Sunday column once a month on the cultural activities of our area - in English of course. I lit up. Louis was speechless. He wanted to answer for me, but he would not dare to say "no" this time. How could my husband deny the wishes of our friend, Freddie, a good client himself, let alone an editor at the city paper?

Naturally, I accepted.

Being that it was the Depression, *the Lynn Telegram and News* could pay me very little - a few dollars each piece depending on the number of words. Compared to the ten cents each I was getting to turn collars, it was a labor of love from God. I wrote like I did for this letter - in English, in longhand, and in ink. I brought my pages to the newspaper office, and they would type it for me. So, began my formal career as a writer. A real writer, for no one is a true writer unless someone pays them for their task, eh? And I was being paid, no matter how minuscule - and I was being paid as a writer for a city newspaper in America!

Louis Seccums - I find Extra Work

The Great Depression changed everything and everyone. My husband had to give up his strong belief that I was to be only a housewife. Economics always changes politics. Economic depression was rampant in all of America. There were even worse dangers. Many people committed suicide who lost all their savings in the stock market or their property. Lynn mostly had little to offer now in the line of opportunity. All the shoe factories were either closed or in a deplorable state of economics. Lynn, Massachusetts fell in stature and no longer was the shoe capital of the world - no longer the capital of anything. Louis was still feeling sick from all the stress and the demands he put upon himself to succeed. But how could one succeed in Lynn? I, too, was sick more often than not. Only by caring for my sons and my husband could I keep my mind from succumbing to my own form of depression - that, and writing. But like everyone else around us, we somehow managed. We had to. There were no choices.

Chapter Thirteen

The Great Depression and Women

In 1933, (a retrospective). Germany in a few short years had gained strength by persuasion and by violence. The party of Nazism was headed by Adolf Hitler who assumed dictatorial power over Germany. Hitler's title was as, "Der Führer," "The Guide." He formed a government something like Mussolini was doing in Italy based on extreme nationalism and fierce pride of heritage. Hitler wanted to vindicate the defeat and humiliation of Germany during the First Great War. The winning alliance demanded too much in reparations, and a rejuvenated Germany would now defy them with nationalist fervor. Hitler was their voice. He came to them at the right place and at the right time. Hitler proclaimed outright the superiority of the German race, especially being superior to the Semitic/Arabic race. Awful persecutions then happened because of this fanatical, half-mad leader.

Here in this country, the New Deal of Franklin Roosevelt gave the first relief of accomplishment to the Depression. Still, people were protesting all over the country. They needed work, mostly the Negroes in big cities and in the South. They felt the discrimination against them in every field, and they felt that they had no hope of advancing out of poverty.

The CWA (Civil Works Administration) was a job-making program for millions of now unemployed workers. The government would create projects just for workers to carry out that need preparation - no heavy material work in the beginning. The CWA was assisted by another organization too, the WPA (Work Progress Administration) which was made to clean up parks and repair public buildings and roads. Many things were finally in progress, but it only got started in 1935, deep into the Depression.

So, it was - jobs were created, but not enough of them. Some workers were painting buildings over fresh paint and building things just to take them down again. Making work for work's sake. In 1936, things were going a little better but we, the small earning people, were still in demand of meaningful work. The few real jobs created didn't pay for all the needs of the people. A big problem was that monopolies had taken over a big sector of the economy. Not enough of these monopolies were broken up. These giants cared little for the workers. Strikes occurred by overworked and badly paid employees. Strikes were a fearful action. The police were ordered in to protect company property. President Roosevelt spoke to these giants of the economy and he told them to respect their workers - that these are the customers that bought their product, etc. He tried, but not hard enough.

Socialistic groups were telling the people that unless they unite in a strong way, they would always have a scarcity of work and nothing in their pockets. Socialists were claiming that wars kept capitalism in power and maintained these giants of industry. At this time, Russia was doing very well in creating an industrial nation - yes, with brutal force like Hitler's Germany. The Russians had extreme Socialism. It was Communism, just the opposite of what we had here. Hunger and a fear for the future was pervasive and seemed everywhere. This condition was no different than the day I was born back in Pratola Serra where the farmers revolted against their land-baron for better wages and for more of a share of the harvest. Exactly the same. Perhaps it all never ended. It just spread.

My brother, Ralfo, was an active member of the Socialist Labor Party. I went with him to a few meetings in Lynn. They made speeches that seemed so easy to convince those in attendance who were needed to join. The speakers declared, "There is nothing to gain if we continue to let capitalists rule us. We produce everything, and they only gain by our fears and indifference." And another man said, "We must unite into an industrial Union where the national income will be divided and spent properly. Any discovery or innovation will be for the benefit of the people! But as it is now, the capitalists gain more power, etc., etc." It was wonderful to be part of the energy, but I understood little about economics and also, I was afraid of any cause becoming a revolt. I did not join my brother as a Socialist member, but I did support his heart for the workers of this country.

In Lynn, people were not directly affected by either of the government programs. They were still unemployed, so they marched to city hall, mostly Negroes. They started from the beginning of the common and marched to city hall. I joined the protest march myself. We got into the auditorium where the mayor, Mayor Manning, a Republican, spoke to the crowd. He said, "Please have patience. Give the President time to organize and get together all his projects that he promised and have started already. We will have jobs! Properly respect the New Deal - Roosevelt will not forget you!"

But President Roosevelt never came to Lynn.

I believed that social evolution will continue if we peacefully protest and avoid revolts and revolutions. Political revolts only bring chaos. By peacefully protesting, as is our right, then and only then will we change as a world, not only as a country.

I had lots more to learn at that time. I avoided even talking about these ideas of economic social revolution or revolts. These subjects always gave me an insecurity and a fear of confusion - in many ways, they still do. I shall stick to what I know best - the evolution of mankind given to us by natural history and the Arts.

As I see even now, in 1979, women are not represented in government. This country contains half women and how many are we in Congress? Only a few. Or how many are there in any federal or state office? If we have two women at a news conference - they both feel proud that another woman is there with them. Half of all the jobs in civil affairs and all parts of the government should be made up of half women. Perhaps they would do a better job. I admit, that with manual labor, men are better, nature gave them more muscles. But women should be represented properly, numerically in any office - Then Democracy would really work. [*Aside: In 1979, when Michelina wrote these words, Jimmy Carter was President. President Carter had twenty-nine members in his cabinet - four were women. In Congress, there were only 18 women in the House of Representatives out of 435 members and only 3 out of 100 in the Senate. Michelina's sentiments here were very much like the 1963 "I Have a Dream" speech by Dr. Martin Luther King.*]

A Birthday Gift From My Sons

In 1936, while our family gathered at the table eating my 35th birthday cake, Reno, then thirteen, said, "Mother, I am giving you a present. You can attend the adult evening classes at the Cobbett School. I know that you want to. You can study any subject you want." I answered him, "Oh! My, what a wonderful gift! I thank you, Sir, for your present and also permission." Importantly he answered, "You are welcome." Then he added, "I shall wash the supper dishes, every time you have school." Then turning to his brother next to him said, "And you my kid brother, shall dry them." Geno answered in the same serious tone, "Yes, Sir! I shall do as you say, Sir!" I got up and kissed them both. "Oh, I thank you so much. You are both such wonderful sons." Both Reno and Geno secretly saved up all their extra coins over many months to do this thing for their mother.

I felt liberated by this thoughtful gift. Both of my sons knew my heart and mind and planned a solution. They knew what was a perfect gift for me. I was relieved of some household duties that kept me away from the opportunity there was for people like myself - night classes for people with no formal education. They gave me the gift to be a student again, but not of domesticities - a student of higher learning. I loved my boys for doing this thing for me. How was I not blessed?

One underlying reason I was so excited was that I would eventually have to go through some formal education to becoming an American citizen anyway. This was always in the back of my mind. These evening classes would serve two purposes. First, they would allow me to move toward citizenship with independent study away from my husband's control. I would have to take a test of the history of this country as a requirement to become a citizen. Second, I could add any subject I wanted besides American history to "formally" advance myself. I was ecstatic about this wonderful gift.

At the evening school, I made many new girlfriends my age and in the same boat as me, mostly self-educated immigrant women from all over the world - places like Italy, Greece, and Poland. Many of the teachers were our age or younger which was, even more, an exhilarating experience. It was heaven. This was our opportunity - my opportunity.

In addition to American history, I took psychology on Monday and on Thursday I took comparative literature - my absolute favorite. I didn't want to say it, but in psychology, I was ahead of the teacher's assignments having already read most of the material. But I shut up and participated in all the lively discourse as it was presented and made myself not raise my hand first. Comparative literature required lots of additional reading, however. It was fun to go to Boston with my brother's Ralfo or with Connie to old bookstores and look for the books I needed. They were excellent company.

Yes, I would have to become an American citizen - sooner or later. My boys were citizens by birth and Louis became a citizen ten years earlier. Somehow, I was still clinging to my Italian roots. But I knew I would forever stay in America and the outside world was dictating to me that I would have to become an American, regardless.

I made many new women friends in association with evening classes at the Cobbett School. They often came by the house, either before or after the classes when Reno didn't come to escort me. I was so very happy that Louis accepted all my new girlfriends so easily - not one complaint. He liked them and they liked him. Perhaps he knew how this settled my heart and thereby settled his own mind. This was a very good time for me.

During these visits with my new girlfriends, the house became very noisy at times. Louis was listening to the radio - so we had to lower our voices as we chatted away so as not to disturb him. But really, I don't think that he ever heard us. He was so absorbed in his own worries and half listened to the radio too. Louis always brought the world news home with him in his newspapers only to reaffirm those worries on the radio. He was forever worrying.

All this extra schooling and energy from fresh minds only aided in my writings for my friend, Freddie Gluck, at the Lynn Newspaper - while it still existed.

"Louis, Reno, Me and Geno about 1936"

The Great Depression Retires Papa

The Great Depression caused Papa to retire his business. The "Golden Needle" of harness-making was closing shop - forever. There was little being transported now in cities using horses. The few places that needed horses were patching their old harnesses themselves instead of buying new ones from Papa. Some of his last clients were the fire stations of Boston which still used horse pulled fire-wagons, but they, too, were dwindling in number. My mother finally convinced Papa that they both should move and share a home together - in Lynn of course, near her grandsons. So, my father retired with enough money to move himself and Mother nearby to us in Lynn and to finally "settle down." Now, Papa, had five sons of his own like his father had, but also two grandsons and three daughters to add to that grand finale. Naturally, Ralfo followed behind him and found some work with Uncle Ferdinando's help at one of Lynn's last remaining shoe factories. Sometimes Papa would tag along with his oldest son to work for creative input and support - and to keep some purpose in his life.

Family dinners at this time, need I say, were major events and always Sunday afternoon at my house. Even during the Depression, the food we shared together was bountiful and freshly made - an Italian feast. No one during this tough time ate better than my clan. We put on phonograph records of opera, we sang, and we toasted to each other endlessly in all the ways possible to cheer. It was the Great Depression, yes - but not in my house.

Rare Photo: "The Family." Sunday Dinner, 1938, during the Depression.

Top Row: Louis Pisano and Michelina's Father, "Pepino" Pirone.

Second Row: Michelina's Mother, Angelina, Brothers; Louis, Frank and Mikele.

*Bottom Row: Bother "Ralfo," Sons; Geno, Reno
and dinner guest (Freddie Gluck).*

Chapter Fourteen

Now Came the Second Great War

This is my quick sense of history about the Second Great World War. My family was following all this in detail because of our strong connections to both Italy and America. There were many discussions and, ultimately, many concerns. My two sons and three of my brothers would be directly involved in this war, which I shall relate later.

With bravado and arrogance, Germany started the Second Great War by suddenly attacking Western Poland on September 1st, 1939 with a massive and rapid attack of German forces which they called the "blitzkrieg." In two weeks, Poland was occupied. Not even the immediate Declaration of War that France and England issued to Germany could save Poland. The specter of a renewed Germanic power hung over Western Europe. The old German Empire was back with a vengeance.

Back in October of 1936, Benito Mussolini declared a coalition and rotation of Rome and Berlin to take on neighboring weaker countries. He called it the "Axis." This Axis would later be joined by Japan. But in Europe, Hitler and Mussolini were joined together, but with Mussolini not as grand or as powerful. Hitler had to cover many of Mussolini's tactical mistakes.

June, Mussolini decided to enter the war against the "Allied Forces" of France and England to share the fruits that came easily and rapidly with German victories. Then Hitler decided to invade Russia - in June 1941. For almost a year, Germany pushed its army near to the doors of Moscow and onto the frontier of The Caucasus toward the desired layer of oil. But the German machine stopped as it did during the First Great War - stuck in the mud.

The Japanese had concluded an alliance with Germany and Italy, called the "Tripartite Pact." On December 7th, 1941, Japan assaulted Pearl Harbor on the island of Hawaii in a surprise attack bombing from the air, inflicting an awful loss. This incident brought America officially into the war although she was already secretly supplying both France and England with relief materials. The conflict now was extended across three continents, four if you include where Japan took some islands near Alaska. The war was now a true World War.

In November 1942, the United States landed in North Africa and teamed in conjunction with the British forces already there. Later, in July 1943, both countries attacked the Axis Powers by choosing Sicily as their entry point. The big risk and surprise was the Allied Forces landing in France, on the coast of Normandy in June 1944. This attack pushed the Germans out from France and a unified thrust was made to toward Germany in sequence with the Russian Army which attacked Germany from the east. There were many stalemates and fallbacks along the way. Finally, In April 1945, the Allies joined the Russians in attacking Belin itself. Germany had truly run out of gas. These events affected my family directly as I said.

So, what was happening inside Italy during all this? This is a complicated question. Which Italy, I say? Mussolini formed a Fascist army which tried to stop the advancing Allied Forces, but he also had to fight the Italian Resistance that battled both him and Hitler. When the Allies attacked Italy, they landed on Sicily and marched up through the south of the peninsula. The soft "underbelly" of Europe it was called. They created a tragic situation with continuous bombing of Italy but were careful trying not to destroy antiquities - but many were lost because the Germans took battle positions in some of these places. Quickly, with each victory, the Allies were breaking all hopes of Mussolini's Fascist army. As soon as the Americans and British reoccupied the region, they were greeted with cheers and support from the paesani as they liberated each street of southern Italy - my Italy. Even Napoli was given special rewards and accolades for its underground resistance.

It was then that Mussolini lost hope. King Vittorio Emanuel, under Allied protection, took the opportunity to arrest Mussolini on the 25th of July 1943. The King then entrusted a new government to General Maresciallo Pietro Badoglio, who was conciliatory to the Allied Forces. But the Germans were not done. No one asked them. They liberated Mussolini from prison, and together they reconstructed a new Fascist government up in the North of Italy that was called "Republic Sociale Italian."

Italy was now completely divided in half - North and South. In the South, King Vittorio Emanuel was protected by the Allies while Mussolini's government in the North was protected by Germany. But still, there were many in the North against the Fascist government, but others were not. Inevitably, an Italian resistance movement in the North against Mussolini emerged.

The Italian Resistance was called the "Partigiani." Secretly, they certainly had help from the Allied Forces. This came by the way of the "Corpo volontari della Libertà" (CVL), the "Voluntary Armed Corp of Liberty." In May 1944, the CVL was a brigade of eighty thousand Italians, both men, and women, who fought the Germans and Mussolini's Fascists hard along with the Partigiani.

In the Spring of 1945 - conclusive - 36,000 Partisans died - 2,000 mutilated or made invalid, and ten thousand civilians, including priests, women, and children. Mussolini, now 61, tried to escape with his mistress to the frontier toward Germany but was caught by the paesani, arrested and executed. He and his mistress were shot and hanged upside down by the Partigiani partisans in the small village of Giulino di Mezzegra in Northern Italy, near Dongo on Lago di Como (Lake Como), 28, April 1945.

Across the world, Japan was continuing until the United States dropped the atomic bomb on two cities. The terrible destruction and number of deaths in Hiroshima and Nagasaki stopped Japan cold. It capitulated on the 15th of August 1945.

Italy became a Republic - peace at last - Amen!

I site these recollections of the Second Great War here because I lived each of these episodes day-by-day due to my family's direct involvement, as I promised to relate now.

Chapter Fifteen

Back Here in America – 1941

At this year, my brother, Ralfo, was working and living in Lynn near Papa and Mother. He was too old to become a soldier, but he was not too old to take on all the powers in the conflagration. As America drew closer and closer to war, Ralfo and I began arguing more and more about his ideas of social betterment for the workers. He kept claiming that the Second Great World War was only to the benefit of giant monopolies. He was involved in a social activist group that was contrary to all that was traditionally American - he was a dye-in-the-wool anti-Capitalist and anti-Fascist. When Ralfo came over, he kept Louis interested by continuously arguing that Mussolini and the Fascists were not truly for Italy or her workers. They were about power and greed. Never did my brother side with Louis. My husband sided with the Fascist and the Italian Nationalist. He liked order, and he thought Mussolini was orderly. But Ralfo knew his limits not to push Louis too much on the subject. The discussion usually concluded with Louis fluffing up his newspaper in front of his face.

I was worried for my brother, mostly because of his radical views on social order. He was a fervent member of the Socialist Party, but this party was becoming more and more anti-American or so many Americans perceived. Many of the protests in the streets were being blamed on Italian working immigrants. This was a bad misperception. Many Italian slurs came from this bias which I will not mention. To gain votes, Roosevelt accepted some of the Socialist Party's concepts in 1936 for his platform, but it became only a campaign promise against the Republicans. The other problem was there was little to differentiate Ralfo's Socialist Party from the Communist Party, a distinction which concerned me more. Everyone seemed to hate the Communists which had sour beginnings in Russia with the execution of Tsar Nicholas II, his wife and their children in 1918. How could any party claim political or humanitarian superiority with these brutal murders as its basis?

Then, when I heard on the radio that Japan bombed Pearl Harbor on December 7th, 1941, my heart again sank.

The Internment Camps

When Japan and America went to war, there were many discussions and fears about being invaded by Japanese forces on America's soil. There were already deep suspicions of sabotage by German or Italian nationals. But the West Coast was in near panic. Why? Not only because of the nearness of Japan, but that was where most Japanese Americans had settled - there and Hawaii. And, Asian people were easy to recognize.

What did the American government do? They gathered all the Japanese they could find who lived in America and sent them to internment camps. Some protested they were American concentration camps like Germany had created for the Jews and millions of other people like Gypsies, Greeks, and Italians. Most of these Japanese people were actually American citizens - unprotected by the Bill of Rights? It was an unthinkable situation. The government claimed that they were "protecting" these people from discrimination or harm because of misidentifying them. But how many Germans were here in America? This was also a big concern. They could blend in unlike the Japanese. To make matters worse, there were more Italian and German American citizens in America than any other nationality - tens and tens of millions. But people got plenty suspicious whenever they heard any foreign accent.

Then, one morning, near the back page of the newspaper, I read something that almost stopped my heart. The American government was newly gathering up "Italian nationals," too, and moving them to internment facilities. There were weak manifestations of this thing years before, but this was now - today. Ten thousand would be moved from California, and three hundred Italian nationals were detained and sent into camps. "Oh, my God! Here in America?!" I thought. "How is this possible? Italians kept as prisoners?"

I ran right to Louis' barbershop. When I got there, I didn't have to say a thing - he already had read it and was pensive about it. Louis informed me that he and the boys were already citizens so they had less to fear. But I was still an Italian national! So, because I was born in Italy and not naturalized (a citizen), the government put me in a category to be one of the "enemy aliens." Me? An enemy alien?

What to do? Pronto, I collected two of my foreign-born girlfriends from night school classes who were in the same boat, one Greek and one Irish. We quickly made plans and took our citizenship tests and became official "American citizens." Was I still scared for me and my family? Of course, yes. But at least I was not technically any longer an enemy alien of America. But I was certainly one peeved citizen.

With this new citizenship came new responsibilities. I had to find work again because of Louis' bad reoccurring issues with his stomach and health. During the Depression, there was little work to be found. But as my brother Ralfo often said, "The business of war is business," and with this new war, the depression became the past. I found part-time work as a seamstress in Lynn in a clothing factory, and I began to save money together with Louis. I left the factory after seven laborious, tedious months and went to work four hours a day in a new Lord and Taylor, in its bridal shop. Mrs. Bidwell, the owner of the shop, was very intellectual, a designer of the type of my old bosses, Rosa and Agnes, on Newbury Street in Boston. I worked there for years until she moved away. Then, I went to work in a boutique shop called, Mrs. T Vogue Design Shop doing design and alterations on fine garments for women. I was saving good money there and Louis complained little about it. I was again in my element of helping to design and build women's fine apparel.

We Bought Our First House

In January 1942, we bought our first house on Hollingsworth Street with Louis' last six hundred dollars down and what I could help with from my new work. The day that we moved in, Louis had a sudden relapse, perhaps from all the pressures. He went immediately to the hospital. It was wintertime. The truck moved the furniture in, and my husband went out at the same moment to the hospital - his stomach was bleeding again. We had not even another cent in the bank. My working carried us through those first few months. It was like being returned back into the Depression. But again - we managed. The new job I had made about thirty-five dollars a week, also extra time on Saturday. It came to about fifty-dollars - fine at that time. It was money. With it, I had to pay for the mortgage which was ten dollars weekly and another ten dollars for the barbershop rent. I also bought coal and I had enough money left over for food. I did this for six months until my husband was well enough to go back to work. Louis would never take any assistance, none of any kind, not even from my family. Through all this, I still went to my night classes, and my boys worked after their schooling when they could to assist.

In the summer of 1942, my husband was finally recovered and feeling fine. I never disturbed him with my wishes, but I yearned to go out with him somewhere or to have some kind of rapport. I wanted desperately to just talk or take a walk together along the beach as we once did, but he only wanted to be left alone. I kept on working and found solace in the company of my many girlfriends and co-workers at the apparel design shop. Days would pass, endless days. There was no other way. Any thought or fear of having been classified as an enemy alien of America quickly disappeared into the immediate past.

Reno Graduates and Goes to Art School

Reno graduated from English High School. Finally! He felt liberated, for now, he could concentrate and study what he really wanted - art. He couldn't enter any college of art he wanted right away for there was a limited number of students admitted, and he didn't have enough money saved for his tuition, so he went to work, and all the money he made, he put into the bank in his name and in mine for his college education. He was accepted for the coming year to the Boston Museum School of Fine Arts, a very exclusive school at the famed museum and also across from my beloved Isabella Stewart Gardner Museum. When he got there, Reno shined like a star. My internal heart was answered. He built and produced many beautiful designs. He proved to himself and others that he was given birth as an artist. I used to go the Museum School on Tuesdays to visit him (it was permitted). I loved to see my son at work. Once, I caught him alone in a room starting a statue first with wires and then slowly adding plaster. "The Wakening," he called it. His first statute - a reclining figure of Adam. In my soul, I smiled a validation, not just of motherhood but a validation of sequence. I know no other way of saying it, but I was to witness it firsthand. Thank you, Matzo Mauriello. Dear fellow, you didn't forsake us after all.

I went again, and Reno had finished the statue of Adam. I loved it so much that he promised to give it to me. I call it "Reno," not Adam, for it looks like him around the mouth. It is a very expressive piece. It was an exhibition at the end of the school year at the Fine Arts Museum and was voted the best piece of art exhibited by the art students of that year.

Both of my boys were full of aspirations and marvelous ideas. Their manhood showed in every way. Geno was now an avid reader and excelled in writing in all of his high school classes. Soon, Geno, too, would graduate. Perhaps I was a little too proud of my children, but I had to be sincere with myself. I expressed openly what I felt with my friends and with my family. And why not? It was a benevolent urge in imparting to all these people the gratifying maternal feeling. It was a pleasure for me to talk to my sons on an intellectual level. They were fully grown men at an early age. I thought it to be a recompensation of my life - a reason for being. Both of my sons were my friends as well. But fears for them were facing me. The monstrous reason that tramped hopes and froze my enthusiasm was the perception and the preparation of war.

The continuous news of what was happening across the sea was felt by us all listening to the radio and attending lectures. It obscured my very will to live. We had to listen to the same subject continuously. Life became oppressive. Nature hates monotony. Even children were carried into the undercurrent. One could see groups of them of every reasonable age talking about Germany's strengths - English defense - America's preparativeness. And so, the psychology of men doped everyone into this same coma. I dreaded the reality of what the awakening might be if those men knew the limitless boundaries of their influence. They created a mess.

I had to occupy my mind to prevent from going mad with worries, but all the modern books dealt with only politics, not philosophy. I went to the library. I read about modern Germany, from Bismarck to Hitler. Nothing. It had nothing to do with the problem of the day, just names and dates of history. But my better self was repeating, "What fools these mortals be." Yes, it had to do with the day's problems.

For years, Germany, since Bismarck, was preparing for supremacy with hard iron will and preparing to be the supermen of the world. And now they were taking the world by force. Why?

Reno, High School Graduation Picture, 1942

Geno, High School Graduation Picture, 1944

Mary Votano, (18), High School Graduation Picture.
May 1944

Chapter Sixteen

The Introduction of "Mary"

Family Service to America

Spontaneously at this time, while Reno was studying at the Boston Museum School of Fine Arts, I introduced him to the daughter of one of my co-workers who I worked with at the Bridal Shop at Lord and Taylor. My longtime co-worker and friend was Constantina Votano. "Connie" was a kind and angelic woman ten years older than me and a very gifted seamstress as well - one of the best workers. Well, Connie had a beautiful young daughter named Maria, seventeen and still in high school. Everyone called this girl, "Mary." I had known Mary since she was born. She became an only child after the death of her four-year-old sister. Many times, Mary would bring lunch to her mother and would sit and chat with the seamstresses during their break. She was a beautiful angel on earth.

Connie would sometimes bring Mary with her to afternoon tea at my house with my other lady friends. I loved them both so much. Well, Reno was coming through the parlor at one of these lady-teas. I had no intentions of anything - no matchmaking, no, because I remembered what embroilments I had to endure with my own father, but these meetings were all innocent on my part, at least that is how I remember it. Soon, Reno took to getting back from his art classes early in order to happen by another one of these scheduled teas which included my friend, Connie Votano. If Mary was not there, he looked very disappointed. He would ask me, "Mother, when is this next tea of yours with Mrs. Votano? Will she bring some company, I hope?" The frequency of coincidental meetings at tea time occurred more and more.

It was very easy to see that Reno, nineteen at this time, and Mary were immediately interested in each other. Neither had much experience as to the art of the courtship dance, so they made little steps at it. Watching their own ballet evolve was something of quiet amusement for me.

Reno and Mary eventually dated under her parents' strict supervision, and neither spoke of anyone else after that. He even took her to his art class once in a while and to the Isabella Stewart Gardner Museum. My son was smitten by essentially the first girl he ever truly looked at. But it was hard not to look at Mary. Naturally, my friend Connie, being of firm Catholic upbringing, expertly moderated these meetings between her beautiful daughter and my son, but she was also supportive - in a traditional Calabrian way. She would say in dialect, "Piano - Piano, mia Cari. Vorrei in guardia!" ("Slowly - Slowly, my Dears. I warn you.") There was no mistaking it, my son had more on his mind than just wire armatures and plaster.

Now, to describe this girl. Mary was a junior, one year behind Geno in high school classes. They also knew each other. Mary was an athletic, thin, dark-haired, beautiful girl and the only other person besides my husband, Louis, at an early age that I would describe as "cinematic." She could have been an actress.

Reno Gets His Notice

The draft was not sudden news to anyone. It was in the air. When it came to your house, it did not ask to come in; it just came in. Yes, we knew it was possible that Reno would be drafted, for a lot of young men were called up of his own age and circumstance. The Second Great War was raging good in Europe, and America supplied much of the resources the Allied Forces needed in everything, including men.

We had some discussions about the draft. Before he was actually drafted, Reno expressed his idea that if chosen, he might declare himself as a conscientious objector. He said, "Yes, I would go, but only to work in a hospital or take care of wounded soldiers. I would do anything except hold a gun in my hand." Oh my, we didn't know what to say. But then we realized, all of us, including Reno, that he was too young to take such a big step. Reno came to realize it would still be war for him regardless, no matter what. They had already mistaken many boys of conscientious objection as being spies, cowards or deserters to avoid going into battle. Reno was none of those categories.

The inevitable arrived. Reno was drafted.

The drafting of my son came to me like a hurricane and tore off one of the best branches of my heart. No more art school. He had to go directly into the draft. How can I express the emptiness I felt when I heard of this notice? The pain was too deep to be able to bring it forth for expression.

The morning that Reno left, I forced myself to be brave. I got up early and I took a little extra care of myself. I didn't want him to lose his morale. He behaved like a real man although I could tell that his heart was breaking. Still, he joined us that morning in light conversation and laughed until the last minute. I wanted him to remember me with composure. I served breakfast with my usual care while my heart was bursting. I refrained from it well enough. My voice only cracked a little when I kissed my son and said goodbye. Reno said goodbye - it was with a smile, a sad smile that had been lingering on his face that entire week. He told me, "Mother dear, don't worry. Take care of yourself, for me. Make believe I am just going away to school this morning. Okay? Training camp - to Camp Davis. Just another school." "Yes," I said, "going just to school." I did not say what I was really thinking, "Oh, but you are going to the school of war!" I was hoping that the lesson he would get in the war wouldn't change his principles and return him a hardened man. But I knew he would never come home the same if he came home at all. Just imagine, he was going to war as the son of a recent alien enemy.

In my final goodbyes to Reno, I said, "Don't let the monsters change you. Use all of your means to stay who you are - capito?" He just smiled his sad smile. "Goodbye, Mother. Take care of yourself, please, okay? I will write to you." "Yes, Dear, I will." And then he thoughtfully said, "Mother, also, please, would you take care of Mary, as well? Go to places with her that you love to go to. Okay? Will you promise? Do like I would do and how I would take her to these places myself if I were here. Okay?" "Of course, I will. I promise." Reno then left with a light kiss to my cheek.

I looked through the window and waved to him. He was walking firm and erect between his father and his brother as if going off to his elementary school again, the same look came back to me, same wave. My son was a healthy grown specimen of a man now with brains, strength, talent, a stout heart and noble intentions.

I stayed at the window and looked as far as I could for as long as I could until they disappeared from my sight. But, even then, I still looked to see him. I had Reno in front of my mind. Reno in all his ages and moods. I saw him in all sizes. It is astonishing how we can see so much in a second. There he was at one year old and four years old when he went to school for the first time.

How immensely lonesome I felt? Reno really was born for my consolation. Now he was gone. It was then I broke down. My son the gifted artist was going where? Three months to training camp. To do what? To learn to kill! And then to war? I shouted the irony and tragedy of life. I could not control my tears any longer. I was glad I was alone. I gave way to my emotions. I cried and cried as if my heart would come out of my throat. Days would go by.

So, as promised, Mary and I became good friends. She came to the house faithfully, once weekly. And we went everywhere together in Boston that she and Reno had visited. We went also to many lectures and recitals in Salem and in Boston. Often, her mother, Connie, joined us, mostly when we went to the movies. It kept our minds off of the reality and uncertainty of the future. We both took comfort in each other's comfort. I kept Reno informed of all our activities and it worked fine.

Reno wrote to Mary from Camp Davis before he left for Europe. He requested of her a picture so that he could place it inside his helmet to remember what it was he was really fighting for and to coming home to. She sent him her graduation picture.

The Second Great War Hit my Pirone Family as Well

Also at this time, 1943, after finishing Harvard, my brother Frank graduated from Tufts Medical School. He was now "Doctor Francis Pirone." Bravo Francesco! I went to his graduation and felt so happy for him. We as a family succeeded through him, and he was so kind about sharing the success. Validation. That word again. Frank had what he wanted, finally. Was I living vicariously through my brother? I admit, perhaps I was when he went to Harvard without me. To change anything? No. Never. We are all of a time and place, and I was comfortable with this and with whatever fate presented. But, my destiny, was mine alone.

Mother and Father joined us at Alice's house where we all had a party for Frank. We were so proud of this young, brilliant doctor and brother of ours.

Then too, my brother Frank, at the age of 29 - was drafted. He had only come to America sixteen years earlier to Ellis Island from Pratola Serra as a twelve-year old boy and Italian immigrant. Now he was back to the Europe from which he came - as an American Army surgeon and officer.

Frank spent his first eight months as an intern at Lynn Hospital and after this short internship, he was called up and went into the Army Medical Corp. Frank served for two and a half years as a surgeon in the parachute division between the borders of France and Germany. My brother would be transported as a rescue surgeon behind enemy lines in a glider - no sound of engines. He protected himself from shrapnel by sitting on his helmet as he glided silently into the remnants of battle to aid wounded paratroopers.

Once, my brother Frank himself was shot down over the territory near Alsace-Lorraine and had to parachute out from his glider. He suffered a few injuries because of this maneuver. Also, another time, he passed a part of Germany where my son Reno was moving through. They briefly saw each other - uncle and nephew in the midst of the great military migration. Frank saw Reno first and shouted out, but neither could stop of course. Uncle and nephew saluted each other from a distance. It was wartime.

By 1944, I had three brothers and my oldest son in the Great Second World War.

My son, Geno, became next.

[Aside: Sunday dinner before World War II: Brother Frank, Lena, Reno and brother Mikele. Not seen, Geno, and brother Louis. All the men joined the war after this picture; Frank and Reno to Europe in the Army and Louis and Geno with the Army Air Forces and Mikele to the South Pacific with US Army Forces in New Caledonia.]

Geno Graduates High School and Enlists

In 1943, Geno's graduation from high school came. I, my husband and my mother went to see him in a procession line with the others. Oh, my God, he was so very straight and handsome - the best looking of all with an extremely intelligent demeanor. He was a confident man at seventeen. My old mother, sick, pale, but full of joy said, "He looks just like his grandfather, Domenico Pisano, when he was young. Remember Lena?" "Yes, he does," I said with a tear. Louis was strangely quiet - no open joy for him. In the back of our minds, we all had that terrible feeling that Geno was going to war, too - and soon.

Geno did not share the same conscientious objector leanings his brother had early in the war, but the war had been going on for two years now. Geno was more nationalistic and proud to defend what he thought was the imminent threat to human freedom. He hated what Nazi Germany was doing and felt concerns for the future - even for America. So, before graduation, Geno signed the papers and volunteered with the Army Air Forces Training Command (AAFTC). His Uncle Louis was already serving the AAF as an engineer. Geno was not yet eighteen so his father had to sign the documents. I did not sign anything. Perhaps that is why Louis was so pensive during the graduation. Geno had already taken the required tests - physical and mental. As I said, Geno was already an excellent specimen of a man at seventeen. He passed easily.

My son wanted to be an Army pilot - another fearful weight on my mind. I could not imagine him in a plane every day flying above the war. Twice the risk to my mind. At that time, airplanes were not trusted by us old fashioned people. Louis and I were born of a time when there were no planes or automobiles or telephones or even electricity. We had no such love for adventure - we aimed only for peace and comfort.

The week before graduation, Geno and a few other boys donated blood. After their ordeal, they all stopped by our house at Geno's invitation. When I came home from work, I found my floors all dirty with footprints, as if a real army had passed through. All the food was gone - eggs, cheese, cold cuts, sodas, wine, milk, and bread - everything! When Geno came home, he shrugged and told us that he took the boys home for a cup of tea, but they attacked everything around. After giving blood, they had that mental and physical urge to replace the precious liquid given away for the soldiers. My husband and I felt so very proud of this test of his confidence in us. He knew that we would have been happy about the visit and would have done the same thing ourselves. That was my Geno in action.

Well, we replenished our icebox easily enough and in time to celebrate Geno's graduation at home with some of his friends. Even Freddy Gluck came to celebrate with us.

Yes, Geno was going now, too.

Another tearful parting. Only one thing was on my mind. At least he was in this country to be trained, and it takes time to make a pilot. I had the conviction that the war couldn't last forever. I was terribly tired of these worries for both of my sons and my brothers. With Geno, I couldn't think of anything else but airplanes for a long time. Since he signed up for the Air Corp, an armada of warplanes flew over my head while I was asleep. They flew over my neck when half awake and I had them in my pockets in and out of the house. Oh, why? Again, no answer came.

When I kissed Geno goodbye, it was a different goodbye than it was with Reno. Tearfully sad of course, but Geno happily went away, as if he was heading toward a goal that he really wanted. His mood helped with the separation. And to my mind he was going away by train to San Antonio, Texas, in the very opposite direction from the death and destruction in Europe where Reno was.

Geno wrote to us often and I kept his letters tied together with his brothers' in a large wooden cigar box for safe keeping. I visited that sanctuary often.

After one year, Geno was scheduled to come home for his first furlough. Louis went to meet him after dinner at the train station in Boston. I was waiting by, nervously pacing the house. It was two o'clock in the morning when Louis finally came home - alone. Geno didn't come. The train had stopped somewhere, he had to change route and no one knew where that would be. The excuse? "It was wartime." Well, Louis and I didn't go to bed. He slept in the chair in the parlor and I laid down on the sofa. Finally, a "knock, knock" on the door came about eight that morning. "Why are you knocking?" We shouted! Geno came bounding in, in uniform. Oh, the joy and a chance of mental rest. One of my sons came back home!

Geno quickly looked around at everything in the house as if he had never been there. "Everything has changed!" He laughed. "Everything looks smaller! Even you, Mother!" Even I was different for him. Geno himself did not look smaller. In fact, my son seemed to have grown two more inches in Texas - almost up to his father's height. They came nose to nose to compare with a huge laugh and hugs. Geno now looked so strong, so mammoth in his uniform. He had not suffered the agony of combat at all. He had enjoyed doing what they taught him. He looked healthy and ready for anything.

That furlough went by like a flash of light, and then Geno went back to pilot training. A tease to me and his father - a promise again to write more letters - a trail of tears to repeat again. We corresponded continuously with more happy thoughts. I tried just to write what good I saw around me and only the beautiful, never the worries.

*1944. Geno, Aviation Pilot Cadet,
at the Army Air Forces, San Antonio, Texas."*

———————⟨⟩———————

In my letters, I think I tried to convey to both of my sons that I was hopeful and that I was waiting for the happy day when both of them were in my arms again. In my prayers and meditations, I told them of thinking of that day when all four of us would be seated around the dinner table as we had done together for so many years.

———————⟨⟩———————

Dreams of Reno

My dreams of prophecy kept retuning to me however - vivid dreams. I didn't push them away from my mind this time. I wanted to know. I wanted to embrace them, to try to make them positive. "Please oh, please give me dreams of positive things." I dreamt one night that Reno was writing me a letter in a green field. It was a happy dream. He looked safe and contented. Another more troubling dream came to me of a deep fog caused by the firing of canon bluster. The fog lifted, and there was Reno almost flying through the air - smiling his sad smile. This dream came to me more than once and I deliberately pushed it away from my mind.

When letters came from Reno, it was as if they arrived from heaven. They didn't come as regularly as Geno's did because of the war. Reno's letters were hard to get because the censor had strict rules, and there were many delays. When his letters finally did come, they usually came in bunches. I knew then, that my son was all right, sad always, yes, but alive! I must have written a dozen letters to every one of his, not knowing if they ever got to him. Yes, he was constantly in some battle - but he never was allowed to describe to us where or when.

My letters to Reno during the war were about local news and whatever was on my mind at that time. They were letters of love from me and from his father who, like me, suffered greatly from his absence. They were letters of consolement and sorrow, of secret fears and of things left unsaid. When Reno wrote to us and to his brother, it was always with cheerfulness. Even so, he didn't want to be there.

My husband seldom showed any emotions, but at this time of waiting for letters, he was in agony. One Sunday morning, I found him standing on the high rock park near us looking out over the sea. He was so absorbed in his own prayers, he didn't hear me approaching. This unreligious man was saying, "Reno, come home! Come back, Reno - come back home!"

Mary came more often to see us. She was now in secretarial school and could do shorthand and type over a hundred words a minute. That was helpful for me of course, and it resulted in additional closeness and affection. Reno had been gone for over a year, but Mary's patience and resolve to be with him again held as true as our own heart, together. In

my soul, I knew Mary, this beautiful angel of mercy, would be the reason
for Reno to return home - alive.

"A Photograph for Reno - Mary, Louis and Me. 1944"

"Photo's Sent to Reno during the War, 1944."

The Midnight Telegram at Our Door

But, did I have any doubts about any of my dreams? No. I believed them to be an open book. That was what worried me further.

One night, at twelve midnight, there was a ring at our front door. Louis and I both got up out of bed and looked through the window to see who could it be at that time of night. There stood that poor, little, miserable-looking woman who brought telegrams to people on her bicycle. "Oh, my God, she was at my door now!"

I began to tremble hard. My husband was as pale as a ghost. He slowly opened the door. "Mr. Pisano?" the messenger asked. "Oh, yes," he said choking on his words. She handed a telegram to him, and he signed something. The messenger then jumped onto her bike and went away into the night. I could not move. I was petrified. My husband immediately took the telegram and ran into the bathroom. He shut the door. He didn't want to shock me with any news.

I stood outside the bathroom with my hands over my mouth. My heart was pounding. No sounds came from inside. My legs became suddenly numb, and I fainted right to the floor.

When I regained my consciousness, I was lying on the top of the bed with Louis placing an ice cloth to my forehead. I looked at his face, he was smiling? Why? "Give me the telegram," I urged him. "What is in it?" "Oh, it is nothing like I feared, really," he said, still smiling. I was thinking, "Well perhaps Reno is just wounded or maybe an accident to Geno." I managed to sit up. "Give me the telegram! Please!" He did and stood up away from the bed.

The telegram was a notification from New York. My Uncle Raffaele, my father's oldest brother, had died! What a relief! I felt guilty not to feel anything for my Uncle's death, but I was happy that my boys were alive and safe.

Still, I saw Reno in my repeating dreams always coming home. These were the dreams that I clung to. I dreamt of him coming home from green fields. I was again at the window. Mary was at his side. In this dream, my son ran up the stairs, hugged and kissed me. The first thing he told me in this dream, "Mother, I didn't kill anyone." Then, I would always wake up from this dream only to daydream it all over again.

Five Sons at War

During the Second Great War, Papa finally had calmed down. He never played cards for money again and was more attentive to Mother. They lived together near us, and we were always visiting each other during this period. My parents, too, worried for my children and also for their own three soldier sons, Frank, Mikele and Louis.

Mother never became an American citizen. She didn't see the need to. Too much trouble, especially for her. "I am too old to change," she would lament. "I am finally here with your Papa now, in America. He is the citizen. So, what is the difference? I would make a poor soldier anyway, no?"

To think back that my mother remained in the category of an "enemy alien" was the irony of all ironies. My elderly mother? Together, she and I committed five sons to America's resolve to win a World War.

Even today, I still kept in my mind the internment camps for the Italian-American nationals and how hypocritical it all was. But my parents and I were in the same boat - we each had traditional Italian sons at war as American soldiers. The first thing we always asked each other whenever we got together was, "Did you get any letters today?" Letters, letters - any letters from our sons?

THREE PIRONE BROTHERS IN SERVICE

FRANK F. PIRONE

MICHAEL PIRONE

LOUIS PIRONE

Dr. Frank F. Pirone, well-known Lynn doctor, left recently for duty with the Army Medical Corps, in which he was commissioned a first lieutenant. He is a graduate of Harvard college and Tufts Medical school and interned at Lynn hospital.
Corporal Louis Pirone, his brother, is now with the Army Air Forces in Texas while another brother, Private Michael Pirone, is in New Caledonia.

PISANO BROTHERS IN SERVICE

RENO PISANO

GENO PISANO

Two sons of Mr. and Mrs. Louis Pisano, 79 Hollingsworth street, are serving in the armed forces. Reno Pisano, a graduate of Classical High and Boston Art school, is now with the Engineers in North Africa.

[Aside: Clipped from bottom: "Geno Pisano, Aviation Pilot Cadet, is also at the Army Air Forces in Texas."]

[Aside: Flash forward. (Undisclosed by redacted letters.) During this time, WWII, Reno was indeed "fighting." He was "boxing" as a welterweight representing the 51st Engineer Combat Battalion of the 3rd Army and fighting for weekend passes. He was "undefeated" which gave him sporadic time off. Sometime during training camp, the pacifist/sculptor became a body builder - a different kind of sculptor. He saw action in North Africa; and he also landed at Normandy Beach, and he survived the Battle of the Bulge with Patton's 51st Engineer Combat Battalion by building

494

bridges near Remagen crossing the Rhine. In 1988, the French government awarded Reno and his small Battalion of less that 125 men, the French "Croix de Guerre" (Cross of War) with Silver Star for rebuilding bridges and protecting a village with diversionary tactics that thwarted the advance of German forces. The Croix de Guerre is "the French Government's highest award bestowed upon foreign military soldiers for heroic achievement." There are only a few recipients. His 51st Engineer Combat Battalion also received a Presidential Citation from the US War Department. Reno was a recipient of both.]

Reno, WWII. Welterweight fighter with Patton's 3rd Army,
51st Engineer Combat Battalion,
Undefeated. Belgium, 1945.

Reno and Beno

A strange friendship for Reno happened when he arrived as a new soldier in North Africa. He was made a guard of both German and Italian prisoners in the remote dessert. I now think of what the Italian prisoners must have thought when they saw this young Italian specimen come up to them in an American uniform. Can you imagine, my son was guarding prisoners of our homeland – Italy! This was his first duty. Well, they gave Reno a camp puppy to train as a guard dog. "Two sad amateurs with mange," Reno would later write. Reno trained this dog himself while they were guarding prisoners together. He taught the puppy to accept commands in German - just in case the dog was captured. This dog was a Belgian Shepherd - a beautiful breed of Shepherd, lean in torso and very tall. They loved each other. This little puppy grew and grew and became one of an enormous size - over one hundred and twenty pounds. Reno named him, "Beno." Geno, Reno and now Beno - another brother?

Beno was more than a dog for Reno, really. It surely must have been a little bit of sunshine in the obscurity of the war. Once we got word of these two partners, we imagined Reno with Beno at his side sleeping on the ground or in the trenches. Reno did write back that his dog's coat was often his bed. Yes, on the ground. Beno, by all descriptions, was a beautiful and useful dog for this artist/guard with whom he was teamed with.

Well, Reno had to leave Beno in North Africa. They shipped Reno away, not Beno. The dog was a valuable guard-dog now, and Reno was a needed soldier somewhere else. So, when the Allied Forces attacked the "soft underbelly" of Europe via Sicily, they kept Beno in North Africa, and they sent my son to Normandy.

Reno landed onto Normandy Beach on the wave of the third day. He volunteered to swim ashore from his craft, one quarter mile away, because orders were not coming and everything was severely backed up. After that landing in Normandy, they put everyone into the eastward push against Germany with General Patton's 3rd Army. This resulted in the Battle of the Bulge. This conflagration lasted many months.

Reno got stuck in the point of this bulge. They went too far, too fast, into France and became surrounded by German forces. They had to retreat and barely got out. During the retreat, he and his engineer company protected a French village by placing campfires all about to confuse the Germans into thinking that there were many more Allied soldiers camped against them. It worked! Because of this Battle of the Belgium

Bulge, they had to get out fast and left everything behind - except their lives. Censorship kept us from knowing any of these details.

To move forward in my story. On the troop-train out of the Bulge, stopping before yet another battle, Reno saw his guard dog, Beno! The dog was in a mob of soldiers in the hands of an Army officer. Reno jumped down from the train and told the officer emphatically that that was "his" dog and his name was Beno. The officer at first refused to believe my son. He said to him, "Can you prove this is your dog? His name is 'Major,' and he has been with me for six months." Reno looked at the dog and demanded to him in German, "Achtung!" Schützen Sie Ihre Position!" Fest!" ("Attention! Guard your position! Firmly!") Reno called out these commands to the dog in perfect German, yes. The dog obeyed immediately and waited for further orders. The Army officer then just handed the leash over to Reno with no more questions. Reno promised the officer that he and Beno would stay in touch with him. After that, for the remainder of the entire war, Reno and Beno were never separated again.

Reno (PV1) and Beno (PV1). Prison Guards, 3rd Army,
51st Engineer Combat Battalion, North Africa. 1943. "Achtung!"

Chapter Seventeen

The War Ends

My Sons and Brothers All Come Home

In central Europe, the war was still going on until the English, American and Russian forces converged onto Berlin. All the territory and countries that Germany had taken by force were pushed backwards and reduced down to the space of Hitler's sorrowful bunker. Hitler, they say, committed suicide on the 18th of May 1945. Germany was divided into four zones; American, English, Russian, and French. They argued the terms amongst themselves as to what spoils each would get in the peace treaty. Germany again, was carved to pieces by its victors.

During this spring of 1945, Geno was home for another furlough. We had a good time with our handsome airman in uniform. While Geno was home, we got word that the war was ending, and we celebrated. But it was tempered because my brother Mikele was still in the Pacific somewhere, so we were always near the radio. We were all together when something heavy and somber came on the radio of a revolutionary kind. Oh, my God, it happened. The atomic bomb was dropped on Hiroshima. Then another on Nagasaki, Japan. Hundreds of thousands died instantly. How terrible a thing. Why? Why did they not just drop the bomb in the harbor and say to them, "See? Surrender now or more will come." I will never know. Japan, the last of the Axis Powers, capitulated and was reduced to a bow. It was ended. The Second Great War came to an end. But in my mind, I felt that there would never be peace in this world as long as there existed greed by men to acquire land.

Yes! This war, however, was over!

We celebrated the news with uncontrollable enthusiasm. People were almost crazy with joy. Bells were ringing from every church and tower, and noises of all kinds were heard even from afar. It was like a wonderful dream, only the reality of it was too good to be true. We went to Central

Square in Lynn, to hilly Union Street, near Louis' barbershop. It became dusk. I never saw so many people in one place in my life. We could see an ocean of human heads - lights, too, were blazing. It was a wonderful sight. People were singing and shouting, "Hub, hub. Hub, hub!" What it meant, I do not know. But Geno, Louis and I were shaking hands, kissing anybody and repeated the, "hub, hub!" Believe me, Geno got plenty of kisses being in uniform from the women - of every age. The noise wrapped around my shoulders. It fell like falling snowflakes. What a joy to share all this with my youngest son. What a wonderful coincidence that he happened to be here with us just in time to see it. In all of the crowd, we found my sister Josephine and Mother near Louis' barbershop. They, too, were crying for joy. This scene lasts forever in my mind.

The next day, Geno was called back after the surrender of Japan. He was still in training, now in Florida. His furlough was canceled, and he had to return, but I knew he would not be involved in any war, and my heart rang like the church bells over my head. Also, I had just heard from Reno that he was safe. When his letter came, I cried out and shouted in Italian, "Thank you! Mother of God!" And then I laughed out loud. Only we Italians could come up with the concept that Almighty God, the supreme creator of the universe, he too had a mother.

Then another letter from Reno came on top of the first. It read:

> "Mother,
>
> I will be home soon. I was preparing to go to the Pacific. They had me on a boat there when we got the news that the war was over. Now the ship is taking me back home instead. We will land in New York. I'm not sure when we will arrive, but soon. I also wrote to Mary.
>
> I'm coming home! Home, Mother.
>
> Your loving son,
>
> Reno"

———————

I revisited the repeating dream I had of Reno floating in a fog and then coming home up the steps with Mary. Now, that dream became all true

- right in front of my own eyes. I was looking through the window, and I saw Reno coming up the street, and yes, Mary was at his side. She had met him at the station. We didn't even know just when he was supposed to come, but Mary was there at the station waiting for him for hours. Anyway, there he was for real, three years later, as handsome as ever. Like his brother, he had grown, in many ways. I came out. He ran up the front porch and hugged and kissed me. Never have I ever had a hug such as this. Mary stood beside him with tearful smiles. Then Louis came out. My husband was crying. I never also have seen Louis cry before or be so emotional. He had finally succumbed. Father and son hugged and slapped shoulders and touched the side of each other's face. No words spoken. Our son was home from war.

Prophetically, true to my dream, the first thing Reno said to me was, "Mother, I have not killed anyone. I wasn't a hero or a coward," he said quietly. "I just worked hard as an engineer. My job was to rebuild what was destroyed. I killed nobody!" We all went inside. Reno, with his beautiful principles, was home. He never mentioned this war to us again.

[Aside: Reno only wrote on the back of this picture, at 95 years of age: "Belgium, Jan. 1945."]

*[After Reno came home from WWII, he unknowingly became
a recipient of two Citations of heroism — one from France
and one from the United States. The reluctant hero.]*

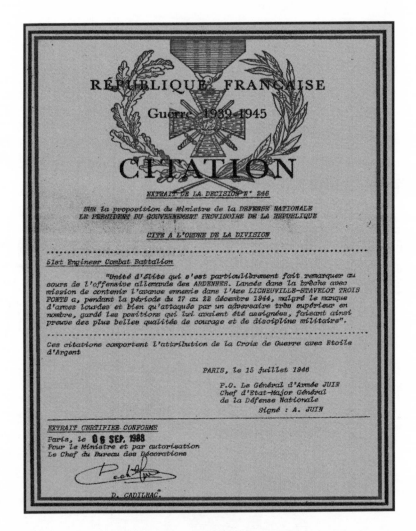

*[In September 1988, the French government belatedly awarded Reno and his 51st
Engineer Combat Battalion the famed, "Croix de Guerre" for protecting a French
village against larger German forces. He and his outnumbered Battalion of only 120
men were also awarded a US Presidential Citation for "its outstanding performance
of duty in action against the enemy from 17 to 22 December 1944, in Belgium during
the Battle of the Bulge" Further quote: "This is the highest honor the United States*

Government can confer upon a unit for extraordinary heroism in action against an armed enemy and was possibly the first time in military history that an engineer battalion had been relieved by five divisions." Two Citations - one G.I.]

Now, What About Beno

Reno came home alone, without Beno. Being just a regular soldier, Reno couldn't bring his dog on the troop transport ship. If every soldier had a pet, it would be like Noah's ark; they all would never arrive. So, once again, dog and master became separated. Reno had to contact the officer who found Beno before, and together they made arrangements for the dog to cross the Atlantic alone. One month later, Beno was in America, but to New York. What must have been on this dog's mind for the ten days it took on the ocean to get here? Yes, Beno was that smart.

Reno went to New York and got Beno out of the boat. He was quarantined for several days - exactly like I had been. Only this Belgian immigrant did not have to wait to be processed on Ellis Island like my entire family had experienced. Thankfully, in 1954, they closed that God-forsaken place down.

Reno was complete. He had finally come home. Beno was home now too.

Beno was so beautiful. Never had anybody seen such a dog as this. He was not a German Shepherd. Like I said, Beno was a Belgian Shepherd with long legs and body with an intelligent face. Everyone who saw Beno loved him. He was smart, obedient, and followed us everywhere. He followed Louis to work one morning when Louis didn't take the bus. My husband had some leftover milk, so he gave it to Beno and sent him home. That night, when Louis closed up, guess who was waiting at the front door? Beno. The dog had memorized Louis' schedule. After that, Beno would show up at closing unless he was told not to.

Once, a bus driver, stopped his bus going up to the highlands where we lived. One of Louis' clients was on the bus. The driver opened the door and called out to the dog, "Hey! Beno! You want a ride home?" The dog jumped in and sat erect next to the driver, dutifully guarding the way.

Everyone in Lynn knew and loved this dog. They also knew his story of being an Army guard in North Africa. To many, Beno was a local war hero. And he understood and enjoyed the accolades bestowed upon him. He took advantage of it, I think.

Another time, we almost had big problems. Our postman, who delivered the mail to our house, wore a stiff postal uniform and brimmed hat that very much resembled that of a Gestapo German officer. Beno would not let the man come or go any further, either way until the poor fellow took off his hat and pleaded, "Beno. It's me! Sam! I don't speak German, remember?" Beno kept a suspicious eye on him nevertheless. After that, our postman, whose name we found out was Sam, always knew to take off his hat before delivering our mail.

I loved that dog so much.

After a while, even my brothers came home. Only Geno now was left in uniform. He had to be in Florida for a while longer.

Reno and Mary's Wedding

Reno and Mary became immediately engaged after the war, and the wedding was scheduled to be on Sunday, December 16, 1945. Life begins afresh. Reno wanted his brother to be his best man. Geno tried to get permission to come back for the wedding but his superiors said "impossible." I wrote to his stern officers myself saying, "These two brothers who had given so much of themselves serving America just when they were flourishing their hopes in college, both of them, with respect and honor, went to the call of war," etc., etc. "No," was the answer again. I was mad about it. That "no" made me detest them. Evidently, no one had told them the war was over.

These two brothers had always been very close. I remember before they parted, they bought two identical rings and wore these rings in remembrance of each other. If one would need the other, they would send the ring. Quixotic? Yes, perhaps, but significant of how they were raised and of their love for one another.

We had no idea of when Geno would be allowed to come home, so Reno chose my brother, Connie, to stand in proxy for Geno at the wedding as best man. It all otherwise went as planned, just before Christmastime, 1945.

I was very busy for a few days. I made the wedding cake and also supervised the design and building of Mary's wedding gown, making the last fitting adjustments myself. Both came out beautifully.

Sunday morning came, and Reno was very calm and collected. With his usual way, he got up after my repeated call for breakfast. It was exactly just how my brother, Ralfo, got me prepared the morning of my own wedding. Two o'clock came quickly, but we were there in time.

When Louis and I entered, the church it was almost full. My brother, Mikele, and brother, Louis, were the ushers. To have them also home and safe from the war was an added blessing for us. They both looked very elegant in their dress suits. I was escorted by Mikele to the front seat and right in the back of me was my dear brother, Frank. He smiled and touched my shoulder in support. My husband, too, looked very nice as usual in his dark suit and white silk shirt.

Reno came out with my brother, Connie, first, and they stood together. I visualized Geno in Connie's place which caused me to take a sudden breath. Reno did look handsome, elegant, magnificent, very natural with a faint and sure smile of an honest man who had so much to offer. No worries about him. A man who was just what he claims to be. Reno searched for me and Louis and smiled. He talked to us with his eyes, repeating what he said before he left the house two hours before. He said that no other man had a better opportunity to imitate goodness and justice taught him from a mother and father. There in the church, Reno's expression repeated those same words.

There was no music in the church because the week before Christmas is the advent observance, a traditional Catholic canon. Well, the ushers were in readiness. Everybody got up - the bridal party was approaching. The white carpet spread in the little church looked very symbolic. "A white road," I thought. I hope it will always be as spotless and smooth as it is today for them both.

Someone whispered, "The bride - the bride," and a beautiful redheaded girl in yellow velvet appeared. It was Marianne, Mary's cousin, the bride's maid. Marianne slowly was leading the party. Behind her, the bride appeared, on the arm of her father.

Mary was stunning - so very, very beautiful. Her father, Mr. Votano, very proud and dignified. He was holding his daughter's arm like one touches a dainty lily. They came up slowly and calmly. Reno was looking at her, smiling, inviting her to come to him. Connie Votano was crying softly as she watched her only child, her daughter approaching. I felt people staring at me. No! I was not crying! Perhaps a little maybe.

Presently, they came up to Reno, and there they stopped. Mr. Votano lifted the veil from Mary's face and kissed his daughter. He stepped aside, and Reno took her right arm, leading her to the altar. The little priest was ready with all his contraptions, incense, book, etc. and dressed in regalia, ready to do his duty. My brother, Connie, looked very dignified, and the contrast of his black and white against Marianne's yellow gown and red hair was very dramatic. Mary's gown was a striking creation. It was so perfect on her. She looked slim and straight like a statue, full of grace and purity. Her raven black hair was also an addition to the combination and line of the gown. The bride did not wear much make-up - she had no need to. The flowers were very beautiful and fragrant.

The vows of the ceremony were done to perfection of the rules, and I could distinctly hear the "I do's." I blessed them both, wishing good luck with my heart full of emotions. They walked back as man and wife.

Louis and Mr. Votano paid the bill together for the wedding, half and half - Italian style. The father of the groom must also share the expense. Okay, we did.

Before they went for the wedding pictures, Reno ran up to me. When he got to me, he again kissed me and said smiling, "Mother! You are still my girl, too! Remember that." Mary also came to me and called me "Mother" for the first time. She, too, was just twenty like I was when I married. It seemed only a heartbeat in time.

After the reception at our house, the bride and groom swiftly ran away to New York City for their honeymoon. After their return, Reno and Mary moved upstairs on the second floor of our house.

Reno went back to the Museum School of Fine Arts right away. He was able to use the bank account we made together for his tuition before the war. There was plenty of savings in it now. Reno had already finished a year before he was drafted, so it was easy for him to get back in and complete his final three years at the School. He went in again without waiting. His three years of war made him less tolerant of wasting time, and Reno gave himself a mission to make up for whatever he lost being a soldier. Also, serving under George Patton and the war itself gave him very little patience for unmotivated teaching.

Nevertheless, Reno had to get side work. He was able to find a job at the General Electric Company in Lynn which helped while going to school. Because he was an engineer during the war, he could easily read blueprints of construction, so he started there. This allowed him to eventually graduate three years later from art school with many more accolades and prizes. He indeed was a seasoned sculptor. The graduation ceremony was in the garden of the Museum of Fine Arts, and we all later celebrated at a fine Neapolitan restaurant in the North End - at my cousin Paolo's.

Becoming a Nonna

The most important thing that came about for everyone at this time was that Mary became pregnant with their first child - just exactly nine months after the honeymoon. A boy! As I said, Reno had little tolerance of wasting time after the war, and he proved it. Reno Victor Pisano became the father to Victor Reno Pisano on September 10th, 1946. Six pounds, eight ounces and already twenty-one inches "tall." A true Pisano.

Dear God! This wonderful arrival changed everything in the family. The baby not only made brand new mother and father; he also made everyone a "new" something - everyone! He made for the first time; a new uncle, seven new great-uncles, five great-aunts, two great-grandfathers, a great-grandmother and two new grandparents - all at once! And that was just on the Pisano and Pirone side of the family! The Votano's had many more first contributions of their own. There was an epiphany.

And for me of course, I was myself a new Nonna at forty-five? Mamma Mia!

The Casualty of War

1946. I was really very fortunate indeed to have both of my sons and all of my brothers survive the Second Great War. I had to be content with this fact if no other. All the agony my husband and I suffered brought us together again, but it was not the same after the war. There was a different kind of relationship between us. We loved each other more like a family relation, not as husband and wife. We lost each other somewhere during the way. After twenty-five years of marriage, we had the same interest in the home and with the children, yes, but I had to deliberately make up my mind to make that part of my life with him work - at any cost. We were alone, but together. At times, his will to control everything became hell-ish, but I came away from it without being burned. My husband was still looking over my shoulder, stopping every impulse toward emancipation. At times, I felt like the unfinished statue of Michelangelo's slave in the Academy Museum of Florence. Encased in stone - struggling to come out - to move - to be completed. Slowly however, I was breaking free - freedom in my own solitude while leaving him to his. I was doing more designing and building of bridal gowns and fine women's clothing. I began writing more poetry and concentrating on other writings. Newspapers and magazines were accepting my pieces. I had many girlfriends to go to lectures with or to share museums. My boys were now grown men. To my mind, the world was yet ahead of me while my husband was content being left in his own. As I wrote before, divorce was never an option. We just had gone through too much history - together.

The Great War finally had its casualty.

Geno Comes Home, Goes to College

Geno came home at last. What a wonderful feeling it was to have him home. All the airplanes in my dreams suddenly went away giving me back my peace of mind. He couldn't get into college right away for colleges were clogged with the soldiers who came home before he did, but he persevered and finally got into Boston College. The beautiful buildings there fascinated me. It was a Catholic college, but the style of the campus was 15th century Gothic. He didn't stay long. Geno, like his brother, was impatient, and I think he didn't want to live at home or in a dormitory. He had already done that, and his unrest was more like his mother's. He felt it was going backwards to live at home or in a dormitory. I also think that he didn't care much for the environment of the place. So, one weekend, he told his father and me that he was leaving Boston College and would be going instead to New York University in New York City. Goodbye Boston, hello to New York City. There are no more surprises left in this world. Geno was gone again.

Not long after, on a blind date, Geno met a beautiful young student nurse while he was at NYU. She was the cousin of one of his friends on the chess club. Geno and his chess club friend went on a double blind-date on a Friday night. Geno's blind date was his friend's cousin. That following Sunday, Geno proposed to her in Central Park. Her name was Janice Beck.

About Janice

Janice Beck was young, blonde and a beautiful student nurse, seven years younger than Geno. I love her still to this day. Janice was very level-headed and direct - a no-nonsense nurse. She seemed very set in her manner and had a serious nature, a very good match for our exuberant "King's pawn to e4" Geno.

They were married three months later in her hometown in Kingston, Pennsylvania - very German, very American setting. Geno loved the differentiation in family style almost as much as he loved Janice.

Louis and I were driven all the way to Pennsylvania by one of Geno's best friends growing up, Hugh Casey. Only Casey, if one could believe, was more demonstrative than my own son - a prankster and jovial fellow. Reno and Mary could not attend because Mary was about to deliver their third child and Reno remained at her side. It was a long ride from Lynn.

The ride took us through many beautiful places that I had never seen before. America is boundless in so many ways, and we were in the heart of it. Casey drove. In his automobile were his fiancée, Geno, me and Louis. On the way, we stopped in New Jersey first to visit Louis' brother, Alfonso. Geno and his Uncle Alfonso were very, very close, especially after Geno moved to New York City. Alfonso was just the opposite of Louis - always happy, easygoing and full of humor. A wonderful man. Alfonso and his wife would take a train to the wedding later, the day of the celebration. Casey got us there the night before.

I had already met the Becks - Mrs. Beck before her husband. At first, I do not think she approved of us. It all was so sudden, and who could blame her? But after, it was just another case of "different types." Anyway, it took some time, but eventually, we became friends and respected one another. But, in the beginning, there were obvious differences and problems, starting with the wedding ceremony.

The first problem came with religion. The wedding was to be in the Holy Trinity Lutheran Church - an ascetic branch of Protestantism. It put my perennial beliefs of universal oneness and love to a firm test. The first surprise was when the Becks found out that Louis, Geno and I were not devout Catholics. Not at all. "How could Italian people not be Catholic?" That raised a lot of curious eyebrows to begin with, but the real problem was with Casey, not us. Well, Casey's Irish Catholic priest back in Lynn refused to let him stand up as best man at Geno's wedding because it was a Protestant ceremony. Oh, boy, not so good. Casey had to defer to Janice's cousin instead. Casey was good-spirited about it and made joking references, but I was livid. Again, it followed me, the dogma of the Catholic Church to deny unity and beauty of humanity if it is not in agreement with its own strict interpretations of God.

The wedding itself, however, was beautiful. I designed and built Janice's gown and constructed a blue garter for her, as well. The small pristine church was illuminated and shining on the beautiful bride, so very young. Her blonde hair, through the veil, had so many colorful rays of gold coming through. As for the ceremony? Yes - my loving God was all around me there too.

Geno, as a groom, stood in front, tall and handsome as ever. He looked just like his father did when he took me to the altar in St. Leonard's Church in the North End. Mr. Beck was German, and Mrs. Beck was Lithuanian - both happy and joyful people through it all. During the small Lutheran reception, my wonderful and very Italian brother-in-law, Alfonso, kept whispering in my ear, "Why are they hiding the cannoli'?" We had a good time.

With the vows of the bride and groom, I felt the final separation of both of my sons - of my children. They graduated now from childhood and war into marriages. I felt the separation, and I accepted it. Did I keep the promise I made to each of them at birth? Looking at them now as two grown responsible men with wonderful wives? I believe I had.

Casey drove us home safely, and eventually, Geno became his best man to complete the circle. Geno and Janice made a home in a small apartment in New York to start their lives and begin together. A perfect couple.

Thinking back, this was a befitting conclusion to the Second Great War and for my family.

Chapter Eighteen

Mother Passes

Going back a bit. Before these two weddings happened, my mother became very sick. She had leukemia. I took care of her here in my house for three months. Papa came for supper every night, so it worked out fine. I left my job and wrote some at home while taking care of Mother. When she felt well enough, Papa took her back home to their apartment. I returned to work at Vogue Bridal Shop in Lynn.

Mother however soon relapsed. While the war was on, she fasted continuously. She thought this form of prayer would bring all her dear soldiers' home. All five did come home which kept her faith alive. She was always anemic anyway. But with all her good intentions, she never should have had those long fasting's. She was a stubborn person - and a devoted Catholic. Again, I had to leave my job and take care of Mother.

For six months, Mother was up and down. I faithfully was there. She became weaker and weaker. My sister, Alice, came from Cambridge and helped as often as she could. She and I were together one-day bathing Mother when she took our hands together and kissed them saying, "Bless you, my two daughters. You are the caress of God. You are the proof of my faith and prayers. Stay friends as you have been all your life, and I thank you both. I was blessed to have such a family. I shall die tomorrow."

And she did.

Mother died as a saint, resigned and so beautiful. She was ready, sure that God was with her. Papa was at her side during her last days with the saddest expression - he knew he would soon lose her. Mother had loads of friends who told us after her death, "Your mother was a woman who knew how to spent her life in charity and she even knew how to die as well. She was like the Mother of all Italy."

Mother was only 69 years of age - an Italian national who managed to get all of her children to America, one by one, so they could have the best of both worlds. She died the same age as my Nonno, Don Carlos and my Uncle Antonio.

September 1946. Papa at Mother's Side "Addio, Mother."

Transitions

One month before my mother died, my first grandchild, Victor, was born.

I asked my brother, Louis, to stay that day with Mother. I went to see my grandson at Lynn Hospital. There he was, near the window of the room where other babies were. A beautiful boy! It brought back memories of when Reno was born, a perfect face. Dear one, you too will be another reason for me to exist. I promise you, I will be a good grandmother. My imagination of this new role for me had no end.

The night Mary went to the hospital to have her baby, Reno made us get up out of bed. They were living upstairs on the second floor. He was so nervous taking Mary out of the door. My husband and I made jokes about his anxiety. Reno sent news from the hospital. "The baby!" he yelled over the phone, "It's a boy! Everything went smoothly. Mother and child are just fine."

Louis and I waited until two o'clock in the morning for him to come back. Reno first visited and woke up his Uncle Ralfo with the good news that his status as "uncle" was now raised up to "great-uncle." We heard Reno come in again to go upstairs and finally to sleep. We greeted him in the back hall with hugs and kisses. He only said, "I'm a father," and started up the stairs in disbelief. I followed him. Halfway up, I kissed him again. He was still repeating to himself, "I am a father. I am a father!" I said, "Reno - I am a grandmother! Good luck my son!"

I went to see Mary. She looked beautiful - she had an easy birth. And when she came home, Reno finally stopped worrying about his time. Being tormented about school and family together was becoming too much for this dedicated student to cope with. Somehow, together with Mary, they would both find a way.

After one week, Mary came home. A few days later, we took the baby to my mother's house. Reno took pictures of the baby in the arms of his dying grandmother. My mother cried and said, "I am now completed." The picture in my mind is so symbolic.

One on the way out, and another starting on the road of life.

Family Picnic, 1948. Mary, (expecting Julie), Victor (2), and Reno.

Final Soliloquy

I should end my story here because to write minutely all that happens in the other thirty-three years since this time, would take another book to describe how hard it was for me to maintain all my promises - especially to myself. Sometimes, I succumbed under the hardship, but in the end, at this date, 1979, I have so many good memories of my life - so many recompenses for whatever I suffered. For, like my mother, I know that I built an honorable family, with both my Pironi clan and with my own - the Pisano.

Lena's Epilogue

They call me "Nonnie."

Pinned to Michelina's Letter mailed in the box. Reverse reading:
"Ballpoint Embroidery on Paper. Still life - Lena, '79"

EPILOGUE

The "Validation of Sequence"

I shall finish my Letter here with this Epilogue and offer some sample writings and perhaps a poem or two or some artwork to finish. Also a few milestones until now - 1979.

Thinking back

In the years of my maturity, I had many moments of a real joy - joy of continuation of myself. I saw this validation in my grandchildren. They, more than my own children, have reproduced many of my own traits. The best of me is there, very evident and satisfactory.

Reno has four children; Victor, Julie, Robert, and Lisa. Geno has three; Susan, Louis, and Laura. With each and every one of them, I had the pleasure of babysitting. With Reno's children first, I gave seven years of sitting - every Saturday night. They lived on the second floor of my two-level home until Reno was transferred as an industrial designer and model-builder for General Electric. Geno too is with GE as an executive of technical writing and worker training. Reno went to GE, Bridgeport, Connecticut, and Geno went to GE, Pittsfield, Massachusetts. Both became very successful men and also teachers in their fields.

When I sat for my grandchildren living upstairs, I made Mary and Reno know that anytime they were free to go out, I was available. Many times, the children would sneak downstairs to have tea with me or just to visit away from their parents. It was a good thing for me, too. I had the grandchildren all for myself. We staged little parties, with Italian cookies and some Postum served in very small cups. Then we sang together - loudly. I told my grandchildren, in great detail, many mythological and biblical stories, or otherwise, I made some up. Always, I eliminated any mention of cruelty or of war. They loved these visits together just as much as I did.

They called me, "Nonnie."

"Captive Audience." Storytelling time and Babysitting Duties with "Nonnie." Julie (the skeptic); Masters, Yale, Public Health. Robert (flummoxed); Architectural Photographer, Me, (co-conspirator with Nonnie); writer, producer, director, educator.

Reaffirmation

In 1955, I took my very first trip back to Italy - for four months. I sailed with the luxury Italian cruise ship, *MS Saturnia*. I pleaded with my husband to come with me, but he had no intentions to go anywhere. I traveled extensively and even rented a house in my old village of Pratola

Serra. It was of course, not as I remembered it even though my welcome by many remaining cousins was warm and engaging. Lots of elderly hugs and tears. Lots of chatter.

But the Second Great War had taken its toll on my old village - more than even centuries of earthquakes and pestilence. I think even now it has not completely healed from the war.

I even visited Roma to find my old friend Annie Chambelli, who was still a nun and still married to God. We walked arm-in-arm all over the Eternal City as we each promised we would do together so many years earlier. We attended all the museums and courtyard recitals that we could squeeze into two weeks' time. Dear Annie was still teaching Mozart to gifted children, but less so and was resolved more now to embrace the protection of the convent and seclusion of the sisterhood. A beautiful, beautiful contented woman. No regrets. Again, we promised to write and to do another visit - perhaps in America next time - perhaps again in the North End.

Coming back on the ship *Saturnia,* I had plenty of time to reflect on what I had experienced as a sad young girl stuck in the bowels of steerage class. Now, I was going to America, well-attended and in Second Class. I thought again of the two little sisters, Stefania and Pina, whom I had pro-tected thinking they were to become orphaned. "Where are they now?" I thought in a dream. "Happy? Married? What was their fate?" I knew their destiny - I saw it in their eyes at Ellis Island. They were destined to be old loving souls.

I wrote a poem for the youngest of the sisters, Pina, on my return voyage to New York. It was published when I arrived home.

loquace sguardo . . .

Leggo negl'occhi suoi o dolce Pina
Desiderio di cose da spiegare e dire
Cose che di bellezza sublime hanno
    sapore
Misti sentimenti nati oltremare.

Il suo sguardo e gesto sanno raccontare,
Dell'orte e coltura da secoli accumulate
Dell'azzurro della riviera, la calma
    marina
Dell'opulente campagna di frutta e fiori.

Se le parole mancano, l'espressione
    spinge
Sulle montagne superbe e maestose
Vestite d'ogni verde ornate di neve
Con pascoli ed uccelli di specie e colori.

Con linguaggio muto ed eloquente
Impartir lei sa a chi la guarda.
Quell'immensità di gioie penetrate
Nella mente e cor recipiente.

Ritinga in se i suoni e colori
Continua a sentir l'incanto d'Europa
Assapora ancor quell'aria, tocca il suolo
Stringa sempre a se tutto il panorama.

Ma lascia ognor, lo sguardo rivelare
Così sempre vivido, agente del core
Finchè vivre, lascia che altri beano
Dei recordi suoi che vorrebbe raccontare.

by LENA PISANO

The Talkative Gaze

I read in in your eyes, dear Pina
The desire to explain and tell of things
Things of beauty so sublime and tasteful
Mixed feelings born overseas.

Your look and gestures know to tell
Of the gardens and harvest gathered over centuries
From the blue of the coastline, the calm of the sea
From the opulent countryside of fruits and flowers.

If words are lacking, expressions Push

On the majestic and supreme mountains
Dressed in every decorated green, sprinkled with snow
With pastures and birds of every type and color.

Dispensing silent and eloquent words
    She knows to whom she is looking.
That immense and penetrating joy
In welcoming the hearts and minds.

Painted in colors and sound
One hears the song of Europa
To relish again that air, touch that ground
Embracing the panorama.

But as it leaves everywhere, the gaze reveals
Something always living, agent of the heart
While she is alive, let others delight
Of the memories that she wants to tell.

The Passing of Another Era

One day my two boys came running up to the bridal shop at Vogue's where I was working. They had bad news. My father was dying. Both of my sons drove me quickly to the hospital. When we got there, Papa had just expired. My Papa was no more. My brother Frank was there and when he saw me, he embraced me, crying. As a doctor, Frank gave our father every comfort until the very end - even as just a son holding his dying father's hand. "He just died Lena," Frank said through his tears. "Papa is gone." My father in death looked very handsome and young as if he were asleep. He was just 80 years old. Yes, we fought and hugged and then fought again over many, many years, but over those coals, he tempered me. The struggles I had growing up not to be dominated, came because of him. Papa was my fire - Papa was my will to resist.

With my father's death in 1953, I became the oldest of my immediate family - the Pironi clan. Guiseppe "Peppino" Pirone had an immense funeral. Every paesani came. The "Golden Needle" of harness making left us, taking with him the horse-drawn era of civilization. Addio, Papa.

"Last picture with Papa. 1953."
[Aside: Lena had surgery on her right elbow after falling on ice.
Her father came every day during her convalescing, rain or shine.]

525

Also, at this same time, 1953, my mother's brother Ferdinando Fabrizio got a heart attack. I went to see him in the hospital. He was told to stay flat on his back, but no, he sat up and even smoked in his hospital bed. I took the cigarette from him and finished it. He looked at me saying, "It tastes good, doesn't it?" "Yes," I said smiling, "but just now you can't smoke, Dear Uncle. Can't you keep still until you get better?" "Okay, Okay," he protested laying back down. He then asked me, "When I get better, will you come to Italy with me? I want to see my home again." "Yes, I will. We shall plan it when you get better." But my uncle was very sick. He fought sleep for several nights because he felt that he was going to die if he closed his eyes, that awful feeling of going far, far away. He asked for pills to keep awake. Frank accommodated him, but more so to keep him calm. But after all efforts, nature finally won. My uncle died of exhaustion.

Uncle Ferdinando, master shoemaker, and actor, also died near 80 years old. He was still full of the desires he lived with for his whole life. Another addio. I made up my mind after the deaths of my father and my uncle, to continue my life freely - not to be afraid to do my duties and to succumb to an early death. I knew I had to keep all of my promises to myself and to my family and to be always adaptable in order to succeed in the final act of my life, Act III - the longest and most rewarding Act of all.

For the next twenty years, I concentrated on my work designing and building elegant gowns and women's apparel of all types and also to write. I wrote voluminously for myself and for others. I sold many small pieces and continued to author reviews of art and culture for local papers and magazines - especially those with bi-lingual readers of English and Italian.

When Reno and Mary moved with the grandchildren to Connecticut, into a new home in the country, we rented out the upstairs apartment for more income. Louis and I accumulated plenty of cash money, in separate bank accounts or course. We had no debt, mostly due to Louis' unyielding mindset of independence. No debt. None. I continued to write pieces for newspapers and magazines and I traveled extensively - always alone. I visited with my families in New York, Connecticut, Canada and California. I stayed months with my sister Josephine and our brother Mikele, both now settled on the West Coast. Louis could not object - he did not object. It wasn't so much a battle won as it was a quiet armistice of forgotten wills. I finally had my sense of self-accomplishment, of my own value. Could I have accomplished more with my life or what I became? In another time or another place? Perhaps. And perhaps not.

December 23rd, 1974, five years ago, I lost my husband. Louis died.

Louis Passes Away

Thinking back, my husband was a man of too much pride who could not accept second place from anybody. And that was the way he lived until he too died. He was 86 years old - I was 70.

Louis died at peace with me and with the world - old and new. He accomplished a part of what he wanted and what he wanted came to him from other voices in his past. At the end, there was still threads of love between us - of commonality - of our long history together. But he never apologized nor truly explained his torments - nor did I to him. Louis was forever faithful to his own self-image which he cultivated and manifested well. He was able to accumulate plenty of money for his children and left them all that he had collected at the end. That was his forever goal, to leave his sons cash money. That was his measure. I received the house we lived in.

When Louis died, I went with his often-spoken wishes on the subject - how could I not? Before we met, he had bought a cemetery plot in Lynn next to his first wife, Tina, and her child, both of whom died during childbirth. Louis never sold that plot, and so there he is buried.

I became reclusive for many months after Louis's death. Again, reflective. I did not go so far as to admit that we were never meant for each other because I could not dismiss the happier times we shared, nor the exceptional sons we had together. And there were many other reasons. But each remembrance blends together into the greyness of truth. Confucius said, "There is no 'is' and there is no 'is not.' Truth lies in between." I loved my husband as well as any man I have ever known. I shall be comfortable living with that as my truth forever.

Louis died a month after our fifty-third wedding anniversary.

Freedom's Call

In 1975, I went back to Italy again for one full year. I had cleaned, painted and repaired my entire home, the way it deserved and how "I" wanted. My continued desire to spent a full year in Italy, to see all the seasons, was nagging me. I rented the second floor upstairs and went by plane this time. My first time in the air. It was another beautiful experience to be above the clouds - to feel levitation. It was wonderful. I stayed mostly in Italy. Six months in and around Naples and Salerno, living with a family in a small apartment. I cooked my own meals. I lived like the paesani did. I paid my expenses with the rent paid by my tenants back in America and had plenty left over. I learned the art of living on my own terms and sensibilities and to take part of everything the paesani did. I took short day trips everywhere, exploring all the islands, staying many nights on the top of Ravello over the Costiera Amalfitana (Amalfi Coast) then down to the beach to have lunch in different towns. Every day, I made new friends along small streets and marketplaces animated by happy laborious paesani - people who would rather die than live anywhere else. I never felt alone. I was in Italy! I went often to my town, Pratola Serra, two hours away on power-ful highways that were never there before. Pompei was near, so too Ercolano, and Paseum. Imagine all my studying and freedoms - all my journals and writings. And everywhere I went, I could speak to anyone, either in pure Italian or pure English - whatever their choice! What freedoms were now afforded me? I was busy as a bee.

I went to all the large cities in Italy - including all of Sicily. I walked and studied all the Greek and Roman ruins and vestiges and other his-torical parts of that beautiful and remarkable island. Another stay with Annie in Roma where again we explored every inch of the Eternal City. In Florence, I even joined the paesani in a march of rebellion for more pay for teachers. I marched in every city that had similar demands for justice - and there were plenty of marches. "Avanti Popolo!" ("Forward, People!") I did this it seemed in all the cities I went to in Europe. People were always marching and always welcoming me to join them - so I did. It was not only fun, but I felt what they felt and it made me a real Italian, or Austrian, or French. I traveled everywhere by train, passing beautiful places in the dark, sitting and talking eagerly with workers who went back to their jobs in the mines of Switzerland from around Milan. And I wrote everything down. More stories came to me, more poetry - in two beautiful languages.

In Paris, I spent many hours on the hill of Montmartre, roaming alone, getting lost, depending always on the taxi driver to find my hotel somewhere in the Latin Quarter. I visited many places I had only read about - only dreamt about. I went to the Commune Barbizon near the Fontainebleau Forest. I touched Van Gogh's shoe. I had coffee at the café's where all the impressionist used to have their breakfast when they had enough money to eat. I wrote as I sat in my own café. I traveled to the Barbizon School where the painter Jean-François Millet painted all his masterpieces that Annie and I once visited that were hanging on museum walls in Boston. I stopped daily at the Louvre to visit with my three best friends - the Mona Lisa, the Winged Victory and the Venus de Milo - each of whom were finally glad to see me in person and welcomed me. "Ciao, Lena!" I was again in another world.

Over additional months, I went to Spain, Portugal, Greece and England. I did the best most invigorating walking of my life at seventy-four. I visited all the real gothic castles I could and traveled by boat up and down the Thames River. On one boat ride in London, I spontaneously sang without fear "Mattinata" (the "Morning") in Italian. Suddenly, I was joined by a French woman who sang with me - in French! We made perfect harmonic accord and received loud claps and cheers from our fellow passengers.

I ended my year in Europe by overstaying a bit. I don't recall how much. I knew that I would probably never have another chance. When I left, I left of course from Naples - how could I not? Too little too late? No. I revisited the intricacies of my own being and again I felt validated by all that was good and humane in this world.

I sadly said goodbye to my town, my old cousins and to my young great-nieces. I remember all of them waving and crying just the same as when I left Pratola Serra for the very first time as a girl of eighteen. They called out, "Arrivederci, Nonna Lena!" And then finally a call out from my oldest cousin who was there with me since we were children ourselves - "Arrivederci - Michelina!!!"

How can I ever forget this? All my people there loved me. Italy loved me. I loved everybody and everything there. I wish someday my sons and their children will have the same opportunity and joy I had in my travels and cherish the memory of it all as I do.

I published two poems when I came back from my first trip to Italy by boat. Both poems returned to my lips after many years. Now this time, I was skipping above the variant clouds in a daze and again remembering my childhood - remembering Italy. The first time I left was as a passenger in steerage class. My last trip from Italy, I came home to America as a passenger on the wing.

April 12, 1957 **THE ITALIAN NEWS**

PATRIA MIA

Mi chiami ed io rispondere non posso,
Vincoli e doveri a questo suol m'attaccano
Mi lacera l'animo questo conflitto strano
Di forti passioni che vincere non posso.

Acuto è il mio desir, almen poter posar
In te o terra patria la spoglia mia.
Spegnermi nel caro suolo e senz'altra nostalgia
In grembo tuo rimaner perenne e riposar.

Con te la voce della cugina intona.
Ritorna cara, qui al tuo focolare
Ai monti, a quell'incanto che senti nel cor.

Più forte, a voi dico, chiamatemi ancor
Storditemi i vincoli, assopite il mio dovere
Tiratemi a voi e tenetemi in catena.
— **Lena Pisano, Lynn, Mass.**

My Motherland

You call me and I say I can't
Your ties and duties are what hold me
This strange conflict tears my spirit
Of strong passions that I will never conquer.

Intense is my desire, at least to place
In you, oh my motherland, my naked self.
Leave me in the dear fertile ground without nostalgia,
In your womb I remain rested and everlasting.

With you, the tuned voice of a cousin,
Return dear, here to your hearth.
To the mountains, to the song you hear in your heart.

Stronger, to you I say, call me again
Break away these ties, assuage my obligations
Pull me to you and keep me in chains.

On the flight, back home to my children and grandchildren in America from Pratola Serra, I could only think of what a wonderful life I had been given via destiny and what gifted people I will someday leave behind me. I am a contented old person now who feels like my mother felt. I did my best and I got back the same.

Michelina Fabrizio Pirone Pisano, 1901 - 1995.
"Nonnie" at age 91, poised for yet another challenge.

[Aside: Besides this monumental handwritten "Letter," Michelina left dozens of photographs, drawings, published and unpublished poetry, short stories, newspaper clippings and articles which she wrote and compiled during her many years, both in English and Italian. Her numerous wedding gowns, which she designed and built, are still being handed down from mothers to daughters in many different families across America. Befittingly.]

Victor's Epilogue to the Letter

FINI

Michelina passed away in 1995 at the age of 94. In her final months, she lived in a nursing home near the beach in Orient Heights, outside of Boston, not far from where her mother and younger siblings first moved to from Pratola Serra. Towards the end of her life, she became almost totally blind after several cataract operations and virtually deaf as well. But my grandmother took solace in the many visitations brought to her in the form of her growing great-granddaughters, all three destined to become women of great success; Jessica, an acclaimed Martha's Vineyard artist, Rebecca, a physical therapist at MGH, and Vanessa, a tough litigator in the courts of Boston - "Orion's belt." Also, my media-guru son Lucas, who as a newborn, rocked in the arms of his own great-grandmother as I once had done. There were always tears at these visits - on both sides. Our "Nonnie" was fading.

After re-reading Michelina's Letter, I am left in overwhelming amazement as to the scope of my grandmother's acute memory and to the depth of her visualization after so many, many years. She brought us back to past whispers in black and white. No doubt these special gifts of memory served her well in her final days of sensory deprivation and isolation. But I also know that she drew upon and relived each of those episodes in her mind and revisited them, "like childhood images, as easily and as clearly as if [she] were looking out of [her] own kitchen window."

Blind and deaf, Michelina left this world about the same way as Helen Keller came in. But she did not leave in remorse or with melancholy. As Michelina herself wrote and believed, "Once we exist, we never cease to exist." And I too believe, each of these iconic episodes in her long vivid memory still exist somewhere - even beyond the pages of this book. The most we can ever hope for is to be confirmed, as she herself believed, as a "validation of sequence."

I hereby complete this book, February 17th, 2019 on Michelina's 118th Birthday. Happy birthday, my dear Nonnie - addio, Michelina.

And thank you Matzo Mauriello for whispering this in my ear.

Made in the USA
Middletown, DE
18 July 2019